A Fine Corps and Will Serve Faithfully

The Swiss Regiment de Roll in the British Army 1794–1816

Alistair Nichols

Helion & Company

To Jane

Helion & Company Limited
Unit 8 Amherst Business Centre
Budbrooke Road
Warwick
CV34 5WE
England
Tel. 01926 499619
Email: info@helion.co.uk
Website: www.helion.co.uk
Twitter: @helionbooks
Visit our blog at http://blog.helion.co.uk/

Published by Helion & Company 2023
Designed and typeset by Mach 3 Solutions (www.mach3solutions.co.uk)
Cover designed by Paul Hewitt, Battlefield Design (www.battlefield-design.co.uk)

Text © Alistair Nichols 2023
Illustrations © as individually credited
Cover: The Regiment de Roll, Egypt 1801, by Henri Garnier (also known as Tanconville),
published in *Les Alsaciens dans la Garde impériale et dans les corps d'élite*, 1910.
Maps by George Anderson © Helion & Company 2023

ISBN 978-1-804511-91-6

British Library Cataloguing-in-Publication Data.
A catalogue record for this book is available from the British Library.

For details of other military history titles published by Helion & Company Limited,
contact the above address, or visit our website: http://www.helion.co.uk

We always welcome receiving book proposals from prospective authors.

Contents

Preface

The raising of what was to become the Regiment de Roll was both a diplomatic and a military project. While it took place during the War of the First Coalition, among the turmoil and rapidly changing environment caused by the French Revolution, it had its roots, indeed its origins, in the often misunderstood tradition of Swiss foreign military service. As, perhaps, the diplomatic aspect faded in significance the military role of the regiment saw it as part of the British Army until the echoes of the last gunfire of the Napoleonic Wars had faded.

Despite its extent and variety, its service has not received much attention from military historians, the only publication that has approached a comprehensive history is Adolf Bürkli's article 'Das Schweizerregiment von Roll in englischen Dienste 1795 bis 1816' printed in *Neujahrsblatt der Feuerwerter-Gefellschaft* in 1893. From the British perspective one reason for this lack of attention has been that all the regiment's service, except for a period in Portugal, was performed in the Mediterranean theatre. This saw men of the regiment deployed from Egypt to Gibraltar, Tarragona in Spain to Dubrovnik in Croatia, the Po Valley in Italy to Malta, not only facing the hazards of battle but also of disease and the sea.

This work seeks to address this omission and recognise the length and variety of the service of the Regiment de Roll and its men. It is the culmination of many years' research and like so many others could not have been completed without the help and encouragement from so many people and institutions that I am afraid to make a list for fear of inadvertently missing a name. That being said, I am sure none would begrudge me for thanking Hubert Foerster in particular for not only providing his encouragement but also his research into the formation of the regiment so that it could be included within this history. I also cannot fail to mention the patient support of my wife, Jane, and the assistance of Hughes de Bazouges and Jean-Philippe Ganascia.

I have given the names of personnel as they were recorded in the army and regimental records, which was generally a French or a mixed French and English version, regardless of their origins. The names of the officers of the Regiment de Roll will be clarified in the biographical notes to be published on the website fortisetfidelis.com. As for place names, those that are in current use have been selected except where this would, perhaps, be unfamiliar and thus cause unnecessary confusion for English language readers.

1

'Many difficulties to conquer'

In London on 9 December 1794 a proposal by the Baron de Roll to raise 'a Foreign Regiment composed of two Battalions of Infantry' was accepted by the British Government.[1] Whilst the capitulation, a legal agreement, did not specify the national identity of the regiment it was clearly to be Swiss, with the baron, as colonel, being empowered to 'nominate all the Officers of his Regiment subject nevertheless to the approval of His Britannic Majesty.'[2]

Ludwig Robert Franz Joseph von Roll von Emmenholz was more familiarly known as Louis de Roll, the version of his name in French, the language of European diplomacy and courtly life as well as military matters, the spheres within which the baron lived. Born in 1750 and raised in France from an early age, he joined the Régiment des Gardes Suisses (the Swiss Guards Regiment) in the service of the French kings, as *enseigne* in 1765 and was promoted *sous-lieutenant* the following year.[3] His family were patricians from Solothurn, the capital of the German-speaking and Roman Catholic canton of the same name, in the north-west of Switzerland. There were strong links between Solothurn's élite and the French monarchy; four members of the Roll family, including Louis, were serving in the Gardes Suisses in 1791.[4]

In common with their peers in other European royal guard units, the officers of the Gardes Suisses enjoyed special benefits, including inflated ranks, so Roll, who served on the regimental staff as *sous-aide-major* and *aide-major* between 1773 and 1783, was commissioned *colonel* in 1781 and honoured as *chevalier* of the Ordre de Saint-Louis two years later. In 1783 he obtained the command of a company and on 5 October 1788 that of the compagnie générale.[5] The general company, second only to that of grenadiers in the first battalion, had a special status, 'If the regiment of the guards was considered as the military personification of the Swiss nation,

1   Copy of the capitulation in The National Archives, Kew (TNA): HO 50/386.
2   TNA: HO 50/386: Article 6 of the capitulation.
3   Rodolphe de Castella de Delley, *Le Régiment des Gardes-Suisses au service de France du 3 mars 1616 au 10 août 1792* (Fribourg: Éditions Universitaire, 1964), pp.352–353.
4   *Etat militaire* 1791. The annual list of units and, by this time, officers in the French army, so equivalent to the British Army List.
5   Castella, *Gardes-Suisses*, pp.352–353. Due to various combinations of first names there is frequent confusion with other members of his family who served in the same regiment, especially François-Joseph (1743–1815).

the compagnie générale was itself "the élite of the élite," resulting from selection. All the Swiss corps supplied their best men to this privileged unit.[6] On 3 May 1791 at a regimental review 147 all ranks, including six officers, are listed in the company.[7] Louis de Roll, however, was not present. On 27 December 1771 Charles-Philippe Comte d'Artois, the youngest of the two brothers of the Dauphin, Louis-Auguste, the future King Louis XVI, had been appointed colonel général des Suisses et Grisons (colonel general of the Swiss and Graubünden) and Roll was appointed one of his aides. When Artois emigrated on 17 July 1789, as the French Revolution developed, Roll was by his side. Artois, 'always talking, never listening, sure of everything, speaking only of force and not of negotiation' became the focus for hard-line émigrés who sought a Counter Revolution.[8]

On 20 June 1791 Artois's two brothers set off, by different routes, to leave France. While the Comte de Provence, the future King Louis XVIII, reached safety, Louis XVI and his family were intercepted and returned to Paris. There they stayed, effectively prisoners, at the Tuileries Palace guarded by the Parisian National Guard. As tension grew in Paris, the Gardes Suisses, reduced by significant detachments, were stationed at the palace in support the National Guardsmen overnight 9/10 August 1792. As dawn broke the first stage of a coup d'état by extreme elements within the National Assembly commenced with an attack on the palace. As the royal family took vain refuge within the assembly, the Gardes Suisses remained at their posts, as *capitaine*, with a commission of *lieutenant-colonel*, Jost de Dürler explained,

> [Overnight] … The two senior officers of the regiment … gave me the command of the posts of the Royal Courtyard, the Swiss Courtyard and a reserve of 300 men who were there in battle order, adding 'If the King withdraws from the Château, as chiefs we will accompany him; we count on you, persuaded that you will never let yourself be overcome and that in no circumstance will you lay down your arms …'[9]

Abandoned by all but a handful of the National Guards, the Swiss steadfastly defended the palace until they were given the order to cease fire. Dürler refused to lay down his arms, without the king's own order, and led the remnants of his command to the National Assembly where he received it. Many of the now defenceless Swiss, wounded or in small groups, were

---

6   Paul de Vallière, 'Histoire du régiment des Gardes Suisses de France (1567–1830)', *Revue Militaire Suisse*, No.5 Mai 1911, p.386.

7   Paul de Vallière, *Honneur et Fidélité Histoire des Suisses au Service Étranger* (Lausanne: Les Editions d'art Suisse ancient, 1940), pp.593–595 and Vallière, 'Gardes Suisses', p.389.

8   Fersen describing Artois in July 1791 quoted in Philip Mansell, *Louis XVIII* (Stroud: Sutton Publishing, 1999), p.59.

9   British Library (BL): Add MS 32168: Relation de Monsieur de Durler Capitaine au Régiment des Gardes-Suisses et commandant environ 500 hommes qui se sont défendus sur l'Escalier de la Chapelle et dans l'Intérieur du Château, le 10 Août 1792. A more polished version, with additional material, was published in *Colonel* Pfyffer d'Alitshoffen (ed.), *Récit de la conduit du régiment des Gardes Suisses, à la journée du 10 Août 1792* (Geneva: Chez Abraham Cherbuliez, 1824); the editor had been *second sous-lieutenant* in Dürler's company but on leave at the time.

slaughtered and others were murdered when mobs invaded the Parisian prisons the following month. Estimates of the regiment's loss on and after 10 August range up to 425 but many of the officers and men escaped, while others were on detached duties or on leave. This event had been preceded by low level attacks and harassment of the Swiss units by revolutionary authorities so at an extraordinary session of the Swiss Diet on 5 September all the Swiss regiments in French service were recalled. This move had, however, been pre-empted by the French National Assembly that decreed on 21 August that the regiments were to be disbanded on the pretext that their capitulations were too restrictive.[10]

Roll became one of Artois's most trusted advisors, travelling with him across Europe or being sent as his personal representative to foreign governments and courts. His proximity and influence was to be envied and resented by others and he was blamed as the cause of the prince's perceived shortcomings. Artois retained a particular attachment to his office as colonel general of the Swiss troops in the French Royal Army, witnessed by his wearing the uniform for his portrait by Henri-Pierre Danloux in 1798. Comte Louis de Bouillé, a French émigré officer, wrote,

> His [Artois's] vain title of colonel general of the Swiss made him attach importance and almost a duty to wear its distinctions, and he was encouraged in it by an officer of that nation, the Baron de Roll, who, without spirit, without talent, without even any charm, but by that sort of cunning and one can say instinct that is peculiar to all intriguers, particularly to those of his nation, had taken a too fatal ascendancy over him.[11]

A Swiss officer, Ferdinand de Rovéréa, noted that, 'the Comte d'Artois … passionately desired to make his return to France in his former post of colonel general of the Swiss and Grisons, and to surround himself for this event [with Swiss troops].'[12] Thus, on 23 November 1794, the Duc d'Harcourt, the French royal princes' chargé d'affaires in London, proposed, on behalf of the Comte d'Artois, to William Windham, Secretary at War, that the Baron de Roll raise a regiment of Swiss infantry in his name for the service of Great Britain.[13] Since August 1794 the British Government had begun raising, by Act of Parliament, regiments to support the return of the monarchy to France. Commanded by French émigré officers, they were organised in the same manner as regiments of the former French royal army and bore symbols of that army, notably the white cockade, by which name these units were often known. Artois was closely involved in this venture and the suggestion

---

10   Rodney Allen, *Threshold of Terror, the Last Hours of the Monarchy in the French Revolution* (Stroud: Sutton Publishing, 1999), pp.238–239.

11   Louis-Joseph-Amour Marquis de Bouillé, *Souvenirs et fragments pour servir aux mémoires de ma vie et de mon temps* (Paris: Société d'histoire contemporaine, 1908), vol.II, p.287.

12   Ferdinand de Rovéréa, *Mémoires de F. de Rovéréa* (Bern, Zürich and Paris: Klinchsieck, 1848), vol.II, p.242.

13   Vicomte Robert Grouvel, *Les corps de troupes de l'émigration française* (Paris: Les Éditions de La Sabretache, 1957–1964), vol.I, p.301.

of raising a Swiss regiment in a similar fashion was embraced, a capitulation being agreed after a little more than a fortnight.

It was to be the first Swiss regiment raised in British service in the era. The Baron de Roll, as a result, became the object of further jealousy, this time from rival Swiss officers such as Rovéréa who described him thus,

> … he looked like he was barely 40. Swiss as much as an inhabitant of Paris where he lived from his infancy can be; without any other local knowledge of his homeland than the houses of his friends; he nevertheless preserved with a seductive facility of elocution, those round and simple forms which opinion attributes to us, that have as a rule allowed him to be readily deemed a frank and good man in the fullest sense of the term; yet he was shrewd, subtle, cunning and glib, as he had to be to obtain and retain preference from a young and fickle prince, surrounded by courtiers. Baron de Roll who previously considered Switzerland as no more than as a regiment of guards and advancement his patrimony, knew how to make a reputation for rectitude that sustained him beyond the wreck suffered by other fortunes of this kind.
>
> Chosen by the Comte d'Artois to accompany him in his emigration, he roamed through diverse courts with him and knew how to profit from it by obtaining in London, the very-lucrative levy of a regiment supposedly composed of the remains of the unfortunate regiment of guards, an urgent resource for the independence of his situation and he was able to avoid the tiresome cares of forming it, by having his prince solicit that he not be removed from his person; thus placed, he acquired greater access to the men then at the helm of affairs … at least as an understudy … he was as unknown to his country as to his regiment … while he quietly devoured the revenues in London.[14]

As Rovéréa observed, and as was customary for regimental colonels in the British service, the Baron de Roll did not take day-to-day command of his regiment, but was closely concerned with its administration. The capitulation of 9 December 1794, written in French, was brief, with only 11 articles and four attached tables, but as stated at Article 10,

> In all the matters which are not detailed in the present Capitulation the Regiment will conform to all that is prescribed by the ordonnances and regulations of the Foreign Troops in the Service of His Britannic Majesty [i.e. the white cockade corps], and enjoy all the honours, emoluments and advantages which have been accorded to them.[15]

As proprietor colonel Roll was responsible for getting recruits to the place appointed for assembling the regiment and ensuring they were 'armed, clothed and equipped in all the points' stipulated in the capitulation. He was to receive 'the sum of fourteen pounds sterling for each NCO and soldier'

---

14   Rovéréa, *Mémoires*, pp.243–244.

15   TNA: HO 50/386. This was later reiterated, 'In all not immediately expressed in that Capitulation, Reference is made to the Capitulation of the White Cockade Regiments'. Woodford to Walker, 7 February 1797 (TNA: WO 4/367).

so produced. He was to be given a third of the money required to form the regiment at its established strength when he received his letters of service and he would get the rest on request, at which time he had to 'provisionally justify the progress of his work to complete his Regiment.'[16] He had leverage, as colonel, as he was entitled to nominate all the officers of the regiment who were then only 'subject to the approval of His Britannic Majesty.' However, he had to work fast as he was contracted to raise the regiment in four months from the date his letter of service was dispatched to him.[17] The final article stated,

> The present Capitulation will last for the War and for one Year afterwards; but in the case where His Very Christian Majesty will be restored to the Throne [of France] His Britannic Majesty is beseeched to employ his good offices, to have the Regiment transferred to the Service of France, and the Capitulation will cease in Consequence from the day when it will be Paid by the King of France.[18]

Table 1: Regimental organisation under the original capitulation dated 9 December 1794.[19]

1	*colonel propriétaire*		
1	*lieutenant-colonel*		
1	*major*		
1	*quartier maître trésorier* (quartermaster) with rank of *lieutenant*		
2	*aides-majors, capitaines*	1	*tambour major* (drum major)
2	*sous-aides majors, lieutenants*	1	*caporal tambour* (corporal drummer)
2	*enseignes*, with rank of *sous-lieutenants*	1	*maitre tailleur* (master tailor)
2	*adjudants*	1	*maitre armurier* (master armourer)
2	*aumônier* (chaplains)	1	*maitre cordonnier* (master shoemaker)
1	*chirurgien major* (surgeon major)		
2	*aides chirurgiens* (assistant surgeons)		

There were to be two battalions each with nine companies, one of *grenadiers* and *chasseurs* and eight of *fusiliers*, each company would consist of a *capitaine*, a *lieutenant*, a *sous-lieutenant*, a *sergent major*, a *fourrier*, three *sergents* and eight *caporaux*; those of *grenadiers* or *chasseurs* were to have 72 *soldats* (soldiers) and one *tambour* (drummer) and those of *fusiliers*, 70 *soldats* and three *tambours*, so each was to have 89 men. Each battalion would thus have 801 men and the regiment, including those in Table 1, would have a total of 1,624 men. If not immediately, soon into the regiment's service the élite companies were formed of *grenadiers* with only a few *chasseurs* in each. The earliest regimental muster roll listing officers and men by company, that of 24 October 1797 when the regiment was significantly understrength, shows 46 *grenadiers* and eight *chasseurs* in the first battalion's *grenadier* company

---

16 TNA: HO 50/386: Articles two, three and four of the capitulation.
17 TNA: HO 50/386: Articles five and six.
18 TNA: HO 50/386.
19 TNA: HO 50/386.

with the same number of NCOs and drummers as above. That of the second battalion is only shown with *grenadiers* but on 24 February 1798 it had 38 *grenadiers* and nine *chasseurs*, while the first battalion's company had 44 *grenadiers* and six *chasseurs*.[20]

Britain did not have a tradition of recruiting in Switzerland although individual Swiss officers and soldiers had served in her army during the eighteenth century, notably Henry Bouquet and the three Prévost brothers in the 60th (Royal American) Regiment of Foot. Thus Britain did not have established networks of well-placed supporters and pensioners in the cantons and other territories of the Confederation to facilitate the raising of men while, at the same time, facing opposition from those working for competitors and, in the case of France, an enemy. The Honourable East India Company had had success in attracting some officers and men to its service.[21] However James Francis Erskine and Jean-Rodolphe Müller had been prevented from raising a Swiss regiment for the company during the American War of Independence. The project faced opposition from cantonal authorities bowing to French pressure and keen to protect their interests in the units to which they were contractually committed. Lacking influential backers, it failed and Müller, from Bern, was imprisoned, banished, fined and had property confiscated.[22]

The events of the French Revolution and the ensuing wars changed the situation for both Britain and Switzerland. When the French Republic declared war on Britain on 1 February 1793, the latter urgently needed to raise troops with experienced and reliable officers. The disbanding of the Swiss regiments in the service of France seemed to offer a source of such men. Not all of the 14,000 or so men in these regiments were Swiss, as they attracted recruits from neighbouring regions as well, but it is estimated that about 8,000 returned to Switzerland and it was considered that they may regard British service positively given the events in France. However there was competition from other powers looking to exploit the same resource, especially Sardinia-Piedmont and Spain, that had the advantages of being traditional employers of Swiss units. Indeed, Sardinia gained the lion's share, expanding the Centurie Schmid to a full regiment in 1792 and, the following year, forming three new regiments; Bachmann, Peyer im Hof, and Zimmermann. Spain, already with four Swiss regiments – Schwaller, Rutiman, Reding and Betschart – agreed capitulations for two more; Yann in 1793 and Courten, in 1796. However, an observer in Spain noted, in 1798, 'As to the regiments calling themselves Swiss … they consist almost entirely of Germans, and excepting the officers there are not perhaps twenty that are either Swiss or French.'[23] The two new Swiss regiments … consist entirely of Austrians'. Furthermore, France had made concerted efforts to divert Swiss

20 TNA: WO 12/11982: pay lists.

21 Cecil C. P. Lawson, *A History of the Uniforms of the British Army* (London: Kaye & Ward Limited, 1967), vol. V, pp.147–148.

22 Ernest Giddey, 'James Francis Erskine et son Régiment Suisse (1779–1786)' *Revue suisse d'histoire*, vol.4 (1954), pp.238–259.

23 Frederick Augustus Fischer, *Travels in Spain in 1797 and 1798* (London: Longman & Rees, 1802), pp.267–269.

soldiers, who would have returned home, into its own forces. It maintained and exercised its influence in Switzerland as an increasingly powerful and belligerent neighbour but also the provider of many pensions, indeed much of the correspondence of François-Marie Barthélemy, the French Minister Plenipotentiary to the Confederation, consisted of claims and enquiries about these very pensions.

Barthélemy's British counterpart was Lord Robert Stephen Fitzgerald who was appointed in May 1792, the post having been vacant for 10 years. When the allies occupied Toulon, from 28 August 1793, he had explored the possibility 'of raising a Corps of men' for service there.[24] Although the allied evacuation of Toulon on 19 December meant the project went no further, the officers Fitzgerald had engaged to assist him were imbedded in the system of Swiss foreign military service.[25] In 1794 Fitzgerald received a number of proposals from Swiss officers to raise units for British service. Former *capitaine de grenadiers* Louis Matthieu Duval of the Régiment de Reinach suggested he and fellow officers could easily attract the majority of the men of his former unit to the British service as, 'the greatest number of the officers and soldiers were born in the [district of] Porrentruy now occupied by the French. The men of this regiment have for the most part left their homeland, are dispersed in Switzerland and are animated with the most righteous resentment.'[26] The region, the rump of the lands of the Prince-Bishop of Basel, and now the Canton of Jura, had been invaded by the French Republic in 1792 and the following year it had been incorporated into France.

Jean-Christophe de Dieffenthaller, of Bremgarten and Luzen, *major* of the Régiment de Castella in 1792 and then *colonel* in the émigré Armée de Condé, proposed to raise a regiment.[27] While Baron Ulysse-Antoine de Salis-Marschlins, of the Graubünden and Zürich, proposed to raise a brigade ultimately of 12,000 men. His submission was detailed and precise as to expected from a man who had been *maréchal de camp* and *inspecteur générale des Suisses et Grisons* in the French service and then, from 1789, *tenente generale* in that of Naples charged with reforming the kingdom's army.[28] Attached to his proposal was a memorandum which began by outlining the problems, and opportunities, that recruitment in Switzerland for the British service would encounter,

> One cannot disguise that there will be many difficulties to conquer … meanwhile, there are none that cannot be overcome with intelligence and sufficient means. The first happens through the selection of the men in charge; the other in a well-

24 TNA: FO 74/4: Fitzgerald to Grenville, 7 January 1794.

25 TNA: FO 74/4: receipt signed 13 October 1793 and Jean Kaulek, *Papiers de Barthélemy, ambassadeur de France en Suisse, 1792–1797, publiés sous les auspices de la Commission des Archives des Affaires étrangères,* (Paris: Félix Alcan, 1889), Tome IV (avril 1794 – février 1795), p.65.

26 TNA: FO 74/4: undated and anonymous memorandum.

27 TNA: FO 74/4: undated, and Jean Pinasseau, *L'Émigration Militaire campagne de 1792 Armée Royale Notices D à Z* (Paris: Éditions A. et J. Picard et Cie, 1964), pp.17–18.

28 Vallière, *Honneur et Fidélité*, p.544 and Plate XXI.

conceived plan and with money, which, in Switzerland as elsewhere, is always the great motivation that drives men.

It would be useless to flatter oneself that in the current circumstances England could obtain permission, even tacitly, to raise troops in Switzerland. There is too much fear of being invaded by the French, …

It is necessary therefore to take care to pursue the point, without compromising, in any manner, either the Helvetic Corps in general or any of the cantons bordering France in particular …

Though in forming this levy one has the double object of procuring troops … and producing a change in the public spirit in Switzerland to render it more favourable to the right cause, it will be necessary to avoid giving this levy the denomination of Swiss but to simply call it a levy of Foreign Troops for the service of England while nevertheless only admitting Swiss officers.[29]

He considered that as Britain was not a traditional employer of Swiss units and any regiments that it raised would not be retained once the war ended which, by implication, meant the restoration of the French monarchy this could be used to advantage, the troops then being available to return to French service. He recommended recruiting in the Graubünden,[30] as, despite ongoing political turmoil, the 'democratic Government of the Republic leaves each individual at liberty to serve where they wish; and whether the current fermentation continues, or calms down, the attraction of a good engagement, the reputation of the English pay and the hope to enter at the peace the service of France, would attract everyone'.[31] Although these projects came to nothing, they not only set the pattern of how the Baron de Roll's regiment would be recruited but they also began to build a network of people, including some influential Swiss officers, who could assist in the venture.

The Foreign Department had been formed at the War Office in London to supervise the raising and administration of the white cockade regiments and the Baron de Roll's regiment fell within its remit. In September 1794 Emperor John Alexander Woodford was appointed 'Chief Inspector and Commissary General of Musters' and he was to be assisted, in time, by five 'Regimental Inspectors'.[32] The expense of all these units was borne by the Foreign Office, one of the inspectors, James Poole, being told by another, 'these accounts were never to be subject to a board of controul [sic], being he believed chiefly borne on the article of secret service money'.[33] This situation was to give rise, at best, to questionable financial administration. However, it meant that the Foreign Office was directly involved in the organisation of

---

29   TNA: FO 74/4: 'Observations on the project of a levy of troops in Switzerland for the service of England' Salis-Marschlins, undated.

30   Now the most easterly, and largest, canton of Switzerland but which in this period was independent but in a close alliance with the Confederation.

31   TNA: FO 74/4: 'Observations …' Salis-Marschlins, undated.

32   TNA: WO 4/154 and 65/167. Woodford's first name, Emperor, was his mother's maiden name.

33   James Poole, *A Narrative exposing a variety of Irregular Transactions in one of the Departments of Foreign Corps during the Late War* (London: J Parson and Son, 1804), p.18.

the regiments, something which was particularly important when facing the specific challenges of recruiting in Switzerland.

In November 1794 William Wickham arrived in Switzerland on a special diplomatic mission and Fitzgerald, whose tenure was not regarded as a success, considered that his mission was usurped, and left the country on 9 December. Wickham was appointed chargé d'affaires and then Minister Plenipotentiary.[34] He was well-regarded by the British Government and even his counterpart, Barthélemy, who described him as having 'ability.'[35] In particular he was trusted by William Wyndham Grenville, the Secretary of State for the Foreign Office, who was an old school friend, furthermore Wickham had studied law at the University of Geneva and married Eleonore Madeleine Bertrand, the daughter of one of the university's professors, in 1788.[36] The raising of the regiment was to be an object of intense diplomatic rivalry between Wickham and Barthélemy.

The first step in raising the regiment was Baron de Roll meeting with Jost de Dürler and Jean-Christophe de Dieffenthaller at Utrecht, in The Netherlands, to draw up a provisional list of its officers, which was sent to the War Office on 6 December 1794, three days before the capitulation was signed.[37] Dürler was to be *lieutenant-colonel* of the new regiment and Dieffenthaller the *major*. A few months later Roll explained his choice of officers for the regiment.

> The aim of the levy of this Regiment was to procure for His Majesty for the service of Great Britain, a Regiment composed of Swiss, formed in more than a large part from the debris of the Regiment of Swiss Guards and Swiss regiments that served so loyally and truly the French monarchy until its last moment.
>
> This Regiment thus cannot be considered as the White Flag [cockade] Regiments under any account, or even like the Regiments raised by capitulation under the command of French or German officers.
>
> The advantages and utility that England will be able to gain from the Royal-Etranger Regiment are of an absolutely different nature, and merit on the part of the Government to be considered simultaneously from the political and military point of view.
>
> I have been so struck with this truth, that my first care was to stir public opinion in Switzerland, in favour of this levy, and make seen the advantage of the service of Great Britain, over the service of the other powers that have agreed capitulations with the different Cantons; to achieve this I principally focused on

---

34   Elizabeth Sparrow, *Secret Service British Agents in France 1792–1815* (Woodbridge: The Boydell Press, 1999), pp.39–43.

35   Kaulek, *Papiers de Barthélemy*, to the Committee for Public Safety 5 January 1795 p.536.

36   William Wickham, *The Correspondence of the Right Honourable William Wickham from the year 1794* (London: Richard Bentley, 1870), vol.I, pp.3–4. Wickham's father is described as having spent some time as a cadet in a Swiss regiment in the service of Sardinia-Piedmont before being commissioned in the First Regiment of Foot Guards, of the British Army (Wickham, *Correspondence*, vol.I, pp.2–3).

37   Staatsarchiv Luzern (SL): Schumacher papers PA 639/22: Dürler to Dieffenthaller, 17 February and 18 March 1795, and to Wickham, 25 May 1795.

Lieutenant Colonel Jost de Dürler (1745–1802), his coat has the 'herringbone' lacing 'à l'anglais' and he wears the decoration of a chevalier of the Ordre de Saint-Louis on the left breast, engraving illustrated in Wolfgang Friedrich von Mülinen, *Das Französische Schweizer-Garderegiment am 10. August 1792.* (Luzern: Gebrüder Räber, 1892)

getting officers from the most distinguished families and who enjoyed great esteem in Switzerland.

On my own account … I have managed to have a corps of perfect officers, who by their influence in all the Cantons and allies of Switzerland, not only will contribute to the prompt success of my recruitment, and thwart the increasing efforts of Barthelemy, Minister of the Convention, against the levy of my Regiment, but also will add infinitely to the number of the partisans for England in all the Cantons …[38]

It is noteworthy that he refers to his regiment by its official name, the Royal Etranger (Royal Foreign) Regiment, which is used in this book until it was changed in 1798. Although it will be seen that British officials and officers generally refer to it in correspondence as the Baron of Roll's Regiment or similar. This differentiation soon became necessary as another regiment called Royal Etranger was formed on 24 December 1795 in Germany under the command of Comte Joseph-Clément Sallier de la Tour for service in the Caribbean.[39] In public Wickham referred to it as 'a foreign corps in which His Majesty would no doubt be pleased to see so many brave Swiss officers offer their services,' thus giving him the pretext to deny it was a Swiss regiment.[40]

While Roll supported the raising of the regiment and took a particular interest in the selection of the *capitaines* of companies, the main burden of the work fell on Dürler and Dieffenthaller. While Dürler, for the first six months of 1795, concentrated on matters in Switzerland Dieffenthaller dealt with those in Germany and one of his first actions was, in January, to obtain permission from the Austrian commanders to establish depots for the assembly of recruits.[41] The point of arrival was Waldshut on the frontier and on the right bank of the Rhine, facing what is now the Swiss canton of Aargau, while the regimental depot and headquarters was placed at Villingen, 65 kilometres to the north and in the Black Forest. This arrangement was possible as both towns were hereditary Habsburg possessions within the Swabian Circle of the German Empire.[42] However permission came with stringent conditions, including that no more than 80 men could ever be at Waldshut at one time. Furthermore, no subject of Austria, or any of the German princes who were allies in the coalition, was to be enlisted nor any deserters from the Austrian

38 Hampshire Record Office (HRO): 38M49-1-59-58: Roll to Windham (copy) 15 March 1795.
39 It was formed by amalgamating troops raised for two different regiments under earlier capitulations (TNA: WO 24/1112: letter of service 13 December 1795).
40 TNA:FO 74/5: Wickham to Grenville 15 February 1795
41 TNA: FO 74/5: Wickham informed Grenville of the agreement in a letter of 15 January 1795.
42 They are now, respectively, Waldshut-Tiengen and Villingen-Schwenningen, both in Baden-Württemberg.

forces, or those of an allied power in the coalition; any such deserters were to be handed over as soon as they arrived at Waldhsut and Austrian officers were to have access to the recruits to identify any that had been undetected.[43] Later Dieffenthaller's chief concern was contracting and supervising the delivery of uniforms, arms and equipment at Frankfurt.

Many officers declined places in the regiment, some because they had property in France which would be subject to confiscation should they enter British service and others had different aspirations or options. One of the latter was Jean-Victor de Constant-Rebecque, who had served in the Régiment de Lullin de Châteauvieux and then the Gardes Suisses in France before joining the Dutch army. After the defeat of the United Provinces he sought a place in the regiment but when, on 31 August 1795, Dürler offered him one he had just taken a place as an aide to Prince Frederik of Orange.[44] The Baron de Roll was an active Freemason, as evidenced by the symbols later used by the regiment, and some officers were also lodge members however there is no evidence that this influenced the choice of officers. Both Roll and Dürler considered officers were dissuaded from accepting places in the regiment they were offered by provisions in the capitulation.

On 14 February Dürler asked Wickham to draw the government's attention to the issues in question, '1st that there is nothing mentioned in the capitulation concerning the wounded, 2nd that it is not positively stated that we ought only to serve in Europe, 3rd that at no point is a fixed term given for the duration of the capitulation, 4th it was not put that we would maintain our justice.'[45] He pointed out that they sought to attract officers who were comfortably off and whose motivation was to continue their military careers. This was certainly unlike the white cockade regiments in which French émigré former officers, destitute after their exile had extended into years, would, if unable to obtain a commission, serve as NCOs simply to earn a living.[46]

Unfortunately, the documents regulating the white cockade regiments that were to guide such matters did not assist. There was no provision for men invalided by wounds, or any other service-related cause, and the units' term of service was the same as that of Roll's capitulation. Furthermore, as well as in Europe, the regiments could be deployed 'in any Part of the Dominions of his late Most Christian Majesty,' thus including present or former French colonies such as in the West Indies which disease made the graveyard of European troops.[47] Lastly the Articles of War dealing with military justice were specific to the white cockade regiments, excluding those raised under separate capitulations such as the Royal Etranger.[48]

---

43 SL: PA 639/22: Dürler to *Capitaine* Henry Dieffenthaller, 30 January 1795.

44 National Archief, The Hague (NA): 2.21.008.01/IN – 19: *Journal de Constant Rebecque*, Volume 1.

45 Copies of this letter are to be found in SL: PA 639/22 and TNA: FO 74/5.

46 Alistair Nichols, 'The Raising of the White Cockade Regiments, 1794–1802' in Robert Griffith (ed.), *Armies and Enemies of Napoleon 1789–1815* (Warwick: Helion & Company, 2022), p.122.

47 Section 1 of the Act, which was printed along with the Articles of War, jointly in English and French, examples of which are held in TNA: WO 24/1112 and HO 42/41.

48 Article II, Section IX 'Administration of Justice' in the Articles of War.

Writing to Grenville, Wickham supported all Dürler's points stating that the first two, 'are absolutely necessary if it is meant that really good men and particularly good non-commissioned officers should be procured.' He continued, 'As to the fourth, if there is no particular objection to it being granted it seems to me of considerable importance, as it is the immemorial privilege of the Swiss regiments in every town in Europe, to be tried by courts martial composed only of their own countrymen.'[49] The system of justice in Swiss regiments stemmed from two sources, both from the early days of the capitulated Swiss units in foreign service. One was to maintain a distinct esprit de corps by making all members of a unit, rather than an external authority, responsible for their comrades' conduct so, in the sixteenth century, in battle, 'every soldier was expected to kill on the spot any comrade trying to turn tail and run.'[50] The other was that the cantons delegated their powers to dispense justice to the colonels and captains in the units raised under capitulation. The criminal code was that of the Habsburg emperor Charles V, thus it was commonly called the Caroline Code, and it was administered by all the officers forming a Council of War that presided in the open in the presence of the regiment.[51] Punishments could be severe and also, at least in name, archaic. Sentencing was carried out by a junior tribunal made up of the *lieutenants* and their decision was then considered by another formed by the *capitaines* and field officers. This second tribunal could only confirm or reduce the sentence of the first, so, in practice, the initial sentence was a maximum which could be reduced.

The regiment was granted permission to administer its own justice, 'a subsequent order' creating the post of a regimental judge advocate and in May 1797 it was noted that such courts martial were held.[52] The case of *Caporal* Bartolomeus Müller who was sentenced on 5 December 1797 for desertion, provides an example of how they worked, 'The Lieutenants forming the inferior Council' condemned him to be shot, the term 'arquebused' being used. The 'superior Council' of *Lieutenant-colonel* Dürler and the *capitaines* reduced Müller's sentence to demotion after which he was to 'pass by the sticks,' wear a black mark on the shoulders until further orders and serve a further four years from the day of the judgement.[53] Passing 'by the sticks' was similar to running the gauntlet in which Müller would have been stripped to the waist and have to march through two ranks of soldiers, 100–200 in number. In this process his arms would be bound and, escorted by four *caporaux* he would have to proceed at a pace set by a drumbeat, each soldier

---

49 TNA: FO 74/5: Wickham to Grenville, 15 February 1795 (with minor spelling corrections).

50 John McCormack, *One Million Mercenaries: Swiss Soldiers in the Armies of the World* (London: Leo Cooper, 1993), p.77.

51 See Franz Adam Vogel, *Code Criminel de l'Empereur Charles V, vulgairement appelé La Caroline: contenant les Loix qui sont suivies dans les Jurisdictions Criminelle de l'Empire; et à l'usage des Conseils de Guerre des Troupes Suisses* (Maastricht: Jean-Edme Dufour & Phil. Roux, 1779).

52 TNA: WO 1/218: table of the regiment, 1 September 1797 and WO 1/217: De Burgh to Charles Stuart, 20 May 1797.

53 TNA: WO 1/218: sentence of Bartholomeus Müller, he received the bounty for re-engaging but in four annual instalments.

striking him with a stick, such as birch, on the shoulders. When finished and the bleeding was stemmed, he would then have to dress and march in front of the assembled regiment.

Later Dürler requested that the regiment be authorised to use the traditional and distinctive Swiss drum beatings, the *batterie Suisse* or *Helvetique*. While there is no evidence of a response, it is very likely that the regiment adopted the *batterie* being raised, as it was, in isolation in Germany without any other guidance. Indeed, the British Army's instructions for an 'established System' of 'Calls and Beats' were only issued on 28 December 1816 before which Scottish regiments, for example, were still using their traditional set.[54]

As some officers resigned or declined commissions, others applied and, in addition, Dürler offered influential figures in the cantons the opportunity to nominate men. Initially Dieffenthaller also interceded in the nomination of some officers, one of whom does not fit the profile described by Roll. Joseph Barbier, a native of Courfaivre south-east of Porrentruy, had risen through the ranks in the Régiment de Reinach from soldier to *sous-lieutenant* in 1792.[55] He was thus known in the French royal army as an *officier de fortune*, to differentiate him from an officer from the nobility who was considered to be serving as a chivalric duty. Barbier reported to Dürler at Solothurn on 17 February 1795 prompting the latter to write to the *major*,

> I freely confess to you that I was very surprised and very embarrassed today, to have seen arrive one named M. de Barbier, saying he was from Porrentruy, and that he is an Officer in our Regiment, without having a single written word from you, … this unfortunate man, finding him woebegone and on the streets, I sought to find the means to place him, [and gave him an advance towards recruiting costs due to] … his air of honesty, and seeing the sorrow he displayed …[56]

Dürler begged him not to nominate any more officers, however Dieffenthaller's choice was soon vindicated when, within weeks, the *lieutenant-colonel* described *sous-lieutenant* Barbier, who was recruiting in Solothurn as 'an excellent acquisition.'[57]

Dürler wanted to attract officers from throughout Switzerland in order that support for the regiment would become widespread and recruitment would be more effective. At the start Basel and the lands of the Prince-Bishop of Basel provided a disproportionate number of officers, something that did not pass unnoticed elsewhere, Dürler explaining to one applicant who was, initially, unsuccessful, 'It is necessary to regard … our regiment

---

54   Henry George Farmer, 'Scots Duty: The Olde Drum and Fife Calls of Scottish Regiments' *Journal of the Society for Army Historical Research*, vol.24, No. 98 (Summer, 1946), p.70. Whilst the conclusion is his own, the author thanks Eamonn O'Keeffe for his advice and guidance in this matter.

55   Service historique de la Defense, Vincennes (SHD): contrôle Régiment de Reinach GR 15 Yc 95. Later his name was sometimes given as Barbié or Berbié.

56   SL: PA 639/22: Dürler to Dieffenthaller, 17 February 1795. He had noted Barbier's nomination in another letter of 4 February.

57   SL: PA 639/22: Dürler to Dieffenthaller, 1 March 1795.

Commission of Eugène de Courten as 'Captain of a Company in a Regiment of Infantry to be forthwith raised for the British Service and to be composed of French Subjects commanded by Colonel Baron de Roll with temporary Rank in Our Army only' dated St. James's 9 December 1794, CH AEV Courten, Cn B 3/2/3. (Courtesy of Nathalie Barberini-de Courten)

rather as an affair of politics rather than as a military matter'.[58] Officers were required to provide a number of recruits, according to rank, *capitaines* 20 and *sous-lieutenants* three; however there seems to have been flexibility in this arrangement as when, in March, a company was allocated to the Comte Eugène de Courten, from Valais, Dürler allowed Antoine-Marie d'Augustini, a prominent local officer, to nominate men from that republic for the places of *lieutenant* and *sous-lieutenant* on the condition that they each provide 20 men who were to arrive at the Waldshut depot within three weeks.[59] The provision of recruits seems to have been the only contribution expected as Dürler was far from pleased when he learned that the *lieutenant* from Valais, Adrien de Preux, had paid Augustini 30 *louis* for his nomination.[60]

Although recruitment took place in Germany the main effort was in Switzerland where it had to be undertaken, more or less, clandestinely. On 30 January Dürler issued a standing order that read, 'Capitaines and officers

---

58   SL: PA 639/22: Dürler to M. Fechter, 10 June 1795.

59   SL: PA 639/22: Dürler to M. d'Agustini, 13 March 1795.

60   SL: PA 639/22: Dürler to Dieffenthaller, 10 June and to Wickham, 4 June 1795; he speculated that this may have been a local practice of which he was unaware. Dürler was surely also unaware that Augustini was simultaneously proposing to raise his own regiment for British service in conjunction with his cousin, Janvier de Riedmatten – Archives de l'Etat du Valais (CH AEV) : Sion, Xavier de Riedmatten, P 298, 299, 302, 306, 308 and 310 (May to November 1795).

will take the greatest precaution to raise recruits with the least fuss, and to be extremely circumspect and prudent on this object, to never have many men assembled in the same place and to send the recruits who engage in Switzerland through to Waldshut immediately'.[61] In a letter to *Lieutenant* Antoine de Champreux d'Altenbourg he specified, 'never have more than two or three men assembled in the same place and never send a transport stronger than three or four men at a time … to avoid the least complaint'.[62] Despite his orders, Dürler later found that up to 15 men were arriving at Waldshut at a time and then they were being sent on to Villingen in batches that were 20 to 30, and sometimes even 40, strong.[63]

All the while Barthélemy applied pressure on the Swiss authorities to act against the recruiters. His efforts were aided by the tactless behaviour of French émigrés trying to raise men for white cockade regiments.[64] Their activities led to the arrest of a *lieutenant* in the Royal Etranger by the Bernese authorities, as Wickham reported,

A very unpleasant affair has happened here to a Mr. Godart [*sic*] a Man of Family – and a Lieutenant in the Regiment of Roll, who has been apprehended on a charge of raising recruits; the proof is so clear that it is impossible to suppress it, and he will be publicly tried … I fear the lightest punishment that will be inflicted will be 4 or 5 years imprisonment.

He has thrown up his commission in the hope of diminishing his punishment. This Gentleman has a wife and children and but a very small Fortune. He had the reputation of an excellent Officer in the Regiment of Ernest where he had a Company. If he be entirely abandoned to his fate, it will I fear have a very bad effect in the Country. I will neglect nothing on my part that may contribute to save him, though I fear every attempt will be totally useless.

The Affair of Mr. Godart would not have happened if the Imprudence of the French Officers had not given rise to such repeated reclamations on the part of Mr. Barthelemy that it was impossible even for the Governments that were the best disposed to connive at the thing any longer.[65]

Barthélemy regularly complained to the cantonal authorities in flamboyant tones, for example when writing to the 'Bourgemaitre of Zurich' on 11 March,

… the enemies of France … do not content themselves, Sir, with establishing the length of the Rhine … depots for Recruits destined to draw your subjects to form a corps that they term as a Swiss Regiment. … They maintain in Switzerland hidden recruiters who work in silence … who occupy themselves in leading their compatriots astray by making them share their crimes in contempt of the laws of their land and breaking the neutrality that the Helvetic Corps has solemnly

---

61 SL: PA 639/22: Standing order, 30 January 1795.
62 SL: PA 639/22: Dürler to Altenbourg, 4 March 1795.
63 SL: PA 639/22: Dürler to Wickham, 24 May 1795.
64 TNA: FO 74/5: Wickham to Grenville, 15 February 1795.
65 TNA: FO 74/7: Wickham to Grenville, 31 May 1795, it is also reproduced in Wickham, *Correspondence*, vol.I, pp.64–73. The officer was Johann Ludwig Gaudard (1760–1810).

adopted. … [He demanded action adding] When during the last American war, England wanted to raise the Erskine legion on the frontiers of the Canton of Schaffhausen, the Helvetic Corps took rigorous measures to prevent its recruitment on its territory …[66]

The French ambassador's humour was not improved when he received a drunken rant from a recruiter for the Royal Etranger, an *officier de fortune* who he had denounced. The officer, who signed his note, 'Schnetz former Swiss of the King,' demanded to know on what grounds Barthélemy had done so, describing France as an 'ungrateful Nation' that gave him a pitiful pension after 32 years' service and had 'unjustly assassinated' its monarch.[67] Despite Schnetz subsequently denying that he had actually penned it, the damage was done and he was demoted to *sergent*.[68]

Barthélemy had successes, particularly when he brought pressure to bear on individuals, 'The most successful measure adopted by Mr Barthelemy was that of gaining the different Bailiffs through whose jurisdiction the Recruits must necessarily pass. Twelve fine Fellows, all Swiss, were seized at once a few days since by the Bailiff of Baden and sent back to their different homes and their Conductors thrown into Prison.'[69] The bailiff at Baden, in what is now Aargau, controlled the Rhine crossing and was particularly active on Barthélemy's behalf, having already, in March, prohibited any boatman 'from taking any unit of men across the Rhine to Waldshut, on pain' of severe punishment.[70] In addition, according to Wickham, the French Ambassador had, 'caused (if I don't mistake) above 40 different officers to resign who had actually accepted their places and begun to recruit.'[71] Nevertheless Wickham considered that Barthélemy's vehement reaction to Schnetz's note came from frustration.

> … your Lordship will have been able to form some judgement of the importance attached by the French Mission to the defeating [of] this measure & of the pains they have taken to accomplish their purpose …I have also reason to know that very large sums of money have been distributed by Mr Barthelemy on this occasion. If I may be allowed to judge from the information that has come to my knowledge I may say with confidence that whatever the raising this regiment may have cost to his Majesty, more than double the sum has been expended in opposing it.
>
> … I feel it my duty to state to your Lordship that its success must be chiefly if not entirely attributed to the zealous and unremitting exertions of the Lieutenant Colonel Monsieur de Durler to whose ability, good Conduct and discretion I must ever bear the strongest testimony. I should mention also that the Baron de Roll

---

66 Copies in TNA: FO 74/5 and SL: PA 639/22.
67 TNA: FO 74/7: (copy), the note is dated 15 May 1795.
68 SL: PA 639/22: Dürler to Dieffenthaller, 3 June, and to Wickham, 12 June 1795. Schnetz gave up his place as *enseigne* to a young applicant of family who compensated him so his pay remained the same for a year.
69 TNA: FO 74/7: Wickham to Grenville, 31 May 1795.
70 SL: PA 639/22: *Lieutenant* George de La Ville to Dürler, 16 March 1795.
71 TNA: FO 74/7: Wickham to Grenville, 31 May 1795.

has to my knowledge expended a very considerable sum in gaining the leading persons in some of the lesser Cantons …[72]

The success in recruitment led Wickham to speculate if even more troops could be raised. One idea was to add a further battalion to the regiment by incorporating most of the Regiment von Wattenwyl, or de Watteville, the former Régiment d'Ernst in French service, which was then employed by the government of Bern – not to be confused with the future regiment of that name in British service – the schemes went no further.[73]

One of the active supporters of recruitment for Britain was *Colonel* Jean Samuel Pierre Roland who commanded the Bernese forces enforcing the cordon along the frontier with Vaud and France. In recognition of his help, his younger son, George, who had served in the Armée de Condé was placed as *lieutenant* in Roll's regiment. Furthermore his older son, Victor, who had served in the May Regiment in Dutch service before the Swiss regiments of that nation were disbanded in July 1795 after it fell under French domination, was later given a captaincy and placed in charge of the recruitment company when it was added to the regiment in March 1796. Support also came from Comte Salomon Hirzel de Saint-Gratien of Zürich, who had served in French service in the Gardes Suisses and then as *lieutenant-colonel* of the Régiment de Steiner and was soon to be a general in Russia. Three of his brothers, Alexandre, Gaspard and Maximilien, served as officers in the regiment.[74] The Baron Salis-Marschlins also provided assistance, indeed Roll was very keen that a member of the Salis family have the captaincy of a company given their prominence in the Graubünden, a potentially fruitful recruitment area. No suitable candidate was forthcoming from the family however Salis-Marschlins strongly recommended that Baron Philipp von Capol be given the company. Capol was well placed, already an officer in the regiment, a native of the Graubünden and a former officer in the Gardes Suisses, Roll and Dürler having been disappointed earlier that, 'There is no one from the Guards who has a company except [Joseph] de Zimmermann who has 43 years' service, 17 years commissioned colonel'.[75]

Given the Graubünden laws, Capol recruited openly and published information about the regiment.[76] Nevertheless, he soon encountered opposition and, after a complaint was submitted to the government on 22 June, his activities were suspended. Although chiefly a political dispute, it was reported that there had been an attempt to assassinate *Lieutenant* Jean Fortuné Juvalta, or Juwalta, of the regiment, while he was recruiting.[77] On 24 September the Bundestag voted on the issue and 30 deputies supported

---

72   TNA: FO 74/7: Wickham to Grenville, 31 May 1795.
73   TNA: FO 74/7: Wickham to Grenville, 31 May and SL: PA 639/22: Dürler to Wickham, 7 June 1795.
74   As an aside, one of his sisters, Marie Catherine, married a Guernsey man and was mother to John Gaspard Le Marchant, a future British general.
75   SL: PA 639/22: Dürler to Salis-Marschlins, 10 March 1795.
76   Staatsarchiv Graubünden, Chur (StAAG): XV 2c/12: 'Hochgebiethende gnädige Herren und Oberen!'
77   HRO: 38M49-1-59-58: Major Walker to Wickham, 21 July 1795.

Capol, 18 opposed him resuming his activities while 15 abstained. Support for recruitment for British service came, in particular, from those who wanted to retain traditional rights, that were dated from 1726 and 1748, one deputy stating, 'The Bündner should not be deprived of the freedom to seek a living as he sees fit.'[78]

Porrentruy, for the reasons already described, provided many recruits for the Royal Etranger Regiment. Broadly speaking fewer officers, and thus men, joined the regiment from the cantons and territories that had existing or prospective capitulations to provide Spain and Sardinia-Piedmont with troops. In Obwalden, however, there was little chance of employment for officers and soldiers returning from French service, or those who wished to pursue a similar calling, as the canton's limited formal interests in foreign service consisted of only a single company in the Regiment Peyer im Hof of the Sardinian-Piedmontese army. It officially rejected recruitment for the Royal Etranger Regiment however such opportunities occurred when officers of the powerful Flüe family raised a company for the regiment. Louis de Flüe, who had distinguished himself in the defence of the Bastille as *lieutenant* in the Régiment de Salis-Samade, was *capitaine* and his two nephews, Michael and Joseph, were *lieutenants*. Companies within the regiment were clearly attributed to specific cantons or territories, particularly in the selection of officers as seen above in relation to Valais and Obwalden. This continued for some time so when *Capitaine* Abraham Frédéric d'Erlach, from Bern, resigned in 1796 *Lieutenant* George Roland, from the same canton, was in line to be given command of the company.[79] However, being too junior this did not, in fact, take place. Another consequence was that foreign soldiers were distributed unevenly throughout the regiment, Germans tended to be recruited more readily into companies identified with German-speaking cantons and, given its proximity, that of Valais attracted Italian recruits.

Henry Dieffenthaller, the *major*'s brother and *capitaine* of the first battalion's grenadier company, commanded the depot at Villingen where the recruits were medically examined, uniformed and equipped. *Capitaine* de Courten arrived there and on 3 July reviewed his company, part of the first battalion; it had 68 men under arms, although this included five who had passed to the grenadiers or chasseurs. He was very pleased with what he saw, informing his brother, 'I must admit that it is superb and that it takes precedence for beauty only after that of the Comte d'Erlach; and for strength above all others of the Regt.'[80] Since the formation of the company one man, a Prussian, had deserted within a day and five men had been claimed by the Austrians as deserters from their own forces. Courten felt that the regiment had 'lost 200 and more men through desertion' but he considered this as a purge, 'The Corps is superb and I have seen 1150 men under arms.'[81] About

78   StAGR: Bundestagsprotokoll AB IV 1/167 24 September 1795 and Kantonsbibliothek, Chur, B 2108, cited in Hubert Foester, *Die Gründung des Regiments von Roll im Dienste Englands 1795–1796* (unpublished article).

79   CH AEV: Cn B 16/1/29: Courten to his brother, 4 March 1796.

80   CH AEV: Cn B 16/1/2: Courten to his brother, 5 July 1795.

81   CH AEV: Cn B 16/1/2: Courten to his brother, 5 July 1795.

Switzerland, Southern Germany, Tyrol, Northern Italy and Corsica (with inset Ajaccio region).

half of the soldiers were 'good and fine Swiss' and 17 to 20 recruits continued to arrive every day.

In Villingen the soldiers were quartered with the local population at the price of a guilder and 30 kreuzers a head. This brought income into the town but as the soldiers' rations were purchased individually local food prices increased.[82] Then, in late summer, a French offensive across the Rhine drew Austrian forces to cover the Breisgau, west of the Black Forest, and Villingen was required for an artillery depot. So the depot of the Royal Etranger Regiment was closed on 28 August, the Austrian *General* Graf von Wurmser ordering the regiment to go to Konstanz on the shores of the Bodensee.[83] The close contact between the regiment's soldiers and the residents of Villingen had resulted in the marriage of at least one of them, *Caporal* Franz Weber, whose new wife, Magdalena Wanger, was granted a passport to follow the him.[84]

The first battalion left Villingen at 5:00 a.m. on 3 September, the second was to follow a day later. The first day's march ended at Donaueschingen where the Princess von Fürstenberg greeted the battalion on horseback and invited the officers to dine; the march then continued to Kirchen-Hausen then Aach. The march had begun when messages arrived from the Konstanz municipality that the regiment could not be lodged in the city due to the presence of large numbers of disbanded émigrés, so the second battalion had been ordered to remain at Villingen until its destination was known. Eventually, after direct contact with Wurmser and the municipality, it was agreed the first battalion and staff would continue to Konstanz while the second, with 730 men, would be cantoned at Radolfzell which was on the Bodensee as well but about 20 kilometres north-west of Konstanz.[85]

On Sunday 6 September the first battalion rested at Radolfzell before marching into Konstanz the next day which Courten described to his brother,

> We arrived around 11 o'clock in the morning, I am persuaded that you would have been enchanted to see our brilliant entrance … The strength of our battalion was 680 men under arms, all in full uniform and in the greatest neatness having made a halt of a good hour for this purpose … 4 leagues from the town. … we [passed through the city], though overwhelmed by the heat, at a regular march, drum beating, flag unfurled, and music en fête, in a word concerning our entry, it would not have been done better if carried out by one of our former Swiss corps …[86]

In the first stages of the regiment's formation British inspectors had not had a great deal of involvement. The first, Captain J. Basset, arrived in May 1795 and he appears to have been pleased leading to a report, 'that the Baron de Rolle's Regiment is twelve hundred strong, and a very fine Corps.'[87] In

---

82   Foester, *Die Gründung*.

83   CH AEV: Cn B 16/1/6 and 16/1/7: Courten to his brother, 28 August and 9 November 1795.

84   Stadtarchiv Villingen-Schwenningen Best, 2.1 AA 36/12 cited by Foester, *Die Gründung*.

85   CH AEV: Cn B 16/1/7: Courten to his brother, 9 November 1795. Radolfzell is given as Zell in a letter, HRO: 38M49-1-59-58: Walker to Wickham, 25 November 1795.

86   CH AEV: Cn B 16/1/7: Courten to his brother, 9 November 1795.

87   BL: Add MS 37875: Lieutenant Colonel Charles Craufurd to Windham, 5 June 1795.

July Major George Townshend Walker, 60th Foot, joined the regiment at Villingen as inspector. Unlike his colleagues he was a serving infantry officer, although most of his career had been spent in staff roles but he was later to prove himself to be an able battlefield commander at battalion, brigade, and divisional levels in the Peninsular War.[88]

Basset, who he had replaced, was sent to Northern Italy to superintend the raising of another regiment, which was to regularly feature in the story of Roll's regiment. Its colonel was Edward Dillon, or the Comte Edouard de Dillon, who although he had begun his career on France's Brigade Irlandaise (Irish Brigade) had served the French monarchy as courtier, diplomat and, since 1780, *colonel* of the Régiment de Provence. His regiment was distinct from those in British service with similar names: the 3rd Regiment of the Irish Catholic Brigade, commanded by the Honourable Henry Dillon, and the second battalion of the 87e régiment de ligne (ci-devant Dillon) that defected to the British in Haïti.

During the four days' march to the Bodensee, the Royal Etranger only lost two men to desertion according to Courten but at Konstanz it increased, possibly due to the proximity of Switzerland.[89] Walker reported,

> ... they are losing severely by desertion to which their want of Exercise & Discipline very much contributes but unfortunately I cannot persuade Durler of this, who is afraid of fatiguing his people indeed the whole Composition & Administration of this Regt is so very bad ... from very bad management they have already considerably overdrawn their funds.[90]

Nevertheless, a statement of the foreign units in British service, dated 25 December 1795, showed the 'Regiment of Rolle's' as 'raised & employed' and with a strength of 1,168 men.[91]

---

88   Ron McGuigan and Robert Burnham, *Wellington's Brigade Commanders* (Barnsley: Pen & Sword Military, 2017), pp.300–307.

89   CH AEV: Cn B 16/1/7: Courten to his brother, 9 November 1795.

90   HRO: 38M49-1-59-58: Walker to Wickham, 25 November 1795, to whom he had already raised the issue of desertions in another of 27 October.

91   TNA: WO 1/898: 'Statement of the strength of the Foreign Corps in His Britannic Majesty's Service employed in the West Indies, Corsica & Europe ...' signed by C. Nesbitt.

2

'A valuable accession'

In 1795 the British Government struggled to deal with a rapidly changing diplomatic and military landscape which led to vacillation and contradictory orders. In Europe, first Prussia and then Spain made peace with France so by July the only remaining power in the coalition with Britain was Austria, along with smaller states including Piedmont. Britain sought to sustain its allies with subsidies as well as supporting counter-revolution in France. A force of émigrés was landed in Brittany and it was planned that this would coincide with advances towards Lyon, over the Rhine and through Franche Comté in the north and from Nice or Savoy to the south. The northern thrust was to include or even be led by the émigré Armée de Condé and Britain took responsibility for financing and strengthening the Prince de Condé's émigrés. Wickham was to assist in the payments and Lieutenant Colonel Charles Craufurd, already liaison officer to the Austrian headquarters in the region, was to act as commissioner.

In the Mediterranean, the British needed to bolster its troops on Corsica, a commitment that had evolved over the previous two years. In 1793 a British fleet had been sent to the Mediterranean Sea under the command of Vice Admiral Lord Hood, among his many tasks was to support allies and neutralise the French fleet at Toulon. Soon, on 25 August, Pasquale Paoli, the leader of the Corsicans trying to expel the French Republicans from their island, invited Hood to assist and so secure a base for the fleet. Despite this approach being overtaken by the chance offered by royalists to take Toulon, Hood detached a squadron of ships to Corsica. The situation on the island was complex, involving traditional social, clan and cultural rivalries along with those of the politics of the age. 40 years earlier Paoli had emerged as a leader of the rebellion against the Genoese rulers of the island but, when Genoa sold its interest in Corsica to France in 1768, overwhelming French forces subdued the island and Paoli went into exile in Britain. The disruption caused by the French Revolution provided Paoli with the opportunity to return to his native land and he quickly re-established his power base, however others, including the Bonaparte family of Ajaccio, sought to use the French authorities to suppress him. As France descended into a struggle between the centralising Jacobins and the Federalists, Paoli asserted independent control over the island except for the coastal strongholds of Bastia, Saint-Florent and Calvi held by French garrisons.[1] Despite optimistic promises, French resistance did not collapse on the appearance of British ships. However, when the allies evacuated Toulon in December the importance of the island as a base grew. On 14 January 1794 a British deputation, led by the civilian commissioner Sir Gilbert Elliot entered negotiations with Paoli, resulting in an agreement that Corsica would become a commonwealth under the British monarch and British forces eventually secured the French-held strongholds on 10 August 1794. Under the constitution Corsica had its own parliament while executive power rested with a viceroy appointed by the king. Paoli, with his party in the ascendancy, expected the post so when Elliot was appointed he became the focus for opposition to the viceroy's rule. In the meantime, the risk of a French counter attack meant that reliable troops were needed to reinforce the island's garrison.

As early as 5 December 1794 London reassured Elliot that the need was recognised and he was informed that steps were in hand, 'for obtaining the Services of a Swiss Regiment, and I think a reasonable hope may be formed of its speedy accomplishment.'[2] The regiment was that to be raised by the Baron de Roll as, on 26 January 1795, Windham wrote to the Duke of Portland, Secretary of State at the Home Office, enclosing a copy of its capitulation, requesting that Elliot be informed, 'that the said Corps should be stationed in Corsica, & that each Company, as soon as completed, should be passed over from Leghorn … to the said Kingdom by single Companies, instead of waiting for the completion of the whole.'[3] In the coming months deployment, in a piecemeal fashion, of Roll's as well as Dillon's regiments was considered essential, 'to afford the only hope of having a sufficient force in Corsica, before an attack shall be made upon it.'[4] Already, however, Livorno, known as Leghorn by the British, with ready access to Corsica and well-established commercial links to Britain, could no longer be used as Ferdinand III, Grand Duke of Tuscany, had abandoned the coalition and declared the duchy's neutrality since 9 February. The port of embarkation would be Savona, west of Genoa, in Sardinia-Piedmont.[5]

Immediately he learned of the proposal to deploy the regiment company by company, without time to train, the Baron de Roll objected,

> I will lose in a moment favourable opinion that had been established in Switzerland, that my Regiment will be a solid and stable Regiment of the Line … much of the officers will leave me at the same instant, and that will cast such disfavour and defiance on this levy, that my recruitment will suffer to such a point that I no longer promise to answer for the ability to fulfil the engagement that I have contracted.[6]

1   Desmond Gregory, *The Ungovernable Rock: A History of the Anglo-Corsican Kingdom and its role in Britain's Mediterranean strategy during the French Revolutionary War (1793–1797)* (London: Associated University Press, 1985), pp.29–48.

2   TNA: WO 1/302: Horse Guards to Elliot, 5 December 1794.

3   TNA: HO 50/386: Windham to William Henry Cavendish Bentinck, Duke of Portland (Secretary of State since 11 July 1794), 26 January 1795.

4   BL: Add MS 58929: Windham to Grenville [?], 2 March 1795.

5   HRO: 38M49-1-59-58: Woodford to Wickham, 7 September 1795.

6   HRO: 38M49-1-59-58: Roll at Osnabruck to Windham (copy to Wickham), 9 March 1795.

For whatever reason, the project was dropped. The British were also concerned to augment the Armée de Condé and one means that was to be taken was to disband most of the white cockade regiments in Germany and transfer the men to the émigré army.[7] In early July Craufurd wrote,

> The Prince is extremely anxious to have the Regiment of Rolle, which is now 1,200 strong … He proposes to augment it with a second [*sic*] Battalion. … and the great advantages that must result from attaching a Swiss Corps to the Condé Army are very evident. There is every reason to suppose that it would become a point of attraction for most of the Non. Comd. Officers and Soldiers who formerly belonged to the Swiss Regiments in the French Service, and I have little doubt but that the second Battalion would be soon completed. The Baron de Roll being a man of such respectable character will increase the advantages to be derived from this arrangement. Should your Lordship consent to the proposal, I beg leave to suggest, that it might perhaps be better to dismiss the Regiment entirely from the English Service, and to let the Prince of Condé take it into his pay upon the same footing that the Swiss Regiments were on in the French Army. He will then of course settle the Levy of the Second Battalion himself.[8]

By neglect or design, key individuals were kept in the dark while this was considered. Elliot was one and another was the Baron de Roll who, although in London through June into July, could not get to see Windham despite repeated requests.[9] Windham, himself, appears to have known little of what was happening as matters were in the hands of Grenville, at the Foreign Office. By August Windham had learned that Grenville had authorised Wickham to make the decision whether the Royal Etranger was to be sent to Corsica or join the Armée de Condé, nevertheless he offered advice that,

> The Baron, I find, as well as most of his Officers, prefers greatly their being employed in Corsica; the reason given by the Baron being, the personal inconvenience likely to result to himself & his Officers, should the Army of Condé, in its passage into France be placed under the necessity of violating Swiss Territory. In every other view the junction of it to the Prince's army is in my opinion to be preferred.[10]

The rates of pay in the Armée de Condé, although better than continental armies, were inferior to the British so Windham pointed out that neither the establishment nor service could be altered, 'without a free & unbiased consent on the part of the Regiment.'[11] For his part, Wickham dismissed Roll's concern about breaching Swiss neutrality considering that, 'The fears of the Baron de Roll were not his own. Nor did the better half of his Regiment partake of them. I see no objection whatever to transferring the Regiment

---

7   BL: Add MS 37875: Woodford to Craufurd, 5 July 1795.
8   TNA: FO 29/5: Craufurd to Grenville, 6 July 1795.
9   TNA: WO 1/302: Elliot to Dundas, 30 April and 4 September 1795 and Roll to Windham, 19 June (BL: Add MS 37859), 23 June, 26 June and 8 July 1795 (BL: Add MS 50851).
10   HRO: 38M49-1-59-58: Windham to Wickham, 7 August 1795.
11   HRO: 38M49-1-59-58: Windham to Wickham, 7 August 1795.

to the Prince'.[12] In this he differed with Craufurd, the British army officer on the ground, who had already identified that areas of Switzerland would have to be secured to prevent the French threatening the flank of any advance through Franche Comté towards Lyon.[13]

However, by 12 August, the decision was taken from Wickham's hands as he had been ordered 'to facilitate the march of the Regiment of Roll to the nearest Port where it might be embarked for Gibraltar.'[14] Remarkably, six days later Henry Dundas, Secretary of State for War, wrote to King George, as part of a chain of communication discussing where to get troops for an expedition to the West Indies,

> A diminution of the garrison of Gibraltar is the other expedient suggested … if the garrison could be speedily supplied by the Swiss regiment commanded by Colonel Rolle, that expedient might with safety be resorted to for one thousand men, but this supply is extreamly [sic] precarious, and without some such resource your Majesty's confidential servants have felt that in the present moment they could not be warranted to advise your Majesty materially to weaken the garrison of Gibraltar.[15]

So, on 20 August Dundas informed Grenville that the king had issued orders for the Royal Etranger Regiment's deployment, it being 'of the greatest Importance that all possible expedition should be used in removing the Regiment to Gibraltar, in order to enable His Majesty to withdraw a part of the British force at present stationed there'.[16] Roll was instructed 'send immediate orders to the Regiment to hold itself in readiness to march for such Port of the Mediterranean as may be fixed upon for its Embarkation.'[17] For his part, Elliot was informed that the Swiss regiment he had so long expected would not be coming to Corsica but he would receive the 100th Foot instead.[18]

If arranging a suitable route through Northern Italy to a Mediterranean port had been considered difficult at the start of the year, French military and diplomatic successes had only made it more so. In view of this, Woodford suggested that the regiment could march for Trieste or Aquileia, at the head of the Adriatic, entailing a march through friendly territory, rather than to the Ligurian coast.[19] Then the regiment's intended destination changed, once again, as Lieutenant General Charles O'Hara, the flamboyant Lieutenant Governor of Gibraltar, 'refused to have Roll in Gibraltar, because the Swiss

12 BL: Add MS 37875: Wickham, at Mulheim, to Windham, 12 August 1795.
13 TNA: FO 29/5: Craufurd to Grenville, 19 June 1795.
14 BL: Add MS 37875: Wickham, at Mulheim, to Windham, 12 August 1795.
15 Arthur Aspinall (ed.), *The Later Correspondence of George III, 1793–1810* (Cambridge: Cambridge University Press, 1962–1970), vol.II, p.382.
16 TNA: FO 74/11: Dundas to Grenville 20 August 1795 (also at WO 6/163).
17 TNA: FO 74/11: Dundas to Roll, 20 August 1795 (also at HRO: 38M49-1-59-58).
18 TNA: WO 1/302: Dundas to Elliot, 23 August and Elliot (unaware of the change) to Dundas, 4 September 1795.
19 HRO: 38M49-1-59-58: Woodford to Wickham, 25 September, and repeated to Gardiner, 2 October 1795 (TNA: WO 4/367).

Guards may long after the Paris Whores, so that finally they will embark ... for Corsica.'[20] O'Hara had been in command at Toulon when he was wounded and taken prisoner on 23 November 1793. Taken to Paris, he was held in harsh conditions as a political prisoner and only released in August 1795. His treatment meant that Frenchmen, even if they were royalist émigrés, were to be regarded with suspicion in Gibraltar.[21] It seems he considered the Swiss in the same light but the style of his objection was somewhat ironic as under his governorship, which was to last from 30 December 1795 until his death on 25 February 1802, the garrison at Gibraltar gained a reputation for indiscipline and drunkenness. Another round of instructions followed and Elliot was now informed that the Royal Etranger was to be sent to Corsica; as soon as it arrived the 100th Foot was to sail to Gibraltar, from where, in turn, part of the garrison would then depart for the West Indies.[22]

Meanwhile the Royal Etranger had remained on the shores of the Bodensee where another unit in British pay soon arrived. As mentioned above, it had been decided to disband the white cockade regiments in Germany, with the exception of the Régiments de Mortemart and Castries which would be sent to Britain, and, after some consideration, the Frenchmen in them were to be transferred to the Armée de Condé while the Germans would form a battalion to be deployed elsewhere.[23] The regiments were disbanded in October and 500 or so men were placed in an old castle at Langenargen, on the eastern shore of the Bodensee, to be organised as the new German battalion by another inspector, Captain Richard Gardiner.[24] It had been considered that the battalion would form a regiment under the command of the Chevalier Charles Jerningham, an English Roman Catholic who had served in the French army rising to the rank of *maréchal de camp*, but soon it was decided that it would be a second battalion for the Dillon Regiment.[25]

When, on 21 September, Major Walker received orders for the Royal Etranger Regiment to march it was in an advanced state of preparedness. The soldiers had canteens, were about to be issued blankets and the final review of the regiment was due three days later.[26] It is probable that this would have been the occasion when the regiment took an oath of allegiance to the British monarchy. If, as likely, it was in the same form as that of the white cockade corps, it was simply to obey orders and 'be faithful, and bear true Allegiance to His Majesty King George, and that I will serve him honestly and faithfully in Defence of His Person, Crown, and Dignity, against all His Enemies or

---

20 TNA: WO 4/367: Woodford to Gardiner, 15 October 1795. The expression was considered so extraordinary that there is an annotation in the copy book 'N.B. I have copied this verbatim.'

21 Sir William G. F. Jackson, *The Rock of the Gibraltarians: A History of Gibraltar* (Grendon: Gibraltar Books Ltd., 1987), pp.182–183.

22 TNA: WO 1/302: Horse Guards to Elliot, 19 October 1795.

23 TNA: FO 29/5, Grenville to Craufurd, 7 July 1795, and Craufurd to Grenville, 6 July 1795.

24 Poole, *Narrative*, p.24.

25 TNA: WO 4/367: Windham to Woodford and Gardiner, 15 October 1795. 300 men were expected to transfer to the battalion but the larger number is given by Walker (HRO: 38M49-1-59-58 to Wickham, 25 November 1795).

26 HRO: 38M49-1-59-58: Walker to Wickham, 21 September 1795.

Opposers whatsoever.'[27] On 15 October Woodford referred to the ceremony in a letter to Walker, 'I have no Doubt but all passed at the taking of the Oath as you co'd wish. But I shall take it amiss that they presented the Colours without you unless you were absent by choice and there was a necessity of not waiting your return.'[28] This suggests, without any other evidence, that this latter ceremony took place about the same time. On 4 June Dürler had described his plans for it, 'Généráls de Salis, de St. Gratien de Hirzel [sic], and other military men must come to the blessing of the flags. I am very sure that they will be amazed by our regt'.[29] But at that stage the flags had not been delivered, indeed he did not even know what colour they would be, Baron de Roll having left this in the hands of Madame Wallier, the wife of his Solothurn banker. Nevertheless Adolf Bürkli, in his early history of the regiment,

Arms of the Baron de Roll: quarters 1 and 4 a golden wheel above a white mountain top with a blue (as the regimental facings) sky and quarters 2 and 3 upper half the top of a black bear with a red tongue and claws on a white background and the lower half red. (Author's collection)

states the presentation of the flag took place in July in the presence of the Baron de Roll, Walker and guests.[30] However it seems he based this on Dürler's wish rather than an account of what happened, as Walker clearly was not there and it is unlikely the baron could have attended as he was fully committed in the arrangements for Artois's involvement in the expedition to Western France during this period.[31] Finally, Courten makes no mention of any such ceremony in his letters although he did indicate, as has been seen, that the regiment carried at least one flag when entering Konstanz on 7 September.

About this time, Walker added an artillery detachment, that had apparently been overlooked in the original capitulation, to the regiment.[32] In line with those of the white cockade regiments, it would have had 35 men: a *lieutenant*, two sergeants, four *caporaux* and 28 *canonniers* (gunners).[33] As for its equipment, Walker was informed, 'The Guns shall meet you at Corsica & be furnished from hence [Britain].'[34]

---

27 Section 1 of the Act and Section 1, Articles 1 and 2, of the Articles of War for the white cockade units.

28 TNA: WO 4/367: Woodford to Walker, 15 October 1795.

29 SL: PA 639/22: Dürler to Dieffenthaller, 4 June 1795.

30 Adolf Bürkli, 'Das Schweizerregiment von Roll in englischen Dienste 1795 bis 1816', *Neujahrsblatt der Feuerwerter-Gefellschaft* in Zürich LXXXVIII 1893, p.10.

31 Roll was certainly in London liaising with the British Government on 7 July (BL: Add MS 37859: letter Roll to Windham) also see Alistair Nichols, '*The Soldiers Are Dressed In Red': The Quiberon Expedition of 1795 and the Counter-Revolution in Brittany* (Warwick: Helion & Company, 2022) pp.228–268.

32 TNA: WO 4/367: Woodford to Walker, 15 October 1795, in which Woodford states his approval of Walker having formed the detachment.

33 Size confirmed in AEV: Cn B 16/1/11 and formation in TNA: WO 24/1112 or HO 42/41: Capitulation for the white cockade regiments.

34 TNA: WO 4/367: Woodford to Walker, 15 October 1795.

As Walker completed the regimental accounts he discovered that there was, by accident or design, an error in the way the officers' pay was calculated, 'Their Pay, from the Field Expenses being consolidated into what was originally intended for it, is now evidently much too high'.[35] Poole explained the issue thus,

> The pay of the officers was divided in two columns [on a table], the first entitled pay, and the second allowances; and from the explanation I have since received of the mode of applying each of them in the ancient French armies, I find the first sum comprehends the whole pay of the officers, while the second was destined to be granted in aid of the pay, on particular occasions, when a certain number of days allowances was added to the pay, as on a march, or on taking the field, &c. and may therefore be compared with our bát and forage allowances. ... I know not how it happened, that the two regiments of Roll and Dillon, were paid the total amount of both, from their first assembling of their corps, making a pay which grossly exceeded that of British officers of infantry; and when compared with the continental powers was enormously excessive, going beyond anything ever heard of.[36]

The regiment could not, of course, march through Switzerland but, by 10 October, Walker had not only received permission to march through the Tyrol but also the assurance of assistance from the Austrian authorities.[37] Two Austrian commissaries were to accompany the regiment so that it was treated as one of their own units as well as an Austrian major to ensure its discipline on the march.[38] However the march was delayed and Walker was becoming concerned, writing on 27 October, 'the route by the Tyrol will become difficult & we are daily losing numbers by desertions. ... The Recruit Parties, except for the completion of one company, are all ordered in & everything will be ready to march in a few days.' Until this point the depot at Waldshut had continued to operate and on 2 October Anton Weidel, from Opava in what is now the Czech Republic, had joined the regiment there, it would be over 21 years before he finished his service.[39] On 6 November Courten noted, 'Today at three o'clock in the afternoon dispatches were sent to all the officers of the Regt commanding the dépôts, and recruits in Switzerland or elsewhere, recruitment ceases totally from today by order of our inspector'.[40]

In this interlude a mysterious episode occurred when Wickham asked that *Lieutenant* Antoine d'Altenbourg undertake a covert mission which was so secret that there is no hint of what it entailed. There is a chance it may have been to do something in Franche Comté as Altenbourg, although of Swiss descent, was a native of the region. The *lieutenant* had the choice of

35   HRO: 38M49-1-59-58: Walker to Wickham, 2 November 1795.
36   Poole, *Narrative* pp.3–4.
37   HRO: 38M49-1-59-58: Walker to Wickham, 10 October 1795.
38   CH AEV: Courten Cn B 16/1/11: Courten to his brother, 6 November 1795.
39   TNA: WO 97/1181/336: pension record. He served nine years as private, over two as corporal and then 10 as sergeant, being discharged on 14 May 1817.
40   CH AEV: Courten Cn B 16/1/11: Courten to his brother, 6 November 1795.

men to take with him and was given an advance payment so that he could buy the equipment they needed. The mission was even kept from Dürler, who had a habit of indiscreetly discussing matters in front of anyone, Walker telling him they were to provide a guard for a consignment of treasure and important papers from Frankfurt. To maintain this story, the party left on the Frankfurt coach and passed through Radolfzell, the location of the second battalion, before heading off to their destination. The need for discretion was paramount and Walker, while trusting Altenbourg's zeal and courage, was concerned he was 'a little too much of a Frenchman for all the prudence necessary on an occasion of this kind.'[41] However, whatever the mission was, it did not come to fruition.[42]

Walker had not made it known that the regiment was no longer to go to Gibraltar as he was concerned about how the news would be received, explaining to Wickham, 'it is inconceivable how every little change of this kind set their hackles in motion.'[43] However in the regiment the concern was about the march itself, Courten remarking, 'we cast our eyes on the Tyrol and there we see all the mountains that have already put on white shirts to greet us.'[44] A fortnight later his frustration was evident, 'our departure had been announced for the 13th, it was moved to the 23 then to the 26 and finally to the 30th several days ago and yesterday evening it was said to me again that it could in fact go to 6 December.'[45] Meanwhile the regiment continued to lose men, not so much to desertion but to the Austrians who had successfully claimed 600 men. Several factors contributed to the delays, including troop movements on the line of march through the Tyrol and prevarication by the Venetian authorities, anxious to appease the French and with no reason to side with Britain, in granting permission to cross their territories.[46] However the main reason was the time needed to prepare the Dillon battalion to march behind the Royal Etranger and it was only ready on 10 December.[47] Walker was not to accompany the march as he was to go ahead to Corsica which left Gardiner as the only British official who would march with the columns.[48]

There is no official record of how the march progressed but a series of letters from Courten traces the route, albeit from an individual perspective. The first battalion marched from Konstanz at 8:00 a.m. on 16 December, although about 200 of the soldiers had marked their last night in the city too enthusiastically and had to be loaded onto the baggage waggons to sober up on the way to Radolfzell. There the second battalion joined and

41　HRO: 38M49-1-59-58: Walker to Wickham, 25 November 1795.

42　HRO: 38M49-1-59-58: Walker to Wickham, 28 May 1796.

43　HRO: 38M49-1-59-58: Walker to Wickham, 2 November 1795.

44　CH AEV: Courten Cn B 16/1/11: Courten to his brother, 6 November 1795.

45　CH AEV: Courten Cn B 16/1/13: Courten to his brother, 20 November 1795.

46　CH AEV: Courten Cn B 16/1/17: Courten to his brother, 27 November 1795 and HRO: 38M49-1-59-58: Walker to Wickham, 15 November 1795 and 38M49-1-59-53: Richard Worsly to Wickham, 31 October 1795.

47　HRO: 38M49-1-59-58: Walker to Wickham, 25 November 1795.

48　HRO: 38M49-1-59-58: Walker to Wickham, 25 November 1795 and TNA: WO 4/292: Windham to Sir Gilbert Elliot, Viceroy of Corsica, 8 March 1796.

the march resumed towards Orsingen-Nenzingen; Courten commanded his own company and that of Charles de Karrer, from Solothurn. Only about four kilometres from Radolfzell, riding at the tail of his company, he noticed that the front had become mixed with the rear of Karrer's that preceded it and a disturbance had begun. Seeing 'muskets raised with bayonets being waved' he galloped to the scene where it was 'an open war between the Italians and Germans of the two companies.'[49] Already one man was on the ground covered in blood and soon another fell, it was an unequal contest as there were four times more Germans, shots were loosed off and a *caporal* hit, but order was soon restored. Courten threatened the men with severe punishment if such an incident reoccurred while ensuring that he did not show favour to either party. The wounded were sent back to Radolfzell and the march resumed, the companies finished the day's march at Orsingen-Nenzingen in good order and there was no further problems.

The regiment seems to have marched along the eastern shore of the Bodensee about 75 kilometres before arriving at Amtzell on the third day. Courten wrote, 'We have horrible marches due to their length and the roads frightful'.[50] He was unhappy that only three captains were with the troops on the march, the others being at the rear with the regimental staff, he was particularly unimpressed that Dürler was not to be seen. The next stage of the march was to Kempten, which was reached on 22 December. Men were beginning to desert, 60 in the first eight days. Prussian crimps dogged the column, spiriting men away by coach, notably 15 men on the night of 21 December.[51] The men were due to rest at Kempten for only a day, but orders arrived that they did not have to march on Christmas Day and would leave 26 December. On 27 December Courten's detachment arrived at Reutte on the northern side of the Eastern Alps. The regiment had no money, the regimental *quartier maître trésorier* was to have obtained cash from a letter of exchange at Kempten but the banker did not arrive, so a regimental council decided to have a chest belonging to Walker broken open in the presence of local magistrates at Reutte. Fortunately, the chest contained 42,603 *livres* so relieving the immediate crisis.[52]

The march continued along a route covered with snow, to Lermoos (29 December) and then Nassereith (30 December). There the first battalion was to wait for the second, that had marched separately since Orsingen-Nenzingen, so they could march together, east along the Inn valley to reach Telfs on 2 January 1796 and Innsbruck the next day. While at Nassereith Marie-Thérèse-Charlotte, Madame Royale de France, the 17-year-old daughter of Louis XVI and Marie-Antoinette, arrived on her way to Vienna and the court of her cousin, Emperor Francis II. She was the last surviving member of her immediate family and had been released from prison in Paris on 18 December in exchange for a number of prominent Frenchmen. His comrades chose Courten to represent the regiment in the expectation

49   CH AEV: Courten Cn B 16/1/22: Courten to his brother, 18 December 1795.
50   CH AEV: Courten Cn B 16/1/22: Courten to his brother, 18 December 1795.
51   CH AEV: Courten Cn B 16/1/23: Courten to his brother, 24 December 1795.
52   CH AEV: Courten Cn B 16/1/25: Courten to his brother, 28 December 1795.

that he would accompany the princess as far as Innsbruck, however, by the emperor's strict instructions, the regiment was prohibited from rendering such honours.[53]

Courten, while recognising his earlier criticisms, paid due credit to Dürler's judgement, 'he proceeds to enter a town as a full parade, he immediately places the two grenadier companies at the head of the column. He says, and we have seen, that he has reason, above all at Innsbruck, where the 180 grenadiers, who in truth are fine, caught attention. It makes the passage of the Regt be viewed favourably.'[54] From Innsbruck the regiment headed south for Italy. It reached Sterzing on 6 January where it had to halt for six days to allow an Austrian column to pass through. More men had been lost but the regiment was still 1,354 strong. Courten lost seven from his company, but he was pleased to report that none had been Valaisans.[55] The march continued to Brixen, Bolzano and Trento towards Verona, which was in Venetian territory so the regiment had to once again march as separate battalions. They could not enter the city, Courten noted, 'It is absolutely forbidden for us to go to Verona, only the Lieutenant Colonel alone will be able to go there dressed in civilian clothes after the whole Regt. has left the territory of the Venetian Republic.'[56] Louis, formerly the Comte de Provence and the legitimate king of France since the death of his nephew the uncrowned Louis XVII, lived in exile at Verona, a situation which the Venetians were increasingly uncomfortable about.

On 6 September 1795 after Louis's accession, Dürler had written to pay homage on behalf of himself and the regiment's officers. In response, Louis acknowledged his debt to Dürler for his conduct on 10 August 1792, declaring, 'the Kings of France will never forget what the Swiss did on this fatal occasion.'[57] Following his visit to Verona, Louis presented Dürler with the brevet of *maréchal de camp* on 25 January 1796 in recognition of 'his military ability and after the proof that he provided of his loyalty and conduct he displayed on 10 August 1792 at the Tuileries.'[58]

Having skirted Verona the regiment went on to Mantua. Courten who was with the first battalion left Mantua on 24 January to arrive at Carpi, north of Modena, three days later where the conditions were uncomfortable, he complained of 'excessive cold … without being able to remedy it, the majority of us being lodged in rooms without chimneys,' and scant provisions so 'disgust is general.'[59] There was a delay which although unexplained, may simply have been the bad weather and, as a consequence, the state of the roads. The second battalion had halted at Mantua. *Sergent* Giachen Giusep Tomaschett from Trun in Graubünden, described being there for 27 days.[60]

---

53   CH AEV: Courten Cn B 16/1/26: Courten to his brother, 4 January 1796.

54   CH AEV: Courten Cn B 16/1/27: Courten to his brother, 9 January 1796.

55   CH AEV: Courten Cn B 16/1/27: Courten to his brother, 9 January 1796.

56   CH AEV: Courten Cn B 16/1/28: Courten to his brother, undated 'near Verona.'

57   BL: Add MS 32168: Louis to Dürler, 6 September 1795.

58   BL: Add MS 32168: dated 25 January 1796.

59   CH AEV: Courten Cn B 16/2/8: Courten to his fiancée, 20 February 1796.

60   P.A. Vincenz (ed.), 'Il regiment svizzer de Roll en survetsch ingles: 1795 entochen 1801: tenor il diari de sergent Giachen Gius. Tomaschett de Trun', *Annalas da la Societad Retorumantscha,*

Courten's next letter is dated 4 March from Modena, his company being quartered at Castelfranco Emilia, just east of the city.[61] There was over 20 centimetres of snow on the ground. The regiment was reduced to about 1,100 men, 'but in all the towns where we are, there are admirers of red coats who follow us to come to take one, and this makes up some of our loss, but in my opinion 3 Italians equate to one Swiss or German'.[62] In addition, recruitment had recommenced in Switzerland with the formation of a recruitment company under *Capitaine* Victor Roland.

Transport had already been waiting at the port of Civitavecchia for a month to receive the regiment, to get there it had to march across the Papal States for which the regiment formed four columns that marched two days apart. The first column of the artillery company, the first grenadier company and four of fusiliers was to leave on 5 March, commanded by Dürler; the second of four fusilier companies of the first battalion, including Courten's, under *Capitaine* Joseph Thüring de Sonnenberg; the third led by *aide-major* Alphonse Antoine de Sonnenberg was of four fusilier companies from the second battalion; and the fourth, under *Major* Dieffenthaller comprised the remaining companies of the second battalion, the grenadiers and four of fusiliers, as well as the regimental hospital with 150 sick. The locations from which Courten sent his letters indicate the route was through Bologna (10 March) and Imola (11 March) to follow the Adriatic shore to Loreto (21 March) before turning inland to cross the Apennine Mountains via Tolentino and Spoleto (29 March).[63] Although Courten visited Rome, the regiment itself marched around the city, Tomaschett remarking, 'We would have liked to stop there, but we had to march on and so we couldn't visit the great and beautiful city of Rome.'[64]

According to Tomaschett the regiment arrived at Civitavecchia on 3, 5 and 8 April but Courten indicates that his column was at the port for three days before embarking on 15 April.[65] In the afternoon Prince Augustus Frederick, King George III's sixth son, witnessed the embarkation having previously attended, that morning, the interment of 22-year-old *Lieutenant* H. Wirtz, from Zürich, who after three days illness had 'succumbed to the fatigues of the journey.'[66] He had joined the regiment at Konstanz after having served as an officer of the Hirzel Regiment in the service of the United Provinces. Courten described the embarkation:

Never has a unit manifested joy as that ours testified yesterday at the moment of its embarkation when only joyful shouts were heard of Vive le Roi, Vive le

Year 11 (1897), p.295. Special thanks are due to Rino Darms for making this article accessible to English readers.

61   CH AEV: Courten Cn B 16/1/29: Courten to his brother 4 March 1796.

62   CH AEV: Courten Cn B 16/1/29: Courten to his brother, 4 March 1796.

63   CH AEV: Courten Cn B 16/1/30, 31, 32 and 33: to his brother and 16/2/9, 10, and 11 to his fiancée.

64   Vincenz (ed.), 'Tomaschett de Trun', p.295.

65   Vincenz (ed.), 'Tomaschett de Trun', p.295 and CH AEV: Courten Cn B 16/1/34: Courten to his brother, 16 April 1796.

66   CH AEV: Courten Cn B 16/1/34: Courten to his brother, 16 April 1796.

Prince Auguste. The royal prince did not leave us a moment since our arrival at Civita Vechia [*sic*], he spent all yesterday afternoon at the port to preside at our embarkation, with tears of joy flowing, on seeing the good spirit that our troops displayed such that we could not have desired a more pleasant time. Despite the losses experienced, we have brought 1257 men under arms onto the vessels, indeed we made several recruits at Mantua and Modena.[67]

Walker, there to supervise the embarkation, wrote, 'The Royal Etranger went on board … in the highest spirits, which was not a little increased by the presence & attention of Prince Augustus'.[68] He did not hide from Wickham his displeasure about the way Gardiner had conducted the march. 'You will no doubt have been greatly surprised at the unaccountable delay in the march of this Corps – more particularly if you know the expense attendant upon it, independent of the loss of its service in so critical a time in Corsica.'[69]

Several of the men, including Courten, suffered sea sickness before they had even left harbour and there appears to have been some desertion before the transports got underway, as indicated by the embarkation return of 18 April.

Table 2: Embarkation return Royal Etranger, Civita Vecchia, 18 April 1796.[70]

Vessels	Officers	Soldiers	Total	Women
	1st Battalion			
Borea	15	260	275	23
Minerva	14	237	251	14
Unity	9	146	155	24
Total	38	643	681	61
	2nd Battalion			
Alliance	9	70	79	7
Anne	11	230	241	9
Parnassus	12	225	237	15
Total	32	525	557	31
Grand Total	70	1,168	1,238	92

The ships arrived off Bastia on 21 April but only two vessels, including that carrying the regimental staff, entered the small harbour while the others remained off shore.[71] The Swiss officers who landed were entertained at the viceroy's residence and, Anna-Maria, Lady Elliot, remarked, 'De Rolle's Swiss regiment is a prodigious fine one. The Lieutenant-Colonel is a most charming man, and was Captain of the Grenadier Guards on duty the famous or rather *infamous* 10th of August. He dined here yesterday, and gave me a full account of that horrid scene and his own miraculous escape'.[72] It was intended that

67   CH AEV: Courten Cn B 16/2/12: Courten to his fiancée, 16 April 1796.
68   HRO: 38M49-1-59-58: Walker to Wickham, 28 May 1796.
69   HRO: 38M49-1-59-58: Walker to Wickham, 28 May 1796.
70   TNA: WO 1/899: return.
71   CH AEV: Courten Cn B 16/2/13: 1 May 1796.
72   Countess of Minto (ed.), *Life and Letters of Sir Gilbert Elliot First Earl of Minto from 1751 to 1806* (London: Longmans, Green and Co., 1874), vol.II, p.337.

the first battalion would join the garrison at Bastia and the second that of Ajaccio but Dürler requested that the regiment be kept together to which Elliot agreed.[73] So, the next day, the Dillon battalion disembarked at Bastia and on the night of 23 April the Royal Etranger set sail for Ajaccio, Elliot writing, 'they are both composed of very fine men, particularly the latter (Roll's) which promises to be a valuable accession to the strength of this Island.'[74]

The reinforcement arrived at an opportune moment. Although Paoli had been persuaded to return to Britain in October 1795, the different Corsican parties continued to compete bitterly but the biggest issue was, as the historian Desmond Gregory observed, 'The Corsicans had got used to not paying taxes and resented having to start doing so again.'[75] The local authorities and forces proved to be unequal, or unwilling, to the task of collecting the taxes when faced with outbreaks of armed resistance across the island. The most significant of which, from March 1796, was in the area of Bocognano, high in the mountains astride the road between Corte (and Bastia) and Ajaccio, the site of the British naval arsenal.

The ships with the Royal Etranger encountered foul weather on their first night out from Bastia and one of the convoy, carrying baggage and no personnel from the regiment, was driven onto rocks. When the storm subsided the vessels were becalmed and so had to be towed by their boats into 'the superb roadstead of Ajaccio' at six o'clock in the evening of 27 April.[76] The town was beleaguered by the rebels from the surrounding mountains. The military governor, Lieutenant Colonel Patrick Wauchope, 50th Foot, was reluctant to act offensively as he considered 'that the whole of the country was utterly opposed to the government'.[77] However Frederick North, Secretary of State, who had been sent by Elliot to galvanise operations, would not accept this assessment.[78] He set about organising militia and brought a detachment of Major George Smith's regiment, that had been raised on the island and bore his name, from Bonifacio; the arrival of the Royal Etranger allowed the strengthened garrison to take the initiative.

On the evening of 8 May three columns, under Dürler's overall command, left the town and converged on Mont-Thabor to establish a camp on the heights above the village of Stiletto. The force was made up of 500 men of the first battalion Royal Etranger, 100 men of the 50th's flank companies, commanded by Major Benjamin Rowe and 200 from Smith's Regiment, supported by some Corsican gendarmes. Dürler was to write a long letter to the Baron de Roll describing in detail the events of the next few days, the regiment's first action.[79] Soon after leaving the town the columns had been fired upon with some casualties but the rebels were driven off by the Swiss

73   CH AEV: Courten Cn B 16/2/13: 1 May 1796.
74   TNA: FO 20/10: Elliot to Portland, 25 April 1796.
75   Gregory, *Ungovernable Rock*, p.113.
76   CH AEV: Courten Cn B 16/2/13: 1 May 1796.
77   Gregory, *Ungovernable Rock*, p.133.
78   TNA: FO 20/11: Elliot to Portland, 16 April 1796.
79   SL: PA 639/22: Dürler to Roll, 23–29 May 1796. The file also contains a copy Dürler sent to his wife.

chasseurs. Dürler was very pleased with his soldiers' conduct, a view shared by North and Wauchope, who were apparently, 'astonished to see the manner that our men make war, and attack the Rebels who place themselves behind Rocks and in the Maquis. The Corsicans even say that they have never seen troops make war like us, and attack with so much courage'.[80] On the night of 9/10 May outposts around the camp were attacked, *Lieutenant* de Preux distinguishing himself in command of an isolated position, and on 12 May a supply convoy was fired on when making its way to the camp. Nevertheless, deputations soon arrived from the neighbouring villages of Afa and Allata to offer their submission. The centre of the local rebellion was Valle-di-Mezzana and on 19 May *Capitaine* Hirzel de St Gratien led a fighting reconnaissance towards the village which resulted in some losses on both sides. Again the chasseurs distinguished themselves and North sent his congratulations and some money to be distributed among the men.

The following morning Dürler, joined by Wauchope, set out towards Mezzana, his columns covered by extensive flank and advance guards but, having received a message that a thousand men were marching on the camp, he immediately turned back to find the new arrivals were Corsican militia sent as reinforcements. Although a deputation arrived late on 21 May from Mezzana there was doubts about the rebels' real intentions. Indeed on the morning 22 May there was an action in which four soldiers were killed and 'a dozen wounded' while 15 insurgents were killed, two taken prisoner and an estimated 30 or so wounded.[81] So Dürler made plans to attack Mezzana in two columns, suspicious of the Corsican troops, especially the militia, they were to march separately in one while the British and Swiss were to be in the other column. Courten considered it was going to be a difficult mission but he had every confidence in the men,

> … we are due to attack a village of 400 houses, with a force of 600 men, it is true that never was there an example of a unit that deports itself as our soldiers do, a bravery that astonishes everyone, a blind obedience in fact all the qualities that one would not expect from a newly formed Regt., my Valaisans I can say are such heroes I look forward to see the moment that a musket shot is loosed, they only seek to fly to the spot where the musket shot was fired …[82]

He attributed the regiment's success to the tactic of rushing on the rebels with bayonets fixed which so unnerved them that their fire was wayward. Of the Valaisan officers, he wrote, 'Thanks to God I am fine, Ebiner also, de Preux is aide de camp en second of our general [Dürler], who commands, in a little affair a few days ago he had a near escape when a ball pierced his hat on his head, he is fine and conducts himself likewise.'[83] However the attack on Mezzana did not take place as it submitted and the troops returned to

---

80   SL: PA 639/22: Dürler to Roll, 23–29 May 1796.
81   CH AEV: Courten Cn B 16/1/35: Courten to his brother, 23 May 1796.
82   CH AEV: Courten Cn B 16/1/35: Courten to his brother, 23 May 1796.
83   CH AEV: Courten Cn B 16/1/35: Courten to his brother, 23 May 1796.

Ajaccio from the Stiletto camp late on 29 May, but not before Wauchope had congratulated Dürler,

> … permit me to say how much I am sensible to your zeal, judgement and conduct in everything since you commanded our troops on campaign. Have the goodness to have all the officers, NCOs and brave soldiers of the Regt. Royal Etranger know how much their merit affects me, and I beg pray you … say the same thing to Major Rowe and to all the English detachment that had the honour to serve under your orders. The good harmony which existed between the two corps, I hope will subsist always and should assure us good success on all other occasions.[84]

At the same time, troops from Bastia, including the Dillon Regiment, had successfully secured Bocognano but Elliot, who accompanied them and concerned about an insurrection in his rear at Corte, made sweeping concessions to the villagers. The effect of this is illustrated by a letter he wrote to Portland, 'I proposed after the Expedition to Bogognano [sic], & after the Pacification of that side of the Country, to place a small Garrison of Roll's Swiss Regiment at that place, but it was judged expedient to know what the inclination of the People was on that point … the answer was of a very seditious & insolent nature … Wishing to avoid a fresh Quarrel, the intention of sending the troops … has been drop'd for the present.'[85]

About this time, however, a detachment of about 150 men was posted at Cargèse, a Greek community, north of Ajaccio, until at least mid-August.[86] Established in the seventeenth century Cargèse was regularly attacked by local Corsicans during periods of lawlessness and *Capitaine* Joseph de Sonnenberg who commanded the detachment wrote years later,

> I … was detached with three Companies from the Regiment de Roll at Cargess [sic], a Greek Colony, where I was attacked by 800 Corsican Rebels, whom I repulsed without Loss on our part, with the Assistance of the Colony people, and drove them to Flight. The Rebels lost a great number of Men.[87]

Meanwhile, the rest of the regiment was at Ajaccio, where space was limited. Indeed Courten had described the regiment as being packed, 'like anchovies in the quarters of the little town of Ajaccio.'[88] Some of the officers were lodged in the Bonaparte's family home.[89] The heat was a problem and many men were hospitalised, Courten considering that the march through Italy and the subsequent voyage contributed to the level of sickness. On 6 July he wrote that, since the regiment had arrived in Corsica, 40 men had died and 30 had deserted. In addition, because of limited engagements, some men, including

---

84   Copy of Wauchope to Dürler 28 May 1796 in SL: PA 639/22: Dürler to Roll, 23–29 May 1796.
85   TNA: FO 20/11: Elliot to Portland, 26 June 1796.
86   CH AEV: Courten Cn B 16/2/14: Courten to his fiancée, 'probably', May 1796 and Poole remembered mustering the detachment at Cargèse 'about July' (Poole, *Narrative*, p.27).
87   TNA: WO 31/1562: return dated 16 October 1813.
88   Vincenz (ed.), 'Tomaschett de Trun', p.297 and AEV: Courten Cn B 16/2/15 23: May 1796 (catalogued as March 1796).
89   Vincenz (ed.), 'Tomaschett de Trun', p.296.

four from his company, would be entitled their discharge in September.[90] Later other detachments were stationed out of the town, according to Tomaschett due to the lack of space, but one, of 120 men, was stationed at the town of Sartène, south of Ajaccio, apparently to exert control over the surrounding area.[91]

Meanwhile in Italy *Général* Napoleon Bonaparte continued a campaign that had already seen Sardinia-Piedmont forced to quit the coalition in April and the Austrian forces besieged in Mantua. He sent troops into the Papal States, which were not at war with France, and neutral Tuscany and by the end of July most of the Italian states, including the Papal States and Naples had signed armistices. French troops reached Livorno on 19 June and over the next weeks took control of the port, Bonaparte arriving on 28 June.[92] This was a severe blow to British commerce and for Corsica it severed the main route for supplies and mail from mainland Europe while the French could send agents and supplies to their adherents on the island more easily. In response the British naval commander, who now was Admiral Sir John Jervis, ordered Captain Horatio Nelson, with a squadron, to blockade Livorno and collaborate with Elliot in the defence of Corsica. Nelson immediately pressed Elliot to occupy Portoferraio on Elba, to hinder an attack by French forces based in Tuscany. The fortified port was Tuscan, while the rest of the island, and much of the adjacent Italian coast, was the territory of the Prince of Piombino and under Neapolitan control.[93] Elliot responded quickly, sending troops from Bastia's garrison, including a Dillon detachment, who arrived off Portoferraio on 9 July, landed that evening and, the following morning, was permitted by the governor to enter the town.[94] The Tuscan officers and, privately, some of the government were apparently sympathetic to the British move.[95] This, Nelson's cajoling, and reports of the situation at Livorno persuaded Elliot to consider an even more ambitious project. On 8 August, in a letter to Portland, he declared that the French force occupying Livorno was reported to be only 1,800 men and he wanted to be ready for any chance of taking the port with little risk, 'altho' such an Expedition cannot be positively determined on … I have judged it right to be prepared for availing myself of such an occasion, if it should occur.'[96]

In consultation with Lieutenant General John Thomas de Burgh, commanding the troops on Corsica, he estimated that a force of 3,000 men could be assembled at Bastia, 1,500 British, foreign and Corsican 'regular troops' drawn from all the island's garrisons, '1000 Corsican Volunteers

---

90   CH AEV: Courten Cn B 16/2/16: Courten to his fiancée, 6 July 1796.
91   Letter of Barbier, quoted in Bürkli, 'Das Schweizerregiment' p.13.
92   Sir Nicholas Harris Nicolas, *Dispatches and Letters of Vice Admiral Lord Viscount Nelson* (London: Henry Colburn, 1845), vol.II, p.197, Nelson to Elliot, 2 July 1796.
93   Nicolas, *Nelson*, pp.199–200.
94   TNA: FO 20/11: Elliot to Portland, 11 July 1796 and Duncan, the officer commanding the force, to Elliot 10 July 1796; see also Nicolas, *Nelson*, vol.II, pp.207–209. Elliot describes Duncan as a major in the Royal Artillery but the only officer of that name with such a rank was Major William Duncan, 1/1st (Royal) Foot.
95   TNA: FO 20/11: Elliot to Portland, 8 August 1796.
96   TNA: FO 20/11: Elliot to Portland, 8 August 1796.

raised for the occasion' and 500 marines and sailors from Nelson's squadron.'[97] Among the regular troops destined for the expedition was a detachment of the Royal Etranger, commanded by *Major* Dieffenthaller. It is unclear when the detachment left Ajaccio for the rendezvous in Saint-Florent Bay but perhaps the last to arrive there was the detachment of the Corsican regiment collected from Bonifacio by the sloop HMS *Sardine*, the entry for 15 August in the captain's journal recording that 'Major Smith came on board with 118 of his Choir.'[98] Three days later they arrived in Saint-Florent Bay where the troops were distributed among nine transports that sailed on 20 August in convoy for Bastia, arriving in the roadstead on 26 August.[99] In the meantime news had arrived that the Austrian offensive in Italy had been defeated so any force that landed at Livorno would be in jeopardy, however Elliot did not cancel the expedition immediately so the troops remained offshore in their transports.[100] Finally, on 31 August, the *Parnassus*, with Dieffenthaller's detachment onboard, weighed anchor in company with two other transports, the *Anne* and *St Mary's Planter*, under convoy of the *Sardine*. On 3 September, after going through the straits, the *Sardine* entered Bonifacio harbour, with the *Parnassus* and *Anne*, anchoring at 8:00 a.m. to disembark Smith's detachment.[101] The vessels set sail again at 7:00 p.m. the same day under a cloudy sky and with fresh breezes. The *Sardine's* journal records,

> … at 8 the 3 Transports in Company … at 10 fired 1 Gun & made the Signal to tack, 3 transports in Sight, at ½ past 10 lost sight of them, fresh Breezes with Showers of   Rain. [Sunday 4 September 1796] … at 5 Strong Gales with heavy Showers of Rain split the fore Sail, bore up for Bonifaccio [*sic*] it bearing NE by N 6 miles, at ½ past 6 Anchored in Bonifaccio harbour … at 8 Two of the Transports came into Bonifaccio, the Parnassus not come in …[102]

On 10 September, in a letter to Franz Xaver von Neveu, Prince-Bishop of Basel, *Lieutenant* Barbier reported what had happened to the *Parnassus*.

> … of the unfortunate fate, which befell a detachment of 230 men of our regiment on Sunday [4 September] at five o'clock in the morning. H.E. the viceroy had summoned it to Bastia for an expedition that he considered and which did not take place. It was returned by sea and arriving in the Strait of Bonifacio a storm arose. The frigate, that escorted the transport vessel, gave the signals to take to the high seas; the captain did not want to obey at all, being drunk it is said. A moment afterwards the vessel struck against a rock and sank soon afterwards. All the crew perished, except fifteen or so persons, among whom no officer was to be found.[103]

97   TNA: FO 20/11: Elliot to Portland, 8 August 1796.
98   TNA: ADM 51/1181: Captain's journal HMS *Sardine*.
99   TNA: ADM 51/1133: Captain's journal HMS *Gorgon*.
100   Nicolas, *Nelson*, p.243, Nelson to his brother, a postscript of 19 August 1796 and TNA: FO 20/11: Elliot to Portland, 28 August 1796, in which he announces the cancellation in a postscript..
101   TNA: ADM 51/1181: Captain's journal HMS *Sardine*. The *St Mary's Planter's* remained off shore.
102   TNA: ADM 51/1181: Captain's journal HMS *Sardine*.
103   Bürkli, 'Das Schweizerregiment', p.13

He then listed the 12 officers who had been lost: *Major* Dieffenthaller, two officers on the regimental staff, two *capitaines*, four *lieutenants* and three *sous-lieutenants*. Comparing the names with those mentioned in Dürler's earlier report of the events of 8–29 May, it would appear that the detachment consisted, wholly or in part, of the regiment's grenadiers and chasseurs. A 'Return of the Royal Etranger that were lost at Sea joining from Bastia to Ajaccio 4th Sep. 1796' shows the loss as 12 officers, along with a surgeon's mate, 10 sergeants, four drummers or fifers, 184 rank and file (corporals and private soldiers) and seven women. Before the shipwreck, the regiment is shown as having 60 officers, 10 staff, 99 sergeants and 50 drummers or fifers present; of the 'effective rank and file' there were 872 under arms and 98 sick – since the previous month, eight had joined, 12 had died and one had been discharged.[104] It seems that the tragedy caused the regiment to be reorganised as future events find Courten in the second battalion and Tomaschett in the first.

One source states that the wreck occurred in the area of 'il Monaci' probably modern day Monacia-d'Aullène, west of Bonifacio.[105] Despite the scale of the disaster there were no official reports of the shipwreck, however, some appeared later in British newspapers, such as that in the *Ipswich Journal*,

> The regiment Royal Etranger, in the British service at Corsica, lately had 11 officers and 218 men drowned in the Parnassus transport, in which they sailed, under convoy of a frigate from Bastia. The Captain of the transport was drunk, and disobeyed the signals made by the frigate, the vessel thrice dashed against the rocks on the 9th of Aug. [*sic*] and only 7 soldiers and 4 seamen were saved.[106]

On 18 September a memorial service was held at Ajaccio for the drowned, as Courten recounted.

> Yesterday we had a divine service for our brothers and friends, which was done with all possible majesty, all the garrison took up arms at 8 o'clock in the morning to go in front of the church [where] the clergy and canons were gathered. There was a magnificent catafalque at the centre of the church, it was surrounded with trophies of arms and with an inscription along it. The church ceremonies finished, we went to the place d'armes where the unit fired three salvoes, during all the time, which is to say from 8 o'clock in the morning until one hour after midday, a 24 pounder cannon fired every minute, nothing was more sombre than this ceremony.[107]

One of the Valaisans, named Brunner, had, according to Courten, survived the wreck by hanging onto a floating hatch for 11 hours before reaching the shore. Courten, himself, was fortunate not to have been on the *Parnassus*.

---

104 TNA: FO 20/12: return of 1 September 1796 to which this return has been added.

105 Grouvel, *l'émigration française*, vol.I, p.304, the source of the information is not provided.

106 *Ipswich Journal*, Saturday 5 November 1796. That month the Foreign Department of the War Office confirmed that they had no 'official account of the accident', TNA: WO 4/378 Woodford to Mr Playfair.

107 CH AEV: Courten Cn B 16/1/36: Courten to his brother, 19 September 1796.

In July, going on regimental business to Naples, he had travelled overland to Bastia where he was poisoned. Whether this was as a result of foul play or an accident is not clear but it meant that he suffered a period of illness and then convalescence. Thus, as he wrote, 'a chain of circumstances having me avoid honourably the shipwreck to which I was destined by position and duty'.[108] He touched upon personal tragedies, 'How much I deplore the fate of Madame de Preux becoming a widow at 25 years on losing a spouse of the same age'.[109] She was not alone, Marie-Anne-Aloyse, but known as Henriette, Dieffenthaller's mother had died at her birth so she had been with her father in the regiment but now, at the age of 13, she had lost him as well although at least her uncle was on hand to care for her.[110] Tomaschett, who stated that five soldiers and two sailors survived, remembered,

> You can easily imagine how sad it was when we received the news that so many brave men had perished. So much the more did this cause sadness in our regiment to have lost so many people in a such an unfortunate way, and just the most outstanding and finest men! Among others we lost one of the most perfect and best officers, who was best able to command the regiment, and many other brave officers and valorous soldiers. To show our sorrow that these people had perished in this sad affair, our regiment fired all its cannons and muskets in a volley 3 Fridays in a row as a sad commemoration of this loss.[111]

In time rumours of the tragedy filtered through to the men's families in Switzerland. The brother of *Capitaine* Joseph d'Appenthel wrote to Dürler three times for news of what had happened. It was only on 7 October 1797 that he received notification, a certificate signed by *aumônier* Becker, that his brother, a former officer in the Régiment de Sonnenberg, had died on 4 September 1796, 'between three and four o'clock in the morning, … by shipwreck on the coasts of the island of Corsica, between Bonifacio and Sartène'.[112]

The British Government had already decided to evacuate Corsica, the letter informing Elliot was written on 31 August and he received it on 28 September.[113] The British presence on the island was made untenable by the Franco-Spanish alliance agreed at San Idelfonso, on 19 August, and ratified at Paris on 12 September. Their combined fleets significantly outnumbered that of the British in the Mediterranean and so resources were to be concentrated

---

108 CH AEV: Courten Cn B 16/2/18: Courten to his fiancée, 17 September 1796.

109 CH AEV: Courten Cn B 16/2/18: Courten to his fiancée, 17 September 1796. Marie-Louise Chaignon had married Charles-Joseph-Adrien de Preux on 20 August 1794. In 1803 she married Pierre Luc de la Fargue who died in 1815 of his wounds received at the Battle of Waterloo while serving as *chef de bataillon* in the 4e Régiment des Grenadiers à Pied de la Garde (TNA: WO 42/64). She continued to receive a widow's pension from her first marriage until her death in 1852 (TNA: PMG 6/10).

110 TNA: WO 4/378: On 24 July 1797 the Foreign Department refused Roll's request that she receive special compensation, on the grounds that it would be unfair treat her differently from other officers' dependents.

111 Vincenz (ed.), 'Tomaschett de Trun', p.297.

112 *Abbé* Ch. Ræmy, *Le Chevalier d'Appenthel* (Fribourg: Libraire J. Labastrou, 1879), p.44. The family later received Appenthel's sword.

113 TNA: FO 20/12: Elliot to Portland, 29 September 1796.

in the Atlantic to defend Ireland and Britain's long-standing ally, Portugal.[114] The decision did not have universal support in the British Cabinet, which resulted in confused and contradictory orders.[115] That planning was not already in place for an evacuation is somewhat remarkable as it was not totally unexpected, Jervis observing to Elliot, 'it was determined to abandon Corsica, in case of a war with Spain, a year ago.'[116] Furthermore this must have been common knowledge as Courten had predicted it in a letter of 6 July.[117]

News that the British were leaving saw a wave of support for the French, exploited by the arrival of republican émigrés to arm and lead their adherents. Jervis's original plan for evacuating the Mediterranean was for all the garrisons, from Corsica, Elba and Capraia, the last having only secured as recently as 18 September, to embark on ships that would rendezvous in Saint-Florent Bay before sailing for the Strait of Gibraltar. As part of this operation, on 6 October Jervis instructed Captain George Henry Towry, of HMS *Diadem*, to evacuate the troops, baggage, artillery and ordnance as well as the naval stores, yard and hospital from Ajaccio,

> I wish as many of the Swiss corps of De Roll's to be received on board the Diadem, and sloops of war, as they can conveniently stow, it being my intention to embark the whole of them in ships of war ... you are not to regard the men being a little crowded during the short passage to that [Saint-Florent] bay.[118]

Then new despatches arrived from London giving Jervis discretion whether to quit the Mediterranean or not. Nelson, who was at Bastia on 17 October co-ordinating the navy's part in the evacuation, commented to his commander, 'The dispatches of this morning are wonderful: do his Majesty's Ministers know their own minds?'[119] The need for a decision was pressing, not least because of the appearance of the Spanish fleet, already superior in numbers, off Cape Corse, on its way to join the French at Toulon. Elliot, for one, wanted to maintain a presence in the region so Jervis compromised. He decided to send the troops to Portoferraio but with sufficient transports and an escort should they be forced to quit Elba in a hurry.

Jervis had originally planned that Ajaccio would be evacuated on 16 October. The process began on 12 October when material was removed from the dockyard and placed on the storeship, HMS *Dromedary*, with the assistance of a party of '30 Swiss soldiers.'[120] The officers of the Royal Etranger seem to have been working to Jervis's timetable as, on 16 October, Courten wrote,

---

114 William James, *The Naval History of Great Britain, from the Declaration of War by France in 1793, to the Accession of George IV* (London: Richard Bentley, 1847), vol.I, pp.310–311.

115 This is illustrated by the series of correspondence reproduced in Julian S. Corbett (ed.), *Private Papers of George, Second Earl Spencer, First Lord of the Admiralty 1794–1801* (London: Naval Records Society, 1913), pp.317–339.

116 Edward Pelham Brenton, *Life and Correspondence of John, Earl of St. Vincent, G.C.B., Admiral of the Fleet, &c.* (London: Henry Colburn, 1838), vol.I, p.224, Jervis to Freemantle, 25 September and p.232 Jervis to Elliot, 2 October 1796.

117 CH AEV: Courten Cn B 16/2/16: Courten to his fiancée, 6 July 1796.

118 Brenton, *St. Vincent*, pp.234–235, Jervis to Towry, 6 October 1796.

119 Nicolas, *Nelson*, vol.II, p.289, Nelson to Jervis 17 October 1796.

120 TNA: ADM 51/1165: Captain's journal HMS *Dromedary*.

> … this evening we embark with all who are English to bring, with us, to the general rendezvous of all the land and sea forces at St Florent which is the principal port of this island. The English fleet which is before Toulon comes to join us at this assembly point to take us under its protection in leaving these seas.[121]

He understood that the regiment would either be placed at Gibraltar or Lisbon or, if not, remain with the fleet, which would sail to Portsmouth from where the regiment would go to Ireland. *Lieutenant* George Roland probably had this schedule in mind when, having obtained a certificate that he had been baptised a Roman Catholic, married Marianna Ottavi, the daughter of the *inspecteur de la marine* at Ajaccio on 16 October.[122]

However, if there had been any urgency it soon diminished, for instance the loading of the *Dromedary* was only completed on 17 October and she made ready for sea the following day.[123] Captain Towry, in HMS *Diadem*, arrived at Ajaccio on 19 October to supervise the evacuation and late in the morning of 21 October '241 Swiss Soldiers' embarked on his ship.[124] The *Diadem* began to leave the harbour at 9:00 p.m. and came to anchor in the bay the following morning. Other Royal Etranger troops were on the sloop HMS *L'Eclair*, they embarked in the afternoon of 21 October, then, the following morning, for some reason they were landed before returning to the *L'Eclair* in the afternoon.[125] Tomaschett may have been in this party as he described the regiment as having completed its preparations to leave on 19 October and did so three days later, the only military equipment that was left behind were the citadel's cannon, which were all spiked.[126] This chain of events is in marked contrast to those given in a later French account of the British evacuating Ajaccio on 16 October to such large-scale demonstrations of support for the French at the departure of 'the unwelcome and detested guests' that Wauchope, to prevent interference, threatened that the warships would fire on the town.[127]

At 8:00 p.m. on 22 October the *Diadem* 'weighed [anchor] & came to sail in [company with] HMS Dromedary, Dolphin, Alliance & L'éclair [*sic*] & 10 Sail of Convoy'.[128] The convoy arrived safely at Portoferraio in the morning of 27 October to join the rest of the ships from Corsica, those with the Bastia garrison having arrived a week earlier.[129]

---

121 CH AEV: Courten Cn B 16/2/20: 16 October 1796.

122 TNA: WO 42/65: the certificate was dated, 17 October, widow's pension claim 1826; evidence shows Roland's conversion to Roman Catholicism, if it took place, was temporary.

123 TNA: ADM 51/1165: Captain's journal HMS *Dromedary*.

124 TNA: ADM 51/1167: Captains' journal HMS *Diadem*.

125 TNA: ADM 51/1139: Captain's journal HMS *L'Eclair*.

126 Vincenz (ed.), 'Tomaschett de Trun', p.298.

127 Maurice Jollivet, *Les Anglais dans la Méditerranée (1794–1797) Un Royaume Anglo-Corse* (Paris: Léon Chailley, 1896), pp.287–288.

128 TNA: ADM 51/1167: Captain's journal HMS *Diadem*. Elliot reported that the convoy sailed on 23 October, TNA: FO 20/12: Elliot to Portland, 26 October 1796.

129 Minto, *Elliot*, vol.II, pp.357–359 and TNA: FO 20/12: Elliot to Portland, 4 November 1796.

3

'Three different Degrees of Red'

The evacuation of Corsica meant that Elliot's post as viceroy had ceased so he decided to quit Elba, placing a heavy responsibility on Lieutenant General de Burgh. Jervis was concerned, 'I entertain the highest opinion of the honour and integrity of General Deburgh; but, inexperienced as he is in business of such a complicated nature – diffident and doubtful, where prompt decision is requisite – I dread the moment of your final departure. I will, however, hope for the best'.[1] Before leaving, Elliot encouraged de Burgh to hold positions on the Tuscan shore, opposite Elba, to ensure supplies reached Portoferraio, as the French extended their military presence south from Livorno. The general agreed to do so, but on the condition that Elliot provided him with instructions to that effect.[2]

The first point to be taken was Piombino, held by a few Neapolitan troops. In the early hours of 7 November a force under Colonel David Douglas Wemyss, 18th Foot, consisting of his own regiment, the two grenadier companies of the Royal Etranger and some artillery embarked on the frigates HMS *Southampton*, *Inconstant* and *Dido* along with the *Sardine* and the cutter *Rose*.[3] Around midday the ships arrived off Piombino, the troops immediately disembarked and the weak Neapolitan garrison gave the town up without a fight. That night Lieutenant Colonel Henry Tucker Montresor with 500 men of the 18th Foot and some artillery took the inland town of Campliglia Marittima, which was held by a French garrison, by a surprise attack.[4] Then Wemyss, having been informed that French troops had evacuated Castiglione della Pescaia, further to the south, decided to try to intercept their retreat to Livorno. De Burgh was to report that, Wemyss having left the force at Piombino too weak by this decision, he ordered 'about three hundred men of Rolle's Swiss Regiment to reinforce it. They did not

---

1   Brenton, *St. Vincent*, p.262, Jervis to Elliot, 11 November 1796. Jervis opened his letter (p.261) with the news that contradictory orders had arrived, 'By the Cygnet cutter, which joined last night, I have orders to support your sovereignty of Corsica; and in case of the evacuation having taken place, to establish ourselves at Porto Ferrajo.'
2   TNA: WO 20/12: Elliot to Portland, 4 November, and to de Burgh, 6 November 1796.
3   TNA: WO 20/12: de Burgh to Portland, 9 November 1796, and captain's journals HMS *Southampton* (ADM 51/1189), *Inconstant* (ADM 51/1179) and *Dido* (ADM 51/1172).
4   Anon., *The Royal Military Calendar or Army Service and Commission Book* (London: A. J. Valpy, 1820), vol.II, pp.362–363.

arrive till it was too late to land them. A gale of wind came on the ship drove from her anchors, and went on the rocks, where I conceive she is totally lost. Four officers, and about sixty soldiers have perished.'[5] *Sergent* Tomaschett was on the transport, which appears to have been the *Anne*.[6]

On 10th November we set out to sea from the port of Porto Ferrjao and on 11th towards evening we were already before the city of Piombino. The captain of the ship ordered to pull ashore and wanted to disembark the same evening because he was afraid of stormy weather. Our commander paid no heed to this and remained on the ship to honourably disembark the following day and to parade with his men. But the next day it was already too late! The captain of the ship had already predicted the weather that happened during the night. A furious wind arose and drove us time and again further out into the high seas, so that already at 8 o'clock in the morning the waves were so big that we couldn't see the mainland anymore. At about 11 we thought we were all going to perish, because the masts started to break one after another making a terrible noise each time. The sailors had to cut the rigging of the sails and throw everything into the sea, so that our ship had no sails anymore and had to let itself be thrown about at the will of the sea's waves. Nobody had hope to escape with his life anymore; death was before everyone's eyes! One moment the ship was as if on the highest mountains and the next as if down in the deep valleys. After a while another wind came for sure and threw the ship to another side, so that we could see mainland again, but the waves returned so furiously, that it was not possible to get to the shore. There were a lot of people on the mainland who saw this sad and terrible spectacle without being able to lend assistance, because the waves were so furious and terrible nobody could have approached to help with other ships. The inhabitants from there avowed that they had never seen such furious waves. There was no hope nor help apart from God! Meanwhile the captain of the ship tries everything possible to approach the mainland, he has the anchors cut and all that was on the ship he has thrown into the sea. Consequently, the ship rushes like a fury between two rocks so that it breaks in two: one piece remained on the rock and the other still attached hung into the water. By this means many managed to save themselves, because this rock was only 40 feet from the mainland, but also alongside another rock. Suddenly there were people on the mainland opposite who were throwing over rope ladders on which you could hook yourself and be dragged over the water and up the rock on the shore. But many who had already hooked in and been dragged [halfway] up the rock were still carried off by the waves, that crashed against the rock, and were thrown into the sea never to be seen again. That's what happened to [*Lieutenant*] *Ludovic de Caprez* from Trun who had been dragged up the rock and had already taken hold of the grass with one hand when a wave came that tore him down into the sea never to be seen again. This also happened to many others! Many froze from the cold because the waves sometimes broke over us and you couldn't get warm in those short days of that harsh season. We were already weak, so that several lost their lives there on this piece of the ship on the rock. – I

---

5   TNA: FO 20/12: de Burgh to Portland, 15 November 1796.
6   TNA: ADM 51/1179: Captain's journal HMS *Inconstant* notes observing 'the Mary & Ann Transport driven on shore.'

however was still on the part of the ship in the middle of the waves half frozen. It was close to night, more dark than light, when I hear them call the name of one or another of those that had been with me. Among others I also hear them call my name; I therefore fumble for one of these ropes and recommend myself to the holy mother of God and let the rope pull me. It also happened to me that a wave came when I was already [halfway] up the dry rock and threw me back into the sea. Luckily, I had fastened myself well on the rope and I didn't lose my senses, so I came out of the water again and was happily dragged to land. Praised be God in eternity! This terrible storm lasted for 24 hours and was the reason why 89 people perished. Among others from our country [i.e. Graubünden] was the son of *Condrau Schmid* from Sumvitg who froze [to death] on this part of the ship. For those who managed to be dragged to land there were suddenly dry clothes ready and tubs with schnapps to overcome the cold and the weakness.[7]

Tomaschett's testimony is supported by Johann Conrad Müller, a *sergent fourrier*, who recalled, 'I was tossed, more dead than alive on the wreckage of our boat broken on a rock, for 20 full hours, from 7 in the afternoon to 3 o'clock the following morning, and that until the storm subsided and I was able to save myself.[8] Again *Lieutenant* Barbier found himself writing to the Prince-Bishop of Basel with bad news, 'We could not be more unfortunate! We have suffered a second shipwreck, on 11 November, near Piombino, on the coast of Tuscany, where we lost 4 officers and 69 men. I was there and was able to save myself by means of a rope.'[9] Courten put the Royal Etranger's losses from the shipwreck at four officers, a *capitaine* and three *lieutenants* two of whom were from the Graubünden, and 71 men from the first battalion, observing, 'This year the Mediterranean has a liking, or to put it more truly, is greedy for Swiss.'[10] The survivors were housed at Piombino before returning to Elba on 19 November, the battalion had lost everything, even their breeches, and were unable to do duty on the mainland. Nevertheless, Courten wrote, 'despite this tragic event all the soldiers re-embarked without a murmur 8 days afterwards. … There is not a unit more brave and more orderly.'[11]

Wemyss's advance on Castiglione was hampered by the bad weather and it was only taken by a further operation, with Royal Navy support, on 16 November, in which the Royal Etranger did not take part.[12] However, within a couple of months, the positions on the Tuscan coast were abandoned as the strength of French forces in the region increased.

It was at this time that the regiment was joined by more Swiss soldiers. A year earlier, on 20 November 1795, as part of British support for its coalition ally, Sardinia-Piedmont, HMS *Lowestoffe* had escorted four transports from

---

7   Vincenz (ed.), 'Tomaschett de Trun', pp.298–300.
8   Bürkli, 'Das Schweizerregiment von Roll', p.14.
9   Bürkli, 'Das Schweizerregiment von Roll', p.14.
10   CH AEV: Courten Cn B 16/1/37: Courten to his brother, 20 November 1796. Tomaschett stated that they returned on '21 October [*sic*]' (Vincenz (ed.), 'Tomaschett de Trun', p.300).
11   CH AEV: Courten Cn B 16/1/37: Courten to his brother, 20 November 1796.
12   TNA: FO 20/12: de Burgh to Portland ,19 and 24 November 1796. Also Journals of HMS *Southampton* (TNA: ADM 51/1189) and *Inconstant* (TNA: ADM 51/1179).

Cagliari, Sardinia, carrying 17 officers and 322 other ranks of the Swiss Regiment Schmid. They were intended as reinforcements for the Sardinia-Piedmont troops fighting on the Ligurian coast but when the convoy reached its destination on 25 November the coalition army had been defeated and was in full retreat from the coast. As a result the *Lowestoffe* made its way with the convoy to sanctuary at Saint-Florent.[13] The Swiss soldiers subsequently landed on Corsica but, given the events in Italy, the government of Sardinia-Piedmont seem to have forgotten about them. The regiment was reported to still be in Corsica in February 1796 but what came of it afterwards is unclear until this point.[14] Some of the men may have returned to Sardinia but Courten, in a letter of 20 November 1796, explains what had happened to the others,

> A hundred and twenty men of the Swiss Regt. Schmidt in the Service of Sardinia who have been disbanded at Corti [sic] in Corsica … evacuated Corsica at the same time as us, and were given to us yesterday by the English General who has finally acquiesced to the demand that these poor forsaken and abandoned Swiss had made repeatedly to him to enter our Regt.. Five officers who were with them, also Swiss, have taken the five last places of sous lieutenants and the 120 men have been to their great joy incorporated into our Companies.[15]

The British forces at Portoferraio were in somewhat of a limbo. The British fleet left Gibraltar on 16 November and by 21 December Jervis was anchored off Lisbon to help defend Portugal.[16] The British Government attempted to direct matters from London without knowing what was happening. On 8 November Dundas issued instructions on the basis of French newspapers' reports of the evacuation of Corsica and the expectation the troops had already reached Gibraltar.

> Upon that supposition … all the Foreign Troops brought away from Corsica … are without a moment's delay to be sent to Lisbon, where they are to be landed & placed under such British General Officer, as His Majesty may have sent there to command them. These Corps are destined to form a Part of the Auxiliary Army which, in the present emergency it is His Majesty's determination to send to Portugal to assist the Court of Lisbon in resisting any attack which may be made upon that Country by the Spanish or French Forces.[17]

On 10 December Jervis sent Nelson with a reinforced squadron to bring the troops from Portoferraio and to land the British at Gibraltar and the foreign units at Lisbon, as Dundas had intended.[18] Jervis also wrote

---

13   TNA: ADM 51/1133: Captain's journal HMS *Lowestoffe*, and ADM 51/1243: Captain's journal HMS *Speedy*.

14   *Giornale di Sardegna*, 20 to 25 February 1796 (my thanks to Bruno Pauvert for so readily and kindly sharing his research on the Regiment Schmid).

15   CH AEV: Courten Cn B 16/2/21: Courten to his fiancée, 20 November 1796.

16   Brenton, *St. Vincent*, p.294, Jervis to O'Hara, 25 December 1796.

17   BL: Add MS 34905: Dundas to O'Hara, 8 November 1796. Also TNA: WO 1/288.

18   Brenton, *St. Vincent*, pp.276–278. There had been a slight amendment regarding the British units (TNA: WO 1/288: Dundas to O'Hara, 8 December 1796).

a note to de Burgh in which he explained the navy's movements and the latest instructions regarding the troops. Nelson arrived at Portoferraio on 26 December, however de Burgh felt he could not quit his post, although Jervis had shared his instructions, he had had none from the government himself. Nelson was not unsympathetic about the position de Burgh had been placed by the ministers, 'the difficulty of your … guessing what may be their intentions at present, I clearly perceive.'[19] However he was unequivocal that his instructions from Jervis were clear and the navy had no further need for a port on the Italian coast.

1797

In the end, Nelson sailed from Portoferraio on 29 January 1797, leaving two frigates and some smaller vessels at Elba, reporting to Jervis, 'The General having declined to evacuate Porto Ferrajo … I have … first completed every Ship to as much stores as her Captain pleased to take. Every Transport is completely victualled, and arranged, that every soldier can be embarked in three days.[20] There were 4,116 troops on the island, 2,067 men in British units, the infantry being the 2/1st, 18th, 50th and 51st Foot, and 2,049 in foreign units – French and Maltese cannoneers, French Chasseurs, Dillon and Royal Etranger.[21]

For at least the first month, the transports were used to house the Royal Etranger, and probably all the troops, Courten had remarked, 'we are in the port, the ships ranged side by side and despite that we parade two good times a day'.[22] They were later brought on land. Tomaschett, noted that during the winter, one of the regiment's battalions was sent to Rio, a commune on the east of the island within Neapolitan territory, while the other camped, presumably outside Portoferraio, which was not uncomfortable as the weather was mild.[23] The *sergent* was pleased with the island and found the living cheap and the officers enjoyed a good social life with a twice weekly ball at Portoferraio.[24]

The first extant muster list of the regiment is from March. *Lieutenant-colonel* Dürler was the only field officer present as the appointments to replace the officers lost at sea had not been received. It was to be on 6 January 1797 that the Baron de Roll was informed that his nomination of *Capitaine* Joseph Baron de Sonnenberg to replace Dieffenthaller as *major* had been approved. It would be the following summer before this and all the other promotions came into effect in the regiment.[25] On the other hand the men

---

19   Nicolas, *Nelson*, p.322, Nelson to de Burgh, 30 December 1796; the exchange can be followed on pp.319–329.

20   Nicolas, *Nelson*, p.329, Nelson to Jervis 25 January 1797.

21   TNA: WO 1/217: return 30 January 1797.

22   CH AEV: Courten Cn B 16/1/37: Courten to his brother, 20 November 1796.

23   Vincenz (ed.), 'Tomaschett de Trun', p.300.

24   CH AEV: Courten Cn B 16/2/22: Courten to his fiancée, 21 January 1797.

25   TNA: WO 4/378: Woodford to Roll, 6 January 1797 et al.

from the Regiment Schmid had been incorporated by 4 March, the officers as *sous-lieutenants* regardless of their rank in their previous service.

Table 3: Return of the Royal Etranger, 4 March 1797, for the period 25 December 1796 to 23 February 1797.[26]

Ranks	Present	Absent
Capitaines	13	3
Subalterns	23	8
Staff, officers	10	2
Staff, other ranks	3	–
Sergents (all)	85	8
Caporaux	121	8
Tambours	45	6
Grenadiers	127	9
Fusiliers	440	34
Total	867	78

At this muster absentees were shown as on leave, duty, or sick, while others were shown as still being at Rio. Of the chaplains, the Roman Catholic priest who was designated *aumônier*, John Becker, was present while his Protestant colleague, *ministre* Berschauer, never served with the regiment.

Obtaining suitable recruits for the regiment had become increasingly difficult due to the progress of the war in Europe and the regiment's deployment. In the two months to 24 April 1797 only 10 men had been recruited, one of whom had to be returned when found to be a Neapolitan deserter, while the regiment lost 19 men in the same period – eight deaths, five desertions and six men who were discharged.[27] There was still a pressure to be selective about the nationality of the recruits, inspectors having been instructed, in June 1796, to reject any, 'who are not Swiss or from the neighbouring German Cantons, but in no account whatever to accept of French or Italians.'[28] This had been reinforced when, six months later, Baron de Roll was pressed 'to take every possible step for completing' the regiment.'[29] He was to be receive £16 for every Swiss or German recruit who, armed and equipped, was approved on arrival with the regiment or on the Isle of Wight, on England's south coast.

On 22 March 1797 de Burgh wrote to London reporting that although 'nothing new has occurred at this Place' since January, the French had recently begun to reoccupy the Tuscan coast and so had prevented some supplies reaching Elba.[30] Without alternative sources, it was likely that the troops would soon be placed on salt rations which would be detrimental to their health with the approach of the summer heat. This letter apparently prompted the Government to send orders to quit Elba which de Burgh received on 13 April. It was just as well as, according to reports in Britain, conditions had

26 TNA: WO 12/11982: pay lists 1797.
27 TNA: WO 12/11982: 'état de la revue', 24 February to 24 April 1797.
28 TNA: WO 4/367: Woodford to Gardiner, 30 June 1796.
29 TNA: WO 4/378: Woodford to Roll, 8 December 1796.
30 TNA: FO 20/12: de Burgh to Portland, 22 March 1797.

deteriorated quickly, as de Burgh had predicted, 'The scurvy and bad fevers raged among the troops, and the seamen and soldiers were in great want of provisions.'[31] There was no delay in leaving and, in the afternoon of 16 April, the Royal Navy warships sailed 'with 40 Sail in Convoy.'[32] At sea the convoy was vulnerable to attack by the French Toulon fleet but, on the morning of 21 April, west of Corsica, it was joined by Nelson with a squadron sent to escort it to the Strait of Gibraltar.[33] Courten, along with 11 other officers, was on board the transport *Campion* with a Royal Etranger detachment that assisted the crew in raising the anchor and working out of the harbour. At one point during the voyage the *Campion* was rundown by a much larger transport, the *Tartar*. In danger of sinking, there was chaos and consternation among the soldiers, 'the unfortunate who have seen the too frequent shipwrecks of their comrades.'[34] However the vessel arrived safely in the Bay of Gibraltar on 23 May. Courten was permitted to go onshore, glad to eat something other than salt meat that could not be desalinated on the transport while the soldiers had to remain on board.[35] However *Sergent* Tomaschett, whose transport arrived on 20 May, states that he and the soldiers with him disembarked the next day.[36]

The officer who had been appointed to command the Auxiliary Army in Portugal was General the Honourable Charles Stuart, described as, 'an able and distinguished soldier, … an extremely complex and prickly character. Very sensitive on any matter that seemed to challenge his own authority.'[37] Stuart arrived in Portugal on 9 January 1797 to liaise with the Portuguese government while his troops were to follow. By 1 June those from Britain had arrived: the Loyal Emigrants, the first French émigré regiment raised by Britain in 1793, and the remaining white cockade infantry regiments, those of Mortemart and Castries, along with the half battalion of French Emigrant Artillery and some French and British engineers; the only British unit present was the 12th Light Dragoons.[38]

Stuart, as Jervis had discovered earlier, had found the Portuguese reluctant to take the steps he considered necessary for their defence.[39] Five days after arriving he had written, 'that the timid apprehension that has so long humbled this Government … inclines the Portuguese Ministers to keep at Lisbon any of the Auxiliary Troops that may arrive, from an ill calculated apprehension that their appearance on the Frontier will excite the Spaniards to commence Hostilities.'[40] Nevertheless he was determined his troops should be ready to take the field so he established an encampment for training the

31   *Staffordshire Advertiser*, Saturday 7 May 1797.
32   TNA: ADM 51/1179: Journal HMS *Inconstant*.
33   Nicolas, *Nelson*, pp.378–384.
34   CH AEV: Courten Cn B 16/2/24: Courten to his fiancée, 27 May 1797 Courten described the larger vessel the *Tartar*, a former frigate in the service of the East India Company.
35   CH AEV: Courten Cn B 16/2/24: Courten to his fiancée, 27 May 1797 and B 16/2/25: 30 May 1797.
36   Vincenz (ed.), 'Tomaschett de Trun', p.304.
37   Gregory, *Ungovernable Rock*, p.87; Stuart, along with all of his command staff, held higher local ranks, dated from 30 November 1796.
38   TNA: WO 17/2460: monthly return 1 June 1797.
39   Brenton, *St. Vincent*, p.294, Jervis to O'Hara, 25 December 1796.
40   TNA: WO 1/217: C. Stuart to Dundas, 12 January 1797.

French units and, when they arrived, the foreign units from Elba would join them there for the same purpose.[41] Furthermore, Stuart was authorised to disband some of the units if they could not recruit men in Portugal although this did not extend to the Royal Etranger.[42]

On 1 June the convoy in the Bay of Gibraltar raised anchor but, as darkness fell, contrary winds and currents, brought chaos among the ships. The drummers on the transports were ordered to beat their drums while other ships rang bells to prevent collisions, to Tomaschett the noise, combined with the sound of the waves, sounded like a battle.[43] The *Campion* collided with a larger vessel and, according to Courten, was only saved, 'by the manual strength of our soldiers who worked with the shafts of large oars to separate the two vessels'.[44] Then, on entering the Atlantic, storms drove the ships towards the Azores, before a calm and conditions on the transports, which in better times a British officer described as 'vile and insupportable prisons' became awful, as Tomaschett described.[45]

Here we were thrown around 20 days across this terrible sea and water, so that we saw nothing but the sky and the water. The roaring of this high big sea, the dreadful waves and the terrible wind caused great horror and fear and this was not without reason. Nobody reckoned to be able to escape with their lives anymore! Many days the waves were so big and furious that the sailors had to surrender and let the ship be tossed about where they [the waves] wanted. Nobody knew where we were going to end up. The worst however was that we had to go down into the bottom of the ship. Here there was a terrible stench. The captain of the ship had even nailed down hatches, so that we couldn't come up. The reason was so all those who weren't sailors wouldn't come to harm or balance the ship more one way than the other. Down here we weren't allowed to move, one row on the one side, the other row on the other side. But sometimes there came such big waves that the ship was thrown so much to one side that often those on the one side were all thrown onto the other side on top of the others and then there came another wave who threw all onto the one side again. So you can imagine what a state it was and an appalling stench. Some screamed! Some yelled! Some swore! But with the swearing there weren't many. Although they were externally dissolute, this also made them come to their senses, so that they all gave thoughts to their human mortality. Many were in so much agony that they had to throw up. The greatest discomfort was the stench and if the captain had made us stay down there like this much longer, most of us would have died. The officers themselves had to obey and remain locked in like us. Although they had a separate compartment, they had to be patient like us, because when you are on a ship, all have to obey the captain of the ship. It didn't last very many days and when the worst of the storm had abated, the captain had us come back up for our needs.[46]

41   TNA: WO 1/217: C. Stuart to Pinto, 12 April 1797.

42   TNA: WO 1/217: Dundas to C. Stuart, 3 December 1796.

43   Vincenz (ed.), 'Tomaschett de Trun', p.306.

44   CH AEV: Courten Cn B 16/2/26: Courten to his fiancée [?], June 1797.

45   Francis Maule, *Memoirs of the Principal Events in the Campaigns of North Holland and Egypt* (London: F. C. and J. Rivington, 1816), p.44.

46   Vincenz (ed.), 'Tomaschett de Trun', pp.306–307.

Finally the convoy arrived in the Tagus, the *Campion* on 21 June 1797, dropping anchor opposite Belem at 6:00 p.m.[47] The Royal Etranger had arrived with 49 officers and staff, 95 sergeants, 49 drummers and 729 rank and file (of whom 25 were sick) along with 54 women and 21 children.[48] They had to remain onboard as there was a possibility the Auxiliary Army would quit Portugal, indeed when they disembarked a week later their heavy baggage was left on the transports for the same reason.

Courten recounts that the troops were brought by boats from the transports early in the morning and landed at Belem, 'there we formed up and we remained on the seashore until 9 o'clock during which time we were seen and reseen by the English and Portuguese generals etc. At 9 o'clock we then had to march to the Camp, our soldiers loaded with their kit, and we at the head of our Companies on foot like the troops'.[49] The march to the camp at Algueirão, northwest of Lisbon, took four hours in the heat and soldiers, who had hardly taken a step for two and half months, dropped by the wayside.

> Finally we arrived nearly 300 men with the flags at the camp, we were 780 under arms before leaving the seashore, with not a single cart to collect our stragglers, who meanwhile arrived all through the night, the cool having given them heart and strength. At midday rollcall the next day there was not a man missing ...[50]

Dillon, marching behind the Royal Etranger, arrived at the camp with only 35 men in the ranks. Stuart was far from impressed with what he saw, 'I never in the course of my service beheld two Regiments more disgraceful to the British Name than the Regiments of Roll, and Dillon'.[51]

Both regiments were placed under the command of Brigadier General John Stuart, of the 3rd Foot Guards, and commenced an exacting regime of training and inspections. Days began at 6:00 a.m. with manoeuvres, there was a break during the midday heat and then further exercises in the evening. Courten wrote, '... we spend every day 7 long hours under arms and are occupied the rest of the day with inspections to receive 4 or 5 generals who pay us the honour of visiting us daily'.[52]

Immediately the number of sick in the regiment rose dramatically. Courten and Tomaschett ascribed this to the 'detestable food' on the transports, exposure to sunshine after being confined on board and the march to the camp.[53] However Charles Stuart put it down to other causes,

---

47 CH AEV: Courten Cn B 16/2/26: Courten to his fiancée [?], June 1797.
48 TNA: WO 1/217: 'State of the Troops arrived in the Tagus from the Mediterranean, 21st June 1797.'
49 CH AEV: Courten Cn B 16/2/27: Courten to his fiancée, 7 July 1797, when he stated that the regiment had been at the camp for nine days.
50 CH AEV: Courten Cn B 16/2/27: Courten to his fiancée, 7 July 1797.
51 TNA/; WO 1/218: C. Stuart to Dundas, 2 July 1797.
52 CH AEV: Courten Cn B 16/2/27: Courten to his fiancée, 7 July 1797.
53 CH AEV: Courten Cn B 16/2/28: Courten to his fiancée, 9 August 1797 and Vincenz (ed.), 'Tomaschett de Trun', p.308.

… the Epidemical Fever prevalent in the Regiments de Roll and Dillon has increased to such an Alarming degree that I am reduced to the necessity of breaking up their Camp and placing them in Barracks at Lisbon. The actual strength of these Regiments united does not exceed seven hundred Men fit for duty, and I have every reason to apprehend from the extreme filthiness and want of Discipline that the active Humanity of Dr Robertson, and his approved ability in every branch that relates to their Management, will not be of sufficient effect to restore them to the Service during the remainder of the Campaign.[54]

The most sickly units, 1st Foot, 50th Foot, Dillon and Royal Etranger, were placed in barracks, 'to avoid the entire loss of the soldiers, and even the officers,' and to be ready for the expected campaign.[55] The change soon had a positive effect on the sickness within the regiment and it was expected that it would be returning to camp at the end of September.

Table 4: Sickness and death rates, as percentages of the rank and file present, in the Royal Etranger and Dillon Regiments, and 50th Foot.[56]

Date	Royal Etranger		Dillon		50th	
1797	Sickness	Death	Sickness	Death	Sickness	Death
1 July	8.74	0.54	14.43	nil	6.38	nil
1 August	26.01	1.68	28.06	6.59	10.64	0.50
1 September	17.50	1.78	18.84	1.86	8.10	nil
1 October	11.23	0.46	9.40	0.85	10.49	0.16
1 November	7.83	0.30	6.77	0.67	7.47	nil
1 December	5.64	0.85	8.33	0.17	6.59	nil

Despite the situation being more widespread, and worse in Dillon, there was concern that there was a particular problem with the Royal Etranger. Dr James Robertson, Inspector of Hospitals and the senior British medical officer present, undertook an investigation into the levels of sickness from fever in the Royal Etranger since its arrival on Corsica. He found that up to March 1797 there had been, on average, almost 78 men sick at any one time, but he could find no clear reason for it, concluding, 'The probable reason why this Regiment has suffered from fever in Corsica & here seems to be that many of the men are older than usual in British Regiments.'[57]

The other issue for dissatisfaction with the regiment was the state of its equipment and clothing. On 31 July James Poole, the inspector, reported that the regiment had 978 stands of arms, of which 302 needed repair, and 241 were of British and 737 of French or German manufacture of very different calibres. The grenadier companies and artillery detachment were armed with the British muskets while the fusilier companies had the foreign made ones. All the clothing was of foreign manufacture and three different qualities, clearly distinguishable by 'three different Degrees of Red Colour.'

---

54   TNA: WO 1/218: C. Stuart to Dundas, 12 July 1797.
55   CH AEV: Courten Cn B 16/2/28: Courten to his fiancée, 9 August 1797.
56   TNA: WO 17/2460: army returns.
57   TNA: WO 1/218: Robertson to C. Stuart, 11 September 1797.

Eighty soldiers had not received their annual issue of new clothing due to a practice of, where possible, giving men a payment in lieu of clothing which was popular with the men while being a saving to the regiment. Poole considered the practice, 'objectionable … because it takes from the uniformity which is so very impressive when we observe a Battalion regularly clothed at one stated Period.'[58] In addition the soldiers did not have cloth greatcoats but items of a similar cut made of 'strong linen which certainly serves to economise the Uniform when off Duty, but I should not suppose it to be of much Utility on real Service.'[59] Issues with foreign made arms and clothing were already being addressed, the Baron de Roll and Edward Dillon being instructed that all their clothing and equipment must be contracted for, and furnished from, Britain.[60]

The regiment's regime of training was not interrupted by the move to barracks at Belem, as Courten wrote, 'we always work, 4, 5 and up to 6 hours per day at manoeuvres, parades etc. … the unit is perfectly lodged and fed. These two things make all the fatigues of the day forgotten …'[61] The daily routine, that took into consideration the heat, began, seven days a week, at 6:00 a.m. precisely when he and the officers walked the 10 paces from their quarters to the soldiers' barracks and commenced drills which lasted until 9:00 a.m. Courten then returned to his chamber where he took breakfast and then did company business for about an hour, after which he was free to read, walk, write or train his seven-month-old pointer dog. At 1:00 p.m. he joined *Capitaine* Louis de Flüe and his French wife, Catharina Josepha, at their nearby lodgings for lunch, Courten having provided one of his Valaisans as a cook for the three of them. After two hours he returned to his quarters where he was kept busy until 7:00 p.m. when he attended parade which continued until sunset, sometimes he was required to oversee the placing of sentries, but then he returned to the Flüe's for supper. His routine was the same unless he did 'extraordinary duty' for a day but this was infrequent as there were many officers to share it.[62]

Meanwhile the future of the regiment was uncertain. Bonaparte's victories in Northern Italy had forced Austria to agree to an armistice on 18 April 1797 which led to peace with the Treaty of Campo Formio on 17 October 1797.

'Grenadier of the Regiment de Roll, 1797.' Although this watercolour has been frequently recreated by illustrators since Lawson it is unlikely that such an ornate uniform was indeed worn – see the uniform section. (Courtesy of the Schweizerisches Nationalmuseum Zürich, inv. no. LM-105115)

---

58   TNA: WO 1/218: Poole to C. Stuart, 4 August 1797.
59   TNA: WO 1/218: Poole to C. Stuart, 4 August 1797.
60   TNA: WO 4/367: Woodford to Poole, 13 June and repeated 8 August 1797.
61   CH AEV: Courten Cn B 16/2/28: Courten to his fiancée, 9 August 1797.
62   CH AEV: Courten Cn B 16/2/29: Courten to his fiancée, undated.

There were rumours that soon there would be peace between Britain and France, and as soon as the Royal Etranger had arrived in Portugal it was clear the British Government wished to reduce the foreign regiments in its pay to single battalions.[63] This happened to Dillon almost immediately, although the new formation was only officially recognised from 1 February 1798.[64] Charles Stuart continued to prepare his force for campaigning while managing these changes to the foreign regiments, a task which was made much more difficult by ministers and government officials in London. He complained that the Foreign Office or the Foreign Department of the War Office interfered with arrangements he had made behind his back. He felt his authority was being undermined and it caused the issue of 'contradictory vexations and orders, of which the Officers justly complain'.[65]

Although he had been critical of his foreign troops, Charles Stuart was clear that they should be treated fairly. He made his anger known when orders arrived in Portugal that the British Army's pay was increased for subalterns, NCOs and other ranks from 25 May 1797 but it was only to apply to British units.[66] Then the Foreign Department circulated the news that the NCOs and other ranks of the foreign units would indeed receive the increment to regiments but no orders were sent to Portugal to put this into effect.[67] Thus on 20 September when John Stuart reported the improvements in Dillon he added that they were,

> [In] danger of being frustrated, by a premature Communication respecting an increase of Pay. As some of the Men have become Clamorous and discontented at not receiving the Augmentation which they already consider their due. Statements to this effect have been likewise made to me by Colonel Durler, of the Regiment de Roll, to whom however, as well as to Colonel Dillon I could give no other Reply than that I had not as yet received your Orders to make any Notification on the subject.[68]

What was worse was that in the specific case of the Royal Etranger the increase in pay for the junior ranks would not take place until agreement had been reached to changes in its formation, effectively a new capitulation. While Charles Stuart considered the regiment's structure and organisation required wholescale reform, he pressed the government to augment the pay of the soldiers, independent of any negotiations with senior officers.[69] He condemned that manner in which the War Office was behaving, telling Windham,

---

63   CH AEV: Courten Cn B 16/2/27: Courten to his fiancée, 7 July 1797.
64   TNA: WO 1/218: C. Stuart to Dundas, 12 July 1797; WO 17/2461: monthly return, 1 February 1798.
65   TNA: WO 1/218: C. Stuart to Dundas, 10 August 1797.
66   TNA: WO 1/218: C. Stuart to Dundas, 10 August 1797.
67   TNA: WO 1/218: Colebrooke Nesbitt to Captain de Courtebonne, Loyal Emigrants, 22 August, and Windham to C. Stuart, 25 August 1797.
68   TNA: WO 1/218: J. Staurt to C. Stuart, 20 September 1797.
69   TNA: WO 1/218: Dürler thanked C. Stuart for this in a letter of 19 November 1797.

… I considered it by no means suitable to the dignity of the British Government, or consistent with my Situation, to propose to a Corps of Officers the direct violation of a Capitulation entered into by the King's Ministers for the purpose of raising a Swiss Regiment for His Majesty's Service, and as every proposition upon the Subject would only prove to them that it was your intention not to grant the men of this Corps similar benefits to those allowed to Soldiers of every other Foreign Regiment in the Army, unless the Officers contributed to it by relinquishing as Part of the Pay and Advantages they possess … at a moment when from the Zeal and Active Exertions of Brigadier General Stuart, I am enabled to assert that both this Regiment, and the Regiment of Dillon, from being among the worst Corps I ever beheld are considerably improved in Discipline, and, in proportion to their numbers, rendered worthy to serve His Majesty. … while on the contrary if an increase of subsistence is withheld from the Non-Commissioned Officers and Men who have hitherto enjoyed no greater Pay from Government than those of other Foreign Regiments in the Service, you must expect a degree of Desertion, threatening the Annihilation of the Regiment.[70]

There were a number of issues that needed to be changed, one of which was the high rates of pay the field officers and *capitaines* received caused by the conflation of pay and allowances and the use of both British and French currency in the calculations. As a result the *capitaines* received £341-1-1 sterling per year while the *lieutenants* got £103-8-4 and the *sous-lieutenants* £85-3-4. To give context to these sums, in 1810 the annual pay of a British infantry captain was £191-12-6, a lieutenant with less than seven years' service £119-2-6 and ensigns £95-16-3.[71] The result was that just 16 officers, *Lieutenant-colonel* Dürler, *Major* de Sonnenberg and the 14 *capitaines*, 13 of companies and the *aide-major*, received over a quarter of the regiment's pay, for instance for the period of 25 December 1797 to 23 February 1798 they received £1,005-7-5 of the £3,812-15-8 ¼ paid to the regiment, of 45 officers and 705 other ranks, as a whole.[72]

Another issue that particularly concerned Charles Stuart was the different justice systems existing across the foreign corps and even before the arrival of the Royal Etranger and Dillon he had complained that of the five foreign regiments he had with him, 'they claim a right to three different modes of Procedure upon Trials'.[73] His objections revolved around the principle of consistency and also the practical issue of assembling impartial members of courts martial. Such issues came to a head following an incident involving one of the Royal Etranger officers in Belem on 4 November.

That afternoon some of the regiment's officers dined at an auberge in town, and one, *Sous-lieutenant* Baron Venceslas de Feldegg, became very drunk, so when the others left to get to parade he trailed behind. On his way he became

---

70   TNA: WO 1/218: C. Stuart to Windham 7 October 1797.
71   TNA: AO 3/56: List 24 June 1798, for the Royal Etranger officers' pay and Robert Burnham and Ron McGuigan, *The British Army Against Napoleon: Facts, Lists and Trivia 1805–1815* (Barnsley: Frontline Books, 2010), p.144, for the British comparison. The money is given as pounds-shillings-pence, 12 pence being a shilling and 20 shillings a pound.
72   TNA: WO 12/11982: Pay list, 23 February 1798.
73   TNA: WO 1/218: C. Stuart to Dundas, 14 June 1797.

involved in a verbal altercation with some servants from a noblewoman's house, resulting in him in forcing his way into the house, sabre in hand, and wounding one of the servants. He was stopped and brought out of the house by three Swiss *sergent majors* but they were attacked by the local populace and when the Civic Guard arrived Feldegg resisted, only making matters worse. Finally the situation was broken up by the intervention of three Loyal Emigrant officers, with drawn swords, and the arrival of *Capitaine* Müller who had Feldegg taken to the barracks under arrest.

After a brief investigation, Dürler tried to deal with the matter swiftly and without invoking a formal Council of War that would bring Feldegg 'dishonour and disgrace.'[74] Dürler ordered an assembly of the regiment's subalterns to discuss their comrade's conduct the next day. They decided his behaviour had been 'unworthy of an officer' and that he should no longer serve in the regiment and this decision was unanimously confirmed by an assembly of the *capitaines* and field officers.[75] Meanwhile, unbeknown to him, Dürler tried to obtain him a generous settlement.[76] On 28 November Feldegg, who had remained in close confinement, appealed to Charles Stuart to be tried before impartial officers as those of his own regiment had already stated their opinion without him being present or having the opportunity to make representations. Furthermore, he suggested his treatment may have not been fair as he was German and not Swiss and his own *capitaine*, Charles de Vogelsang, had not been present.[77]

As a result Charles Stuart instituted a Court of Enquiry of three British generals. During their questioning Dürler admitted Feldegg had not had a chance to explain himself in the process so any decision had not been a court's judgement but he insisted it had been done with Feldegg's interests in mind. Feldegg, in turn, admitted that his behaviour, while drunk, was 'extremely irregular and improper' but not 'infamous or dishonourable;' he reiterated his request for a trial by independent officers.[78] That was not an option as the administration of justice was maintained by the regiment and the only recourse was the holding of a Council of War which would have been unjust, for the reasons already stated. This was solved when the regiment's officers agreed to relinquish to Charles Stuart their role in administering justice in this case. He had his decision published in the army's general orders of 13 December, that Feldegg was 'not legally displaced from His Military Situation in the Regiment of Royal Etranger' and so was free to return to duty.[79] However he asked Brigadier General John Stuart to pass on his thanks to the regiment's officers for allowing a solution to be found and

74   TNA: WO 1/218: Court of Enquiry's report 6 December 1797.
75   TNA: WO 1/218: Report bearing all the officers signatures 5 November 1797.
76   TNA: WO 1/218: Dürler to C. Stuart, 19 November 1797. The former applied for him to paid up to 24 December and be given six months' leave, dated so that he would receive the improved pay, in the hope, not having been sentenced, he could find employment in Germany or elsewhere.
77   TNA: WO 1/218: Memorial of 28 November 1797. Feldegg's promotion from cadet and *sergent* was dated 14 November 1796 but had been effective from 25 April 1797.
78   TNA: WO 1/218: Court of Enquiry's report 6 December 1797.
79   TNA: WO 1/218: extract from General Orders, 13 December 1797.

also to assure Dürler of his, 'complete & entire disapprobation of the Baron de Feldegg's Conduct'.[80] Finally the brigadier was to inform Feldegg that he had only escaped punishment through an 'error in proceeding' and one which had been done in his interests; whether Swiss or German, he was an officer in the Royal Etranger and so had to comply with 'the Laws by which the Regiment is governed & from which there is no appeal'.[81]

A clear picture of the Royal Etranger is provided by the muster roll for 24 October 1797, the first to list the officers and men by company. The regiment had two battalions with 19 companies, including the artillery company of a *capitaine*, a *lieutenant*, a *sous-lieutenant*, four *sergents*, four *caporaux* and 34 *cannoniers* but the recruit company had disappeared. The staff consisted of 14 officers (of which three were absent) and five other ranks. The 53 company officers (16 absent) were almost up to establishment; this was also the case for the 91 *sergents*, 123 *caporaux* and 40 *tambours*. The shortage of manpower was manifest among the soldiers. The first battalion's *grenadier* company, *Capitaine* de Zimmermann, had 54 soldiers and the second battalion's, *Capitaine* de Dieffenthaller, 53 (the soldiers being *grenadiers* or *chasseurs*). But the number of *fusiliers* in the rest of the companies varied between 29 and 19, the average being just over 26.[82] Few recruits had been obtained in Portugal – between 1 July 1797 and 1 June 1798 only 55 men joined the Royal Etranger while 40 had died, 99 were discharged and 99 deserted.[83] The number of rank and file in the Royal Etranger had reduced from 732 to 553 during that period, yet it still had the officers and NCOs for two battalions. A review on 5 November found that the situation was likely to only get worse as the engagements of many of the men were due to end imminently, 54 by 1 November 1798 and a further 227 between then and 1 November 1799. Indeed 36 *sergents*, three *fusiliers* and 12 musicians were 'engaged without term' thus able to leave once they had completed three months' notice, in the case of the last group this had been done due to the 'difficulty of procuring good or even tolerable musicians'.[84]

The need for change was clear and on 3 October Woodford had sent the Baron de Roll,

> … a provisional agreement for the continuation of your Regiment in His Majesty's Service until a Capitulation can be regularly made. It being intended that your Corps should as nearly as possible be put in regard to pay upon a footing with an English Regiment. … But your claim for the continuation to the Field Officers and Captains of their present high rate of pay the Secretary at War does not feel himself justified to lay before the King.[85]

---

80   TNA: WO 1/218: C. Stuart to J. Stuart, 21 December 1797.
81   TNA: WO 1/218: C. Stuart to J. Stuart, 21 December 1797.
82   TNA: WO 12/11982: muster roll October 1797.
83   TNA: WO 17/2460 and 2461: Monthly returns.
84   TNA: WO 1/218: J. Stuart to C. Stuart, 6 November 1797.
85   TNA: WO 4/378: Woodford to Roll, 3 October 1797.

The regiment was to lose its artillery company as well as the posts of *aide-major* and *sous-aide-major* on the staff, in addition the *petit état major* was to disappear, the *tambour major* and *caporal tambour* to be counted among the drummers and the three craftsmen among the privates. Over the next few months correspondence went to and fro between the *colonel* and the War Office but finally a new capitulation was agreed that fulfilled the British Government's wish to reduce the regiment to one battalion, paid and formed as the country's own regiments of foot. Unfortunately, a full copy has not been found, only a document reproducing three articles. The first of which states 'A Capitulation shall be granted to the Baron de Roll for ten years from the 25th June 1798;' Article 21 gave the British Government the right to reduce the regiment should it fall below 100 rank and file, 'unless such loss proceeds from Death or any Misfortune of War' and after the expiration of this capitulation, if it was not renewed and the regiment was reduced, the officers would be entitled to receive half pay (article 23).[86]

The new arrangements for the Regiment de Roll, or Regiment of Roll, came into effect on 25 June 1798, the name Royal Etranger ceased to be used and ranks were now, generally, referred to in English.

Staff
1 colonel, 1 lieutenant colonel, 1 major, 1 quartermaster, 1 adjutant, 1 surgeon, 2 assistant surgeons, 1 chaplain; along with 1 sergeant major, 1 quartermaster sergeant, 1 paymaster sergeant

Flank (Grenadier and Light) Companies – officers
1 captain, 2 lieutenants

Colonel's Company – officers
1 captain lieutenant, 1 ensign

Lieutenant Colonel's and Major's Companies – other officers
1 lieutenant, 1 ensign

Other Battalion Companies – officers
1 captain, 1 lieutenant, 1 ensign

Other ranks – all companies
5 sergeants, 5 corporals, 2 drummers, 55 soldiers

Evidence suggests that there were to be, also, two fifers and it appears that there was no regimental paymaster due to the continuing role of Foreign Department inspectors.[87] The alterations meant that the services of both *aide-majors*, 15 *capitaines*, seven *lieutenants* and seven *sous-lieutenants* were terminated.[88] Despite the swingeing cuts, the men of the regiment received comparatively generous treatment, the reduced officers who were present in Portugal receiving a years' pay, at the old rate, while those of Dillon had

---

86   TNA: WO 1/940: Undated or signed (ff.487) the date and term of the capitulation is confirmed in a briefing document of 1800 (FO 74/28 'The Foreign Corps in the Service of Great Britain and under the immediate direction of the War Office').

87   TNA: WO 1/388: Baron de Roll 'Establishment of a Regiment of Infantry of two Battalions referred to in the accompanying Capitulation' July 1798.

88   TNA: AO 3/56: List of recipients of the payments, 24 June 1798, and WO 4/353: List showing officers who had received the payments and those who had not, 23 January 1799.

only received six months' pay.[89] Furthermore the reduced officers were soon offered an equivalent of half pay, on condition that those who had received the lump sum return it, and *Capitaine* Joseph de Zimmermann took this option presumably regarding it as the equivalent of a retirement pension, receiving payments until his death in 1819.[90] The supernumerary NCOs were retained on strength and in their ranks.[91] Almost immediately the changes came into effect, Baron de Roll submitted another proposed capitulation for his regiment to, once again, have two battalions, along with a recruit company, although organised as a British regiment of foot of a similar size; it appears however that he received no response.[92]

Courten had already left the regiment. Having been granted six months' leave he had sailed to England on his way home and on 20 November 1797 he met the Baron de Roll in London. It was then that he learned of the state of the negotiations, 'to put the regiment on the British establishment and formation, pay as well as the organisation.'[93] Courten also found that, as he was eleventh in seniority amongst the captains, he was among the officers whose services were to be terminated. He returned home as the wars were brought to Switzerland. In January 1798 France discarded any pretence of respecting the Confederation's neutrality by sending troops into Vaud and then, on 1 March, Bern. The city's treasury was emptied and its contents sent to France, where money was immediately passed to Toulon to finance Napoleon Bonaparte's expedition to Egypt. The Confederation collapsed and the French presented the country with a new centralised constitution as the République Helvétique. However, as French troops widened their occupation, the rural cantons of Uri, Schwyz and Unterwalden – the home of the first Confederation – erupted in armed insurrection as did Valais. There Courten with 5,000 local men prevented the French advance for 17 days. However, resistance was suppressed throughout the country and many of the leaders, including Courten, had to leave. The new republic's client status was soon evident when, on 2 August, a treaty was signed giving France perpetual access through the Alpine passes into Northern Italy. France also demanded the service of Swiss troops so in July 1798 recruitment for any other foreign service was prohibited and on 19 December 1798 the new republic undertook to supply 18,000 men, voluntarily enlisted, to 'act in concert with the French troops as auxiliaries against the enemy designated by the French government.'[94]

---

89 TNA: WO 1/218: C. Stuart to Dundas, 10 August 1797.
90 TNA: WO 4/379: Woodford to Roll, 17 October 1798, and WO 65/168: Foreign Army List.
91 TNA: WO 4/379: Woodford to Roll, 1 June 1798.
92 TNA: WO 1/388: Baron de Roll 'Articles of a New Capitulation proposed by Col. Baron de Roll' July 1798.
93 CH AEV: Courten Cn B 16/2/31: Courten to his fiancée, 21 November 1797.
94 Jacques Schalbetter, 'Le Régiment Valaisan au service de l'Espagne 1796–1808', *Annales valaisannes: bulletin trimestriel de la Société d'histoire du Valais romand*, vol.15, no.3, 1969, p.298 and Stephen Ede-Borrett, *Swiss Regiments in the service of France 1798–1815* (Warwick: Helion and Company, 2019), p.117 reproducing a capitulation translated by George Nafziger.

The invasion, as well as Bonaparte's capture of Malta on his way to Egypt, added to the simmering tensions that had not been resolved by the Treaty of Campo Formio. From mid-1798 various countries, suspicious or afraid of France's ambitions, began to form alliances which developed into the Second Coalition. At the same time those Swiss émigrés opposed to the République Helvétique had gathered in Southern Germany and Britain agreed, should hostilities commence, to pay for Swiss auxiliary units, formed by the émigrés, to serve alongside the Austrians.

Meanwhile, in Portugal, the British auxiliary army remained peacefully stationed around the mouth of the Tagus as the immediate threat from Spain had passed. On 13 June 1798 Charles Stuart left the army, handing over command to Lieutenant General Simon Fraser. The Regiment de Roll remained quartered in Belem and for some there were opportunities for family life. Among the 51 women and 21 children listed with the regiment in April 1798 had been Henriette de Dieffenthaller and her maternal aunt, Louise Baronne de Wimpfen.[95] The latter, a *channonoise noble de Sainte Glossinde*, had arrived to help care for the orphan and both stayed in Lisbon where an émigré remembered meeting the 'venerable abbess de Wimpfen … and her lively and pretty niece, Henriette de Dieffenthaller, … who followed the fortune of a regiment as a young girl'.[96] The following year, on 18 July 1799, Henriette married the 41 year old Captain Charles de Vogelsang, she being only 16 this was with the permission of her guardians, her paternal uncle and maternal aunt, and the ceremony was performed by John Becker, the regiment's chaplain.[97]

The build-up of troops and ships at Toulon for Napoleon's expedition had drawn the British to re-establish a naval presence in the Mediterranean and on 8 May Nelson, now a rear admiral, left Gibraltar with a squadron to reconnoitre Toulon.[98] However the French fleet and troop transports managed to get out from Toulon to Malta, which was quickly captured, before it continued on to Egypt. Nelson, his squadron reinforced, eventually encountered the French fleet on 1 August, anchored in a strong position in Aboukir, or Abu Qir, Bay after landing the troops. Nevertheless, Nelson attacked and destroyed the French fleet in what was to be known as the Battle of the Nile. Furthermore, a force was sent to capture Menorca, known to the British as Minorca, as part of Britain's war with Spain and the initial stage of a campaign against the country's Mediterranean ports.[99] Charles Stuart was chosen to lead this expedition and received his instructions on 29 August. On 18 September he arrived at Lisbon where he was joined by some officers, including Major General Sir James St Clair Erskine and Brigadier General John Stuart, before sailing on 6 October to Gibraltar to collect four battalions

95   TNA: WO 12/11982: Return, 24 April 1798.
96   Jacques Scévola Cazotte, *Témoignage d'un Royaliste* (Paris: Adrien Le Clerc et Cie., 1839), pp.273–274.
97   TNA: WO 42/64: Application for a widow's pension.
98   Nicolas, *Nelson*, pp.11–12.
99   J.W. Fortescue, *A History of the British Army* (London: Macmillan and Co., 1906–1920), vol. IV, Part II, pp.605–606.

for the expedition.[100] These troops landed on Menorca on 7 November and by prompt and bold deployment the island was taken, the last Spanish stronghold of Ciutadella capitulating on 15 November.[101]

The Spanish forces on the island included three battalions from Swiss regiments, both battalions of the Regimiento de Rutiman as well as the first battalion of the Regimiento de Yann, detached from the garrison of Mallorca (Majorca). Soldiers from these regiments readily deserted to the British, many being found to have been Austrian prisoners of war sold, in Italy, 'for two hard dollars a-piece to the Spaniards by these rascally French.'[102] When the Spanish garrison left Menorca on 17 November, the 'Swiss' stayed behind, 'to a man anxious to enter into the King's service.'[103] They were soon formed into a new regiment with John Stuart, appointed 26 December 1798, as colonel which was named the Minorca, or Stuart's, Regiment. Some sources, such as Fortescue, suggest that Charles Stuart sent for the Regiment de Roll to assist in the organisation of this new unit, in fact he did so for a slightly different purpose.[104] He explained this, immediately after Menorca had been secured, in a letter to Jervis (now Earl of St Vincent), 'I must beg of you to embark and send the Regiment de Roll and its Supernumerary officers here without delay, for I am in hopes with that allure to entice many Germans from Majorca.'[105] The garrison of Mallorca not only included the second Yann battalion but also the recently formed Regimiento de Courten, in which the majority of the men were also former prisoners of war.[106]

When they learned of this request the Portuguese government protested about the use of a regiment that had arrived as part of the Auxiliary Army against Spain.[107] Such considerations may have been anticipated when troops were taken from Gibraltar, and not Portugal, for the expedition against Menorca. The British Government accepted Fraser's advice not to send the Regiment de Roll, 'to avoid furnishing the Court of Madrid any pretext' to cancel negotiations with Portugal.[108] Nevertheless, to aid the formation of the Minorca Regiment, Fraser was to send, 'as soon as possible, such supernumerary officers of the Regiment de Roll as are now in Portugal'.[109] However Dundas, gave these instructions on the false assumption that the surplus Roll officers in Portugal had been placed on half pay and so at the disposal of the British Government. Enquiries revealed most had returned to Switzerland and only eight remained in Portugal, the most junior three, Feldegg, Henry Zwicky and Henry Matthey, had already rejoined the regiment and four had obtained commissions in the Portuguese army; only

---

100 TNA: WO 17/2461: Army returns and Fortescue, *British Army*, vol.IV, p.616.

101 *The London Gazette Extraordinary*, 24 December 1798.

102 Alexander M. Delavoye, *Life of Thomas Graham, Lord Lynedoch* (London: Richardson & Co., 1880), pp 158–159.

103 Delavoye, *Thomas Graham*, p.161.

104 For example, Fortescue, *British Army*, vol.IV, pp.619–620.

105 TNA: WO 1/220: Stuart to St Vincent (copy), 19 November 1798.

106 Schalbetter, 'Le Régiment Valaisan', pp.295–296, 307–308.

107 TNA: WO 1/220: Fraser to Robert Walpole, ambassador to Portugal, 20 December 1798.

108 TNA: WO 1/220: Fraser to Dundas, 22 December 1798, and Dundas to Fraser, 18 January 1799.

109 TNA: WO 1/220: Dundas to Fraser, 18 January 1799.

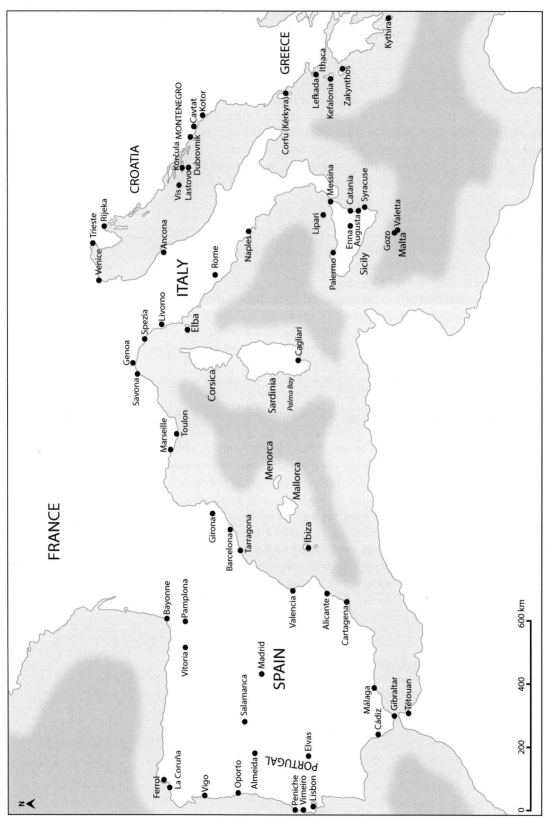

The Mediterranean Sea.

Jean Baptiste Marie Joseph Baron de Tschoudy, a lieutenant, was available and Fraser undertook to send him 'at the first opportunity'.[110] Tschoudy was appointed lieutenant in the Minorca Regiment on 26 January 1799 and later he was joined by another former Roll officer, Louis de Girard, who resigned from the Portuguese army and was appointed lieutenant on 15 September 1799.[111] The rest of the Minorca Regiment's officers came from a variety of sources including British regiments as well as Dillon, Castries and Mortemart. Several of them had previously served in the French royal army's Brigade Irlandaise and then in Britain's Irish Brigade, sometimes called the Irish Catholic or, more recently, Pitt's Irish Brigade, created in 1794 but disbanded in 1798.[112] One of these was Ernest Missett who had been *lieutenant* in the Régiment de Walsh in France and captain in the 2nd (Walsh de Serrant) Regiment of Britain's Irish Brigade before joining the Minorca Regiment in the same rank.[113]

Then the strategic situation changed in the summer of 1799 when the new coalition allies under Alexander Suvarov achieved a series of victories in Northern Italy. With the French armies committed elsewhere, it was considered unlikely that they or the Spanish posed a threat to Portugal. So on 17 June Dundas wrote to the new British commander in Portugal, Lieutenant General Cornelius Cuyler, instructing him 'as soon as any ships shall arrive at Lisbon' the 2/1st and 50th Foot, the last remaining British infantry in Portugal, as well as 'the Regiment of Roll' were to embark and go to Gibraltar 'or such other Place within the Mediterranean as may be pointed out to you by the Earl of St Vincent, or by the Officer commanding His Majesty's Land Forces in the Mediterranean'.[114] Charles Stuart was, by this time, no longer in the Mediterranean, having returned to England to recover his health, leaving Major General Sir James St Clair Erskine commanding Menorca.[115]

However, unaware of these instructions, when ships arrived at Lisbon on 23 June, Cuyler sent the 2/1st Foot to Cork. He was preparing to send the 50th to the same destination when news of the presence of a Franco-Spanish fleet that had evaded the British squadrons in the Mediterranean and had entered the Atlantic arrived.[116] Independent of these events, St Clair Erskine, was increasingly concerned about the defence of the island due to a build-up of forces in the adjacent Spanish ports. So on 17 June St Clair Erskine wrote to St Vincent outlining his concerns and requested that reinforcements be sent from Portugal, namely the 2/1st and 50th Foot and, 'at least, one of the Foreign Regiments either that of de Rolle, or Dillon: I particularize those Regiments, because they are both of them, for the most part, composed of Germans'.[117] Furthermore he asked that Brigadier General Patrick Wauchope

---

110 TNA: WO 1/221: Fraser to Dundas, 13 February 1799.
111 *The Army List*, 1800.
112 *The Army List*, 1800 and *Etat militaire*, 1791.
113 *Etat militaire* and *Army Lists*; Missett had served in the French Chasseurs after the disbanding of the Irish Brigade in 1798.
114 TNA: WO 1/221: Dundas to Cuyler, 17 June 1799.
115 Fortescue, *British Army*, vol.IV, p.625.
116 James, *Naval History*, vol.II, pp.370–388.
117 TNA: WO 1/221: St Clair Erskine to St Vincent, 17 June 1799.

be sent with them, if he could be spared. The request arrived at Lisbon on 12 July and Cuyler immediately set preparations in hand for the 50th, Roll and Dillon to embark as soon as further transports arrived. Indeed, he determined to send them as a brigade fit for immediate service with, 'Camp Equipage, Blankets & Kettles, and not a moment shall be lost in sending these Corps from hence, which form a very excellent Brigade, under the command of B. Genl. Wauchope'.[118]

Delay was caused by obstruction from the Portuguese, even after they had acquiesced to the units leaving, fearful of doing anything that might be construed as hostile to Spain, and concern about the presence of the joint Franco-Spanish fleet.[119] However when the Royal Navy reported that the enemy fleet had passed by, heading to the north-east, the 50th marched from its quarters at São Julião and Dillon from Cascais to join Roll at Belem where the brigade embarked on 6 August and sailed the following morning under convoy of HMS *Mermaid*.[120]

Table 5: Embarkation return of the brigade under Brigadier General Wauchope, Belem, 6 August 1799.[121]

	'50th or West Kent Regiment'	'Dillon's Regiment'	'De Rolle's Regiment'	Total
Officers	29	24	26	79
Staff	3	5	6	14
Sergeants	33	51	62	146
Corporals	29	50	74	153
Drummers	22	22	22	66
Privates	500	495	450	1,445
Women	57	33	49	139
Children	73	20	33	126
Servants (not soldiers)	–	5	13	18

The convoy arrived at Mahón in Menorca on 20 August 1799 and St Clair Erskine reported 'that the Health of the men has in no degree suffered from their Passage.'[122] He expressed his gratitude to Cuyler for the manner in which the brigade had been sent, complete with additional medical personnel and supplies, appreciating as he did the difficulties Cuyler would have experienced from the Portuguese authorities.

118   TNA: WO 1/221: Cuyler to Dundas, 13 July 1799.
119   TNA: WO 1/221: Cuyler to Dundas, 20 July, 5 and 7 August 1799.
120   TNA: WO 1/221: Cuyler to Dundas, 7 August 1799.
121   TNA: WO 1/221: embarkation return.
122   TNA: WO 1/296: St Clair Erskine to Dundas, 22 August 1799.

4

'Like as many lions'

The threat to Menorca was averted with the arrival of Wauchope's brigade, indeed it seemed clear the Spanish had given up the project when they learned of its departure from Lisbon.[1] By August 1799 the garrison on Menorca was a respectable size, 7,425 officers and men, from the nine battalions, including the foreign regiments of Roll, Dillon and Stuart, and artillery and artificer detachments.[2] In Italy, where the French had invaded Naples in January, as summer turned into the autumn of 1799, the tide of war turned and the French were in full retreat. Nelson, who was a guest of the Neapolitan royal family as he recovered from a severe head wound received at Aboukir, wanted his hosts to gain from the retreat and requested assistance from St Clair Erskine, the senior army officer in the Mediterranean. However he had no instructions from the government regarding offensive operations and his ability to act on his own discretion had been curtailed, as he pointed out to Dundas, 'having been led by your dispatch of the 24th June to look to the probable arrival of a Governor or Superior Officer to take the command of the Troops; who will of course be charged with His Majesty's Commands and your Instructions.'[3] In particular Nelson encouraged him to send an expedition to Rome, which, '… would throw open her gates and receive you as a deliverer; and the Pope would owe his restoration to the Papal Chair to an *heretic*. This is the first great object, as it would not only be the complete deliverance of Italy, but restore peace and tranquillity to the torn-to pieces Kingdom of Naples.'[4]

St Clair Erskine recognised that he had up to 2,500 available troops but he refused to send an expedition. Rome's population was in a state of anarchy but there was no indication whether it supported the coalition or, indeed, was even particularly hostile to the French. Wauchope's brigade was the obvious choice to send but as St Clair Erskine explained to Dundas,

---

1 TNA: WO 1/296: St Clair Erskine to Dundas, 22 August and 2 September 1799.
2 TNA: WO 1/296: Return of 22 August 1799.
3 TNA: WO 1/296: St Clair Erskine to Dundas, 2 September 1799.
4 Nicolas, *Nelson*, vol.IV, pp.14–15, Nelson to St Clair Erskine, 13 September 1799. The news had not arrived of the death of Pope Pius VI on 29 August 1799, a prisoner in France.

> I should think myself inexcusable if I had sent one British Regiment only with the Regt. de Rolle under any Officer on the Expedition as it is represented to me; & committed the Credit of His Majesty's Army upon the specie of so doubtful an Adventure.
>
> It is true that foreign Regts from Portugal as well as the 50th have arrived in most excellent order, but I should decline to venture either De Rolle's or Dillon's upon the Roman State at present where the temptations to desert would be almost inevitable.[5]

Nevertheless, he undertook to ensure troops would be ready to leave for Italy or Malta, where French troops continued to hold out in Valletta, as soon as the expected commander arrived.[6]

In 1799 Switzerland was also the scene of fighting between the armies of the Second Coalition and France. Following the agreement described above, a Swiss corps was raised to serve alongside the Austrians but paid for by Britain as part of its contribution to the coalition. It consisted of three regiments, named after their colonels, Ferdinand de Rovéréa, Baron Rodolphe-Antoine-Hubert de Salis-Marschlins and Nicolas-Léodegard-François-Ignace Baron de Bachmann as well as a Valaisan battalion formed by the former *capitaine* of the Royal Etranger, Courten. Two more former officers in the regiment, the Ryhiner brothers, served with the corps. Benoit, the younger, as *capitaine* in Bachmann's regiment while his brother, Henry, was a *major* on the corps staff.[7] Even after the coalition allies retreated from Switzerland following defeat at the Second Battle of Zurich, 25 to 26 September 1799, the Swiss corps continued to serve alongside the Austrians.

In November 1799 Lieutenant General the Honourable Henry Edward Fox was appointed to replace St Clair Erskine in command on Menorca.[8] Charles Stuart retained the post of 'Commander in Chief of the King's Troops in the Mediterranean' and he proposed that for the 1800 campaign the British Government send sufficient troops to Menorca from where he could make a significant intervention on the coast of either Provence or Liguria. Despite accepting the plan ministers then sought to divert troops to other missions. Henry Bunbury, who served in the Mediterranean and later wrote a history of this stage of the wars, observed, 'Whenever our ministers found that they had a large body of troops at their disposal they shewed symptoms of *wanting to do something*; but they never were prepared beforehand, and they seldom looked to the main objects of the contest in which they were engaged.'[9] As a result the first reinforcements only arrived on Menorca in May 1800 by which time a frustrated Stuart had resigned. Sir Ralph Abercromby was appointed to replace him as commander-in-chief in the Mediterranean and

5   TNA: WO 1/296: St Clair Erskine to Dundas, 5 September 1799.
6   TNA: WO 1/296: St Clair Erskine to Dundas, 2 September 1799.
7   TNA: WO 25/772: Half pay returns.
8   TNA: WO 1/298: Fox to William Anne Villettes, 17 January 1800, and Fortescue, *British Army*, vol.IV, p.781.
9   Henry Bunbury, *Narratives of some Passages in the Great War with France, from 1799 to 1810* (London: Richard Bentley, 1854), p.72.

on 5 May he received his instructions, but due to bad weather he only got to Gibraltar on 6 June.[10]

In the meantime, the Regiment de Roll remained in barracks at Georgetown, now called Es Castell, that had been established as a military town on the harbour southeast of Mahón and described by a British officer as 'a neat, comfortable place, containing excellent barracks for the troops.'[11] There an incident occurred which illustrates how some members of the regiment sought to profit from garrison life. Sergeant Antoine Lacombe of the Colonel's Company and his wife, Francisca, ran a wine house in part of a shoemaker's house in which they also lodged. However, on 4 January 1800 he was killed in an altercation with a group of soldiers from the 90th Foot who had been served by Fifer Joseph Woolf from Roll, working as a waiter, when there was a dispute about payment. Lacombe intervened and when they refused to pay or leave he put on his greatcoat, sword and hat and warned them that, if they did not leave, he would take them to the guardhouse or call out the guard. One of the soldiers, Grenadier Thomas Carron, then got into a fight with Lacombe who fell, or was pushed, and hit his head, apparently fracturing his skull. Undeterred Carron continued his assault, with such savagery that his companions seemingly wanted nothing more to do with it, and struck at Lacombe at least twice with his own sword killing him. An officer of the 90th Foot, who was passing and heard the disturbance, immediately arrested Carron and seized the sword. Within a week, on 10 January, Carron was tried for 'wilful murder' of which he was found guilty and so sentenced to be hung.[12] However the court asked that consideration be given to reducing the punishment apparently after taking heed to Carron's submission that 'Serjeant Lacombe had departed from the Character of a Non Commissioned Officer and had become a wine house keeper' when the fight began but this was not heeded and the sentence was confirmed.[13]

This seems to have been an isolated incident and Tomaschett, by now in the Lieutenant Colonel's Company, simply wrote of the regiment's stay on Menorca, 'Here we stayed for almost a year and we had it very good.'[14] The regiment's return to the Mediterranean saw recruiting parties sent to Gibraltar, apparently working among prisoners of war held there, as well as to Sardinia, this party consisted of Ensign Henry Zwicky, who had previously been in the Schmid Regiment that had been stationed on the island, as well as a sergeant.[15] Meanwhile, a few men remained employed at Lisbon, one

10   Fortescue, *British Army*, vol.IV, p.783; Abercromby had held the local rank of general on the 'Continent of Europe' since 13 August 1799 (*Army List* 1800).
11   Aeneas Anderson, *Journal of the Forces which sailed from the Downs , in April 1800, on a Secret Expedition under the Command of Lieut.-Gen. Pigot, till their arrival in Minorca, and continued through the subsequent transactions of the Army under the Command of the Right Hon. Sir Ralph Abercromby, K.B. in the Mediterranean and Egypt* (London: J. Debrett, 1804), p.25.
12   TNA: WO 1/298: Transcript of the court martial.
13   TNA: WO 1/298: Brigadier General Moncrieff, 90th Foot, to Fox 13 January 1800 and transcript of the court martial; WO 90/1: f.50.
14   Vincenz (ed.), 'Tomaschett de Trun', p.309.
15   Zwicky was promoted to lieutenant in the Minorca Regiment on 18 April 1800, but it took some time for the transfer to take place.

being Sergeant Michel Krumm who was attached to the Paymaster General's department.[16]

While at Menorca the Regiment de Roll took part in a spectacular military display to celebrate King George's birthday on 4 June. The troops were deployed on either side of Mahón harbour with six battalions on the northern shore.

> Immediately opposite, on the George Town side of the river, the line commenced on the banks, and stretched, in an oblique manner, along the glacis of Fort George [now San Felipe] for about three quarters of a mile. The regiments that composed this part of the line were the 8th or king's, the two battalions of the 17th, the 48th and 90th, the Minorca regiment, and De Rolle's Swiss guards; they were also wheeled by signals into line. At half past eleven the Lieutenant-Governor [Fox], with numerous retinue, arrived in barges at Fort George, when the signal was made for the lines on either side of the river to prime and load. The men then came to ordered arms, and within a few minutes of twelve o'clock the whole shouldered arms.
>
> At twelve, the great guns began to fire from Citadella [sic], and the firing continued successively along the whole coast of the island till it reached Fort George, where every piece of artillery was regularly discharged. A similar cannonade then continued on the side opposite … The infantry then commenced a *feu-de-joye* from … [the right of the line on the north shore] and continued like the roll of a drum along the whole line till it terminated [on the left]. It was then renewed on the opposite shore, and run on without the least interruption to the end of the lines. This firing was repeated twice, and followed by three cheers … The scene was grand and impressive, and received no small addition from the beauty of the day. The whole concluded with a general salute, the regimental bands joining in the animating air of 'God save the King!'[17]

Having left his army in Egypt, Napoleon Bonaparte had returned to France on 9 October 1799 and soon took power as First Consul on 25 December. Then in 1800, exploiting control of Switzerland, the French armies took the initiative in Italy and on 2 June Bonaparte entered Milan while the Austrians sought to concentrate at Alessandria. Despite the tide of war turning against them, the Austrians had brought the siege of Genoa to a successful conclusion when its French garrison surrendered on 4 June. However, defeats elsewhere meant that the Austrians could only leave 5,000 men to defend the city. As a result Lord Keith, who had led the Royal Navy's support for the siege, was asked on 5 June to reinforce the city's garrison, as well that of Savona, with British troops from Menorca.[18]

On 7 June 1800 Keith wrote to Fox asking him to send without delay all the troops he could spare as he considered, 'that an English Garrison being instantly thrown into Genoa may prove the means of saving all Italy,

---

16   TNA: WO 12/11984: Pay lists 1800.
17   Anderson, *Journal*, pp.17–18.
18   Fortescue, *British Army*, vol.IV, p.784.

and giving a favourable turn to the affairs of the Allies.'[19] Anticipating that Abercromby may not have arrived at Menorca, Keith enclosed an extract from Abercromby's instructions, 'to give every assistance which a light moveable force, acting in conjunction with a superior Fleet, can afford, either in the way of diversion, coup de main, or occasional co-operation with the Austrian Armies acting against France on the side of Italy and Piedmont.'[20] The decision of what operations were to be undertaken rested with the army and navy commanders for the theatre. Initially it was impossible for Fox to comply as there was only one transport at Menorca available for troops.[21] Keith repeated his entreaty on 12 June but Fox, without his own instructions, was anxious not to derail any plans the new commander may have drawn up. Nevertheless, with regard to Keith's 'requisition for Troops for Genoa to co-operate with the Austrian Force,' he informed Dundas, 'I shall hold them in readiness and embark them as Vessels arrive but shall defer their sailing with the expectation of the daily arrival of Sir Ralph Abercrombie [sic] … unless further urged by Lord Keith.'[22]

His dilemma did not last long as Abercromby arrived the next day, 22 June, and orders were immediately issued for troops to embark for Genoa.[23] The units that were allocated to go were the 18th, 28th, 40th, 42nd, 48th, 90th, Roll and a company of Royal Artillery.[24] However, the 28th had not arrived from Gibraltar at this point and the 42nd, which was stationed at Ciutadella, could not get to Mahón in time.[25] The men of the Regiment de Roll embarked at 6:00 a.m. on 23 June on the troopship HMS *Expedition* at Georgetown, along with Brigadier General John Doyle, and sailed that afternoon.[26] The regiments had been instructed to 'carry all Camp Equipage, Necessaries & Ammunition & will leave their Women, heavy Baggage and Sick' behind under the supervision of a small detachment.[27] Roll left two NCOs and 18 privates on Menorca.[28] It was as the ships were at sea, on 26 June, the news arrived that the Austrians had evacuated Genoa and Keith was now off Livorno, so Abercromby headed towards that port. It was there, on 1 July, that he learned the Austrians had been defeated by Bonaparte at Marengo on 14 June and an armistice had been concluded that saw the Austrians withdraw over the River Mincio.[29] There was nothing to be gained by landing at Livorno in breach of the armistice.

In the urgency of the departure, the 40th Foot had been crammed into HMS *Hindostan*, a storeship, without adequate water.[30] The situation was so

---

19   TNA: WO 1/298: Keith to Fox, 7 June 1800.

20   TNA: WO 1/298: Extract of the orders provided by Keith to Fox in his letter of 7 June 1800.

21   Fortescue, *British Army*, vol.IV, p.785.

22   TNA: WO 1/298: Fox to Dundas, 21 June 1800.

23   Anderson, *Journal*, p.19.

24   TNA: WO 1/298: Distribution of the Forces, 23 June 1800.

25   Anderson, *Journal*, p.20 and TNA: WO 17/2238: Return 1 July 1800.

26   TNA: WO 28/351: General Order, 22 June 1800 and ADM 51/1331: Captain's journal HMS *Expedition*.

27   TNA: WO 28/351: General Order, 22 June 1800.

28   TNA: WO 17/2238: Return 1 July 1800.

29   Fortescue, *British Army*, vol.IV, p.785.

30   Anderson, *Journal*, pp.27–29.

serious that 150 men of the 40th were transferred, at sea, to the *Expedition* that also sent water to the *Hindostan*.[31] Both ships then returned to Mahón where the men of the 40th were disembarked. The Regiment de Roll remained on the *Expedition*, except for the morning of 29 June when the ship was brought alongside a wharf and the soldiers were briefly put ashore while their accommodation was washed and fumigated. An illustration of the different standards of hygiene and internal management experienced on hired transports and their Royal Navy counterparts.[32] Finally, having taken ammunition on board, the *Expedition* was towed out of harbour on 1 July and set sail the next day in company with the *Hindostan, Dover, Pegasus* and 10 transports, with the 28th, the 40th, a detachment of the 11th Light Dragoons and some of Abercromby's staff.[33] The *Expedition* arrived in Livorno roadstead on 6 July, where Keith and Nelson's flagships were at anchor, and the other ships arrived over the next two days.[34] Abercromby had already left on 4 July for Malta and on 11 July the remaining ships off Livorno, including the *Expedition* with Doyle and the Regiment de Roll on board, sailed. The winds were unkind and it was only in the afternoon of 21 July that the ships arrived off the entrance to Mahón harbour. The wind was a northerly and there was a heavy swell so most of the ships remained off shore but the *Expedition* and the *Pegasus* got into the harbour, 'not without some damage; the former having got on shore'.[35] There were, however, no ill-effects for the troops on board. Despite the arrival of more troops meaning that accommodation was in short supply, the Regiment de Roll appears to have been placed in barracks at Mahón although at some stage one company was quartered at Sant lluis, six kilometres inland.[36]

Abercromby had discounted any prospect of useful intervention in Italy and awaited further instructions.[37] Having returned to Menorca, he ensured the troops he intended to take with him on any expedition were ready for active service, once again the Regiment de Roll was the only foreign unit among them. His first step was to place his infantry in two divisions with two brigades, each with three battalions; the second division was commanded by Major General John Moore and his first brigade, under Brigadier General Hildebrand Oakes, consisted of the 42nd, 90th and Roll.[38] Over the next few weeks the units 'were continually perfecting themselves in those evolutions, which it was generally expected and desired that they would be called upon to employ in actual service.'[39] The emphasis on training under realistic conditions was continued in field days as brigades or individual battalions.

31   TNA: ADM 51/1331: Captain's journal HMS *Expedition*.
32   TNA: ADM 51/1331: Captain's journal HMS *Expedition*.
33   TNA: WO 1/298: Fox to Dundas, 4 July 1800. Anderson states the 1st Battalion, 40th, was still on the *Hindostan* and the 2nd Battalion sailed in two of the transports (Anderson, *Journal*, p.29).
34   TNA: ADM 51/1331: Captain's journal HMS *Expedition*.
35   Anderson, *Journal*, p.37; TNA: ADM 51/1331: Captain's journal HMS *Expedition* states that the ship struck some rocks.
36   TNA: WO 28/351: General Orders 8 and 23 August 1800.
37   Fortescue, *British Army*, vol.IV, pp.786–787.
38   TNA: WO 28/351: General Order 4 August 1800.
39   Anderson, *Journal*, p.43.

General Orders specified, 'On these occasions they should be practised in performing with exactness and precision a few simple measures; and in order to accustom the soldiers to a free use of their arms, when encumbered with their necessaries, they ought, when ordered to fire with blank cartridges, sometimes to parade in full marching order.'[40] Efforts were made to ensure that the units were clothed, armed and equipped in the best possible manner. Abercromby inspected all the units on Menorca and the Regiment de Roll and 2nd Foot were seen 'on the Parade' at Mahón on 13 August.[41] The General Order of 16 August expressed Abercromby's satisfaction with what he found and also the tenor of his command:

> The Commander in Chief having now finished the Inspection of the Troops near Mahon, has in many particulars reason to be satisfied with their appearance. … he has the fullest reliance on the Exertions of every Officer from the General to the Ensign, in the forming of Troops, so worthy of their Care, whom they may command in action, & on whose Conduct their own honour & the Welfare of the public so much depends.[42]

The strength of the Regiment de Roll stood at two field officers – Lieutenant Colonel Dürler and Major de Sonnenberg – six captains, eight lieutenants and five ensigns, with a staff of a chaplain, adjutant, quartermaster, surgeon and two assistant surgeons. Present were 54 sergeants and 22 drummers and fifers and of the rank and file, 565 were fit for duty, one was recruiting and three were on furlough. What is remarkable is how healthy the regiment was, only having two men sick, both in hospital.[43]

On 24 August Abercromby received new instructions. The British Government had decided to use its available troops to destroy Spanish naval arsenals and shipping in harbour. Abercromby was to sail to Gibraltar where he would be met by a force from Britain, commanded by Lieutenant General Sir James Murray Pulteney, which was to have already attacked Ferrol and Vigo. Abercromby was then to lead the combined force against Cádiz.[44] As soon as 26 August the units destined for the expedition were ordered 'to hold themselves in readiness to embark at the shortest notice, carrying with then Camp Equipage & heavy Baggage.'[45] Abercromby selected to take 15 battalions by including the foreign units of Dillon, Minorca and the newly formed Corsican Rangers in his force which was reorganised into three brigades and a reserve; the third brigade of Roll, Dillon and Minorca being commanded by Brigadier General John Stuart.[46] The Regiment de Roll embarked in the morning of 29 August at English Cove, now called Cala

40   Anderson, *Journal*, p.44, quoting General Order 11 August 1800.
41   TNA: WO 28/351: General Order 12 August 1800.
42   TNA: WO 28/351: General Order 16 August 1800.
43   TNA: WO 17/2227: Return of 1 August 1800, of comparative size the 2nd Foot had 149 sick and the 18th Foot 48.
44   Fortescue, *British Army*, vol.IV, pp.788–789.
45   TNA: WO 28/351: General Order 26 August 1800.
46   TNA: WO 28/351: General Order 27 August 1800.

Figuera, to the east of Mahón, on four transports, the *Wakefield* (with 235 men), *Betsey* (200), *Telemachus* (174) and *Fanny* (58).[47]

The fleet of warships and transports sailed on 31 August, the almost 11,500 troops on board unaware of their destination.[48] Abercromby arrived at Gibraltar on 11 September and the fleet came in three days later. There he was informed Cádiz was gripped by a yellow fever epidemic so he considered abandoning the expedition but Keith persuaded him to press ahead.[49] On 20 September Pulteney, having aborted the attack on Ferrol and Vigo, arrived and after watering the vessels off Tétouan, Morocco, the fleet sailed on 2 October 'with 22 ships of the line, 37 frigates and sloops, and 80 transports, having on board about 18000 men'.[50] Arriving off Cádiz on 4 October, it was learned that at least 200 people a day were dying of the fever in the city and 'that it prevailed in all the villages around, and was equally fatal among the [Spanish] troops. There could be no reason to hope that the British army, if it should be landed could escape the effects of the pestilence'.[51] Nevertheless preparations to land commenced, including a botched attempt to assemble boats laden with troops, but they were finally cancelled when it became clear that only a small proportion of the troops could be landed at any one time and the navy could not guarantee to provide continued support to them once they were ashore.[52] On 7 October the signal was given for the fleet to sail for Tétouan Bay and by the afternoon they were all underway.[53] Among the soldiers the rumour ran that the attack had been called off by bribery, Sergeant Tomaschett describing the decision having been made after barrels of money had been delivered to the admiral by a boat from Cádiz flying a flag of truce.[54]

The vessels anchored in and around the Strait of Gibraltar changing station as the wind changed direction. Conditions for the troops were far from comfortable with scurvy and other sickness appearing on several vessels while the poor state of many of the transports resulted in men being continually soaked. Then on 13 October an easterly gale struck that drove several vessels ashore or to crash into others, 80 ships losing their anchors in Tétouan Bay.[55] The 16 year-old Richard Church, ensign in the 13th Foot, described the conditions when writing home to his mother, 'We, the army, certainly go through more than any people in fatigue,

---

47   TNA: WO 28/351: General Orders 27 and 28 August 1800.
48   Anderson, *Journal*, p.59 and TNA: WO 17/2227: Return of 1 September 1800.
49   Bunbury, *Narratives*, p.74.
50   James, *Naval History*, vol.IV, p.38.
51   Bunbury, *Narratives*, p.75.
52   Details of this ignominious episode are given in James Abercromby (Lord Dunfermline), *Lieutenant-General Sir Ralph Abercromby K.B. 1793–1801* (Edinburgh: Edmonston and Douglas, 1861), pp.227–239.
53   Anderson, *Journal*, pp.82–83.
54   Vincenz (ed.), 'Tomaschett de Trun', p.310. His conclusion is implicitly supported by the Coldstream Guardsman in Anon., *A Faithful Journal of the late Expedition to Egypt ... by a Private on Board the Dictator* (London: J. Lee, 1802), pp.17–18.
55   Robert Thomas Wilson, *History of the British Expedition to Egypt; to which is subjoined, a Sketch of the present state of that Country and its means of defence* (London: T. Egerton, 1802), p.1, footnote.

hardship, dreadful living, and storms; living on salt pork ... so full of salt you cut it with the greatest difficulty; foul water, maggoty biscuits: such living is common to us'.[56]

While in this position, the welcome news arrived that the French garrison at Valletta had surrendered on 5 September, thus all of Malta was now in British hands. Finally new instructions arrived from England on 24 October, Abercromby was to proceed to Egypt and expel the French troops that Bonaparte had left there. Peace negotiations between Britain and France were inevitable with Austria about to sue for peace in the spring. The Mediterranean and Egypt were bound to be important considerations in the ensuing negotiations so the British Government wanted French control of Egypt to be at least contested if not completely broken. However, in deciding to order the expedition the strength of the French forces in Egypt was grossly underestimated and that with Abercromby was inadequate. It was chronically short of cavalry, artillery and engineers, lacked horses, not only for the cavalry but also the artillery and transport, and was so short of money that the men had not been paid for three months.[57]

The ships had already begun to sail eastwards, some directly to Malta, such as that with Abercromby onboard, who arrived there on 26 November, and others to Menorca. Those carrying the Regiment de Roll appear to have been among the latter, Tomaschett, the only source providing any detail of the regiment's movements at this time, states that the vessel he was on sailed for Menorca on 22 October.[58] The regiment's musters show that two men deserted on 21 October, perhaps having slipped away from a watering party at Tétouan Bay before their transport departed.[59] What is clear is that others had already arrived at Menorca, even if they had only brought those who were sick, at the muster of 24 October Ensign Jean Guignard, two sergeants, a corporal, a drummer and 11 privates were 'sick at Mahon' when they had not been there the previous month.[60] The troops that were now arriving, including the Regiment de Roll, remained on their transports although everything possible was done to alleviate their conditions.[61] Although Tomaschett does not give the date he left Menorca he states that the regiment, or at least the detachment he was with, arrived at Malta on 29 November where it disembarked.[62] More ships were to arrive over the coming days.[63]

---

56 E.M.Church, *Chapters in an Adventurous Life: Sir Richard Church in Italy and Greece* (Edinburgh: William Blackwood and Sons, 1895), p.3. The 13th Foot had been part of Pulteney's force.

57 Abercromby, *Abercromby*, p.254 and G. le M. Gretton, *The Campaigns and History of the Royal Irish Regiment From 1684 to 1902* (Edinburgh: William Blackwood and Sons, 1911), p.107.

58 Vincenz (ed.), 'Tomaschett de Trun', p.310.

59 TNA: WO 12/11984: Paylist, 24 October 1800.

60 TNA: WO 12/11984: Paylist, 24 October 1800. Four privates were left at the General Hospital at Gibraltar, two as patients and two as attendants.

61 Thomas Walsh, *Journal of the Late Campaign in Egypt: including descriptions of that Country, and of Gibraltar, Minorca, Malta, Marmorice and Macri* (London: T. Cadell and W. Davies, 1803), p.12.

62 Vincenz (ed.), 'Tomaschett de Trun', p.311.

63 Walsh, *Journal*, pp.17–18.

At Malta, Abercromby inspected different units each day, his concern being practical competence and discipline rather than parade ground display.[64] He recognised the particular conditions under which his foreign units served so when the order was published that British regiments were to only take three women per company with them, the others being left at Malta, it continued, 'From the Peculiarity of their Situation; the Whole of the Women belonging to the Foreign Regiments are Permitted to accompany them.'[65] Sergeant Tomaschett states that the regiment remained on Malta until 16 December.[66] This date may well have been the date the regiment embarked but it left no earlier than 20 December as that was when the first part of the fleet sailed, followed by the second part the following day.[67] The original destination was Rhodes or Crete where Britain's ally, the Ottoman Empire, was to deliver horses and supplies but bad weather caused the fleet to seek shelter on the Turkish coast and the first part of the fleet entered Marmaris Bay on 28 December and the second on 1 January 1801.[68] Officers and men were struck by the scenery that surrounded them in the bay, while some provided dramatic descriptions Tomaschett simply wrote, 'It is good wine country with abundant forests, so that we could provision there with all we needed until Egypt.'[69]

Planning was hampered by a lack of reliable information about Egypt and the French forces there but Abercromby decided to land at Aboukir Bay for an attack on Alexandria. Possession of the city would sever the French army's communication with its homeland and provide a port to serve the needs of his own army and the fleet. He had initially favoured landing at Damietta, on the east of the Nile Delta, to link with the Ottoman army advancing from Syria and use water transport to capture Cairo and the French arsenals there. But he discarded this plan on learning of the condition of the Ottoman forces he was expected to co-operate with. He considered he could not rely on them for the critical first stage of the expedition.[70] The Ottoman army in Syria commanded by the Grand Vizier was, to British eyes, a medieval horde which was furthermore ravaged by plague. There were also some concerns about its aims and how this may impact future operations. Bonaparte's invasion of Egypt had broken the power of the Mamluks, who had previously controlled Egypt, as George Baldwin, the former consul warned Abercromby, 'The ambition and hope of the Mamluk is to reign; to recover his sovereignty. The known, and now become necessary, policy of the

---

64   Piers Mackesy, *British Victory in Egypt: The End of Napoleon's Conquest* (New York: Taurus Parke, 2010), p.34 and Anderson, *Journal*, p.105.
65   TNA: WO 28/351: General Order 10 December 1800. Women of the foreign regiments could have accompanied the regiments on the Cádiz Expedition, orders prohibiting them have not been seen, otherwise they would have been brought by ships coming to Malta from Menorca.
66   Vincenz (ed.), 'Tomaschett de Trun', p.311.
67   TNA: ADM 51/1331: Captain's journal HMS *Expedition*, Wilson, *British Expedition*, pp.2–3 and Anderson, *Journal*, p.108.
68   Wilson, *British Expedition*, pp.2–3 and Anderson, *Journal*, p.108.
69   Vincenz (ed.), 'Tomaschett de Trun', p.312.
70   Mackesy, *British Victory*, pp.22–26.

Turk, is to annihilate the Mamluk, and to despoil the country of its wealth.'[71] Unfortunately successful co-operation with the Ottomans had already been put in doubt as the expected supplies were delayed and when the first batch of horses arrived they were in such poor condition they could not be used. Officers had to use their own money to buy the small horses that could be found locally.

Nevertheless, the time in Marmaris Bay was not wasted. To ensure the chaotic scenes off Cádiz were not repeated, the process of embarking the troops in boats and landing them ready to immediately go into action was planned and practiced jointly by the two services. In addition, the troops were put ashore for exercise as frequently as possible but some, particularly in the Minorca Regiment, took the opportunity to try to desert, although none are recorded doing so from the Regiment de Roll in this period.[72] Another reason troops were landed was to form fatigue parties, particularly to fell and retrieve wood which was expected to be in short supply in Egypt. As well as fuel the wood was used to make articles such as tent pegs, fascines and sledges to manhandle supplies – to make up for the lack of horses and wheeled transport. A General Order shows that the Regiment de Roll and 300 men of the 92nd provided the fatigue parties on 6 February.[73] While at Marmaris Bay a long overdue reform was made which, if it had been made earlier, would have alleviated many of the problems the Regiment de Roll had previously faced. While being transported by sea troops only received three quarters of their daily ration on the grounds that they were doing little work and their stay on board was of short duration. However in the Mediterranean the soldiers, 'on board troop-ships weakly manned, are obliged to do as much work as the sailors, and detained on board for months together, the pittance is too small, and it is but fair, that they should receive the same allowance as the sailors.'[74] Abercromby represented this to Keith, who was responsible for such matters, and the latter 'immediately placed the soldier on the same footing with the sailor in this particular.'[75]

As a result of changes made at Malta, the infantry now formed six brigades, one of Guards battalions and five from the line, as well as a reserve, with four battalions, the flank companies of the 40th Foot and the Corsican Rangers. The Regiment de Roll was in the 5th (Foreign) Brigade commanded by Stuart, along with the Minorca and Dillon Regiments; the Brigade Major was Captain Hyacinthe Saint Pern of Dillon.

71   George Baldwin, *Political Recollections relative to Egypt* (London: Author, 1802), pp.84–85, reproducing a letter he wrote on 1 February 1801.
72   TNA: WO 17/1757: Monthly returns for 1 January and 1 February 1801.
73   TNA: WO 28/351: General Order 5 February 1801.
74   Walsh, *Journal*, p.49.
75   Walsh, *Journal*, p.49.

Table 6: Strength of Abercromby's army and its 5th (Foreign) Brigade, 14 February 1801.[76]

	Officers	Staff	Sergeants & QMs (cavalry) present	Drummers & trumpeters present	Rank & file fit for duty	Sick present	Total rank & file present
Army							
Infantry	641	105	985	424	13,146	1,028	14,174
Cavalry	39	10	83	20	1,035	28	1,063
Artillery*	31	7	12	9	644	22	666
5th Brigade							
Roll	21	5	52	21	523	6	529
Minorca	34	6	52	21	928	13	941
Dillon	21	5	50	22	525	20	545
Bde. total	76	16	154	64	1,976	39	2,015
* includes the Horse Department							

Finally, on 16 February, Greek transports arrived with 500 horses and the fleet could now head for Egypt. An officer recalled, 'the army all embarked on the 20th of February, yet it was not till the 23rd that the fleet could weigh anchor, when it sailed with a very fresh breeze. The quantity of vessels was such, about 175 sail, as to require a compete day for the whole to assemble.'[77] Captain Francis Maule, of the 2nd Foot, remembered the occasion,

> On the morning of the 24th of February, the usual signal was made to sail.
>
> Scarcely had the favourable breeze filled our sails, when our neighbours, the regiment de Rolle, accompanied us with their noble music.
>
> Their vicinity, indeed, was always coveted by me, and on subsequent occasions, I have been still more gratified in an acquaintance with that regiment. At all times, when on duty with them, I have observed with delight their correct discipline and military deportment.[78]

This passage, and praise, is notable as Maule studiously avoided identifying particular units or individuals in his memoirs 'with very few exceptions.'[79] Three days later the breeze turned to a gale that only abated on 28 February and the fleet was dispersed, the Greek horse transports and the Turkish gunboats had taken shelter in harbour and would only return weeks later.[80]

The fleet finally came into sight of Alexandria on 1 March and then entered Aboukir Bay the following morning. The ships had to anchor five miles offshore due to the shallowness of the bay and the weather was boisterous so the landing could not be attempted until 8 March. The French were thus given ample time to prepare. The landing was made by the Reserve, the Guards, and 1st Brigade. Despite fierce and determined resistance, led by *Général de Division* Louis Friant, it was successful and by nightfall most of

---

76   TNA: WO 1/345: return 14 February 1801.
77   Wilson, *British Expedition*, pp.6–7.
78   Maule, *Principal Events*, pp.69–70.
79   Maule, *Principal Events*, p.iv.
80   Mackesy, *British Victory*, pp.50, 82.

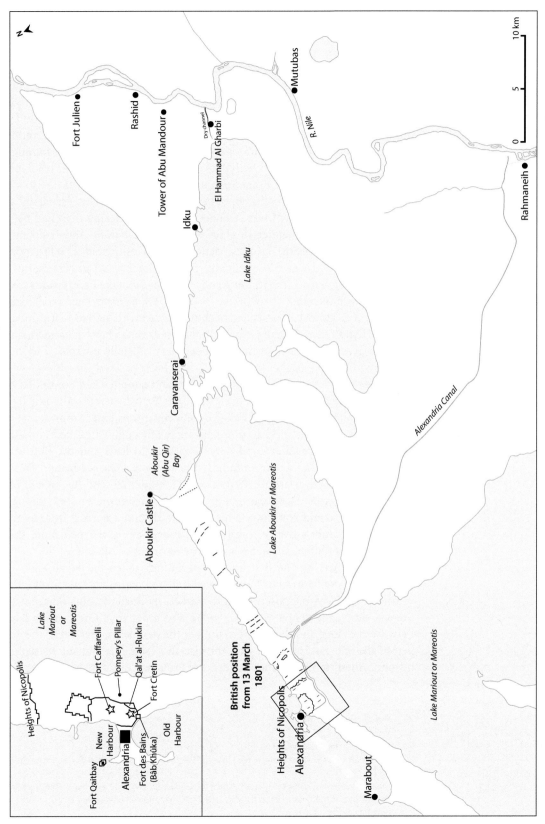

The region around Alexandria, with an inset of the city's defences.

the infantry, but only a handful of the cavalry, was ashore. A defensive line was established about three miles from the beach and the elements of the 4th and 5th Brigades that were ashore were placed before Aboukir Castle, on the northern tip of the bay, 'which had refused to surrender on being summoned.'[81] The next day, however, they were replaced by the 2nd Foot and 400 unmounted light dragoons and the two brigades, up to full strength, took their places in the line.[82] Each British soldier had landed with food for three days, the wisdom of this was proven the next day when the operation to land the remainder of the troops and supplies was suspended due to rough seas until 10 March. The line, with the head of Lake Aboukir on the left flank, was consolidated with the Reserve occupying the advanced posts.

The situation for Abercromby and his men was perilous especially as the French force in Egypt was stronger and in better shape than had been expected. Their commander in chief *Général de Division* Abdallah (after his conversion to Islam) Jacques Menou had an estimated 22,000 troops supported by 8,000 in auxiliary legions – Syrian, Greek, Copt and Janissaries – and supporting arms.[83] The training and effectiveness of the French units had, however, declined since their first arrival in 1798, as historian Yves Martin has observed, 'almost all units had been reinforced with 'native' recruitment. The 21st Light Demi-Brigade, especially, has in its ranks Egyptians and many former slaves from Darfur who have been very officially purchased to join the army. Likewise Maltese and Copts had been pressed into the service of various units.'[84] However reinforcements and supplies had continued to arrive piece-meal from France, even while the British were in Aboukir Bay. Before the landing Menou had had to deploy his troops to face four points of attack: Sinai, from the Turkish troops advancing through Palestine; Damietta and Aboukir, where Abercromby was expected to land and the Red Sea, from another British force from India, while keeping a reserve around Cairo. Now Abercromby was ashore Menou could confidently send the bulk of his troops to deal with the threat he posed. In the meantime Friant, although outnumbered, could concentrate his forces to defend a narrow front as the British could only advance towards Alexandria along the peninsula that separated the Mediterranean Sea and Lake Aboukir, or Maadie.

That advance, on the first line of the French defences, began early in the morning on 13 March.[85] Their line stretched across the peninsula, the northern end was on raised ground marked by ancient ruins adjacent to the sea shore, the centre was on a ridge and a patch of lower ground lay between the ridge and the southern limit of the peninsula, marked by the dry bed of the Alexandria Canal with the also dry Lake Mariout (or Mareotis) beyond. Abercromby planned to turn the French position by exploiting the

---

81   Walsh, *Journal*, p.70.

82   Walsh, *Journal*, p.81.

83   Mackesy, *British Victory*, pp.55–56.

84   Yves Martin, *The French Army of the Orient 1798–1801* (Solihull: Helion & Company, 2017), p.97.

85   Maule, *Principal Events*, p.83, says the men were under arms at 4:00 a.m. but Walsh states that the advance should have begun an hour later but 'owing to some untoward circumstances' it only began at 6:30 a.m.

gap between the ridge and the canal and turning its flank. It was known that the French had received reinforcements, who had arrived with *Général de Division* François Lanusse who replaced Friant in command, and Abercromby wished to try the defences of Alexandria before more arrived, however he did not know what lay between this first line and the city itself.

Initially the British advanced in two principal columns, with the Reserve forming another on the right flank to head for the ruins. The left column, under Abercromby's second-in-command Major General John Hely Hutchinson, was formed by the 3rd, 5th and 4th Brigades, in that order. In Stuart's brigade the Regiment de Roll took the lead, followed by Dillon and then Minorca.[86] The heads of both principal columns were preceded by regiments deployed as skirmishers, that on the left being the highlanders of the 92nd Foot. Progress had to be slow as the cannon of the supporting artillery had to be dragged by sailors and soldiers. However soon the fire from the superior and well-served French guns were causing mounting casualties so the principal columns redeployed; Hutchinson's with the 3rd and 5th Brigades in a line and the 4th Brigade behind, still in column, ready to threaten the enemy's flank. The 5th Brigade, forming from the right, lined up with Roll on the right, Dillon in the centre and Minorca on the left. Soon Lanusse sent infantry to attack Hutchinson's column while cavalry charged that on the right. The 92nd, still skirmishing, held firm despite heavy losses in the ensuing fire-fight, in which the French were able to bring their artillery so close they could use grape-shot. This attack was only repelled when two or three companies of Dillon came up on the highlanders' left flank. The British lines continued to press on, disputed by French skirmishers supported by artillery that exploited its mobility, without fear of interference from British cavalry or counter-fire. Finally, the French abandoned their positions, it was at this stage that the Dillon Regiment distinguished itself when it, 'charged with the bayonet, and carried two guns placed on the canal of Alexandria, turning them immediately against the enemy.'[87]

It was about midday and the British continued forward as the French retreated, in some confusion but largely inatct, towards the defences that lined the escarpment of the Heights of Nicopolis. The British had not expected the breadth of the sandy plain between the two positions but plans were made to attack the heights on the right, by Moore's Reserve, and Hutchinson's three brigades on the left. In preparation Hutchinson advanced to a piece of rising ground, sarcastcially called the Green Hill. Here, as his troops took shelter from the French artillery placed on the heights beyond, Hutchinson was able to get the first sight of the defences before Alexandria, they were stronger and further from the city than expected. The losses his units were already suffering showed what the cost of an assault would be and, if taken, the position would have to be entrenched. It was already after 3:00 p.m. and the infantry did not have the required tools with them. Abercromby agreed

---

86   Walsh, *Journal*, plan facing p.86.
87   Wilson, *British Expedition*, pp.21, 26.

that an attack should not be made and had his troops withdraw to the ridge of sandhills they had captured.[88]

The action of 13 March, which the British would call the Battle of Mandora, had tested the whole army as it had deployed, manoeuvred and fought against a determined enemy over rough ground under formidable artillery fire, especially in the plain in front of the Heights of Nicopolis. The preparations and training on Menorca, Malta and in Marmaris Bay had paid dividends. Abercromby wrote his official despatch on 16 March, 'I have the greatest Satisfaction in saying, that the Conduct of the British and Foreign Troops under my Command is deserving of the highest Praise; their Courage and their Discipline have been equally conspicuous.'[89] It had, however, come at a cost, Abercromby remarking, 'These victories make me melancholy.'[90] His army reported 186 killed and 1,135 wounded, including sailors and marines, The losses of the 5th Brigade were: Minorca, two killed, 15 wounded and one missing, all of whom were rank and file; Dillon, 13 rank and file killed and three officers, 10 sergeants, five drummers and 80 rank and file wounded; Roll: two sergeants and eight rank and file killed and three officers, three sergeants and 41 rank and file wounded.[91]

As is generally the case entries in the muster lists do not correlate exactly with these reported casualties. The former show that eight men were killed, Sergeant Joseph Fernkes and seven private soldiers, and three sergeants, five corporals and 29 privates were wounded.[92] The disparity in the number of wounded is explained by the musters only recording those men whose wounds were so severe that they had not returned to the regiment by 24 March. Of the wounded officers, Lieutenant Aloyse Baron de Bachmann of the Light Company, was on a hospital ship on that date but the other two who were wounded, Lieutenant Colonel Dürler and Major de Sonnenberg, did not have to leave the regiment.[93]

Over the next week measures were taken to strengthen the line facing the Heights of Nicopolis, the priority being to bring up heavy guns, ammunition and entrenching tools. Abercromby, despite the doubts of several of his senior officers, planned to attack the French on the heights which, as soon as they were taken, would be entrenched before the heavy guns were brought up to attack the walls of Alexandria's Arab town in which the French field army was quartered. He would not countenance withdrawing without making the attempt and, indeed there were good reasons to act now rather than later.[94] Delay allowed more French reinforcements to arrive and sickness, notably ophthalmia, was increasing among his troops. On 18 March, the overall strength of the Regiment de Roll had increased by six since 14 February,

88   Maule, *Principal Events*, p.86 and Mackesy, *British Victory*, pp.94–97.
89   *The London Gazette*, 5–9 May 1801.
90   Baldwin, *Political Recollections*, p.136.
91   *The London Gazette*, 5–9 May 1801.
92   TNA: WO 12/11985: 24 March 1801.
93   Aloyse de Bachmann had served in France in the Régiment de Salis-Samade and his father had been *major* of the Garde Suisse at the storming of the Tuileries Palace who was a victim of the massacres of prisoners on 2 and 3 September 1792 (Valliere, *Honneur et Fidelité*, p.637).
94   Mackesy, *British Victory*, pp.102–106.

apparently by the arrival of men from Menorca who had recovered their health. However out of the 535 rank and file, 66 were sick and it was a similar story in the other regiments of the brigade: Minorca having 867 fit and 78 sick and Dillon had 443 and 95.[95]

It was during this period that Paymaster John Harley, 47th Foot, had an encounter with one of the Roll officers that, as well as conveying an engaging scenario, indicates the continuing communication between the troops onshore and the ships anchored in Aboukir Bay,

> On the 17th, as I had charge of the provisions of our regiment, about halfway from the landing place to the lines, I was met by a foreign officer in a very exhausted state, who addressing me in broken English, informed me … that he landed that morning at an early hour from a transport, and had been ever since travelling about in quest of rations, having been refused by the commissariat depot to which he had applied, as he had no return or document to show them.
>
> Knowing that his regiment was in front of the lines, and that he was unable from fatigue and want of refreshment to reach them, I willingly produced my store, and we sat down together to partake of it. When he had eaten a hearty meal of cold pork and biscuit, and taken a glass or two of rum and water, of which I usually contrived to have a tolerable supply, he turned to me with joy beaming on his countenance, and said, 'I have dined at the table of princes, but may truly say, I never enjoyed a dinner before; and I only wish, my dear sir, that I may, one day or other, have it in my power to show my gratitude.' He then told me that he was the Baron Capolle, and that before the French revolution he was a colonel in the old Swiss Guards in Paris, and fought in the defence of the unfortunate Louis the Sixteenth.[96]

On 17 March the garrison of Aboukir Castle surrendered and two days later 500 Turkish soldiers landed at Aboukir Bay, with a few thousand more expected.[97] Meanwhile Menou had arrived at Alexandria on 18 March with cavalry and the Régiment de Dromadaires, a unit formed for scouting and raiding in which the men were carried by camels but fought on foot. Infantry were following and arrived on 20 March. Both he and Abercromby were in an analogous position. Neither had overwhelming strength to attack the enemy in a defensive position yet, if they hesitated, their opponent would be reinforced, Menou by troops who were known to be on their way from France and Abercromby by Ottoman troops. Menou, pressed by subordinates who had no respect for him, acted first, launching an attack an hour and a half before dawn on 21 March.[98]

---

95   TNA: WO 1/345: 18 March 1801 return.

96   John Harley, *The Veteran or 40 Years' Service in the British Army: The Scurrilous Recollections of Paymaster John Harley 47th Foot – 1798–1838* (Solihull: Helion & Company, 2018), p.76. Harley makes some errors as he described his guest as an officer of the Chasseurs Britanniques but this regiment was yet to be formed and Capol was *second lieutenant* of the Gardes Suisses without any additional rank (*Etat militaire*, 1791).

97   Walsh, *Journal*, pp.92–94.

98   Mackesy, *British Victory*, pp.112–113.

The British held a line running north to south, right to left. On the sandhill ridge at its centre were the Guards' and 1st Brigades, with a battery between them. To the north of the ridge was a valley, through which the Alexandria to Aboukir road ran, with higher ground between it and the sea. This higher ground was broken up and dominated by ancient ruins which were somewhat in advance of the centre. This position was held by the Reserve commanded by Moore. On the left of the line, the ridge fell away to flat ground between it and the banks of the Alexandria Canal on the edge of Lake Mariout. This extensive position, from the ridge to the canal and then back to the head of Lake Aboukir was held by the 2nd Brigade. Supports were deployed behind the line, the 3rd Brigade for the 2nd, the 4th as a reserve in the centre, behind the ridge, the 5th Brigade in the valley, so aligned between the Reserve and the Guards and finally the cavalry, both mounted and those on foot, were behind the 5th, in terrain considered suitable for this arm.[99] To reinforce the defences, a redoubt had been constructed in front and to the left of the Reserve's position and others were built on the canal, on the left of the line, however none were completed and were open at the rear. Furthermore 'several small flêches, with one or two guns, [were] disposed at intervals along the front of the line.'[100] This somewhat neat description neglects the deployment on the Alexandria Canal, on the arm of land that projected southwards and so separated Lakes Aboukir and Mariout. Events indicate that this was held by elements of Stuart's 5th Brigade, indeed when, on 18 March, some British cavalry had rushed to engage some of their French counterparts south of this point, it was a company of the Minorca Regiment that supported them.[101]

The British positions along the Alexandria Canal were the target of Menou's opening attack, in a feint designed to entice the British to commit reserves to this sector. French troops had made a wide arc into the dry bed of Lake Mariout and just after 4:00 a.m. 300 French light cavalry skirmished with the left wing while another force, made up of 200 men of the Régiment de Dromadaires, supported by 30 cavalrymen, attacked the fieldworks on the canal. The attack happened just as the British regiments were preparing to stand to and the picquets were being called back. Walsh related that,

> In this false attack on the left, the enemy, rapidly advancing, entered a small flêche at the same time with the out centinels. They immediately turned the twelve-pounder, which was mounted in it, upon our men, and had actually fired one shot from it, when a redoubt in the rear of this flêche opening its fire upon them, they quickly retreated, carrying off with them three officers, one sergeant, and ten rank and file of the fifth brigade. They had one officer and four privates killed in the flêche, but took away their wounded.[102]

---

99   Mackesy, *British Victory*, pp.108–109.
100 Walsh, *Journal*, p.95; flêches were arrow-shaped outworks that were open at the back.
101 Walsh, *Journal*, p.93.
102 Walsh, *Journal*, p.96.

The captured officers and men can only have been from the Regiment de Roll. Three days later Captain Anton Mohr, Lieutenant Nicholas Fuchs of the Major's Company and Lieutenant Fidel Weissenbach of the Grenadier Company along with a sergeant, a corporal and six privates were recorded as prisoners.[103] Two things are remarkable about this detachment, the surprisingly high number of officers and that it was drawn from across the regiment's companies, the prisoners being Sergeant Conrad Hoffmann of the Light Company, Corporal Mathias Cruset of Capol's Company and privates from four different centre companies.

Perhaps because the detachment was supplied by his brigade, as soon as this firing was heard Stuart set his regiments in motion towards the source. However, Moore, the general officer on duty overnight, was less concerned.[104] Before anything further developed a fierce fire-fight commenced on the right, signalling that this was where the true contest was to be and Moore immediately returned to his own units. Stuart turned his column about and back to his starting position, this manoeuvre meant that his regiments were now aligned, left to right, Roll, Dillon and Minorca.

Over the next four hours, the Battle of Alexandria as the British were to name it, became a contest for the position among the ruins which Moore's Reserve stubbornly defended drawing attacks not only from the French left but also their centre and cavalry as well. The strong French right wing had to contend with the British centre and left. Moore's units fought within the defences that had been constructed in and around the ruins except for the 42nd (Royal Highlanders) placed on the left flank of the redoubt in front of his position. There it faced wave after wave of attacks, which were countered with musketry and charges, indeed Abercromby, always keen to be at the front, was caught up in the fray. The highlanders' battle lines eventually became fractured and, charged by cavalry, they stood their ground as individuals or in small groups. Captain David Stewart of the 42nd, described the situation:

> The regiment was now much reduced, and if not supported, must soon have been annihilated. From this fate it was saved by the opportune arrival of the brigade of Brigadier General Stuart, who advanced from the second line, and formed his brigade on the left of the highlanders, occupying as far as his line extended, part of the vacant space to the right of the Guards. No support could have been more seasonable. The enemy were now advancing in great force, both of cavalry and infantry, with a seeming determination to overwhelm the small body of men who had so long stood their ground against reiterated efforts. To their astonishment they found a fresh and more numerous body of troops, who withstood their

---

103   TNA: WO 12/11985: Paylist, 24 March 1801.

104   Moore considered that it was a false alarm that only confirmed his observation of 'a want of intelligence and confusion the evening before in the officer who commanded the picquets in that quarter.' J.F. Maurice, *The Diary of Sir John Moore* (London: Edward Arnold, 1904), vol. II, p.13. It not clear if he was referring to another officer, such as the duty field officer, or Mohr.

charge with such firmness and spirit, that in a few minutes they were forced to retreat with great precipitation.[105]

Stuart had brought his brigade, apparently on his own initiative, in line 'in the most perfect order, and poured in such a heavy and well directed fire, that the enemy fled or perished.'[106] The alignment meant the Minorca Regiment was immediately adjacent to the 42nd so that some of the highlanders formed up with it. Sergeant Tomaschett wrote, 'Roll, Dillon and Stuart together with a Scottish regiment No.42 were unyielding as walls in their positions and fought like lions until finally the enemy is forced to retreat with a terrible loss of men'.[107] The struggle was not over and it certainly was not a set-piece battle, of line engaging line. The confusion is illustrated by the later account by Private Antoine Lutz, Minorca Regiment, of how he seized a French standard. As the French retreated after an attack, he and other soldiers of his regiment charged forward and Lutz saw a French officer, on foot, carrying a standard who he shot. Lutz then reloaded his musket, picked up the fallen flag and started to run back to his regiment. However, he was overtaken by a French cavalry charge so he dropped flat into a hollow, covering his prize as best he could but as he got up again he was attacked by two dragoons. He shot at one but hit his horse which trapped the dragoon, when Lutz approached him he surrendered and Lutz returned to the line with the standard and prisoner.[108]

Finally, the French retreated back to the Heights of Nicopolis and it was only now that Abercromby allowed it to be seen that he had been severely wounded. He was taken out to HMS *Foudroyant* in Aboukir Bay where he died on 28 March. Some have criticised Abercromby for exposing himself to danger, in the midst of the fight. However Tomaschett, who used 'German' as a generic term for the foreign regiments, provides a different perspective when he wrote about the battle.

> What helped us most was that we had with us this generous Abercromby, the principal general, who was always in front of the army, once he was even in the middle of the enemy. But when our German regiments saw this, they threw themselves into them like as many lions and instantly freed him. This general received two mortal wounds there but this day still commanded all the time.[109]

The admiration and regard for Abercromby from the British soldiers is well documented, Tomaschett clearly shows that the foreign soldiers he commanded shared those sentiments in no lesser a degree.

In the orders of the day, 24 March, Hutchinson, to whom the command of the army now fell, passed on Abercromby's thanks to the army and to its

105 David Stewart, *Sketches of the Character, Manners, and the present State of the Highlanders of Scotland* (Edinburgh: Archibald Constable and Co., 1822), pp.469–470.
106 Wilson, *British Expedition*, p.35.
107 Vincenz (ed.), 'Tomaschett de Trun', p.315.
108 *Cobbett's Political Register*, 18 December 1802.
109 Vincenz (ed.), 'Tomaschett de Trun', p.314.

commanders, beginning with Moore, to whom 'no acknowledgements are sufficient.'[110] After he had given fulsome praise to the Reserve, he continued, 'The support given to the reserve by Brigadier General Stuart, of the 5th brigade, was as gallant as it was prompt, and entirely confirmed the fortunate issue of that brilliant day.'[111]

Then on 5 April, Hutchinson wrote the official despatch. After giving a brief resumé of the battle, he paid homage to Abercromby's memory and then began the recognition of individual officers and units with:

> It is impossible for me to do Justice to the Zeal of the Officers and to the Gallantry of the Soldiers of this Army. The Reserve, against whom the principal Attack of the Enemy was directed, conducted themselves with unexampled Spirit. They resisted the Impetuosity of the French Infantry, and repulsed several Charges of Cavalry. Major-General Moore was wounded at their Head, … [after mentioning further officers of the Reserve, he continued] Brigadier-General Stuart and the Foreign Brigade supported the Reserve with such Promptness and Spirit; indeed, it is but Justice to this Corps to say, that they have, on all Occasions, endeavoured to emulate the Zeal and Spirit exhibited by the British Troops, and have perfectly succeeded.[112]

Stuart considered this faint praise for his contribution to the victory, feeling that Moore had made sure the glory was his own and he was to hold Moore a grudge from then on.[113] The losses, in killed and wounded, recorded at the end of the despatch indicate that Stuart, whose brigade major, Saint Pern, died of his wounds, may have some grounds for these feelings. This measure, however crude it may be, shows the commitment of his brigade, alongside the 42nd, in repelling the assaults into the valley.

Table 7: Killed and wounded (all ranks) on 21 March 1801 with indication of these casualties as a percentage of those present.[114]

Unit	Killed	Wounded	Total	Total present	% of those present
Guards Brigade	49	156	205	1,548	13.24
1st Brigade	17	162	179	1,907	9.38
2nd Brigade	1	6	7	1,882	0.37
3rd Brigade	3	67	70	1,811	3.86
4th Brigade	7	63	70	1,868	3.74
5th Brigade	66	268	334	2,090	15.98
Minorca	*44*	*162*	*206*	*980*	*21.02*
Roll	*9*	*59*	*68*	*567*	*11.99*
Dillon	*13*	*47*	*60*	*543*	*11.04*
Reserve	86	359	445	2,740	16.24
42nd	*52*	*261*	*313*	*787*	*39.77*
Reserve without 42nd	*34*	*98*	*132*	*1,953*	*6.75*

---

110   Order of 24 March 1801 reproduced in Wilson, *British Expedition*, p.44.
111   Wilson, *British Expedition*, p.44.
112   *The London Gazette*, 15 May 1801.
113   Mackesy, *British Victory*, p.133.
114   *London Gazette*, 15 May 1801 and TNA: WO 1/345: 18 March 1801 return.

In the official despatch the Regiment de Roll was shown as having nine rank and file killed and two officers, five sergeants, a drummer and 51 rank and file wounded; the officers being named as Lieutenant Ignace Metzger and Lieutenant and Adjutant Ferdinand Comte de La Ville Sur-Illon. The muster of 24 March shows that the casualties were distributed fairly evenly across all the regiment's companies. Corporal Wilhelm Koenig and eight privates were listed as killed and, on this date, four sergeants, 10 corporals, a drummer and 35 privates had received wounds three days earlier that were so serious to require them to be on board ship.[115] One of the sergeants was Tomaschett who would lose a hand as a result of his wound.[116]

---

115   TNA: WO 12/11985: 24 March 1801.
116   Vincenz (ed.), 'Tomaschett de Trun', p.318.

5

'We have served so well'

Hutchinson was faced with a dilemma, the battle had changed nothing in the balance of the forces facing each other before Alexandria, each side were of comparative size and occupied strong positions, however the French had superiority across Egypt as a whole. Reinforcements from the Nile could cross the bed of Lake Mariout to the city and more were on their way from Toulon, causing Keith to detach part of his fleet on 27 March to blockade Alexandria to prevent their arrival.[1] The first option Hutchinson tried was to offer the French troops at Alexandria passage to France if they evacuated the city, as the British Government had authorised from the start. Menou flatly refused the offer but news of it spread amongst his troops and was to have a steadily corrosive effect on morale, already undermined by years of exile.[2]

Flooding Lake Mariout would strengthen the British positions as well as making inland access to Alexandria much longer and more difficult for French reinforcements. Conversely the rising waters would reduce the front the French would have to defend and could also impede the flow of supplies the British had been receiving from the Arabs. This last could be mitigated by securing Rashid (Rosetta) on the western branch of the Nile and so gaining access to the resources of the delta. The arrival of Kapetan Pasha and Ottoman troops, most of them regulars, enabled Hutchinson, on 6 April, to send 1,000 British troops and 4,000 Turks to test the French hold on Rashid.[3] The French abandoned Rashid and Fort Julien, down-river, surrendered on 19 April after a brief siege. To cover this last operation, the British and Turks occupied a strong position across the gap between the Nile and Lake Idku, centred on the village of El Hammad Al Gharbi, to block the passage of any troops that may come down the river from Cairo. With the news that Rashid was secured, the dyke of the Alexandria Canal was breached on 13 April and Lake Mariout began to fill with water, reaching its full height around 7 May.[4] Troops were then sent to El Hammad for operations on the Nile, Hutchinson himself arriving there on 26 April.

---

1   Mackesy, *British Victory*, p.151.
2   Mackesy, *British Victory*, pp.149–150.
3   Mackesy, *British Victory*, p.155.
4   Walsh, *Journal*, p.122.

Individual NCOs and soldiers from the Regiment de Roll, such as Sergeant Etienne Metry and Privates Jean Macka and Pierre Pahen of the Major's Company accompanied this force being shown as 'employed in the army,' however in what capacity is not clear.[5] The regiment, as a whole, along with the rest of Stuart's Foreign Brigade, was among the troops left to defend the static line before Alexandria, commanded by Major General Eyre Coote. As historian Mackesy observes, 'Coote's was not the glorious role, but it was a vital and an anxious one.'[6] Wider responsibilities fell to Lieutenant Colonel Dürler and Major Sonnenberg, the field officers of the Regiment de Roll, as from 12 April each day a colonel did duty for all the line brigades, the Guards retaining their own arrangements, along with four field officers who were assigned responsibility for the picquets.[7] Dürler was one of the four field officers that day and Sonnenberg took his turn the next. On 14 April it was directed that Dürler 'will do duty of Colonel till further orders' and the next day he was colonel of the day.[8]

Trachoma, or 'Egyptian' ophthalmia, which sometimes left sufferers with the permanent loss of their sight in at least one eye, affected the British soldiers, like their French counterparts. This led to high levels of sickness among Coote's men and then, from early May as the temperature rose, plague appeared in the General Hospital at Aboukir where the patients were tormented by fleas.[9] Coote's division was further reduced when the 28th and 42nd, along with some artillery and light dragoons, marched to join Hutchinson on 4 June, Walsh, his aide-de-camp, observed, 'This diminution of major-general Coote's force left his entrenched position very destitute of troops, and without a second line. His entire division consisted of about five thousand men, of whom upwards of fifteen hundred were afflicted with sore eyes and fluxes, which reduced it to little more than three thousand fit for duty.'[10]

Plague was virulent at Aboukir; from April to July 1801, 318 cases were identified, of whom 150 (47 percent) died.[11] The disease took its toll on the medical staff at Aboukir so Assistant Surgeon Hartvig of the Regiment de Roll was detached to the hospital there.[12] Plague was successfully contained and did not spread to the soldiers on the line by the establishment of a sanitary cordon across the narrow point of the isthmus, to which the Regiment de Roll contributed men.[13] Due to a lack of surviving returns it is not possible to say how the Regiment de Roll was affected, although it can be seen that eight rank and file from the regiment died, from all causes, in April.[14]

---

5   TNA: WO 12/11985: Musters 24 May and June 1801.

6   Mackesy, *British Victory*, p.158.

7   TNA: WO 28/351: General Orders 12 April 1801.

8   TNA: WO 28/351: General Orders 14 and 15 April 1801.

9   Walsh, *Journal*, p.131 and Mackesy, *British Victory*, p.227, citing a soldier of the 92nd Foot who was a patient there at the time.

10   Walsh, *Journal*, p.166.

11   Walsh, *Journal*, Appendix 32 report of Inspector General Thomas Young.

12   TNA: WO 17/1757: Return 1 August 1801.

13   Walsh, *Journal*, p.167 and TNA: WO 12/11985: Muster 24 June 1801.

14   TNA: WO 17/1757: Return 1 May 1801.

Duty on the static line was trying. It was only 15 minutes march from the French positions so every day began with stand to an hour before daylight – in mid-June duty commenced at 3:00 a.m.[15] There were some clashes with the enemy; Adjutant de La Ville Sur-Illon being wounded by a sabre blow while carrying out a reconnaissance in June.[16] As the fieldworks were of sand they required constant maintenance. Furthermore work was required to build a dyke after the French attempted, on 23 June, to flood part of the front with water from Lake Mariout.[17] Much of the spadework would have been carried out by the Maltese Pioneers, a unit raised by Abercromby for such service, but in July the Regiment de Roll provided a sergeant, a corporal and three privates to serve with the pioneers.[18] Other men from the regiment had a range of duties such as serving in the hospitals, the artillery (five privates) and other roles such as Private Stephan Kovatsch who was 'employed with the mules.'[19]

In July reinforcements arrived for Coote and by the end of the month he had about 9,000 men. They allowed Coote to prepare for offensive operations and on 14 July he reconnoitred the French positions west of Alexandria from the sea.[20] One of the new arrivals was Lieutenant T. Marmaduke Wybourn of the Marines who joined those of his corps doing duty on land. In a letter of 15 July he portrayed what service in Coote's division was like,

Camp before Alexandria 4 o'clock in the Morning. … We always beat to arms two hours before day, to be ready in case of surprise, and when day breaks, Ravellen [sic] beats and everybody is dismissed to their Tents till sunset, except the various guards and centrys [sic]. It is the most (I was going to say – awfully grand sight I ever saw) at daylight the colours are hoisted, the whole Army drawn up along the position in battle array, and all the Bands, Trumpets, Drums, fifes and Bugles strike off at the same time; it may be heard many miles.

The plain is the most miserable of any in Egypt, not a tree or even a bit of grass, all sand, and scorching as a furnace. Vermin of all sorts but most fleas and ants, scorpions and beetles crawling over one in the night and getting under the clothes, and no man is permitted to undress, or even take off his sword, and in this manner and under Tents only have the Army been ever since they came …

Adieu … I am melting with heat tho' not yet six o'clock. Nor is it possible to write, for vermin.[21]

The final reinforcements joined Coote in the first days of August, among them were the Chasseurs Britanniques and the Watteville Regiments. Both had been formed in Slovenia as recently as 1 May after the Armée de Condé

---

15   Mackesy, *British Victory*, p.159.
16   Archives du Musée Condé, Château de Chantilly (AMC): Fonds Grouvel 1 GR 142.
17   Walsh, *Journal*, p.179.
18   Robert Gould, *Mercenaries of the Napoleonic Wars* (Brighton: Tom Donovan, 1995), p.77 and TNA: WO 12/11985: Muster 24 July 1801.
19   TNA: WO 12/11985: Musters 24 July 1801.
20   Walsh, *Journal*, pp.181–183.
21   Anne Petrides and Jonathan Downs (ed.), *Sea Soldier: An Officer of Marines with Duncan, Nelson, Collingwood and Cockburn* (Tunbridge Wells: Parapress Ltd., 2000), pp.40–43.

and the Swiss émigré corps had been disbanded after having served alongside the Austrians as auxiliary troops in British pay. This ceased after Austria had made peace with France and, in general, the former Condéens joined the Chasseurs Britanniques while the Swiss went to Watteville. Courten, however, had suggested that his two companies, the remains of his Valaisan battalion, be incorporated into the Regiment de Roll, but this did not happen and they contributed more soldiers, in proportion to their size, to Watteville than any of the other Swiss units.[22]

While Coote remained before Alexandria, Hutchinson had led his force up the Nile joining the Grand Vizier's army that had marched from Syria as well as Mamluks who had opposed the French. At Cairo, on 28 June, the French capitulated on the terms Menou had been offered at Alexandria and it was at this stage that news arrived that the force from India had finally reached Qena on the Upper Nile from the Red Sea. The Cairo garrison marched with their arms and baggage to Rashid where they embarked to go to a port in France at allied expense and the last convoy with the troops, civilian officials, women and children left Egypt on 9 August. The capture of Alexandria was to be the final stage of the campaign and the first of the brigades from the Nile returned to the camp east of Alexandria on 9 August. Before they arrived, Coote took the opportunity to issue an order to the division he had commanded,

> … to express, in the strongest manner, his best thanks for the zeal, activity, and attention shown by the troops, seamen, and marines under his command, upon all occasions. … It will always be with much pleasure, that the General will bear testimony of the uniform good conduct and behaviour of the troops he has had the honour to command, during a long and harassing period of three months, which must reflect the highest credit upon every individual.[23]

Daniel Nicol, 92nd Foot, on returning from the Nile, noted the work that had been done on the line before Alexandria.

> Great alterations had been made since we were here; deep trenches were cut, breastworks raised, pits dug in front to prevent an attack from cavalry, redoubts well finished and mounted with heavy cannon from the fleet from the sea to the lake. Wells had been built … Everything appeared in a state of security; officers' marquees were screened by date branches and gravel walks made round them very comfortable indeed.[24]

---

22   CH AEV: Courten Cn B 30/3/37: Roll to Courten, 2 October 1801 and Alistair Nichols, *Wellington's Switzers: The Watteville Regiment in Egypt, the Mediterranean, Spain and Canada* (Godmanchester: Ken Trotman Publishing, 2015), pp.35–41, also Alistair Nichols, *Wellington's Mongrel Regiment: A History of the Chasseurs Britanniques Regiment 1801–1814* (Staplehurst: Spellmount Limited, 2005).

23   Order of 2 August 1801 reproduced as Walsh, *Journal*, Appendix 18.

24   Daniel Nicol, *Sergeant Nicol: The Experiences of a Gordon Highlander during the Napoleonic Wars in Egypt, the Peninsula & France* (Milton Keynes: Leonaur, 2007), p.81.

The army was reorganised to incorporate the new arrivals, Stuart's Foreign Brigade was now the 3rd and had been joined by Watteville. The Brigade Major was Captain Ernest Missett of the Minorca Regiment.[25]

When the Reserve arrived on 13 August offensive operations immediately began against the French holding Alexandria and 26 vessels with shallow draughts moved into Lake Mariout to suppress the French gunboats. The British troops were placed in three divisions, two, including Stuart's brigade, were to operate to the east of the city while Coote, with 4,000 troops, embarked on the lake in the evening of 16 August to open a new front on the west of Alexandria. To cover this landing, the divisions on the east were to press towards the French positions and commence active siege operations early on 17 August. Half an hour before daylight, Stuart led some troops, including the Minorca Regiment, onto a sandhill only 820 metres or so from the French line of defences and work commenced on an entrenchment to provide cover for the troops behind the sandhill. Troops from the Reserve held the position over night and at about 2:00 a.m. the French attacked the picquets, wounding two men, but did not continue with the attack but, 'This occasioned an alarm, and the picquets and sentries across the plain … ran in.'[26] The following day, 18 August, the Reserve units were relieved by Roll and Watteville, under the command of Dürler, and that night, 'some of the enemy again crept near our sentries in the plain and wounded one of them' and took Sergeant Joseph Botzhoffer, of Roll, prisoner.[27]

Coote had landed successfully on 17 August and maintained the initiative by pushing on to Alexandria, supported by diversions on the east of the city. Progress was such that, on 26 August, Menou requested an armistice and for negotiations to commence, he stretched these out as long as he could so that the capitulation, the conditions of which were the same as for the Cairo garrison, was only signed on 2 September. British and Turkish troops took up posts in Alexandria the same day.[28] The capitulation meant that the officers and men of the Regiment de Roll who had been held prisoner by the French were released. The officers, at least, had been confined in Fort Qaitbay, built on the site of the Pharos lighthouse, on Alexandria's harbour where, as the British officer Robert Wilson wrote, 'their treatment had not been good; close confinement perhaps was justified, rigour was never necessary, and therefore the officers had some reason to complain.'[29] Their condition would have been worse but for *Chef de brigade* Jacques Cavalier, who commanded the Dromadaires, the unit that had captured them, who 'on his own responsibility, advanced them money, when the French commander in chief had refused.'[30] After his own capture, in May 1801, Cavalier had been thanked by Hutchinson and paid what was owed to him. Dürler, while making no comment about the conditions, noted of Lieutenant Weissenbach,

25   Walsh, *Journal*, Appendix 20.
26   Maurice, *Diary*, vol.II, p.41.
27   Maurice, *Diary*, vol.II, pp.41–42 and TNA: WO 12/11985: Muster 24 August 1801.
28   Mackesy, *British Victory*, pp.221–224.
29   Wilson, *British Expedition*, p.214.
30   Wilson, *British Expedition*, footnote p.214.

Sultan's Medal, 1801 on the original chain and hook suspension. Issued to officers in four sizes according to their rank, the suspension was frequently changed to a European pattern with a sandy coloured ribbon. (© Noonans)

'his imprisonment for six months has aged him a little; he is a brave and honest boy.'[31] Nevertheless the officers had fared much better than the other ranks, as witnessed by Nicol, 'Some of our men taken prisoners in the month of March were sent in to our lines; they looked as if they had been badly kept, were like skeletons, dirty and ragged.'[32] On the other hand there were Swiss among the Alexandria garrison and Dürler was able to assist one of them, *Chef d'escadron* Peyer-im-Hof, who left for Marseille on 12 September.[33]

Since Republican France had declared war in 1793, the British Army had had scant success but the result of the campaign in Egypt provided the British Army with a rare victory. Its services were recognised by a unanimous vote of thanks passed in both Houses of Parliament on 12 November 1801. That of the Commons included, 'That the House doth highly approve of and acknowledge the zeal, discipline, and intrepidity uniformly displayed during the arduous and memorable operations of the army in Egypt, by the non-commissioned officers and private soldiers.'[34] Furthermore, the Ottoman Government established an order of knighthood, the Order of the Crescent, for the senior officers as well as, 'gold medals of different sizes have been given to all the officers of the army, according to their respective ranks. These medals have on one side a crescent and star, and on the reverse the sultan's name, with the date of the year.'[35] Finally, on 6 July 1802, the units that served in the campaign, including the Regiment de Roll, received 'His Majesty's Permission to bear on its Colours & Appointments a Sphinx with the word "Egypt".'[36] This was the first battle honour to be awarded generally in the British Army.[37]

There were material rewards as well, Dürler receiving a richly decorated Mamluk sabre from Colonel John Abercromby, the Adjutant General and the general's son, and he was later given another, similar, sword from Menou for assisting as an interpreter during the negotiations for the capitulation.[38] Later all the officers and men who had been present in the campaign received prize money, a share of the value of the material captured at Alexandria, Rashid and Cairo. It was paid in four instalments, the first quite soon after

---

31   Bürkli, 'Schweizerregiment von Roll', p.18, quoting Dürler to *Avoyer* Honnegger 1 April 1802.
32   Nicol, *Sergeant Nicol*, p.86.
33   Bürkli, 'Schweizerregiment von Roll', p.20.
34   Walsh, *Journal*, Appendix 35.
35   Walsh, *Journal*, Appendix 35, as a result the Sultan's Medals are often identified, although wrongly, as of the Order of the Crescent.
36   TNA: WO 380/5: Regimental record.
37   Mackesy, *British Victory*, p.236.
38   Bürkli, 'Schweizerregiment von Roll', p.17.

the campaign and the rest in 1808, 1812 and 1823.[39] The money was shared out in six classes, according to rank, irrespective of how long or where the unit served in the campaign. In 1808 the instalment received by those of the Regiment de Roll was, for Dürler and Sonnenberg in the Second Class, £42-1-4; those in the Third (captains, paymaster, surgeon and chaplain) received £7-10-7, in the Fourth (lieutenants, ensigns and assistant surgeons) £3-8-7, Fifth (sergeants) £1-11-10 and the Sixth (rank and file) 4/10. Although the amount the Sixth Class received was paltry, it was the equivalent to just over three weeks' net pay for a private soldier who received, after stoppages, 1/6 per week.[40]

Negotiations for peace between France and Britain had already commenced following the fall of Pitt's administration in February 1801 and, although it was only in November that talks began for a final treaty, preliminary agreement had been reached on 30 September. On 15 September Hutchinson received despatches from the Government, dated 24 July, informing him that his command was ended and the army was to be dispersed, the destination of each unit being specified. Despite the change of administration the habit of directing operations in detail from London, with no account of delays or the reality of events on the ground, continued leaving Moore to observe, 'Upwards of 20,000 men are thus disposed of, whereas the effective force does not exceed 15,000 or 16,000.'[41]

Nevertheless, by 1 November the only troops that remained in Egypt were 12 battalions at or about Alexandria and the Indian contingent at El Hammad. The former Minorca Regiment, renamed the Queen's German Regiment in recognition of its conduct on 21 March, left for England soon afterwards.[42] The British Government decided to retain a garrison in Egypt until a conclusive treaty had been signed and on 21 November Fox received instructions, dated 12 October, that this would include foreign regiments as well the contingent from India.[43] The latter, of British and East India Company units, had to stay until the prevailing winds in the Red Sea changed with the season. When it left for Suez on 11 May to return to India the contingent took with it 135 men from the foreign brigade who had volunteered for service with British regiments in the sub-continent. This was despite, certainly in the case of Watteville, their own officers being opposed to the recruitment, however none came from the Regiment de Roll.[44] This would seem to indicate either a stronger esprit de corps or control in the regiment, or perhaps both.

---

39   TNA: WO 164/141: 1808 payment, the others being WO 164/147 and WO 164/153. The record of the earlier payment has not been found.

40   Burnham and McGuigan, *The British Army*, p.198.

41   Maurice, *Diary*, vol.II, p.48 also Mackesy, *British Victory*, p.236.

42   On 9 January 1805 it was brought into the line as the 97th (or The Queen's German) Regiment of Foot and on 6 June 1808 the designation 'German' was dropped as recruits were being obtained from Ireland.

43   TNA: WO 1/300: Lord Hobart, now Secretary of State for War and the Colonies, to Fox 12 October 1801.

44   TNA: WO 17/1758: Monthly returns 1 May and 1 June 1802.

Immediately the French had departed rivalry between the Ottomans and Mamluks was renewed. The British were in a difficult position as they were allies of the former but had, along with the Ottomans, guaranteed the safety of the Mamluks to gain their assistance against the French. However, the Ottomans wanted to finally break the power of the Mamluks who still held sway over the Nile above Cairo. This led to an incident when a party of Mamluk chiefs, beys, with some of their followers arrived to visit the Kapetan Pasha who was camped outside Alexandria. The next day, while still guests of the Pasha, the Mamluks were ambushed by Turkish troops with cannon and almost all were killed. At the sound of artillery the British troops were immediately under arms and, according to a British newspaper account, when Brigadier General Oakes learned of what had happened, he,

> … commanded the Captain-Pacha [*sic*] to appear before him. … he was arrested and disarmed by the Swiss grenadiers of the regiment of Roll, who received orders to this effect from General Oakes. The General reproached the Captain Pacha in the severest terms; but the latter excused himself, by declaring that he had received an order from the Grand Seignior, to put all the Beys and Mamelukes to death, and declared he was to answer with his head for the execution of the order.[45]

The Mamluk survivors were recovered while the dead were buried with due honours. Although it may seem incredible that the Pasha should be treated in such a manner, credence is given to the overall story by Walsh, although he was not present at the time. He states that Stuart was ordered 'with guns and lighted matches, to proceed to the Turkish camp … and to insist upon the bodies of the beys being given up to the British.'[46]

As senior officers departed the command of the army in Egypt devolved to Major General Richard Lambart, Earl of Cavan, and, in time, that of the Foreign Brigade, now made up of Roll, Dillon, Watteville and Chasseurs Britanniques, to Brigadier General the Honourable John Hope.

The negotiations for peace between Britain and France continued through the winter, finally concluding in the Peace of Amiens on 25 March 1802. It was evident, from an early stage, that the British Government wanted to exploit the peace by reducing the cost of the army and the foreign regiments were clearly among the first to be considered for disbandment. A document held in the Foreign Office papers shows that another option was also considered, to transfer the Regiment de Roll to the service of another country. The scoping paper noted that as the regiment was among those that had, 'served the whole, or a very considerable part of the War,' the officers on disbandment would be entitled to three years' pay, 'being an equivalent to

---

45   *Cobbet's Weekly Political Register*, 30 January 1802
46   Walsh, *Journal*, pp.163–164, footnote. He states the incident occurred in October and that Hutchinson was the commander who gave the order to Stuart; although Hutchinson would appear to have quit Egypt by this time.

Half Pay'.[47] This, the grant of six months' pay to the NCOs and three months' to the other ranks, as well as the annual issue of clothing meant the cost of disbanding the regiment was estimated to be just over £20,540. A cheaper option was to transfer it, along with five other regiments, to the Neapolitan service and four more to that of Portugal. This was even after adding, 'an Estimate of the Sum which might be required, as a Compensation to the Troops, on being transferred to a Service, where their Pay Allowance, would be considerably inferior, to those which they receive from Great Britain. … likewise a proposed annual subsidy for five years, … to be paid by Great Britain [to Naples]'.[48]

In London the Swiss colonels lobbied for their regiments to remain in British service. The Baron de Roll submitted a plan for the retention of a Swiss brigade in British service which Frederick de Watteville supported in a letter to William Wickham on 30 November 1801.[49] The brigade was to consist of both the colonels' regiments as well as that of Major General Charles-Daniel de Meuron. His regiment had transferred from Dutch service in Sri Lanka and had recently fought in the Mysore Campaign of 1799. It is noteworthy that Watteville described the Regiment de Roll as attracting the Roman Catholics of Switzerland while his regiment, and that of Meuron, the Protestants. Whatever the merits of the arguments, it was the presence of the Regiment de Roll in Egypt that ensured its preservation, like Watteville, in British service while those that had already departed were soon disbanded.[50]

Uncertainty of their futures only added to the burden imposed on the regiment's officers by unhealthy conditions and boredom in Egypt. Some took advantage of the changed diplomatic environment, that made travel easier, to take leave and go home, the Baron de Bachmann, captain from 1 May 1801, to Switzerland and Lieutenant François d'Altenbourg to Franche Comté. Captains Vogelsang and Roland, and Lieutenant Metzger, also took three months leave on 8 May.[51] Their wives had remained at Menorca but on 16 June 1802 that island, in compliance with the terms of the peace, was restored to Spain and so they, and all others connected to the Regiment de Roll moved to Malta. Men invalided by wounds or disease also went to Malta to be discharged. The majority had been sent there in 1801 but small batches continued to arrive from the regiment in Egypt in the following year, for example nine men were discharged on 24 April and another nine on 24 October 1802.[52] Tomaschett had been invalided in 1801 and he recorded what happened in his journal. At Malta he was given the choice of being sent to Britain where he would receive a pension for life or to take a payment

47   TNA: FO 74/28: Scoping document, unsigned and undated but clearly from 1802. The other units that were suggested for Neapolitan service were Dillon, Stuart's, Watteville, and the two foreign cavalry regiments, the York Hussars and Hompesch Mounted Rifles, and for the Portuguese, the Chasseurs Britanniques, Loyal Emigrants and the two former white cockade regiments of Castries and Mortemart.

48   TNA: FO 74/28: Scoping document.

49   HRO: 38M49/3/4/50–52: Watteville to Wickham, 30 November 1801.

50   Examples being Lowenstein's Jägers in May 1802 and the Corsican Rangers two months later.

51   TNA: WO 17/1758: Returns Egypt 1802.

52   TNA: WO 12/11986: Pay and muster lists 1802.

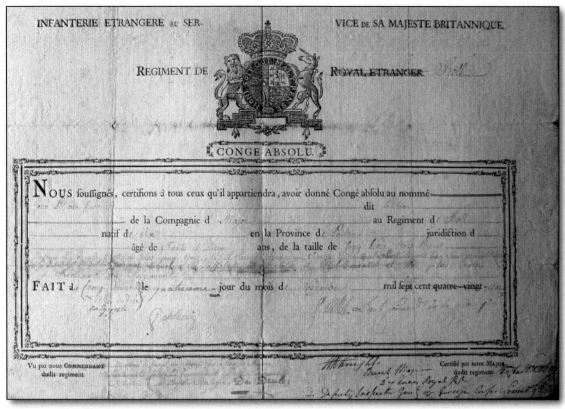

Discharge certificate Private Jean Petito or Petiteau, from Vix, France, of the Major's Company, dated 14 November 1801 and bearing the signatures of Dürler, Sonnenberg as well as Lieutenant Nicholas Fuchs, commanding the company – the use of obsolete stationery of the Royal Etranger is of note. (Courtesy of Fonds La Sabretache)

Certificate of Corporal René Bernard's entitlement to prize money having served in the 1801 Egyptian campaign, dated 15 June 1802 at Valletta, Malta. (Courtesy of Fonds La Sabretache)

Discharge certificate of Frenchman Corporal René Bernard as an invalid, dated 15 June 1802, who had lost the sight in his right eye as well as having been wounded. He received a payment of £75 in lieu of a lifetime pension. (Courtesy of Fonds La Sabretache)

and return home, and he chose the latter. On 17 June he, with other invalids, sailed from Malta to Messina and then Livorno which they reached on 20 July. There they were paid their money and discharged.[53] Advised that the roads were poor and subject to thieves, he took another ship to Genoa, arriving on 24 July, from there he continued overland through Northern Italy to Lake Maggiore and crossed to Bellinzona in Switzerland, to arrive home in Graubünden on 2 August.[54] Soon after his return, he wrote his journal from notes that he had kept.[55] At Malta the soldiers who were invalided were given certificates of their entitlement to prize money and these could be sold to agents thus giving the soldiers ready money who would otherwise find it very difficult to benefit from the entitlement.

On 1 April 1802 Dürler wrote a letter to his brother-in-law, to be taken to Switzerland by Bachmann; he touched upon his hopes and fears as well as reflecting on his service in the campaign.

> If we do not enter into a campaign anew, to join us to the Turks and make war on the Mamluks in upper Egypt, I nourish the hope to have the pleasure to embrace you next winter.
>
> You would have learned that we made a really arduous campaign in this country, where our regiment served perfectly well; but in the two battles we lost many both killed and wounded. I was seriously wounded at the battle of 13 March by a musket shot and very slightly by a shell in that of 21 March; finally I have been fully recovered. I have twice had ophthalmia or in other words affliction of the eyes, very common in Egypt, and moreover an illness that necessitated an operation, from which I pulled through to the entire satisfaction of the surgeon. Apart from these illnesses I have always born up well despite that we were here without tents for a long time and that I have quite often slept in spite of the weather at the advance-posts, wrapped in my cloak and soaked by the heavy dews, common in this country and causing a great deal of sickness. Indeed! I have been fortunate in all manners; providence has taken care of me in an outstanding way. We have spent a year camped, and before arriving in Egypt we were nine months at sea. We have been in Asia and Africa and experienced storms and continual changes in climate; despite all that I have never had reason to complain.
>
> We blockaded Alexandria for five months, where three days in a row I found myself on duty at the advance-posts with the workers spending the nights there. It has been almost two years that I have not slept under a roof and that I have quite often made do with bad food; notwithstanding all that I would have been devastated if I had not made this campaign in Egypt. ... It is seven years since I left my wife and more than eight months that I have had not the least of her news. Finally I have hope that between life and death I will spend again some happy and tranquil moments with her and that I will have the pleasure to drink a bottle of good wine and have a good dinner at your home ...
>
> Do not believe the news that the gazettes tell of the plague in Egypt; until this moment our regiment has not lost a single man by this sickness. Thanks to God

---

53　The date of 20 July is confirmed in TNA: WO 12/11985: Paylist 24 August 1801.
54　Vincenz (ed.), 'Tomaschett de Trun', p.318. Tomaschett later married and had a daughter.
55　Vincenz (ed.), 'Tomaschett de Trun', p.291.

I do not fear it and I am firmly convinced that it is He who has marked the time of my death.[56]

Soon Brigadier General Hope, in turn, left Egypt. Before doing so he issued an order of the day in which he complimented each of the regiments he commanded and continued by writing, 'It is a particular satisfaction … to confer the command of the foreign brigade to the hands of an officer whose character, talents and experience, demand the esteem of those who have the good fortune to serve with him.'[57] The officer to whom he was referring was Dürler who was naturally proud of the personal and professional compliment that he had been paid. The rank of *maréchal de camp* he had received from the exiled Louis XVIII entitled him to such a command in the French royal army and now, from 25 April 1802, he was to exercise that function as a brigadier in the British Army. He wrote to his wife, enclosing Hope's order,

It is to him that I owe what has just been rendered to me, in giving me the command of the Foreign Brigade, which is composed of the regiments de Roll, Dillon, Watteville and the Chasseurs Britanniques. I hope that I will have the pay of brigadier while we are here; but this is not for very long, for it is said that we will leave soon. We will surely be quarantined at Malta, where perhaps we will be disbanded. One way or another I will go to England to see the Baron de Roll. The 'word' is, that all the foreign regiments will be disbanded as well as many of the most junior English regiments. But as we have served so well during this campaign and that due justice has been rendered to us in eulogies I do not doubt that the regiments de Roll and Dillon, that were so well conducted in the two battles of 13 and 21 March of the year past, will have the same treatment as the English regiments that will be disbanded.

Tell Steiger's father, that his son [Albert Bernard], the captain, is at this moment my brigade major, a duty that gains him twelve livres a day more than his salary, that it is General Hope who recommended him to me and that he is an excellent fellow.[58]

Men from the Regiment de Roll also fulfilled staff roles in this period, Sergeant Heinrich Fohrer was Assistant Provost Marshal on 1 February 1802 and Lieutenant Weissenbach was Town Major at Alexandria by 1 September 1802.[59]

On 29 August Dürler wrote a letter to his daughter, Sophie, to give his blessing to her engagement and to assure her that his pay as brigadier would go a long way to assure the financial security of the family. However, it would be the last letter the family received as soon afterwards he contracted a fever and died on 18 September 1802. He was buried with full military pomp and honours, as reported in a British newspaper:

---

56   Bürkli, 'Schweizerregiment von Roll', pp.17–18.
57   Bürkli, 'Schweizerregiment von Roll', p.19, in which it is reproduced in French.
58   Bürkli, 'Schweizerregiment von Roll', pp.19–20.
59   TNA: WO 17/1758: Monthly returns 1802.

Colonel De Durler, of the Regiment De Roll, who commanded the foreign Brigade here, died the night before last, regretted by his friends, and the whole army; he was buried yesterday with all the honours due to his rank; the procession was very grand and solemn; the coffin was carried on men's shoulders; Colonel Beresford , of the 88th, Cols. Barlow and Saunders, of the 61st, Colonel Gordon, of the 26th light dragoons, Colonel Laird, of the 54th, and Captain Donnelly, of the Narcissus frigate, were pall-bearers. His own regiment marched in front, with arms, four field pieces followed, then the corpse, after which came on Watteville's, Dillon's &c. with side arms, which were followed by the officers of the English regiments, according to their rank. When the procession began near Pompey's Pillar, where he died, minute guns were fired from Fort Caffarelli, until it arrived at the Catholic convent, where he was interred. The whole ended with three rounds of musketry and three of the field pieces.[60]

On 25 October Lieutenant Colonel John James Barlow, 61st Foot, took command of the brigade and Steiger continued as his brigade major.[61] Finally, in compliance with the terms of the Peace of Amiens, the remaining British units left Egypt and the Regiment de Roll was one of the last to go, on 12 March 1803, just as plague returned to the country.[62] The regiment sailed to Malta; it is not clear exactly when the Regiment de Roll arrived but it is included in a 'General Return of Troops arrived at Malta from Egypt' of 1 April.[63] The troops arriving on the island had to undergo 42 days of quarantine, a British soldier who arrived at the same time recalled they, 'were obliged to burn everything we had in Egypt, for fear of the plague.'[64] Immediately after their quarantine ended the Regiment de Roll, Dillon and the 10th Foot sailed for Gibraltar, arriving there on 16 June 1803.[65] They disembarked on 20 and 21 June, replacing three regiments of the garrison which immediately left for England.

Table 8: Strength of the regiments arriving at Gibraltar, June 1803.[66]

	Officers	Staff	Sergeants	Drummers	Rank & File	Women	Children
Roll	18	5	48	22	411	36	21
Dillon	22	4	51	20	399	8	9
10th	19	3	37	19	712	5	0

No rank and file were sick in Roll while in Dillon there was one and 11 in the 10th Foot.

60   *Saunders's News-Letter*, 1 January 1803, citing a letter of 20 September from Alexandria.

61   TNA: WO 25/679: Watteville history and WO 17/1758: Monthly returns.

62   TNA: WO 380/5: Regimental record and WO 25/679: Watteville history; a wing of Watteville had to remain in isolation near Marabout because of an outbreak of plague, they only left after it had ceased, on 29 April.

63   TNA: WO 17/2119: Monthly returns Malta 1803.

64   Gareth Glover (ed.), *The Military Adventures of Private Samuel Wray 61st Foot 1796–1815* (Godmanchester: Ken Trotman Publishing, 2009), p.21. Also, Richard Cannon, *Historical Record of the Tenth, or the North Lincolnshire, Regiment of Foot* (London: Parker, Furnivall & Parker, 1847), p.51.

65   TNA: WO 1/289: Trigge to Lord Hobart, 22 June 1803.

66   TNA: WO 17/1791: Return of regiments arrived from Malta 19 June 1803.

The garrison at Gibraltar had undergone turbulent times since O'Hara's tenure as governor had ended. His successor was Prince Edward, Duke of Kent, the king's fourth son, and he was determined to bring the garrison back to a high state of discipline. However, he went about his task with pettiness and brutality and the situation boiled over into a series of mutinies over Christmas 1802, that were put down with bloodshed. The Duke was recalled and he left reluctantly on 1 May 1803, to never return, however he was not removed from the office of governor so command of Gibraltar rested with lieutenant governors. The first of these was Lieutenant General Sir Thomas Trigge who immediately rescinded 35 of the Duke's 169 regulations while continuing the latter's work, but in a more measured manner.[67]

The peace had been uneasy and mutual suspicion turned to hostility resulting, on 18 May 1803, with Britain declaring war on France. However when Nelson, returning to command in the Mediterranean, arrived off Gibraltar on 4 June 1803, he found that 'the news of actual War had not reached this place'.[68] He had been absent during the Egyptian campaign and in his letter to the Prime Minister he expressed the traditional suspicion of foreign troops in garrison at Gibraltar.

> I shall only say one word of GIBRALTAR, on which I had a serious conversation with Sir Thomas Trigge, on the impropriety of placing Dillon's Regiment as part of the Garrison of Gibraltar. When we reflect how that Regiment is composed, and that fifty men, the usual Guard at Land Port Gate, by being corrupted, might lose the place, who shall say Gibraltar is secure with those Troops? If it is said, do not trust them with the Guard, then you show your distrust, and, naturally, they become your enemies. The Regiment de Rolle is a fine Corps, and will serve faithfully; but I would not trust them at Gibraltar.[69]

His distrust was not shared by Captain Maule, serving in the garrison with the 2nd Foot, who had another occasion to be 'gratified in an acquaintance' with the Regiment de Roll. Its 'correct discipline and military deportment' was to be sorely tested before two years were out.[70] On arriving at Gibraltar the regiment had to reorganise in accordance with its new establishment dated from 25 December 1802. Crucially this involved the reengagement of the soldiers, their service having ended a year after the peace. This was an issue the foreign regiments, raised under separate capitulations, shared with many British units as enlistments that were limited for the war had been common across the army. Problems were anticipated and Lord Hobart, Secretary for War, had authorised Fox to disband the Regiment de Roll should insufficient men reenlist.[71] However the process went well, indeed it gained about 50 men, chiefly Germans, from Dillon which, in contrast, was effectively

67 Sir William G. F. Jackson, *The Rock of the Gibraltarians: A History of Gibraltar* (Grendon: Gibraltar Books, 1990), p.195.
68 Nicolas, *Nelson*, vol.V, p.79, Nelson to Addington, 4 June 1803.
69 Nicolas, *Nelson*, vol.V, p.106, Nelson to Addington, 28 June 1803.
70 Maule, *Principal Events*, pp.69–70, previously quoted in full.
71 Jason R. Musteen, *Becoming Nelson's Refuge and Wellington's Rock: The Ascendancy of Gibraltar during the Age of Napoleon (1793-1815)* unpublished PhD dissertation, Florida

reduced to its cadre of officers with only 34 rank and file on 1 August 1803. Nevertheless, the Regiment de Roll was still significantly under strength with only 477 rank and file against its new establishment of 40 corporals and 710 privates in 10 companies.[72]

The Regiment de Roll was in all regards, except personnel, like any other unit of the British Army. From 1804 the regiment's establishment was officially recognised and subject to full parliamentary scrutiny. The officers' commissions were published in the annual Army Lists. Their commissions were now permanent, meaning they were entitled to half pay when they left active service or the regiment was disbanded and two of them took immediate advantage of this. Captain Henry Dieffenthaller and Lieutenant François de Reding were placed on half pay, and replaced, by a War Office decision, by the brothers Ryhiner, Henry and Benoit respectively, who returned to full pay as from 25 December 1802. Commissions could be also be exchanged or sold according to the army's practice and regulations, so on 19 November 1803 Lieutenant Henry Matthey exchanged with Lewis (Ludwig) Müller, a German officer with extensive service in the British Army, to take the latter's place on half pay of the 5th Foot.[73] The promotions following Dürler's death, although dated from 25 September 1802, were now put into effect, Sonnenberg to lieutenant colonel and Vogelsang as major.

The new establishment included the post of paymaster to which William Ancrum was appointed on 25 September 1802, and he arrived in August 1803. Another additional post was that of second major which went to the Baron de Roll's nominee, Eugène de Courten who was restored to full pay from 25 December 1802. Courten had enhanced his reputation during the previous campaign in Continental Europe and he had been offered, but declined, the lieutenant-colonelcy of the Watteville Regiment. The Baron de Roll was keen for Courten join the regiment as soon he could to work with Sonnenberg to repair some dissension, 'a spirit of factions' and 'little cabals' that had arisen among the officers.[74]

The situation in Switzerland had changed yet again. In compliance with the peace between Austria and France in 1802, the latter had withdrawn its troops from the country. An insurrection, the Stecklikrieg (War of Sticks), broke out and soon the Helvetian Republic collapsed. Napoleon Bonaparte intervened between the parties and imposed a new constitution, the Swiss Confederation, now of 19 cantons, by the Act of Mediation of 19 February 1803. Switzerland was nominally independent but was subject to hardly concealed direction, and occasional insult, from Bonaparte. One result was the agreement that four new Swiss regiments would be raised to serve within the French army. One officer who soon joined the Regiment de Roll was

---

State University. 2005 p.134 citing Fox to Pelham 3 July 1803 in Despatches from Gibraltar, 1802–08 at the Gibraltar Government Archives.

72   TNA: WO 17/1791: Returns; WO 380/5: Regimental record and WO 24/887: Establishments 1804.

73   *Army Lists* 1803 and 1804. Müller was suspended from 14 July 1804 for a year by a court martial, but the reason is not stated, however during this period he was 'employed overseer of King's Works' (TNA: WO 17/1792: Monthly returns and WO 12/11988: Pay list).

74   CH AEV: Courten Cn B 30/3/41: Roll to Courten, 25 September 1803.

Jacob Frey, a former *lieutenant* in Rovéréa's regiment, who had been active in the Stecklikrieg and thus attracted the enmity of the pro-French authorities in his native canton of Aargau. He was appointed lieutenant on 22 December 1804.

Many more young men, from leading Swiss families, over the next years came to join the regiment in preference to building a career under Napoleon's shadow even though their journeys to England were difficult and even dangerous. Ulysses Gougelberg who had been appointed ensign on 25 December 1802 made such a journey which he described in a journal. On 8 June 1804, aged 20, he left his home at Maienfeld in Graubünden and, travelling via Heidelberg and Frankfurt, he reached Kassel on 24 June. There he obtained a passport from the French ambassador to travel to Hamburg purportedly to visit a Swiss commercial house. The French authorities suspected the true purpose of his journey and, on the next leg, an agent tried to get him to incriminate himself and, when that did not work, had him arrested. However, with foresight, Gougelberg had entrusted letters that would have condemned him to the temporary safekeeping of a servant girl. Without this incriminating evidence and a passport that was in order, he was released and continued to Hamburg, from which he travelled with a British family to Husum, arriving on 8 July. Three days later he took the packet and reached Harwich on 17 July. At London, Alexander Routh, the regiment's agent, arranged for Gougelberg to be supplied with his uniform and outfit and he paid a visit to Baron de Roll; for his stay he was fortunate enough to be looked after by relatives, of the Planta and Salis families, who were resident in London. He later travelled to Lymington, Hampshire, where on 3 December 1804 he sailed to Gibraltar.[75]

In addition, a small number of young men were appointed to the regiment in this period whose families were part of the Comte d'Artois's intimate circle of courtiers. One was Anne-Louis-Henry de Polastron whose mother, Louise, had been Artois's mistress and constant companion in his exile until her death on 27 March 1804. Although there is no evidence that Louis, as he was known, was not Louise's husband's son, the prince maintained 'the tenderest interest' in him.[76] The Baron de Roll proposed the 18-year-old Polastron for an ensigncy in his regiment which was duly published on 5 May 1804 and he joined the regiment by August that year.[77]

The British Army's Foreign Depot had been established at Lymington after the resumption of hostilities, its small port meant that troops could be readily transferred to and from ships in the Solent, including at Spithead off Portsmouth. The depot was the rendezvous for newly appointed officers, and those returning from leave, before being sent abroad. It was also where foreign recruits for the British Army, especially former deserters and prisoners of war, were received, enlisted, vetted, allocated to units and

75   Marie Gugelberg von Moos (ed.), *Erlebnisse eines Bündners im Regiment Roll (1804–1819)* (Maienfeld: privately published, c.1910), pp.5–11.

76   CH AEV: Courten Cn B 30/3/43: Roll to Courten, 21 July 1804.

77   Vicomte de Reiset, *Les Reines de l'Emigration, Louise d'Esparbès, Comtesse de Polastron* (Paris: Emile-Paul, 1907), pp.318–338, the commission was back dated 25 March 1804.

equipped before commencing their training and being sent to their units. All the foreign regiments were directed to keep a subaltern officer and sergeant at the depot for 'taking charge of and instructing any Recruits.' Those sent from the Regiment de Roll were expected to be German speakers and, preferably, to be conversant in English.[78] The regiment responded to this instruction by sending Lieutenant Nicholas Fuchs, Sergeant Heinrich Fohrer, Corporal John Jacob and Private Klein Michel to the depot. Fuchs was promoted captain on 20 October 1804 and subsequently returned to the regiment on 27 September 1805, having been replaced at Lymington by Charles Bronner, an Alsatian who had formerly been a *quartier-maître* in the Armée de Condé, who was appointed temporary lieutenant on 4 April 1805.[79] A batch of recruits from Lymington reached the Regiment de Roll on 17 November 1804 but after this the Foreign Depot was not a fruitful source of recruits as it only provided 30 men from 1806 to 1810, all Swiss except for one from the Netherlands.[80]

Recruitment was particularly difficult in this period as Napoleon tightened his grip on Continental Europe and the British Army was not engaged in active operations in the theatre, so did not have access to sources of men. Captain Henry Ryhiner and Lieutenant Barbier had some success recruiting men at Lisbon, presumably from soldiers discharged after the foreign units of the British auxiliary force were disbanded in 1802, 45 men reaching the regiment between May and September 1804.[81] Recruits also arrived from Italy, as Courten describes in a letter to his brother, 'There often falls from the sky some 12, 15, 20 Hungarians and Germans for us; we know who sends them; it is an old protector of the regiment of whom I decline to name … It is he who sends us these gifts, I say gifts because they do not cost a penny.'[82] He was cryptic for fear of the letter being intercepted but, by giving information only his brother could know, he identified the benefactor as Prince Augustus Frederick, King George's son. These men not only replaced those who were discharged but also enabled the regiment to steadily increase in strength to 550 rank and file on 1 September 1804.[83]

The situation for the garrison at Gibraltar was not comfortable due to the state of their accommodation, in a letter to the War Office Trigge described the Rock as having the, 'worse Barracks for Officers and men, than in any Country in the world. It is extraordinary, that after our having this place so long, the Regiments should be in ruinous Barracks, and only enough of them in general, to allow a Bed about four feet wide for three men. No Hospital

---

78   TNA: WO 7/73: Lieutenant Colonel Howard to officers commanding regiments, 24 May 1803.

79   TNA: WO 12/11989: Pay list 1805 and *Army Lists*.

80   TNA: WO 25/669–670: Foreign recruit books February 1806 to September 1809 and September 1809 to July 1810, respectively.

81   TNA: WO 12/11988: Pay lists 1804.

82   Courten family papers (Courten): *Souvenirs à Gibraltar 1803–1805*, transcriptions of letters written by Eugène de Courten, Eugène to Pancrace, 1 March 1804. Edited versions in Alistair Nichols with Antoine de Courten (eds), 'The Letters of Major de Courten of the Roll Regiment, Gibraltar, 1803–1805', *Journal of the Society for Army Historical Research*, vol.94 No.379, pp.177–192, and No.380, pp.276–293.

83   TNA: WO 17/1792: Monthly returns Gibraltar 1804.

whatever'.[84] When Courten arrived on 31 October 1803 he experienced, at least initially, the shortage of quarters first hand.

His letters home provide details of life in garrison and in the Regiment de Roll. One of the first things he noticed was the expense involved in having the correct dress required. It seems that it was at this stage that the regiment adopted the additional items and distinctions for which it became noted, for instance all ranks had a frill from the shirt displayed through the coat buttons.[85] He described the routine, in the winter the regiment paraded at 3:00 p.m. and afterwards, at 4 o'clock, the officers dined together; in the summer, dinner was at the same time but the parade took place at sunset. When on duty, he also attended the Garrison Parade at 7:30 a.m. along with the staff. The officers maintained an active social life and, as all the regiments in garrison had served in the Egyptian campaign, celebrations were held to mark the key dates of 8, 13 and 21 March. Regiments took the lead on the days that they had been particularly distinguished, so the Regiment de Roll hosted comrades on 21 March, the anniversary of the Battle of Alexandria.[86]

Each regiment was allocated one day a week for field days, that for the Regiment de Roll being Friday. Men were not provided for garrison duties that day and the regiment exercised manoeuvring and live firing. Their intensity increased as the day of the regiment's inspection approached, 'We exercise in strength, and almost always with firing to prepare us for the annual review … where we are obliged to do in succession all the manoeuvres of the Dundas regulations.'[87] The regiment was reviewed 10 April 1804, 'to the satisfaction of the Lt Governor and the generals … We manoeuvred in front of a large public crowd ... we did twelve manoeuvres in the execution in which we used up 35 cartridges per man'.[88]

Trigge was indeed satisfied, reporting that the officers were,

> … Well instructed and attentive to their duty in the Field, and to their garrison duty.
> Non Commissioned Officers: Good and well instructed in their duty.
> Men: Of a good size, able and fit for service; but many rather old …
> Manual Exercise: Well performed.
> Movements: Very good. Evolutions: Exact and well executed.
> Firings and Manoeuvres: Well executed & according to His Majesty's Regulations.[89]

Accompanying lists provide information on the 561 men, including the sergeants and drummers, present with the regiment. Nationality: 256 Swiss, 217 Germans, 58 Italians, 20 French, nine Portuguese and one 'English.' Age: 18 years old – 14; 20 to 25 years – 188; 30 to 35 years – 235; 40 to 45 years – 99 and 50 to 55 years – 25. Only 68 were under 5 foot 6 inches (1.68 metres)

84 TNA: WO 1/289: Trigge to John Sullivan, Undersecretary at the War Office, 23 August 1803.
85 Courten: *Souvenirs*: 10 November 1803 to Eugénie.
86 Courten: *Souvenirs*: 2 April 1804 to Eugénie.
87 Courten: *Souvenirs*: 1 March 1804 to Pancrace.
88 Courten: *Souvenirs*: 1 May 1804 to Eugénie.
89 TNA: WO 27/88: 10 April 1804.

in height while 14 were 6 foot (1.83 metres) or over; 382 had eight or more years' service while 75 had a year or less.[90]

When Courten had arrived at Gibraltar, although peace continued between Britain and Spain, communication with the latter was tightly controlled as an outbreak of yellow fever was ravaging the population of Málaga, killing an estimated 12,000 people that year, and it was feared the disease might spread into the intervening countryside. The Rock, however, remained unaffected and when the outbreak passed the restrictions were lifted on 17 February 1804.[91] In the summer and autumn of 1804 the disease returned to Málaga and was even deadlier, possibly killing over 26,000 residents of the Spanish city.[92] Thus restrictions were reintroduced at Gibraltar on 27 August.[93] This time the disease was not kept at bay and about 10 September the first deaths occurred in Gibraltar town.[94] It began to take its toll among the troops a fortnight later and from 1 October nearly all the garrison, including the Regiment de Roll, was camped on high ground above Europa Point, the southern point of the Rock.[95] However, whether it was the duties required of the men in the town or, as has been suggested, typhus was now rampant, the change to the healthier environment did not stop the progress of the epidemic immediately.[96]

The effects on the Regiment de Roll were stark and, on 14 October, Major de Courten informed his brother of the death of Captains Aloyse Bachmann (died 5 October) and Ignace Metzger (died 1 October and soon followed by his wife), Ensigns Julien de Courten (the major's cousin who had travelled with him to Gibraltar and who died 8 October) and Polastron (died 3 October) and Assistant Surgeon Pierre Lodron (died 12 October). Courten, himself, had been ill and reported that all but two of the officers had been attacked by fever, 'several have been very ill'.[97] One of the officers who Courten mentioned as having been unaffected was Lieutenant François d'Altenbourg, who had just returned from leave in Franche Comté and, by seniority, was due to take over one of the vacant companies, but he died on 19 October. He was the youngest of three brothers who had joined the regiment at its onset, his oldest brother had died in the shipwreck off Bonifacio in 1796 and the other, Charles, had drowned in an accident on Menorca in 1799.[98] A task he gave his brother was to inform families in Valais of the death of brothers or sons in the regiment, namely Sergeant Joseph Pfammatter (died 6 October) and Corporal Elois Lorétan (1 November).[99] It was not only the men of the regiment who

90　TNA: WO 27/88: 10 April 1804.

91　Edward Nathaniel Bancroft, *An Essay on the disease called Yellow Fever, … partly delivered as the Gulsonian Lectures, before the College of Physicians, in the Years 1806 and 1807* (Baltimore: Cushing and Jewett, 1821), p.318 and Courten: *Souvenirs*: 1 March 1804 to Pancrace.

92　Bancroft, *Yellow Fever*, p.319.

93　Courten: *Souvenirs*: 28 August 1804 to Eugénie.

94　Bancroft, *Yellow Fever*, p.327.

95　Courten: *Souvenirs*: 1 October 1804 to Eugénie and Maule *Principal Events* p.288. The

96　Jackson, *The Rock* p.196.

97　Courten: *Souvenirs*: 14 October 1804 to Pancrace.

98　Courten: *Souvenirs*:22 October 1804 to Pancrace.

99　Courten: *Souvenirs*: 14 October and 25 November 1804 to Pancrace; CH AEV: Courten Cn B 30/2/54 and TNA: WO 12/11988: Paylists.

suffered, by 22 October Courten estimated the regiment had lost 'more than 15 women and as many children' and the garrison, as a whole, was reported to have lost 270 women and children between 1 September and 20 December.[100]

The progress of the fever meant that, 'The duties of the garrison now became arduous and severe upon those officers, who continued in health.'[101] The soldiers had their normal guard duties to perform as well as burying the dead from the town in the neutral ground before the Spanish lines. Bombardier Benjamin Miller of the Royal Artillery remembered,

> We frequently threw 40 into one hole, clothes and all and some quite warm, and scarcely dead. Every person in the garrison had a shock of it more or less.
>
> There was a strong party of soldiers every day ordered for digging holes and burying the dead, and frequently half of the party would be buried in the same holes they had themselves dug the day before.[102]

Maule paid tribute to how the soldiers of the garrison performed their duties at this time,

> … in the midst of a populous town, I saw nothing, but heard on either side a confused noise of voices, intermingled groans, and the doleful lamentations of the sick and dying. The sentinels on duty, alone seemed mindful of their usual employment, and unmindful of their danger, and of the fate which probably awaited them.
>
> Accustomed to view perils, and to undergo hardships with indifference, they seemed cheerful amidst the general consternation, and performed everything required of them with alacrity.[103]

Courten reflected dolefully to his brother on the toll shipwreck and disease had had on the regiment, 'Understand, my good friend, that [of] 70 officers that we were at the formation of this regiment, which was then of 1,800 men, we find ourselves no more than 14, … All the rest are new. We have a young man from Solothurn, de Glutz, who entered as ensign in 1799, and who takes a company at this moment, and all those who follow him, … [in line for captaincies], have at the most three years of service.'[104] Later he wrote, 'We have had irreparable losses in our NCOs; 18 sergeants, almost all of the best we had, and in our excellent band 7 members, three of which were of such talent that we will not be able to replace them.'[105]

---

100 Courten: *Souvenirs*: 22 October 1804 to Pancrace and *Public Ledger and Daily Advertiser*, 12 February 1804.

101 Maule, *Principal Events*, p.289.

102 M.R.Dacombe, B.J.H.Rowe and J.Harding (eds), 'The Adventures of Serjeant Benjamin Miller, during his service in the 4th Battalion, Royal Artillery, from 1796 to 1815', *Journal of the Society for Army Historical Research*, vol.7, no.27 (January 1928), p.39.

103 Maule, *Principal Events*, pp.296–297.

104 Courten: *Souvenirs*: 10 October 1804 to Pancrace. Joseph de Glutz had been appointed *sous-lieutenant* 5 September 1796 but only joined the regiment in 1799, he was promoted captain on 5 April 1805.

105 Courten: *Souvenirs*: 16 November 1804 to Eugénie.

Despite rain arriving in November the fever, and deaths, persisted. There was, however, a feeling that the corner had been turned and on 8 December Courten commanded a detachment of 184 men from the Regiment de Roll that returned to quarters in the town. All the men had had the fever and since recovered; the other regiments sent in similar detachments at the same time.[106] Finally on 3 January Courten was able to write,

> I am very well; the plague is extinguished ... I began my year by treating our lt-colonel, Mme la Baronne de Vogelsang and her husband who came from the camp only for this day. I had almost all the corps of officers at coffee after dinner, and for the first time since the sickness, we were reunited. ... We had a very good dinner; this is new for us all, as all have lost the habit. ... The plague has taken leave of the Rock.[107]

The official death toll was put at 5,946 (1,082 military and 4,864 civilians) out of a total population of 15,000.[108] The Regiment de Roll that had had 550 rank and file on 1 September 1804 had 398 four months' later, on 1 January 1805.[109]

Table 9: Sickness and deaths, since the last return, amongst the rank and file of the Regiment de Roll, 1 August 1804 to 1 January 1805.[110]

	Sick	Dead		Sick	Dead
1 August 1804	36	2	1 November 1804	93	118
1 September 1804	35	1	1 December 1804	No return made	
1 October 1804	103	21	1 January 1805	8	16

In the meantime, on 12 December 1804, Spain had declared war on Britain. This coincided with the arrival, five days later, of the new lieutenant-governor, Lieutenant General Henry Edward Fox. Trigge had been promoted to general and, knowing of the change since April, he had resigned his post in August but had remained to command the garrison through the epidemic until Fox arrived. Fox soon appointed Captain Anthony Mohr, described by Courten as having a 'quiet and gentle character, added to quite a great education' as one of his aides de camp.[111] Such an appointment for an officer of the Regiment de Roll again indicates the progress of the regiment's integration into the army.

106 Courten: *Souvenirs*: 10 December 1804 to Eugénie.
107 Courten: *Souvenirs*: 3 January 1805 to Eugénie.
108 Jackson, *The Rock*, p.196.
109 TNA: WO 17/1792 and 1793: Gibraltar monthly returns 1804 and 1805.
110 TNA: WO 17/1792 and 1793: Gibraltar monthly returns 1804 and 1805.
111 TNA: WO 17/1793: Monthly returns, from 1 April 1805 and Courten: *Souvenirs*, 16 November 1804 to Eugénie.

6

'Like grass before a sharp edge'

1805

The losses incurred by the Regiment de Roll in the epidemic brought promotions and changes to the officer cadre. Despite Courten's observations there was a strong sense of continuity among the captains, seven of whom had been officers in the regiment from its formation and two more, Steiger (on leave in Switzerland) and Glutz, had been commissioned in 1796. The only exception was Nicholas Müller, whose maternal grandfather was Nicolas-Léodegard-François-Ignace de Bachmann. He had held officer rank in both his grandfather's regiments, as a boy in Sardinian service and then as *aide-major* in the Swiss corps in British pay. He joined the British Army on 5 May 1803 as a lieutenant in the 60th Foot before his appointment as captain, with temporary rank, in the Regiment de Roll.

Table 10: Captains of the Regiment de Roll, 1805[1]

Name	Date of captaincy
Philip Capol	9 December 1794, brevetted major 1 January 1805
Anthony Mohr	9 December 1794, brevetted major 1 January 1805
Albert Steiger	27 August 1802
Elias Reinach	25 September 1802
Henry Ryhiner	25 December 1802
Nicholas Müller	5 January 1804
Joseph Barbier	1 October 1804
Nicholas Fuchs	20 October 1804
Ferdinand de La Ville	21 October 1804
Joseph Glutz	4 April 1805

Of the regiment's medical staff, only Assistant Surgeon John Rouvier had survived the fever. On 22 December 1804 John Augustus Romheld, formerly assistant surgeon in the artillery of the King's German Legion, was appointed surgeon to replace Louis Desguerrois who had died 25 October 1804 and another German, Assistant Surgeon William Heyn, transferred from the

---

1   *Army Lists*, 1805 and 1806.

Joseph Glutz (1781–1838), officer in the Regiment de Roll from 1796 to 1816, the small piece of ribbon on the left breast may have been to attach the hook of the Sultan's Medal without damaging the coat. Photograph by José R. Martinez, Solothurn. (Courtesy of Historisches Museum Blumenstein, Solothurn, inv. no. 1955.61)

68th Foot to replace Pierre Lodron. Both were with the regiment by 1 April 1805.

On 8 April 1805 Courten left Gibraltar on leave to return home. Due to the war with Spain he had to return via England and the convoy in which he sailed had to take a wide arc to evade the Franco-Spanish fleet as the Trafalgar Campaign commenced. Then on reaching England his vessel was quarantined off Portsmouth, before continuing his journey via London, by the Harwich to Husum crossing, and then through Germany to Basel. From there he had to journey through Switzerland incognito, staying in the homes of comrades' families, before arriving safely at home in Valais. There the authorities placed him under surveillance and he had to agree to certain conditions, specifically 'not to speak against France, its government, its august leader, nor in favour of England or its service'.[2] He did not return to the regiment and retired on 21 October 1806 having been granted three years' pay.

As Courten's transport made its way from Gibraltar to England others were sailing in the opposite direction and facing the same hazards. On 19 April a convoy sailed from Portsmouth with reinforcements for Gibraltar as well as Malta where they would 'create a strategic reserve of some seven thousand troops for active operations'.[3] This force was commanded by Lieutenant General James Craig, a general senior enough to make decisions on the spot, with Major General John Stuart as his deputy. Craig's primary mission was to occupy Messina with or, should it be necessary, without the consent of the Neapolitan Court to ensure Sicily did not fall to the French who had gathered troops in Apulia, Southern Italy. To this was added an instruction to be ready to defend the Kingdom of Naples in co-operation with the Russians who were now allies in what was to become the Third Coalition, after Austria joined on 9 August. This task was complex as the Neapolitans, whose policy was now under the personal direction of Queen Maria-Carolina, veered between joining the alliance and submitting to French demands that the kingdom be neutral.

Craig landed at Valletta on 18 July and eventually Russian and British troops arrived in the Bay of Naples on 20 November. The Neapolitan army was found to be in no condition to co-operate effectively with the allies but this was irrelevant after Napoleon's victories over the Austrians at Ulm on 17 October and the Russians at Austerlitz on 7 December destroyed the coalition with Austria suing for peace which was agreed by the Treaty of Pressburg on 26 December, in which Austria made significant concessions

---

2   Courten: *Souvenirs*: attached correspondence.

3   Piers Mackesy, *The War in the Mediterranean 1803–1810* (Cambridge: Harvard University Press, 1957), p.58.

of territory to France. Intervention in southern Italy was of no significance to the strategic situation so the allies re-embarked and on 19 January 1806 Craig sailed for Messina while the Russians returned to their base at Corfu (or Kérkyra). The Neapolitan court hesitated to allow the British to land on Sicily as it tried to ingratiate itself with Napoleon but he had already decided to sweep the Bourbon monarchy from power and place his brother, Joseph, on their throne. Finally, reality became clear and on 13 February King Ferdinand, who was to take sanctuary on Sicily, granted permission for Craig to land. He immediately called for reinforcements from Malta and Gibraltar as French troops arrived on the opposite, Calabrian, shore of the Straits of Messina. Having secured Sicily Craig, ill for some time, returned home handing command to Stuart. Sicily was not only to be defended for the rest of the war but it would also a base from which offensive expeditions could be launched.

Meanwhile the naval campaign had culminated on 21 October in Nelson's victory at the Battle of Trafalgar and three days later the first of the damaged ships arrived at Gibraltar.[4] Many of the wounded were taken ashore to be treated at Gibraltar's Naval Hospital and Assistant Surgeon Heyn was detached to help with the influx of patients.[5] Prisoners of war also arrived at Gibraltar, including soldiers who had been on board the warships of the combined fleet. Between 28 and 30 October, 13 enlisted in the Regiment de Roll, followed by a further 81 in November. This had a significant effect on the number of rank and file in the regiment, which had hovered around, or just below, 400 for most of 1805 but on 1 December it was 479.[6] Although Gougelberg described the recruits as Germans it seems the intake was more diverse, with names such as Stephen Fiorelly and Augustin Casapietra.[7] Their recruitment was approved by Fox who seems to have considered men of any nationality were now suitable recruits for the regiment.

On 1 December Fox inspected the regiment and found the officers were, 'Attentive, properly dress'd & appointed; swords according to His Majesty's regulation' and the soldiers were, 'A good body, in general, but some of the men very old.' He continued, 'I saw every officer exercise his company, they appeared well instructed & capable of the duty required of them. I called upon a Captain, a Lieutenant & an Ensign to exercise the Battalion according to His Majesty's order, & they appear'd well acquainted with their duty.' Those recruited since the last review in April 1804 were described as, 'Very good.'[8]

The returns attached to the report show details of the 538 men, including sergeants and drummers. The balance of nationalities had changed: 299 Germans, 116 Swiss, 97 Italians, 16 French, eight Portuguese and two English. At the previous review the proportion of Swiss had been 46 percent it was now 22 percent, that of Germans had increased from 39 percent to

4   James, *Naval History*, vol.IV, p.136.
5   TNA: WO 25/762: Return of service.
6   TNA: WO 17/1793: Monthly returns 1805 and WO 12/11989: Muster and paylists 1805.
7   Gugelberg (ed.), *Bündners*, p.13 and TNA: WO 12/11989: Muster and paylist 25 November 1805.
8   TNA: WO 27/89: 1 December 1805.

56 percent and of Italians from 10 percent to 18 percent. Of the other data sets: Age: 18 years old or under – five, 20 to 25 years – 175, 30 to 35 years – 290, 40 years or older – 68; only 37 were under 5 foot 6 inches (1.68 metres) in height and six were 6 foot (1.83 metres) or over and 232 had eight or more years' service while 108 had a year or less. The changes reflected how the epidemic had particularly affected the older soldiers from the regiment's original formation and also the difficulties of recruiting Swiss at this stage of the wars. The returns also provide a glimpse to the other duties performed at Gibraltar. The officers and men who were on duty but absent at the review were shown as: 'Recruiting in England' – a subaltern, a sergeant, a corporal and a private; 'Regimental Guard' – a subaltern, four sergeants, a drummer and six privates; 'King's Bakery, Gibraltar' – a private; 'Cooks & Barrack Orderlies' – 16 privates and 'Attending sick' – a corporal and three privates.[9]

1806

Once Craig had returned to England, Fox was appointed commander-in-chief in the Mediterranean. On the face of it, he was a strange choice as he lacked vigour and was considered old beyond his years. However, the death of Prime Minister William Pitt, on 23 January 1806, led to a new administration, the so-called Ministry of All the Talents, that included politicians from across the parties for the sake of unity. Fox's brother, Charles James, was appointed Foreign Secretary and, in addition to his military role, Lieutenant General Fox was to direct relations with royal court of King Ferdinand or, more accurately, of Queen Maria-Carolina. He left Gibraltar on 28 June, arriving at Messina on 22 July.[10]

In the meantime, Stuart had led an expedition to the mainland and won the Battle of Maida on 4 July, leading the French to evacuate their forces from Calabria but on his return to Sicily he was greeted by Fox. Stuart had expected to be superseded by a senior officer but he learned that he was not to resume his role as second-in-command as Fox had been given a deputy to not only support him but to take a leading role in military matters. This was none other than Sir John Moore, it was to be too much for Stuart to take and he left for Malta on 5 September to wait there for a ship to England.

While Fox had commanded at Gibraltar he had maintained good, even friendly, relations with his Spanish counterpart despite the nations being at war and their officers and men followed their lead. However, at the same time, there had also been a relaxation in discipline in the garrison. This, and boredom, may have led to the only significant event within the Regiment de Roll in early 1806. This was a duel between 23-year-old Captain Nicholas Müller and Lieutenant Rudolph Wilhelm, a former sergeant major who had been promoted ensign in 1801 and lieutenant in 1803. Wilhelm died, on 4

9   TNA: WO 27/89: 1 December 1805.
10   TNA: WO 1/281: Fox to Windham, 29 July 1806.

April, but Müller was acquitted by a subsequent court martial.[11] Moore, who arrived on 28 June only hours after Fox's departure, was not impressed with what he saw at Gibraltar,

> I was sorry to see the very bad state of the garrison. It looked more like a place where the inhabitants did occasional military duty than a military station … Now there is no general parade; the detachments are marched from the regimental parades to their posts. The soldiers off duty are all dirty, and the regiments in the worst state of discipline. The duty is of course done in a slovenly way, and everything seems neglected and going to decay.[12]

However, it is unlikely that he saw the Regiment de Roll as it embarked on 1 July to be ready to leave in the convoy with Moore. This sailed on 5 July and arrived at Messina on 5 August, Moore disembarked immediately but the regiment remained on board for a further three days before doing so.[13] The Baron de Roll regarded the move from Gibraltar positively, 'I think that the change will be rather advantageous, and agreeable for the regiment.'[14]

The British force held Messina and posts in the northeast of the island along with garrisons at Syracuse and Augusta as well. The Regiment de Roll stayed at Messina until November when it moved to the north coast. The regimental staff and four companies were posted at Gesso, another with additional men on the coast at Rometta and the rest a little inland at Bauso, presumably occupying the castle there. However, most of Captain Henry Ryhiner's company – Ryhiner, his two subalterns, Lieutenant Frey and Ensign Amanz Glutz, with three sergeants, two drummers and 54 rank and file – were detached to the Calabrian mainland at Scilla.[15] These deployments were maintained into the following year.

The regiment no longer had an assistant surgeon serving with it. Rouvier had resigned to remain at the Naval Hospital at Gibraltar as a surgeon mate and his replacement, Frederick Herring, a Hanoverian, did not join the regiment until the end of 1807. Surgeon Heyn had been granted six months' leave on 1 February to go to England for his health but the transport he was on was captured by a French privateer and he was held as a prisoner of war at Nantes for two and a half years.[16] As a result a Sicilian, Joseph Catanoza, was 'attached' to the regiment on 8 September 1806 to fulfil the role.[17]

---

11   CH AEV: Courten Cn B 30/3/48: Roll to Courten, 16 May 1806. This is the only evidence of the event that exists.

12   Maurice, *Sir John Moore*, vol.II, p.121.

13   TNA: WO 12/11990: Pay and muster lists 1806. The regimental record (WO 380/5) shows the date of arrival as 26 July. However, the regiment is not on the return for 1 August, but four battalions that arrived on 26 July are, but is on that of 1 September with the note, 'The Regiment de Roll arrived from Gibraltar since last Return' (WO 17/1931: Monthly return).

14   CH AEV: Courten Cn B 30/3/48: Roll to Courten, 16 May 1806, when writing he thought the regiment had gone to Malta.

15   TNA: WO 17/803: Regimental returns, the remainder of Ryhiner's company were the additional men at Rometta.

16   TNA: WO 25/762: Return of service and WO 12/11990: pay list 1806.

17   TNA: WO 12/11990: 4th quarter pay list 1806.

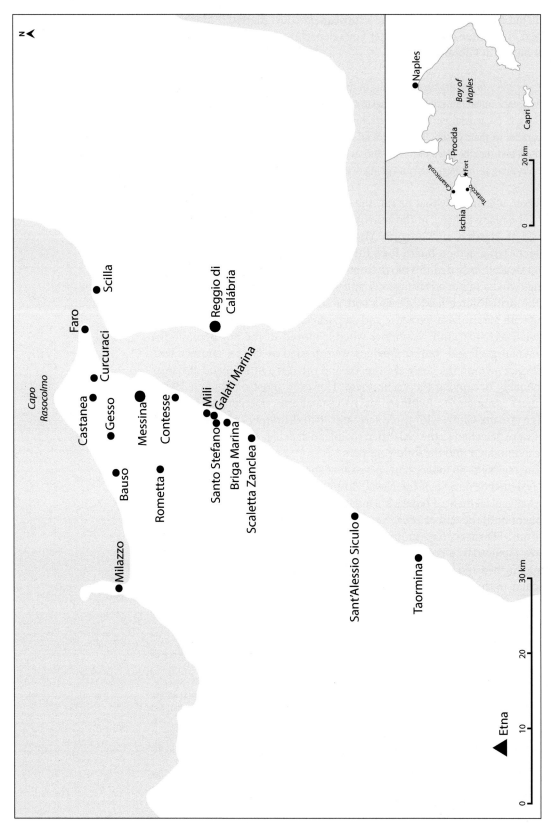

Northeastern Sicily, with Bay of Naples inset.

During the Maida campaign up to 3,000 prisoners had been taken, among them were men from the 1er Régiment Suisse and 1er Régiment Polonais.[18] On 23 July Stuart wrote to Fox about them,

> … there are several hundreds of <u>Poles</u> & <u>Swiss</u> who are Prisoners – & who have offered to volunteer for our foreign Regiments – they are the former description of people of which my own [Minorca] Regt. was composed – Austrian prisoners constrained by the French to serve – I have given <u>no</u> authorities as yet for their appropriation to <u>particular</u> Regiments – they will now receive your Orders on the subject – the <u>Swiss</u> I think are to some measure a due to Watteville's – who assisted materially in taking them.[19]

As Stuart observed the Poles, in fact mainly men from Galicia in today's Ukraine, had been serving in the Austrian Beaulieu Regiment and captured by the French, in Northern Italy, as recently as the end of the 1805 campaign.[20] From his own experience with the Minorca Regiment, he had confidence in their potential. The recruits were distributed in August and the lion's share went to units that had taken part in the campaign, Watteville took 283 and the Chasseurs Britanniques 323.[21] Nevertheless the Regiment de Roll received 164 of these recruits between 16 and 25 August and judging by their names they would all, with the possible exception of a handful, appear to have been 'Poles', the exceptions having names that may indicate a German origin.[22]

1807

During 1806 Napoleon had drawn the Ottomans into an alliance before demanding that they close the Bosphorus and Dardanelles straits to Russian shipping. With no access to the Mediterranean from the Black Sea, Russian opposition to the French in the Adriatic would be severely curtailed. The British Government sought to support its ally and coax the Ottomans into keeping the straits open to Russia by sending warships to appear off Istanbul to overawe the Turks into accepting the British ambassador's arguments. However, it was only on 19 February 1807 that British warships entered the Dardanelles and approached Istanbul but they were unable to make any impression on the city and returned through the straits on 3 March. The mission had been a failure.

At the same time as orders went to the Royal Navy, separate instructions were sent to Fox on 21 November, signed by the Foreign Secretary, Lord

---

18 Bunbury, *Narratives*, p.265.
19 BL: Add. MS 37050: Stuart to Fox, 26 July 1806.
20 Milton Finley, *The Most Monstrous of Wars: The Napoleonic Guerrilla War in Southern Italy, 1806–1811* (Columbia: University of South Carolina Press, 1994), p.16 and Henri de Schaller, 'Le Régiment de Watteville au service de l'Angleterre', *Revue historique vaudoise*, November 1894, p.334.
21 TNA: WO 17/1931: Monthly return, 1 September 1806.
22 TNA: WO 12/11990: 4th quarter pay list 1806, a further 16 joined on 4 September.

Howick, Charles James Fox having died on 13 September. Lieutenant General Fox was to prepare to send a force of 5,000 men to Egypt.

> The object of His Majesty's Government in determining upon this measure is not the conquest of Egypt, but merely the Capture of Alexandria for the purpose of preventing the French from regaining a footing in that Country and of enabling His Majesty's Forces there to afford countenance and protection to such of the Parties in that Country as may be best disposed to maintain at all times a friendly intercourse with Great Britain.[23]

Thus what was at first a clear purpose was immediately muddled and inevitably entailed involvement in the politics of Egypt. However, the commander of the expedition was to be told, 'on such questions it will be advisable that he should communicate with Major Missett and that he should pay such attention to the opinion of that Officer as, from his local information and experience, it shall appear to merit.'[24]

If the aim was to support Russia, the choice to send an expedition to Egypt, that was largely independent of the rule of the Ottoman Emperor, was strange. Mehmet Ali, who had arrived as commander of the Albanian troops in the army that marched from Syria in 1801, was now recognised by the sultan as viceroy and establishing himself as an independent ruler. The decision, according to historian Macksey, illustrated 'the British obsession with Egypt, kept alive by the uncertain future of the Ottoman Empire.'[25] The British Consul General, Ernest Missett, had been pressing for Alexandria to be garrisoned by British troops. Still a captain in what was now the 97th (or Queen's German) Foot and brevetted major on 22 December 1803, he had remained in Egypt in a diplomatic role. He considered British occupation of Alexandria, as part of a complex competition for influence with his French counterpart, Bernardino Drovetti, would assist in his aim to support the Mamluks.[26]

The situation required a commander with good judgement in both military and political matters but Fox was reluctant to be without Moore's aid and counsel. A growing chasm was developing between the British and the court in Sicily, the queen was already suspected of negotiating with France, if not for a return to Naples then for another realm as compensation. So, Fox chose Major General Alexander Mackenzie Fraser to command the expedition with Patrick Wauchope, now major general, as his deputy, although both were well regarded personally, they would be found wanting in independent command.

Along with supporting arms, including a detachment of the 20th Light Dragoons, seven infantry battalions were allocated to the expedition: the 31st, 1/ and 2/35th, 2/78th (Highlanders), the Regiment de Roll, Chasseurs Britanniques and the comparatively newly-raised Royal Sicilian Volunteers,

---

23   TNA: WO 6/56: Howick to Fox, 21 November 1806.
24   TNA: WO 6/56: Howick to Fox, 21 November 1806.
25   Macksey, *Mediterranean*, pp.184–185.
26   Macksey, *Mediterranean*, pp.50–51, 185.

5,252 rank and file in all.[27] Remarkably none of the senior officers had had experience of Egypt from 1801, indeed only the Regiment de Roll and Chasseurs Britanniques had served there before.[28] There may have been uneasiness about the number of foreign troops on the expedition because, when Fox gave Fraser his instructions on 2 February 1807, he continued,

> A considerable proportion of your Force is composed of Foreign Troops, but it cannot be avoided. They are all of a good description and Two Regiments [Roll and the Chasseurs Britanniques] well disciplined and no doubt fully to be depended upon. But I should at the same time recommend their being mixed in Brigade with the British.[29]

He was also keen that every opportunity to recruit men for the very same regiments was exploited, authorising Fraser, 'to enlist men of any nation, or Country, that you think may be depended upon for increasing the strength' of the Regiment de Roll and Chasseurs Britanniques.[30]

The Regiment de Roll embarked at Messina on 21 February 1807, with 32 officers and staff, 29 sergeants, 21 drummers, 36 corporals, 643 privates, 29 women and 15 children.[31] All the units had been ordered to take their heavy baggage and were accompanied by women and children, suggesting a long-term deployment. The convoy, with HMS *Tigre*, *Apollo* and *Wizard*, set sail on 6 March and proceeded along the eastern shore of Sicily to be joined by vessels carrying the 2/78th from Syracuse. However, on the night of 7/8 March a heavy squall scattered the ships and when it subsided there were only 14 transports, about a third of the convoy, remaining with the *Tigre*, her captain, Benjamin Hallowell, being the naval commander on the expedition. They pressed on towards Egypt and arrived off Alexandria on 16 March. Missett, even when he was told that there were no more than 1,000 troops immediately available, assured Fraser and Hallowell that no resistance was to be expected. Indeed, he insisted that only by acting swiftly would reinforcements, Albanians called by Drovetti from Rashid, be prevented from joining the defenders.[32] His summons to surrender Alexandria having been rejected by the governor, Fraser felt compelled to attack. The next day, 17 April, launches rowed towards the shore west of the city with 600 to 700 troops, five field pieces and some sailors, all that the available boats could take. Due to the distance the transports were from shore and a headwind it was night when the men landed 'a few Miles to the Eastward of Marabout.'[33] Then the surf came up preventing the rest of the troops and supplies from being landed until late the following afternoon. Given the scattered convoy

---

27   TNA: WO 1/304: Embarkation return, 21 February 1807.
28   *Public Ledger and Daily Advertiser*, 21 August 1807, printing a letter from an anonymous officer in Sicily.
29   TNA: WO 1/304: Fox to Fraser, 2 February 1807.
30   TNA: WO 1/304: Fox to Fraser, 27 February 1807.
31   TNA: WO 1/304: Embarkation return, 21 February 1807.
32   *The London Gazette*, 9 May 1807, Fraser to Windham, 25 March 1807.
33   *The London Gazette*, 9 May 1807, Fraser to Windham 25 March and Hallowell to Duckworth, 24 March 1807.

and the piecemeal landing, the troops derived from various units but it is clear that some of the Regiment de Roll had come ashore in this first landing as Lieutenant Gougelberg commanded a picquet that night.[34] Once all his available troops were ashore, at 8:00 p.m. on 18 April, Fraser advanced on the city's defences. The first obstacle was 'a palisaded Intrenchment, with a deep Ditch in front of it … stretching from Fort des Bains [Bâb Khûkha] to Lake Mariotis [sic], strengthened by Three Batteries mounting Eight Guns, exclusive of Fort des Bains on its Right Flank, mounting Thirteen Guns.'[35] A detachment, commanded by Captain Henry Ryhiner, of 50 men of the Regiment de Roll with two small cannon under an artillery lieutenant made a false attack on Fort des Bains and Gougelberg described what happened,

> … we advanced and got nearer to the fort, nay nearer than we had thought, and began the attack, but lost some men at the first canister shot, and, under almost constant cannon-fire, battled until three o'clock in the morning; but the object was achieved, the other columns seizing the line, while the enemy, who had expected the main attack from this side, turned chiefly against our detachment.[36]

While this feint was taking place the entrenched line was attacked by three columns, one of which, Colonel John Oswald's storming party, was headed by 150 volunteers.[37] As Capol later testified,

> … Capt. Fuchs was the Officer selected by the General Commanding to Head the Advanced Volunteers … the Works having been carried, [Brigadier] General [the Honourable William] Stewart observed to me, how bravely & how much to his satisfaction Capt. Fuchs had executed the object entrusted to his directions.[38]

Having cleared this obstacle the columns advanced on the southern, or Pompey's, gate of the old walls in the hope of forcing their way into the city. However, the gate was found to have been barricaded and the walls too well defended, so Fraser, conscious of how few men he had, decided not to make any further attempt. His troops marched to the east of the city to halt, at about 2:00 a.m., in the positions the French had held six years earlier.

Meanwhile the Roll detachment under Ryhiner was in a precarious position as the Turks had reoccupied the entrenched line. Fortunately, Major Marc du Faure of the Chasseurs Britanniques had been sent with a party of men from his regiment to collect the supplies that had been left at the beachhead. Finding the enemy in the lines he immediately launched an attack that dispersed its defenders, collected the wounded he could find and then continued to the shore. There he was joined by Ryhiner's detachment with the field guns and both parties then removed the supplies and embarked for Aboukir Bay.

---

34 Gugelberg (ed.), *Bündners*, p.14.
35 *The London Gazette*, 9 May 1807, Fraser to Windham, 25 March 1807.
36 Gugelberg (ed.), *Bündners*, p.15.
37 Alfred H. Miles (ed.), *With Fife and Drum* (London: Hutchinson & Co., 1899), p.123.
38 TNA: WO 71/222: Capol's evidence at a court martial, November 1810.

Plate 1
Officer *petite uniforme*, Régiment
des Gardes Suisses, after Hoffmann.
(Courtesy of Fonds La Sabretache)

There are notes on the colour plates at
the end of the book.

Plate 2
Louis de Flüe (1752–1817),
lieutenant de grenadiers of the
Régiment de Salis-Samade, later
capitaine in the Royal Etranger.
(Courtesy of Historisches Museum
Obwalden)

Plate 3

Chasseur, Royal Etranger 1795. (Original artwork by Alexandr Chernushkin © Helion & Company, 2023)

Plate 4
King's and Regimental Colours, Regiment de Roll, c.1806–1816 (Original artwork by Alexandr Chernushkin © Helion & Company, 2023)

Plate 5
Assistant Surgeon William Heyn (c.1777–1840) who served in the Regiment de Roll 1804–1815. (Courtesy of Chris Bryant)

Plate 6
Charles de Sury (1782–1834), lieutenant commanding the Grenadier Company, Regiment de Roll, from 1808 to 1811. (Courtesy of Dr Felix von Sury)

Plate 7

Regiment de Roll, 1805–1816, contemporary watercolour: Left to right – drummer, drum major, grenadier, sergeant of a flank company (seated), two grenadiers, rifleman, rear of battalion company sergeant (background). (Courtesy of the Schweizerisches Nationalmuseum Zürich, inv. no. LM-69461)

Plate 8

Regiment de Roll, 1805–1816, contemporary watercolour: Left to right – drummer, drum major, grenadier, private, centre company (seated), rifleman, officers (background). (Courtesy of the Schweizerisches Nationalmuseum Zürich, inv. no. LM- 69462)

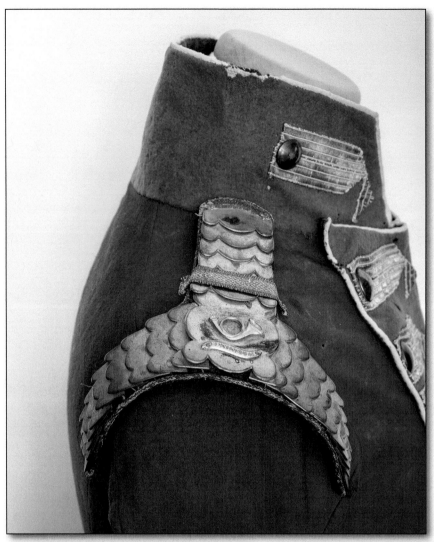

Plates 11 to 13
Wing, cuff and turnbacks, officer's coat, Light Company, Regiment de Roll c.1816. (Photograph Julie Masson, courtesy of the Collection Château de Morges et ses Musées, Suisse, Inv. 1005547)

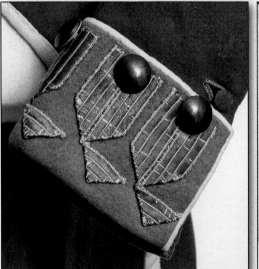

The British losses from the night's action had been light, seven killed and 10 wounded.[39] The Regiment de Roll is shown as having had Assistant Surgeon Catanoza and two rank and file killed and one wounded. It would seem that Catanoza met his death when he stayed behind in the entrenchment to tend to some wounded. A second-hand report stated that when the columns had moved on towards the city's gate, he 'and a few wounded men fell into the hands of the Turks … and were murdered by them'.[40] The two soldiers from the regiment who were killed were Privates Charles Chervany and Martin Oberschnik, respectively from Fuch's and Glutz's companies.[41]

As the sun rose, on the morning of 19 March the troops on the east of Alexandria had to move out of the range of the city's guns and there was little food or water to be had. However, in the evening, the *Apollo* and the 19 missing transports were seen approaching Aboukir Bay and they anchored the following morning. Aboukir Castle had surrendered and soon Alexandria followed suit. On 21 March the British took over the city's defences and the Regiment de Roll entered under Brevet Major Mohr. There seems to have been some indecision as Gougelberg recalled, 'our detachment was obliged to remain in the streets almost until nightfall, when Sir William Stewart finally came and led us himself to Fort Pharo [Qaitbay]'.[42] The following morning it rejoined the bivouac outside the city where a camp was established and the regimental baggage arrived that day. At the capture of the city substantial amounts of military and naval equipment were captured, so once again men of the Regiment de Roll were entitled to prize money, this time distributed in two equal payments from 1814. For those in the regiment these ranged from 9 shillings and 8 ½ pence for rank and file to £138-16-3 for Lieutenant Colonel de Sonnenberg.[43]

On 23 March, only two days after the British had entered Alexandria, Missett informed Fraser that very soon the city's population would be starving and the troops reduced to salt rations unless Rashid and El Rahmaniya, the sources of the city's food, were occupied and he added that Albanian reinforcements were continually arriving at Damietta.[44] Missett wanted the mission to be more extensive than just holding Alexandria in order to make a greater impression on the competing parties in Egyptian politics. Fraser recognised this and asked the British Government for specific instructions about the Mamluks as well as requesting reinforcements, however he could not risk ignoring Missett's warnings.[45] Assured that there would be little or no opposition, on 29 March Fraser sent Wauchope with Brigadier General Robert Meade's brigade, the 31st Foot and Chasseurs Britanniques, four guns and six light dragoons, about 1,400 men in all, to take Rashid.[46] Two days

39   *The London Gazette*, 9 May 1807, Fraser to Windham, 25 March 1807.
40   *Public Ledger and Daily Advertiser*, 21 August 1807 the anonymous officer provided '… the best account I can procure … collected from several of the Officers who were engaged in it.'
41   TNA: WO 12/11991: Pay list 1807.
42   Gugelberg (ed.), *Bündners*, p.15.
43   TNA: WO 164/181 and WO 164/525.
44   BL: Add MS 37050: Missett to Fraser, 23 March 1807.
45   Mackesy, *Mediterranean*, p.189.
46   *The London Gazette*, 14 June 1807, Fraser to Windham, 6 April 1807.

later Wauchope led the assault on the town but its defenders, 700 Albanian troops led by the town's governor, Ali Bey Al-Selaniki, put up a fierce fight. Wauchope was killed and Meade was severely wounded and ordered the retreat. Enemy cavalry emerged from the town and fell on some of the wounded, who had been brought out during the fighting, and those who could not escape were killed and beheaded. The brigade had 185 men killed and 282 wounded.[47]

News of this defeat arrived at Alexandria on 31 March and Fraser hesitated over how he should respond but Missett continued to press for Rashid to be occupied. He persuaded Fraser that continued British possession of Alexandria was impossible without it and, furthermore, that the Mamluks would soon march from the north to join the British. So the first expedition had hardly returned to the city when another, larger, one left.[48] It was commanded by Stewart and consisted of a strong artillery detachment, half a troop from the 20th Light Dragoons and the 1/35th, 2/78th, Regiment de Roll and a Light Battalion.[49] This last unit had been formed by combining the light companies of the Regiment de Roll, Chasseurs Britanniques and the four British battalions. At about 2,500 men the expedition had over half of Fraser's available troops.

The artillery and cavalry having gone ahead, the infantry marched from the camp outside Alexandria on 3 April. The Light Battalion was at the head of the column followed, in order by 2/78th, Roll and 1/35th. Their march which was hard, slow going and hampered by each battalion being accompanied by its field equipment, rather than it all, collectively, following at the rear of the column, so it was already night when the column reached the Aboukir wells, the 35th losing its way in the dark.[50] The following day was spent getting the camels and infantry across the mouths of the lakes, Aboukir and Idku, to the caravanserai on the far side. It was here that the expedition was joined by 200 sailors who were to assist in moving the artillery and also received three days salt rations, which had been already cooked on the ships in anticipation of the lack of water on the march. A detachment of Royal Marines held the caravanserai having been placed there since the retreat of the first expedition.

Interference by enemy cavalry was anticipated when the advance guard, commanded by Lieutenant Colonel Patrick Macleod, of the 78th, and formed of the Light Battalion, three companies of the 78th, two 6-pounders and a detachment of light dragoons, set off in the evening of 4 April towards Idku. Stewart, with the main column, followed, the 35th and Regiment de Roll marching with the artillery and baggage in close formation and the 78th was at the rear with a gun. Some enemy cavalry had been spotted by Macleod, so when it set off again from Idku, on 6 April, the march continued along the shores of Lake Idku, to approach Rashid from the southwest rather than directly across country. The eastern flank of this route was lined by

47   *The London Gazette*, 14 June 1807, Fraser to Windham, 6 April 1807.
48   Miles (ed.), *Fife and Drum*, pp.134–135 and *The London Gazette*, 14 June 1807, Fraser to Windham, 6 April 1807.
49   Fortescue, *British Army*, vol.VI, p.18.
50   Miles (ed.), *Fife and Drum*, pp.136–137.

sandhills and troops were sent as a screen, among whom was Gougelberg who recalled how difficult it was to make progress when continually sinking deep 'into the loose, hot sand.'[51] As Macleod approached El Hammad Al Gharbi, he encountered some enemy cavalry who were driven off after 'a slight Skirmish'.[52] The village was held by enemy infantry, so the advance was reinforced by the grenadier companies of the Regiment de Roll and the 35th Foot, however the enemy retreated and it was taken without opposition. That night the advance guard held El Hammad, while the rest of the troops stayed behind the village and closer to the Nile.

Early on 7 April El Hammad was occupied 'by a Detachment of Two Hundred and Seventy-six Rank and File of De Rolle's Regiment, under the Command of Major Vogelsang' and the advance guard took the Heights of Abu Mandour without opposition.[53] A sortie from Rashid that afternoon proved that there were not enough troops to invest the town so one end of the siege line was on the bank of the Nile, south of the town, and the other was in front of the Alexandrian, or western, Gate of the town. As soon as the line was established the troops had another task as Captain John Slessor, commanding the Light Company of the 2/35th Foot, described. 'Our next care was to send out fatigue parties to bury the headless corpses [of the men killed on the earlier expedition], that lay about the sands, in a shocking putrid state.'[54]

Stewart had been ordered to bombard the town rather than risk another assault and the first guns came into play late on 7 April and very quickly further batteries were established. The governor was summoned on 8 April but asked for time to receive instructions which was refused. The plan to get him to submit by bombarding the town was inherently flawed, the nature and construction of the buildings meant that any damage was limited and, in any case, the Albanian defenders had no regard for the welfare of the residents. There were sorties and counter-attacks while enemy cavalry were able to leave the northern side of Rashid and so threaten the left of the British line. Furthermore, without command of the river, the British were unable to stop supplies and reinforcements entering Rashid from the right bank of the Nile. The ammunition for the British guns and additional supplies, ready for when the Mamluks arrived, was brought by boat to the shore of Lake Idku where a depot was established. As Stewart had not been provided with enough camels for this task, he had ordered that those carrying the troops' camp equipment be used.[55] Slessor described the living conditions for the troops without tents, 'We suffer much from the scorching heat by day and the excessive dew by night. A few branches of the date tree shelter us a little. We lay on the ground with a blanket or great coat; often nothing but rations of salt provisions, sea biscuit and burning *acqua dente* [*sic*], with soft Nile water.'[56]

---

51   Gugelberg (ed.), *Bündners*, p.16.
52   *The London Gazette*, 18 July 1807, Stewart to Fraser, 18 April 1807.
53   *The London Gazette*, 18 July 1807, Stewart to Fraser, 18 April 1807.
54   Alethea Hayter (ed.), *The Backbone: Diaries of a Military Family in the Napoleonic Wars* (Bishop Auckland: The Pentland Press Ltd., 1993), p.96.
55   TNA: WO 1/348: Missett to Fraser, 22 April 1807.
56   Hayter (ed.), *The Backbone*, p.96.

Officer's shoulder belt plate, silver with eye and garter gilt. (Historisches Museum, Basel inv 1948.392, courtesy of Jean-Philippe Ganascia)

The El Hammad position was about eight kilometres (five miles) from the siege line before Rashid and it not only protected the rear of the siege line but also the supply line from Lake Idku. The position is described as being along a canal, or wide irrigation channel, that, when the Nile flooded, carried water to Lake Idku, with banks, or dykes, that commanded the surrounding ground. It was just over three kilometres (two miles) long before it petered out at what was the high water mark of the lake but in April 1807 the bed of the canal was dry and the edge of the lake was a further 800 metres (half a mile) or so away, leaving a dry patch of land that was good for cavalry between it and the canal's end. There were two recognised passages across the canal, one by the bank of the Nile and the other giving access to the village of El Hammad that stood on the south side of the canal. The occupation of the position was problematic due to its length, given the number of troops available for its defence, and its retention meant that Stewart's already inadequate force was divided between two positions that were too distant to be mutually supporting.

Vogelsang seems to have had six companies of the Regiment de Roll with him and he placed them at two posts covering the main passages across the canal, each with a 6-pounder; he commanded that on the left by the Nile and Mohr that of El Hammad. The companies, each with about 50 men of all ranks present, are not specified but Gougelberg, in Barbier's company, was with Vogelsang and it appears that those of N. Müller, J. Glutz and Fuchs were with Mohr.[57] Initially there was only some minor skirmishing along the front of the position but the enemy grew in numbers, so Stewart reinforced it on 12 April with another gun and a captain's detachment of 23 rank and file, bringing Vogelsang's strength to 300 men.[58] It would appear that the captain was Henry Ryhiner, with his brother, a handful of men from his own company and perhaps more from the companies already at El Hammad. A few days later the enemy placed a gun on the right bank of the Nile to fire on Vogelsang's post that killed a sergeant on 16 April.[59] Meanwhile, on 15 April, two Regiment de Roll privates, both apparently Spaniards, deserted but were returned by Arabs, they appeared before a court martial on 20 April and were shot six days later.[60]

---

57 Gugelberg (ed.), *Bündners*, p.17; TNA: WO 12/11991: Pay list March to June 1807.
58 Miles (ed.), *Fife and Drum*, p.147; *The London Gazette*, 18 July 1807, Stewart to Fraser, 18 April 1807.
59 Miles (ed.), *Fife and Drum*, p.145 also Gugelberg (ed.), *Bündners*, p.17.
60 Miles (ed.), *Fife and Drum*, pp.152, 158; TNA: WO 12/11991: Pay list March to June 1807 shows them as Joseph Escobar and John Nafsnar.

Vogelsang had reported that the El Hammad position had significant problems so on 17 April Stewart direct Colonel John Oswald to visit it and report its state.

> He found that Major De Vogelsang had entrenched himself on the left, having his gun well secured, and making the best of a bad position. The Colonel passed along the southern bank of the canal, which he found equal in height to the northern. They were both steep, so that an enemy once at the foot of either was protected from the superior fire. At Major Mohr's, in the centre, he found the gun exposed, and that but little had been done to fortify the village of El Hamet [*sic*], with which it was connected; but there were here so many chasms in the bank by which the village might be turned, that nothing could render it secure as a defensive position. The right … was quite uncovered … Colonel Oswald reported that the line of El Hamet might be maintained against the desultory attacks of a few Bedouin Arabs, but was untenable against a combined force of cavalry and infantry acting in concert.[61]

That evening, 17 April, Gougelberg led a patrol south along the Nile and discovered, 'a considerable enemy camp' and he had difficulty escaping from the cavalry sent after him.[62] That the enemy were gathering forces on the left bank of the Nile clearly showed they were strong enough to not only to defend Rashid but to take the offensive as well. Despite the continued promise that he would be joined by the Mamluks, on 19 April Stewart informed Fraser that his position was untenable. However, he would need time to send the artillery and supplies he had with him away before retreating. To make matters worse, the only sources of reliable intelligence were agents who reported to Missett at Alexandria and, if anything needed instructions from Fraser, there were further delays as he, due to ill health, was now on a warship in Aboukir Bay. While he waited for orders, Stewart decided, despite Oswald's damning assessment, to retain and reinforce the position at El Hammad to hold the enemy at bay and keep the way open for the Mamluks to join him. That morning, 19 April, the enemy made a concerted attack on Vogelsang's position before retreating and although Gougelberg described it as a skirmish, with the enemy attacking 'in their usual untidy manner,' he had three of his men wounded.[63] Gougelberg had wanted to follow the enemy's retreat and drive them from a grove of date palms but Vogelsang would not permit it considering that they were trying to lure his men into an ambush.

At the same time, the men of the Regiment de Roll in the siege line before Rashid were subject to a sortie directed against the right of the line when, 'the infantry stole through the clumps of trees to the redoubt in front of De Roll's. The attack appearing serious, the three corps on the right were placed under arms, and their respective picquets in the redoubts reinforced.'[64] However, the sortie, like the simultaneous attack, developed no further.

---

61   Miles (ed.), *Fife and Drum*, p.153.
62   Gugelberg (ed.), *Bündners*, p.17.
63   Gugelberg (ed.), *Bündners*, p.17.
64   Miles (ed.), *Fife and Drum*, p.155.

That evening Stewart sent two light companies to the El Hammad line under Captain Henry Tarleton; they were his own, of the 1/35th Foot, and Captain Casimir de Reinach's of the Regiment de Roll. Tarleton's orders 'were to drive the Enemy across the Nile, either during that Night, or early next Morning.'[65] By chance both captains had begun their military careers in the pre-revolutionary French royal army, Reinach in the Régiment de Reinach and Tarleton in the Régiment de Dillon.[66] Gougelberg, for one, considered such an attack reckless given the strength of the enemy, which he now estimated to be around 5,000 men.[67] They were part of a considerable Ottoman-Egyptian reinforcement that had come down the Nile from Cairo and outnumbered Stewart's total force four to one, the vanguard, mainly of cavalry under Hasan Paşa, was on the left bank while the infantry, under Tabuzoğlu, was on the right.[68]

Tarleton advanced from the Nile position at daybreak on 20 April. Lieutenant Frederick de Rusillion, of Roll, led the vanguard, followed by the rest of the Roll Light Company and then that of the 35th Foot; Vogelsang posted a detachment under Gougelberg on high ground to cover Tarleton's line of retreat.[69] Rusillion was soon attacked by Bedouin Arab cavalry but these were driven back when the rest of the company arrived, however columns of Turkish cavalry were seen advancing so the retreat was ordered. Vogelsang sent a company strength detachment under Captain H. Ryhiner to support the light companies with orders to retreat to his position, on the Nile. Rusillion managed, with difficulty, to reach Gougelberg's post where together they held off the enemy 'without great loss.'[70] They then fell back to join Vogelsang as did Tarleton, whose company had not advanced as far as Reinach's. However, Tarleton ordered the rest of his command, under Ryhiner and Reinach, to retreat to Mohr's position in the centre.[71]

As the body of about 100 men crossed the open ground towards El Hammad it was overtaken by the Turkish cavalry. Stewart, in his later report, was highly critical, 'While crossing the Plain, the latter Detachment, under Captain Reinack's Orders [sic], was suddenly attacked by 200 Cavalry, and as it should appear, was with little Opposition routed; Two Thirds were cut in Pieces.'[72] The criticism of Reinach, in particular, may be somewhat unfair as Ryhiner was the senior officer. Gougelberg reflects this in his account, 'Ryhiner was forced to try to cross the open field, but was overtaken by Turkish cavalry, more than six times stronger, and after heroic resistance and terrible carnage, only a few of our men escaped.'[73] Stewart received the initial

---

65   *The London Gazette*, 18 July 1807, Stewart to Fraser, 25 April 1807.

66   *Etat militaire*, 1791 and AMC: 1 GR 142.

67   Gugelberg (ed.), *Bündners*, p.17.

68   Bruno Mugnai, *The Ottoman Army of the Napoleonic Wars, 1784–1815: A Struggle for survival from Egypt to the Balkans* (Warwick: Helion & Company, 2022), p.285.

69   Gugelberg (ed.), *Bündners*, p.18.

70   Gugelberg (ed.), *Bündners*, p.18.

71   *The London Gazette*, 18 July 1807, Stewart to Fraser, 25 April 1807 and Gugelberg (ed.), *Bündners*, p.18.

72   *The London Gazette*, 18 July 1807, Stewart to Fraser, 25 April 1807.

73   Gugelberg (ed.), *Bündners*, p.18.

report of the defeat at about 11:00 a.m. and an anonymous British officer sheds light on why Stewart was so critical of the way the detachment had been commanded,

> This express [report] was soon followed by Captain Reinach himself, who gave a similar account, stating his loss to be about sixty men. Although the Captain did not admit his having been overtaken by the cavalry marching in an irregular and disorderly manner, yet it appears to have been the case. … It is manifest … he apprehended no attack … Captain Reinach asserted that he was charged in square; but experience, both before and since, proves that such was not the enemy's ordinary mode of fighting.[74]

As soon as he returned to his bivouac, Gougelberg was ordered to take 28 men of his company to reinforce Mohr's post and he was placed in the village. All was quiet, so he and Ensign Jost Müller went to where the Regiment de Roll detachments had been cut up earlier in the day, he recalled, 'It was a ghastly sight! Over 50 of these unfortunates lay headless, close together.'[75] Soon dense formations of enemy cavalry were seen to be approaching, however Gougelberg's men were ready at their posts and as the enemy swept by to cross the canal several men and horses were killed or wounded. The village was almost completely surrounded but the cavalry withdrew as quickly as they had arrived.

On receipt of the news of the failure of the morning's attack, Stewart sent Lieutenant Colonel Macleod to take command of the El Hammad position with reinforcements; two companies of the 78th Highlanders, one of the 35th Foot, a picquet of the 20th Light Dragoons and a 6-pounder gun. Later that afternoon Stewart sent Macleod two more companies of the 35th Foot, under the command of Captain Charles McAllister, 'with a Day's Provision for his whole Force, Ammunition, &c.'[76] Macleod now had about a third of Stewart's troops but McAllister was unimpressed with his new commander,

> I had not a high opinion of Colonel MacLeod's judgement. I knew that as a regimental officer his character stood high, and that his courage was unimpeachable, but I had observed his conduct when at the head of the advance of the army, and it did not please me. He appeared to be a man incapacitated for separate command in consequence of a lack of firmness … If an exigency arose he never seemed to be prepared for it; and the plan which he formed this minute he abandoned in the next, without there occurring any apparent reason for the change.[77]

---

74   Miles (ed.), *Fife and Drum*, pp.158–159.
75   Gugelberg (ed.), *Bündners*, p.18.
76   *The London Gazette*, 18 July 1807, Stewart to Fraser, 25 April 1807.
77   Miles (ed.), *Fife and Drum*, p.183. McAllister's account entitled 'The Disaster of El Hamet' (pp.175–236) is presented anonymously 'By an Officer in Command' however his identity is clear from the circumstances and events he relates.

Macleod placed the Light and a battalion company of the 35th, the Grenadier Company of the 78th, the detachment of Light Dragoons (Captain John Delancey) and a 3-pounder gun, under Tarleton's command, on the right to cover the lakeside plain. Mohr was in the centre, around El Hammad, with three companies of Roll, Gougelberg's detachment and a company (McAllister's) of the 35th. On the left was Vogelsang with four companies of the Regiment de Roll, including the remnants of Ryhiner and Reinach's detachments, with a company of the 35th and two of the 78th.[78] In front of the canal Macleod placed several isolated detachments and outposts. That night, 20/21 April, Stewart rode out to see Macleod's position for himself, avoiding a body of 150 to 200 enemy cavalry that, at sunset, had skirted Tarleton's position and were roaming behind the line. In his official report Stewart explained,

> Having reconnoitred the Line of Defence, which I found to be weak in many Parts, and very extensive, I confirmed my former Instructions to Lieutenant-Colonel McLeod, viz. that he should defend the Post to the utmost, but if likely to be forced or turned by a numerous Cavalry, that he should concentrate and *appuyer* himself upon the Lake; and if this was feasible, he should fall back on the main Army. I at the same Time concerted Measures for a general Retreat on the succeeding Night, unless certain Intelligence of the Mamelukes should arrive on the 21st.[79]

Through the night Macleod received reports from his outposts of djerms – heavy cargo boats – loaded with troops on the Nile, including one from McAllister that specified that each djerm contained about 200 Albanian infantrymen, however he did nothing.[80] Following Hasan Paşa's success of the previous day, Tabuzoğlu was moving his infantry over the river for a concerted attack on the El Hammad position.

As dawn approached a thick mist arose so when Macleod arrived at his outposts in front of El Hammad there was nothing to see until the early morning sun began to burn off the mist. According to Gougelberg, Macleod initially mistook the newly arrived troops for Mamluks but still sent his detachment closer to the village and gave him command of a group of men, inhabitants of El Hammad, who had offered to fight to defend the village.[81] McAllister, who was ordered by Macleod to defend the village, states that as the mist dispersed the enemy's army in battle array, about 6,000 combatants of which 2,000 were cavalry, came into view.[82] Macleod sent a brief message to Stewart,

78 BL: Add MS 37050: 'Captain Delancey's (20th Lt. Dragoons) Account of the Affair at El Hamet' with clarification of Mohr's detachment from Gougleberg's and McAllister's accounts.
79 *The London Gazette*, 18 July 1807, Stewart to Fraser, 25 April 1807.
80 BL: Add MS 37050: Delancey's Account; Miles (ed.), *Fife and Drum*, pp.191–192.
81 Gugelberg (ed.), *Bündners*, p.19.
82 Miles (ed.), *Fife and Drum*, pp.196–197.

The Cavalry were not to be seen this Morning; but, to my utter Astonishment, from Sixty to Seventy large Germs [*sic*], and a large Brig, are now coming down the Nile upon us. I do not know what to say of this; it appears, undoubtedly, a Reinforcement to the Enemy, and one of considerable Magnitude. … I must make Preparation, and be ready to retire upon you; let me know as soon as possible.[83]

Macleod, apparently concerned that the larger vessels, that carried four or five cannon, would dominate Vogelsang's post, he ordered the major to withdraw, with his gun, away from the river, to a sand hill about three quarters of a mile behind Mohr's post. At the same time he sent an order for Tarleton to join Mohr by marching along the northern bank of the canal. He then returned to El Hammad where he personally ordered McAllister to evacuate the village and withdraw with a gun to the post Vogelsang was to take.[84] Gougelberg, stationed near the village, was left behind. He had placed the Egyptians about 20 paces from his own men, which was just as well, as soon as the enemy's attack developed, they turned and fired on the Roll soldiers.[85]

Vogelsang had to make an oblique march to reach the post he had been assigned, so he had to leave a reserve, that McAllister estimated to be half his force, in his original position to cover the movement. However his reserve was soon overrun and enemy infantry and cavalry poured across the canal. Nevertheless McAllister had managed to join him, 'We formed square together, keeping our guns in the centre, and found that we mustered in all about three hundred and seventy or eighty bayonets.'[86] At the same time at least 500 cavalry had already got through on the right and threatened Tarleton's detachment as it marched to the centre.[87] Macleod now joined Tarleton and lined the detachment's infantry as two sides of a triangle, pointing northwards, the open side on the high bank of the canal which, however, provided scant protection as the enemy's infantry had crossed the canal and fired down from the bank.

Mohr had maintained his post but was almost surrounded and he signalled for Gougelberg to join him. The latter's detachment had already lost about 12 men and, to reach Mohr, it pushed its way through the enemy cavalry fortunately with few casualties.[88] Rather than continue on to Mohr's post with Tarleton's men, Macleod now decided to drive the enemy from some heights behind the canal and occupy them while sending Captain Delancey to get Mohr to join him there, 'This order was complied with immediately, but with such precipitation, that the 2 Companies [*sic*] of de Roll's; Grenadiers of the 78th and the 2 Companies of the 35th were indiscriminately mixed together.'[89] They were surrounded by the enemy whose infantry, closing in behind cover and even in the sand itself, did great execution, as Sergeant

---

83   *The London Gazette*, 18 July 1807, Stewart to Fraser, 25 April 1807.
84   BL: Add MS 37050: Delancey's Account; Miles (ed.), *Fife and Drum*, p.201.
85   Gugelberg (ed.), *Bündners*, p.19.
86   Miles (ed.), *Fife and Drum*, pp.196–197.
87   BL: Add MS 37050: Delancey's Account.
88   Gugelberg (ed.), *Bündners*, p.19.
89   BL: Add MS 37050: Delancey's Account.

Alexander Waters of the 78th Grenadier Company explained, 'by reason of their musquets [*sic*] carrying so much further than ours.'[90] Waters wrote,

> Our men were falling from these heights like grass before a sharp edge. It was at this awful moment that the much lamented Colonel Macleod fell … For nearly the space of an hour I can give you little or no account of, for nothing but dreadful shouts of terror & piercing groans of dying men were to be heard.[91]

Macleod and Tarleton were dead. Commissary Charles John Forbes, who had joined the detachment wrote,

> The Turks drove the party I was with about a mile along the heights, when we found ourselves completely surrounded by the cavalry in our front, and infantry on both sides and rear. As our greatest loss took place on this spot, it was thought advisable to attempt to cross a field and join another party under Major Vogelsang, of De Rolle's regiment, which had formed into a square for the defence of the cannon. However, we had not half crossed the field, when the Turkish cavalry came in upon us and cut us up most cruelly.[92]

Gougelberg was less reticent as to why the formation was broken up.

> We were surrounded on all sides, … shot after shot, 2-3 and even more people fell. The artillerymen were dead, the guns in the ditch, my servant shot at my side, Capt. Müller, his brother [Jost], and [Ensign] Stettler were wounded, [Lieutenant] Ledergerw was missing and soon there were only about 90 men left, who now sought to flee to a square formed by Major Vogelsang on the plain.[93]

Gougelberg tried to keep his men together but was severely wounded by a mounted Albanian officer who, thinking he was dying, was about to behead him but as Gougelberg still showed fight he took him prisoner. Forbes, who was also taken prisoner, estimated, 'that the party I remained with … consisting of 275, were all killed to 30, of whom 15 only escaped without being wounded.'[94] The guns were now in the enemy's hands.

As they approached, a detachment was sent from Vogelsang's square to assist the fugitives in joining it but only a few, including Sergeant Waters, managed to reach its shelter. The enemy had sent considerable forces towards Rashid but those that remained could devote all their effort against the square in wave after wave of attacks. Waters continued,

---

90   BL: Add MS 37050: Letter of Sergeant Waters to a comrade, 9 May 1807.
91   BL: Add MS 37050: Letter of Sergeant Waters to a comrade, 9 May 1807.
92   *The Oxford University and City Herald*, 5 September 1807. 'Extract of a letter from a young gentleman … to his father at Gosport' 9 May 1807. Although published anonymously, he identifies himself as a commissary and Forbes, who was born in Gosport, was the only such person taken prisoner at the time.
93   Gugelberg (ed.), *Bündners*, p.19.
94   *The Oxford University and City Herald*, 5 September 1807, Forbes 9 May 1807.

… I had the gratification to observe that the Officers were unanimous in their resolution to resist till the last extremity, In this doubtful situation we remained for better than an hour & a half during which time our square was much reduced especially our front face which was instantly completed from such part as was less exposed & the number of wounded began to crowd the square very much, many of them were expiring fast. In this situation we thought to hold out till night when we had the hopes of a reinforcement from Rosetta lines, but a shot from our own six pounder followed directly by a second which they had every opportunity of laying to their advantage almost totally disconcerted all ranks, still what was to be done?[95]

The sun was now high in the sky and men wilted through lack of food and especially water. There was no sign of help arriving and ammunition was beginning to run short, for McAllister it was clear that there was little hope,

Yet … there was not one heart in all the gallant band that quailed, not one countenance that changed colour. We stood leaning upon our weapons, without a complaint being uttered, and fully prepared, from the highest to the lowest, to submit to whatever fate it might be God's will to cast upon us.[96]

The square could not move closer to Rashid without abandoning both the guns and wounded. McAllister remembered how steadfast the British were,

I have the more satisfaction in recording this fact, that the portion of De Roll's regiment which acted with us, though composed entirely of foreigners fell in, heart and soul, with the determination of their English friends; indeed I may state, in general terms, that men more brave, more steady, more enduring, than these strangers proved themselves to be, throughout the whole of the day's operations, have never, in the course of thirty years' hard service, came under the observation of my senses.[97]

McAllister's compliment is not a hollow one when it is considered that his 'hard service' included commanding his battalion at the Battle of Waterloo. Finally, as the ammunition was running out, an enemy officer approached the square with a flag of truce and the order was given to cease fire. Vogelsang left the square 'with a Handkerchief in his hand,' and instantly the enemy cavalry and infantry rushed in, taking all the men prisoner those who resisted were instantly dispatched.[98]

In a brief report, of 1 May, Vogelsang stated that Macleod had ordered the retreat of the three columns between 6:00 and 7:00 a.m. and 'after three consecutive hours of defence, we succumbed one after another, leaving two thirds of our number on the ground killed or wounded.'[99]

---

95   BL: Add MS 37050: Letter of Sergeant Waters to a comrade, 9 May 1807.
96   Miles (ed.), *Fife and Drum*, pp.211–212.
97   Miles (ed.), *Fife and Drum*, p.212.
98   BL: Add MS 37050: Letter of Sergeant Waters to a comrade, 9 May 1807.
99   TNA: WO 1/348: Vogelsang to Fraser, 1 May 1807.

The prisoners did not expect quarter to be given, as Waters explained, 'however in this we were deceived for altho' we were roughly handled at first & plundered & stripped no sooner had they made good their prize & had all the prisoners conveyed sufficiently to the rear where they knew they were secure, than they began to use us quite different, to those who shewed no symptoms of obstinacy they behaved uncommonly lenient & generous.'[100] It appears that, since the last expedition to Rashid, the French consul, Drovetti, had persuaded Mehmet Ali that 'it would be more humane, as well as prudent, to offer to his soldiers, for a live man, double the sum that formerly was given for a head!'[101]

That morning, once the mist had cleared, the British lookout in the tower at Abu Mandour spotted the djerms on the Nile and at about 7:00 a.m. Macleod's message was received. All Stewart's force, before Rashid, would be required to save Macleod. The field guns were withdrawn from the siege line and camels were loaded with stores and ammunition, everything else was destroyed and the heavy guns buried. The artillery train, wounded and stores were gathered in the plain on the left of the line guarded by the 78th, the Roll companies taking over its positions before in turn being relieved by the 35th. The Roll and 78th companies then formed a square around their charges with the 35th at the rear, a movement covered by the Light Battalion. The enemy immediately emerged from the town and their cavalry tried to attack the baggage but were driven off by the fire of the 78th and Roll. The square then moved off, flanked by the Light Battalion.

The last report from the lookout had been that the troops around El Hammad had quit the canal, 'formed square, and repulsed the enemy who charged it.'[102] It was expected that all or most of them would join the troops from Rashid on the march and Stewart set off towards Lake Idku at about 10:00 a.m. The enemy's attempts to interfere with his column were stopped by the field guns and musketry, despite the troops being only two deep so they could cover all of the baggage. The shore of the lake was reached at about 1:00 p.m. but there was no sign of Macleod's force nor the sound of combat from the El Hammad position. The formation was changed as the lake side did not have to be covered, the contingent of the Regiment de Roll formed one face and the Light Battalion the other, with the flank covered by the 35th and part of the 78th. Stewart decided that he had to try to find out where Macleod's men were, so the column, with the light infantry to the fore, advanced away from the lake and onto higher ground. After a march of a mile, with the enemy being driven before it, a point was reached from which El Hammad could be seen clearly. 'There was nothing visible except some Turkish cavalry leisurely retiring on the other side of the position, and some enemy's tents pitched upon the bank itself. With glasses the ground was minutely examined, but no trace of a field of battle was to be discovered.'[103] With no trace of Macleod's force to be seen, there was nothing to do but turn back to the lake and continue retreating.

---

100 BL: Add MS 37050: Letter of Sergeant Waters to a comrade, 9 May 1807.
101 Miles (ed.), *Fife and Drum*, p.173.
102 Miles (ed.), *Fife and Drum*, p.162.
103 Miles (ed.), *Fife and Drum*, pp.167–168.

The same formation was adopted with the lake on the left but there was no interference from the enemy and the site of the lakeside depot was reached by 7:00 p.m. where the troops could take some food and drink and the sick and wounded, as well as most of the heavy baggage, were embarked. This took quite some time, so it was 10:00 p.m. before the march resumed and Idku was reached at 1:00 a.m. on 22 April. Despite encountering the enemy most of the day, there had been only 50 casualties, killed or wounded, and none lost as prisoners.[104] The column set off again the next day without interference from the enemy and reached the caravanserai at 3:00 p.m. where, with naval assistance, the troops and equipment crossed to the Aboukir side. All was over by early 24 April and the troops marched to their previous position on the eastern heights outside Alexandria.

As Stewart retreated along the shore of Lake Idku, a Royal Navy boat brought a despatch from the army's (Acting) Deputy Adjutant General, enclosing a message from Missett. It stated that on 18 April one of his informants had seen a large body of troops from Cairo moving down the Nile, by boat and land, on their way to relieve Rashid.[105] The messenger, presumably travelling via Rashid, had passed the information onto Missett at Alexandria who sent a message to Fraser who received it on HMS *Canopus* in the night of 20 April.[106] In the evening of 21 April, unaware of the day's events, Fraser sent a letter, marked secret, to Missett. In it he expressed his dismay that, despite the latter's assurances that the people of Egypt were friendly but for the Turks and Albanians, a party Bedouins had surprised and captured a detachment of Royal Marines from those at the caravanserai. Enemy reinforcements were arriving from Cairo and there was no sign of the Mamluks, Fraser came as close as politeness allowed in accusing Missett of giving him misleading information. He concluded, 'I fear I shall still be under the disagreeable necessity of ordering the troops to fall back on Alexandria, thereby subjecting them and the inhabitants to all the miseries [of starvation] stated officially by you.'[107]

Moore, having read the reports about both attempts to capture Rashid, concluded, 'All the accounts agree as to the good conduct and bravery of our troops. It is to be lamented that they have been so miserably directed.'[108] The historian, Fortescue, was damning about Macleod, 'The one unfortunate fact which seems certain is that Macleod lost his head … he showed neither vigilance nor caution to anticipate danger, and when he suddenly awoke to his situation, ruined everything by hurried and faulty dispositions.'[109] It must be asked why Macleod was employed in such a critical role after he had already mismanaged his battalion at the Battle of Maida, something that was known in military circles despite a cover up.[110] An explanation may be

---

104   *The London Gazette*, 18 July 1807, Stewart to Fraser, 25 April 1807.
105   Miles (ed.), *Fife and Drum*, p.170.
106   TNA: WO 1/348: Fraser (secret) to Missett, 8:00 p.m. 21 April 1807.
107   TNA: WO 1/348: Fraser (secret) to Missett, 8:00 p.m. 21 April 1807.
108   Maurice, *Sir John Moore*, vol.II, p.175.
109   Fortescue, *British Army*, vol.VI, pp.22–24.
110   He and another battalion commander seem to have lost their heads, to use Fortescue's expression, in the battle. For an explanation of the events and cover up see Nichols, *Wellington's Switzers*, pp.83–84.

that Macleod was being given a second chance by Fraser, described as 'a just, worthy, and honourable good man,' who was his regimental colonel.[111] It would also explain why Sonnenberg, who was senior to Macleod, was not at El Hammad.

The prisoners were treated quite roughly at first. Gougelberg, for example, who was severely wounded, was thrown into the bottom of a djerm where he found about 20 severed heads. He had been stripped of everything but his shirt, trousers and boots. However that evening, carried to the other side of the river, he was reunited with other officers, placed on another vessel and given somewhat crude treatment for his wounds.[112] Others remained on the left bank of the Nile where they spent the night in tents.[113] The following day Gougelberg and his companions were taken to a house at Mutubas where some of the wounded who died were beheaded and their severed heads prepared for display.[114] While at the house some high ranking individuals came and took some of the prisoners away to be slaves.[115]

The majority of the prisoners, including Gougelberg, McAllister and Forbes, went up the river by boat to Cairo, accompanied by their former comrades' heads. Some of those left behind wounded, including Captain Nicholas Müller and his brother Jost, were also enslaved, in terms that they were considered as property to be bought and sold at the whim of an owner. At Cairo the prisoners had to participate in a ceremonial triumph as described by Forbes,

> [With the heads] carried before us … upon poles. … we were marched along amidst the acclamations of the people, and were received before the Pacha's palace with music playing and guns firing. After waiting in ranks for above an hour, we were ordered before the Pacha, Mahomet Ali [sic], who received us in a very becoming manner …[116]

Waters had remained on the left bank of the Nile from where he and his fellow prisoners were marched, in small parties, to Cairo. He stated that it took four and a half days to reach the city but the men were 'well used in the march' and the wounded were carried on asses; their later arrival was not marked by ceremony.[117] All the testimonies bear witness to the good treatment that the prisoners received from Mehmet Ali and also other nation's diplomats, especially Drovetti.

Lieutenant John Matheson, 78th Highlanders, was released and arrived at Alexandria on 6 May with messages from the prisoners at Cairo. These included a report from Vogelsang that not only gave a brief account of the action on 21 April but also a report on the condition, number and identity of the prisoners. In it he stated there were 22 officers at Cairo, including

---

111 Maurice, *Sir John Moore*, vol.II, p.175.
112 Gugelberg (ed.), *Bündners*, p.22.
113 BL: Add MS 37050: Letter of Sergeant Waters to a comrade, 9 May 1807.
114 Gugelberg (ed.), *Bündners*, p.22.
115 Miles (ed.), *Fife and Drum*, p.227.
116 *The Oxford University and City Herald*, 5 September 1807, Forbes 9 May 1807.
117 BL: Add MS 37050: Letter of Sergeant Waters to a comrade, 9 May 1807.

nine from the Regiment de Roll, while seven officers had been left behind at the enemy camp on the Nile, four of whom were from Roll and wounded. Nine officers had been killed, including Lieutenant Nicholas Ledergerw. In all there were 466 prisoners, including some from the 31st Foot and Chasseurs Britanniques who had been captured during the first expedition, as well as two officers and eight men of the Royal Marines captured at the caravanserai.[118] He requested surgical instruments and medicines be sent to Cairo, on behalf of the doctors, noting that some of the wounded had as many as five severe wounds.

Vogelsang did not remain at Cairo for long as on 6 May he and Second Lieutenant John Love, of the Royal Marines, were sent to Istanbul; Fraser, for one, was somewhat baffled by this noting that it ran contrary to Mehmet Ali's portrayal of himself as an independent ruler of Egypt.[119] Their journey apparently took 48 days, as they travelled by camel through Palestine, Syria and Turkey.[120] Gougelberg indicates that soon afterwards all the prisoners were ordered to prepare to make the same journey but this was countermanded.

In the middle of May Captain Delancey also returned from Cairo accompanied by a confidential emissary from Mahomet Ali. The latter's mission was to ascertain the purpose of the British intervention in Egypt and to assure Fraser of his master's wish to have better relations with the British.[121] Except for two minor skirmishes, on 9 and 10 May, the British troops at Alexandria had been undisturbed by enemy action and Fraser's position was improved further by the arrival of two further battalions from Sicily on 25 May. With them came convalescents of the regiments already serving at Alexandria including two sergeants, two drummers, three corporals and 31 privates from the Regiment de Roll.[122] Mehmet Ali's diplomacy and his treatment of his prisoners soon created a position whereby, to Missettt's chagrin, Fraser had more confidence in the viceroy than in the unfulfilled promises of the Mamluks. Soon supplies to Alexandria were uninterrupted and on 30 May Fraser informed Fox that the city was secure.[123] In essence the situation that was reached between Mehmet Ali and Fraser was that the former would accept, and indeed condone, the temporary occupation of Alexandria but would retain the prisoners until the British left the country.

The first of the captured Regiment de Roll officers returned in early May, Ensign James Sonnenberg 'who was sold as a slave at Rosetta was brought to an Outpost … and his freedom purchased by Lieut. Colonel Baron de Sonnenberg for 4,000 Turkish Piastes or £222-4-Sterling.'[124] Fraser requested that the older Sonnenberg be reimbursed the cost of buying his nephew's freedom. The following month Drovetti bought the Müller brothers from

---

118 TNA: WO 1/348: Vogelsang to Fraser, 1 May 1807.
119 TNA: WO 1/304: Fraser to Fox, 19 May 1807.
120 Gugelberg (ed.), *Bündners*, p.26.
121 TNA: WO 1/304: Fraser to Fox, 19 May 1807.
122 TNA: WO 1/304: Fraser to Fox, 19 May 1807 and WO 1/304: Embarkation return 17 May 1807.
123 TNA: WO 1/304: Fraser to Fox, 30 May 1807.
124 TNA: WO 1/304: Fraser to Fox, 14 May 1807.

slavery and they joined the other prisoners of war at Cairo.[125] The effect of the expedition to Rashid on the Regiment de Roll can be seen in the paylist ending 24 June 1807, see Table 11.

Table 11 – Regiment de Roll's casualties on 21 April 1807 from paylist ending 24 June 1807, with additional notes.[126]

	Missing (all)	Subsequently recorded as:
Mohr's Company		
Bt Major Mohr	X	[at Cairo wounded*]
Lieutenant Frey	X	[at Cairo wounded*]
Sergeants	–	
Corporals	–	
Drummers	–	
Privates	3	1 dead
Additionally 1 Pte killed on 21 April indicating he was with the Rashid element		
A. Steiger's Company		
No losses – indicating that the company may not have been on the expedition. Capt. Steiger was Town Major at Alexandria.		
Reinach's Company		
Captain Reinach	X	[at Cairo*]
Lieutenant Russilion	X	[at Cairo*]
Sergeants	2	–
Corporals	4	1 dead
Drummers	1	–
Privates	57	22 dead
Ryhiner's Company		
Captain H. Ryhiner	X	[at Cairo*]
Lieutenant B. Ryhiner	X	
Sergeants	–	–
Corporals	–	–
Drummers	1	1 dead
Privates	3	2 dead
Müller's Company		
Captain N. Müller	X	[at Nile camp wounded*]
Ensign J. Müller	X	[at Nile camp wounded*]
Sergeants	1	–
Corporals	2	2 dead
Drummers	2	–
Privates	45	21 dead
Barbier's Company		
Captain Barbier	X	[at Cairo wounded*]
Lieutenant Gougelberg	X	[at Cairo wounded*]
Sergeants	1	–
Corporals	3	–
Drummers	–	–
Privates	42	20 dead

---

125 TNA: WO 17/1758: Monthly returns. Assistant Surgeon Alexander Leslie, 78th, accompanied them, and Gugelberg (ed.), *Bündners*, p.27.

126 TNA: WO 12/11991: Pay lists 1807.

	Missing (all)	Subsequently recorded as:
Fuchs's Company		
Captain Fuchs	X	[at Cairo*]
Lieutenant Ledergerw	X	Killed 21 April
Ensign Sonnenberg	X	[at Nile camp wounded*]
Sergeants	3	–
Corporals	2	1 dead
Drummers	–	–
Privates	47	15 dead
In addition Cpl David Naeff was killed on 18 April		
Laville's Company		
Sergeants	2	–
Corporals	3	1 dead
Drummers	1	–
Privates	45	17 dead
In addition Sgt John Bruderer had been killed on 16 April		
Glutz's Company		
Ensign Stettler	X	[at Nile camp wounded*] Died of his wounds 17 May
Sergeants	1	–
Corporals	1	1 dead
Drummers	1	–
Privates	40	23 dead
L. Steiger's Company		
Sergeants	–	–
Corporals	2	–
Drummers	–	–
Privates	41	16 dead
* situation as recorded by Vogelsang in his report of 1 May 1807		
The two deserters from the El Hammad position on 15 April were from Fuchs's and L. Steiger's Companies.		

In June the Regiment de Roll, posted in the Alexandria lines, was joined by 151 recruits, 27 had enlisted at Gibraltar and another five at Messina, while the rest, 119, had been transferred from Froberg's Regiment.[127] This regiment had begun to be formed in May 1804 on Malta but recruitment had initially been very slow and it was only in 1806 that its numbers had become more respectable. Most of the recruitment, often by dishonest means, took place in the eastern Mediterranean and the Balkans, attracting men from a wide range of nationalities. The officers also came from a variety of sources, including foreign regiments in the British Army in which case all received a step up in rank, apparently for payment.[128] Two officers from the Regiment de Roll had been promoted in this manner, Ensign Jules de Clermont to lieutenant and Ensign Frederick de Watteville, who had been promoted lieutenant in another regiment three

---

127 TNA: WO 17/803: Regimental return 1 July and WO 12/11991: Paylist 1807.
128 TNA: WO 1/305: Fox to Castlereagh, 1 July 1807.

weeks before, to captain.[129] By September 1806 the Froberg Regiment, stationed at Fort Ricasoli, had 683 men but there were only five officers present, one being Clermont who had joined on 26 August 1806.[130] The lack of officers, the racial mix, the introduction of strict British Army discipline and resentment over the way they had been recruited led some of the men plot mutiny. On 4 April 1807 one such plan was discovered and as steps were taken to deal with it the mutineers attacked the officers. Watteville was among those killed and others, along with about 200 loyal men, were taken hostage and it was to be eight days before the mutiny was completely suppressed.[131]

The subsequent inquiry uncovered wide scale wrongdoing in the recruitment and formation of the regiment so the majority of the men were discharged and sent home. However, it was always recognised that there were reliable soldiers in the regiment. On 9 April 1807 Lieutenant General William Anne Villettes, commanding on Malta, wrote,

> I find there are about 300 good men in Froberg's Regt, Germans, Poles, Swiss, & some Russians, whom the officers consider at least as much to be depended upon as those of the other Foreign Corps in general, the rest to the amount of about 400, consisting of Albanians, Bulgarians, Wallachians, & Greeks of other descriptions, all late subjects of the Turkish Government … will never be fit for any regular Service, and indeed are so dreaded by the others, that I am now obliged to separate them from each other.[132]

The soldiers who were considered dependable, described by Fox as 'in general very good men,' could choose the foreign regiment they wanted to join.[133] The majority, 16 sergeants, 13 corporals, five drummers and 85 privates, chose to join the Regiment de Roll, 53 went to the Chasseurs Britanniques and six to other units.[134] Some of the Froberg sergeants who joined Roll were experienced men. For example, Francis Degensfeld, an Austrian, had served for eight years as a sergeant in the Hompesch Mounted Riflemen and been discharged for almost a year before joining Froberg in the same rank. Ambrose Fritz, a German, had served for six years in the Hompesch Hussars and then four more in the 44th Foot, all as a private, before transferring to Froberg as sergeant.[135] No breakdown of the nationalities of the other men is available but the indications are that most were in fact from the Balkan region. Officers from the regiment were distributed in a similar fashion. By 1 July three were in Egypt, attached to the Regiment de Roll, Captain Clermont and Ensigns Anton Segesser and Aymar de Roquefeuil. Fox suggested that

129 *Army List*, 1807

130 TNA: WO 12/11735: Froberg paylist and WO 1/305: return of officers 21 June 1807. Watteville joined after the Froberg Regiment had been inspected on 9 March 1807 (TNA: WO 27/91).

131 Guy C. Dempsey, 'Mutiny at Malta, The Revolt of Froberg's Regiment April 1807', *Journal of the Society for Army Historical Research*, vol.67, no.269 (Spring 1989), pp.16–27.

132 TNA: WO 1/293: Villettes to Fox, 9 April 1807.

133 TNA: WO 1/305: Fox to Castlereagh, 1 July 1807.

134 TNA: WO 12/11735: Froberg paylist.

135 TNA: WO 97/1178/258: and WO 97/1178/414 invalid discharges.

Clermont, who was commended by the enquiry into the mutiny, could return to the Regiment de Roll.[136] However he and Roquefeuil were soon appointed to the Sicilian Regiment and it was only Segesser who joined the Regiment de Roll. He had not been part of the original Froberg cadre, but had been a private who had been promoted ensign on 9 May, by Fox, in recognition of his conduct during the mutiny.

The Regiment de Roll remained at Alexandria, on 1 August it was quartered in the 'Triangular Fort,' Qal'at al-Rukin, in the south-west corner of the old city walls, and this was to be the regiment's home for the rest of its stay in Egypt. On the same date a small detachment, Ensign Segesser, a sergeant, a corporal and seven privates, was posted as a guard at the cut in the Alexandria Canal.[137]

Developments elsewhere finally ended the Egyptian adventure of 1807. In London the Ministry of All the Talents had fallen and been replaced by a new administration, described as, 'all Pitt's friends, but without Pitt.'[138] On 14 June, in London, the order was given for Alexandria to be evacuated and the troops to return to Sicily. In addition, the premise for the expedition was soon over as the same day, 14 June, Napoleon crushed a Russian army at the Battle of Friedland that forced the Czar to make peace with France at Tilsit on 7 July so, as a result, Napoleon abandoned his alliance with the Ottoman Empire. The order arrived in Sicily on 9 July, accompanied by another recalling Fox on the grounds that he was not physically fit for an active command in the field and he was replaced by Moore.[139] However, the troops were to remain a little longer at Alexandria to allow a new British ambassador to the Porte to establish himself at Istanbul. It was only about 16 September that Fraser received the final instructions to quit Egypt and his troops evacuated Alexandria three days later.[140]

In anticipation of the evacuation, on 2 September, Major Francis Rivarola of the Sicilian Regiment, arrived at Cairo to negotiate the release of the prisoners and they were brought down the Nile by boat, arriving at Rashid on 17 September. In doing so they passed the El Hammad position, Gougelberg recalled, 'On our unfortunate battlefield, which we looked at with sorrow, a large number of Turkish tombs had been erected, the number of which permitted us to infer the equally great loss which we had inflicted on our enemy.'[141] At Rashid the men were taken to Missett's vacant house in the town where they were surrounded by guards and told that they would probably return to Cairo due to some disagreement about the terms of their release. Finally, late in the evening of 20 September, they were informed they would continue on their journey the next day and at Fort Julien they were met by Captain Steiger, sent by Fraser to accompany them on their way to Aboukir Bay. Gougelberg wrote,

---

136 TNA: WO 1/305: Fox to Castlereagh, 1 July 1807.
137 TNA: WO 17/803: Regimental returns.
138 Maurice, *Sir John Moore*, vol.II, p.169.
139 Maurice, *Sir John Moore*, vol.II, p.181.
140 Maurice, *Sir John Moore*, vol.II, p.194.
141 Gugelberg (ed.), *Bündners*, p.27.

… we continued our journey unhindered, … and only got to our transport ships at night, which we could only board with danger because of the high waves of the sea. Only now did we feel redeemed and saved and thanked God with a happy heart for liberation. The anchors were raised and the next morning we were embraced by friends who had long thought us lost and who now welcomed us as if resurrected.[142]

Six captains, three subalterns, 12 sergeants, four drummers and 199 rank and file of the Regiment de Roll returned. The last of the ships left Aboukir Bay on 25 September and the convoy reached Messina on 17 October 1807. The strength of the regiment, when it sailed from Egypt with the returned prisoners, was two field officers – Lieutenant Colonel Sonnenberg and Major Capol – nine captains, 14 subalterns, four staff, 45 sergeants, 22 drummers, 678 rank and file, 34 women and 22 children.[143] An unknown number of the British prisoners who had been enslaved remained behind but efforts continued to recover them and one, Private Metry Harpanin, returned to the Regiment de Roll the following year.[144] However others were never found.

---

142 Gugelberg (ed.), *Bündners*, p.28.
143 TNA: WO 1/304: Embarkation return Aboukir Bay 23 September 1807.
144 TNA: WO 12/11992: Paylist 1808.

7

'They would distinguish themselves'

1807

Following the Treaty of Tilsit, with no opposition in Central Europe, Napoleon was able to bring his ambitions to bear on Portugal and, in turn, Spain. The superficial aim was to force Portugal to join the Continental System which was designed to strangle British commerce. Napoleon's first act was to start to assemble an army corps, commanded by *Général de division* Jean-Andoche Junot, at Bayonne in July 1807. In response to the changing strategic situation, on 15 September Moore received orders from the British Government to sail with a force from Sicily to Gibraltar where he would receive further instructions. The orders specified the units that he was to take with him, amounting to 7,258 rank and file, and that he was to leave immediately the troops arrived from Alexandria. Thus Moore, and the troops, left Sicilian waters on 29 September and command of the British forces on the island devolved to Major General Sir John Sherbrooke.[1] In October 1807 Junot's troops began to cross the frontier into Spain, still France's ally, on their march to Portugal. On 28 November they began to enter Lisbon and the Portuguese royal family left for safety in Brazil. Moore arrived at Gibraltar on 1 December and, learning of the events in Portugal, he proceeded to England.[2]

The reduction in the British force on Sicily came at a time that the island was under increased threat. In compliance with secret clauses of the Treaty of Tilsit Russia not only evacuated the Ionian Islands and Kotor, on the coast of Montenegro, but also ensured they were handed over to French forces. The first notice of the handover came in a message from the British consul on Corfu that French troops were already on the island, that arrived at Messina on 25 August.[3] Napoleon now had almost complete control of the Adriatic Sea. Sherbrooke only had a British force of 10,335 rank and file so Moore, before leaving, had recommended its deployment at Syracuse (1,200),

---

1   Maurice, *Sir John Moore*, vol.II, pp.193–196.
2   Maurice, *Sir John Moore*, vol.II, pp.196–200.
3   Maurice, *Sir John Moore*, vol.II, p.193.

Augusta (about 1,000), in and around Messina (4,000 to 5,000) and with the remainder at Milazzo.[4] On its return from Egypt the Regiment de Roll was sent to Syracuse, arriving there on 19 October 1807.[5] Soon three of the regiment's companies, those of N. Müller, Barbier and Fuchs, were detached to Augusta under the command of Major Capol.[6] The regiment stayed at Syracuse and Augusta for the remainder of 1807 and into 1808, Gougelberg, for one, had pleasant memories of his time at Syracuse.[7]. Immediately after arriving Captain Albert Steiger was appointed Town Major at Syracuse, a post he held until September 1808 when he became aide de camp to Brigadier General Stewart and then, when Stewart left Sicily, to Brigadier General Frederick Charles White.

1808

Napoleon recognised the opportunity he had to capture Sicily and his first step was to reinforce Joseph's army with troops that could now be released from Central Europe. The French returned to Calabria and by 18 February 1808 Reggio and Scilla had fallen. The way was now open to the French to bring arms, ammunition and supplies along the coast to the eastern shore of the Straits of Messina for an invasion of Sicily. The British Government had recognised that it had left its forces on the island too weak to counter the threat and reinforcements arrived in the spring: 1,000 men drafted to the British infantry units, 500 artillerymen and four line battalions (3rd, 4th, 6th and 8th) of the King's German Legion, in addition the Watteville Regiment returned from Gibraltar and the Royal Regiment of Malta was sent from its island home.[8] Furthermore John Stuart returned as commander, having received among other recognition of his earlier victory, the title of Count of Maida as well as the local rank of lieutenant general. Unfortunately, he apparently returned anxious to avoid hazarding the laurels he had won at Maida on any risky ventures.

In the summer the Regiment de Roll left Syracuse and Augusta, as Gougelberg wrote, 'we moved into cantonment fifteen miles south of Messina. The area is bad and unhealthy; 7 officers, including myself, quartered in the same house, fell ill with malaria at the same time and even after recovery we were only able to regain our strength slowly. In mid-August we returned to Messina in garrison'.[9] The cantonment was at Scaletta Zanclea, about 20 kilometres south of Messina, the army's returns shows the regiment there on 1 July 1808 when sickness increased, despite the deployment only being about a month long.[10]

---

4   Maurice, *Sir John Moore*, vol.II, p.196.
5   TNA: WO 12/11991: Paylist 1807.
6   TNA: WO 17/803: Regimental returns.
7   Gugelberg (ed.), *Bündners*, pp.28–30.
8   TNA: WO 17/1933: Monthly returns, Sicily.
9   Gugelberg (ed.), *Bündners*, p.30. He gives the date as 18 June but the army return would indicate it was the following month.
10   TNA: WO 17/1933: Monthly returns, Sicily.

Table 12: Sickness among the rank and file of the Regiment de Roll, 1 May to 1 November 1808.[11]

First day of the month	Regiment's Location	Regiment's rank & file sick		Army in Sicily (all) – rank & file sick	
		In quarters	In hospital	In quarters	In hospital
May	Syracuse	16	44	258	1,067
June	Syracuse	23	46	538	1,265
July	Messina	0	38	495	1,450
August	Scaletta	15	42	500	1,626
September	Messina	28	64	599	1,616
October	Messina	11	103	261	1,855
November	Messina	20	66	165	1,547

During the brief stay at Scaletta Zanclea an incident occurred involving Captain Reinach. From the existing correspondence it is not clear what happened but it was sufficiently serious not only to have come to the attention of the army's adjutant general, James Campbell, but also to bring with it the prospect of a court martial. Reinach considered he had to resign and Lieutenant Colonel Sonnenberg informed Campbell, 'The unfortunate vivacity of his over hot head that took place on … [4 July] against Asst. Surgeon Herring, is the only cause for which he wishes to leave the service of His Majesty, & without a General Court Martial.'[12] With no other income and wishing to leave Sicily, Reinach requested a pension as he had a wife and child to support but on 22 July he offered his resignation and Sonnenberg commented that its acceptance would 'relieve the Regiment of many difficulties & grief in the future … I have to hope that this affair will be closed in this manner & you will no longer hear speak of it.'[13] Although a pension could not be provided Stuart seems to have had some sympathy for Reinach as he was soon appointed to the Calabrian Free Corps, in a position that equated to a captaincy, and in 1812 he obtained a British commission, albeit as ensign, in the Royal Corsican Rangers.[14]

Napoleon continued his attempt to dominate the Iberian peninsula by placing his brother Joseph on the throne at Madrid and replacing him at Naples with his flamboyant cavalry commander, and brother-in-law, Joachim Murat, who arrived in his capital on 6 September 1808. He immediately resolved to drive the British from Capri, just across the bay from Naples, which had been held since the Maida campaign. It was garrisoned by the Royal Corsican Rangers, a reincarnation of the earlier unit, under its lieutenant colonel commandant, Hudson Lowe who, in time, appears to have wanted to leave. As on 23 May 1808, with Stuart's arrival, Bunbury informed him, 'I hope to succeed in getting you relieved – probably by De Roll's'.[15] Stuart, however, kept Lowe, and his regiment, at Capri and in September he was joined by the Royal Regiment of Malta. On 4 October

11   TNA: WO 17/1933: Monthly returns, Sicily.
12   TNA: WO 31/1559: Sonnenberg to Campbell, Scaletta, 12 July 1808.
13   TNA: WO 31/1559: Sonnenberg to Campbell, Scaletta, 23 July 1808.
14   TNA: WO 25/748: Half pay officers' returns and *Army Lists*.
15   BL: Add MS 20190: Bunbury to Lowe, 23 May 1808.

Plate from a dinner service of the Regiment de Roll's officers' mess, with detail inset. (Historisches Museum, Basel inv. 1948.392, courtesy of Jean-Philippe Ganascia)

French, Italian and Neapolitan troops landed on the island, in the absence of the Royal Navy ship that guarded it, and by the following morning the western end of the island was taken and almost all of the Maltese defenders were prisoners. Lowe and his Corsicans continued to resist in Capri town, however, with no sign that a relieving force would arrive in time, he agreed a convention on 16 October by which he and all his troops could return to Sicily with their arms and equipment. The weather hampered the evacuation and it was only completed by 21 October and, in breach of the convention, inducements, threats and even violence were brought to bear on the Corsicans to desert, mainly by officers and men of the Neapolitan Regimento Real Corso (Royal Corsican Regiment), some of whom were relatives of those in British service. While the feat was celebrated by the French and their supporters, there was, to Lowe's disgust, official silence from the British. Bunbury, Lowe's friend, observed, 'the loss of so strong a post threw discredit on our arms, and awakened a distrust of our foreign corps.'[16]

Even while Lowe was holding out on Capri, Stuart complained to the Secretary of War about the number of foreign troops under his command,

> … there are besides five Regiments of Strangers the Men of which have been collected from every nation – and who having made Desertion in fact a Trade certainly cannot be considered as proof against Circumstance or Seduction – nor are they regarded by our Enemies or our Allies in an equal Scale of Respect with which they estimate the British Soldier.[17]

His attitude had changed from when he had commanded a brigade of such men in 1801 or even after Maida, perhaps coinciding with him exchanging the colonelcy of the 97th (Queen's German) Regiment for that of the 74th Highlanders on 8 September 1806. He did not specify the regiments he was describing but, having specifically excluded the King's German Legion battalions from his complaint, it seems they were the Regiment de Roll, Watteville and the Chasseurs Britanniques, along with Dillon and Meuron, which were on Malta at the time. However, the indiscriminate recruitment that had taken place under Fox's command meant that there were some grounds for Stuart's observation.

On 1 December Stuart complained about desertion from the foreign corps that 'in several Instances [had been] for the express purpose of joining the Enemy at their Posts distributed along the Shore of Calabria'. He continued,

---

16 Bunbury, *Narratives*, p.353.
17 TNA: WO 1/305: Stuart to Castlereagh, 6 October 1808.

The superior Comforts of these Soldiers enjoying the regular Payment and liberal Ration of Provisions as supplied by the British Government, with the other manifold advantages of our Service possesses in comparison with that of the Enemy, leaves little room to doubt that a fixed Disinclination and Disaffection is the Motive of these frequent Breaches of Trust, more particularly as whole Guards have gone off with their Arms – which renders it very questionable how far any of these Corps could in the event of a still more active campaign be entrusted to occupy the advanced Posts of the Army or placed in any other Situation of Confidence whereby the Security of the whole might be committed. …

In other respects it must be admitted that all these Corps are quiet, subordinate and exemplarily regular and orderly in their Conduct. In Justice also to their Commandants and every Class of Officers acting under them their habitual Attention to their Duties must be owned to be such as to merit particular and favourable Observation.[18]

Attached to his letter was a table showing the number of desertions from the foreign corps, on each month from January to November 1808. It showed the Regiment de Roll lost 29 men in the period: two in February, one in April, 13 in August, seven in October and six in November. In comparison the Chasseurs Britanniques lost 24, the 8th Battalion of the King's German Legion 21 and Watteville 16.[19] In addition some cases were described and one of these examples related to Roll,

…Within the last Fortnight a Corporal and four light infantry men of Roll's Regt. deserted from an out Picket on the Beach near Cape Rasocolmo – took with them their arms – seized a Boat and proceeded to join the Enemy in Calabria.[20]

Stuart may have overstated his concerns as they contrast with other decisions he took in the same period. One was to form an élite battalion by combining the light companies of his foreign regiments along with two others, one light and the other of grenadiers from the British units present. The formation of flank battalions, which Stuart had had when he was last in command on Sicily, had been mooted in March and some foreign light companies had been deployed independently in the summer.[21] On 9 November Brevet Lieutenant Colonel Victor Fischer, of Watteville, was appointed to command the 2nd (Foreign) Light Battalion, formed by the light companies of Roll, Watteville, Chasseurs Britanniques, Dillon and two of the King's German Legion battalions. The three flank battalions were to be a strategic reserve and the 2nd Light was first deployed to Castanea in the high ground above the Punta del Faro, the north-easterly point of the island.[22] This explains how Roll light infantrymen were at Capo Rasocolmo, which is immediately north of Castanea.

---

18   TNA: WO 1/306: Stuart to Castlereagh, 1 December 1808.
19   TNA: WO 1/306: Undated extract attached to Stuart to Castlereagh, 1 December 1808.
20   TNA: WO 1/306: Stuart to Castlereagh, 28 December 1808. The paylist (TNA: WO 12/11992) shows four privates deserting on 15 November and one the next day, but no corporals.
21   BL: Add MS 20190: Bunbury to Lowe, 29 March 1808, the Chasseurs Britanniques' light company was deployed independently from June (TNA: WO 12/11635).
22   Nichols, *Switzers*, pp.106–107.

The only cavalry Stuart had on Sicily was a detachment of the 20th Light Dragoons so he also turned to his foreign units to address this deficiency. On 5 September, the Regiment de Roll, Watteville, and Chasseurs Britanniques were ordered to each provide 15 men to serve with the light dragoons. The men were to remain on their regiment's strength but be paid the additional sum, due to cavalrymen, from central funds. The measure appears to have worked well as each regiment's contribution was raised to 20 men on 2 November, to form a troop of 60 men.[23] Stuart specified that the men should be German or Hungarian, however the troop's future sergeant major, Norbert Landsheit, later described them as 'the natives of almost every country under heaven' and the discharge records of three men supplied by the Regiment de Roll show them to have been Dutch, German and Polish.[24] The men were attached to the 20th Light Dragoons until 25 December 1809 when they formed the newly established Foreign Troop of Light Dragoons, which was also known as the Foreign Hussars.

On 25 November 1808 the Regiment de Roll's establishment was increased significantly. Since the end of 1807 there were supposed to have been 76 privates in each of the 10 companies and this was raised to 114. While the regimental staff and the number of drummers and fifers remained the same, the number of lieutenants, sergeants and corporals increased. The establishment now stood at one colonel, one lieutenant colonel, two majors, 10 captains, 22 (from 12) lieutenants, and eight ensigns. The staff consisted of a paymaster, an adjutant, a quartermaster, a surgeon, two assistant surgeons, a chaplain, and a judge advocate. The sergeants were made up of a sergeant major, a quartermaster sergeant, a paymaster sergeant, an armourer sergeant and 60 (from 40) sergeants serving with the companies. There were 20 drummers and two fifers, and the rank and file consisted of 60 (from 40) corporals and 1,140 privates.[25]

Ten lieutenants were appointed between 13 to 22 December 1808, four had been ensigns in the regiment and the rest were promoted from other units in the army – three from the King's German Legion, one each from the 60th Foot and Dillon and another was John Peter Sorgenfrey, a Dane who had been serving on the British staff in Portugal. This increase may, on the face of it, appear over optimistic, given that the Regiment de Roll in Sicily was already 136 rank and file short of its 1807 establishment at the end of 1808.

Events in the Iberian peninsula were to influence the Mediterranean theatre, indeed they would soon overshadow it, as Britain was more willing and able to intervene at scale in a theatre that was so much closer and more accessible than Sicily, Italy or the Adriatic. Resistance to Napoleon's invasions grew in Portugal and Spain and the Peninsular War, as it is known by the British, began. A small British expeditionary force commanded by Sir Arthur Wellesley landed in Portugal and defeated a French division at Roliça on 17

23   TNA: WO 1/307: Stuart to Castlereagh, 3 February 1809.
24   G.R. Gleig (ed.), *The Hussar* (London: Henry Colburn, 1837), vol.II, p.31 and TNA: WO 12/11993: Paylist 1809 and pension records of Willhelmstal (WO 97/1179/228), Landaur (WO 97/1180/8) and Bernesky (WO 97/1178/94).
25   TNA: WO 24/887: Estimates.

August 1808 and then, four days later, Junot at Vimeiro. By the Convention of Cintra (or Sintra), signed on 30 August, it was agreed that Junot and all of his army would be repatriated in British ships, taking their equipment and personal property with them. The terms of the convention, while not unprecedented, became a cause of political contention in Britain.

1809

Nevertheless, more proximate developments were to affect the Regiment de Roll on Sicily. A peace treaty was concluded with the Ottoman Empire thus, in May, Major Vogelsang returned. During his captivity his wife, Henriette, had been drawing just short of half of his salary from the regimental paymaster under her own signature, this unusual arrangement had been authorised by Sherbrooke in December 1807.[26]

Events in Central Europe came to the fore as Austria prepared to fight France once more. Although Southern Germany was to be the main theatre of operations there was also to be an offensive in Northern Italy. A senior officer in the Austrian service had met Stuart in March and an expedition from Sicily to the Italian coast was to co-ordinate with Austrian action but, as Bunbury, explained,

> Sir John Stuart … could not make up his mind. He dawdled and fretted in his quarters; issued no orders, nor even looked at the troops. The spirit of discontent and even of contempt … became every day more general and more mischievous in the army. And thus passed away in worse than idleness the important month of April. Then we were roused from our sulky languor by repeated salvoes from the cannon of Scilla and Reggio; and by the French accounts of their victories at Eckmuhl and Ratisbon [22 and 23 April 1809].[27]

The Regiment de Roll remained at Messina Citadel, with detachments at Forte Gonzaga on the landward side of the city and on 9 April the 2nd Light Battalion was ordered to move to Contesse, immediately south of Messina. Then, finally, in May, the expedition was organised at Milazzo, on the north coast. The only element of the regiment to go was the Light Company, in the 2nd Light Battalion that formed a brigade with the Royal Corsican Rangers and detachments of the Calabrian Free Corps in Major General Robert Macfarlane's Advance Corps.[28]

The battalion embarked on transports at Milazzo on 19 May. However, departure was delayed further, indeed five days later orders were issued that the troops on board were to be brought ashore every day for exercise.[29] Finally

---

26 TNA: WO 12/11993: Paylist 1809. She drew £33 for the first quarter of 1809 during which period Major Capol received £71-1-3.
27 Bunbury, *Narratives*, p.362.
28 TNA: WO 1/307: State dated 11 June 1809.
29 Bbliothek am Guisanplatz, Bern (BiG): Diary of Major General Louis de Watteville, 24 June 1809.

the fleet sailed on 11 June but light and adverse winds hindered progress and it was on 24 June that the fleet finally anchored off the island of Procida in the Gulf of Naples. A reconnaissance of the island and its larger neighbour, Ischia, found that the enemy's batteries appeared stronger than expected, nevertheless landings were to go ahead and orders were issued for three days' provisions to be cooked for the troops. After midnight the launches from the transports carrying the infantry of the first two brigades of the Advance Corps that were to land on Ischia assembled and HMS *Warrior* and *Success* with a flotilla of Sicilian and British gunboats prepared to engage the batteries. At daybreak the warships and gunboats commenced the attack on the batteries and Lieutenant Gougelberg, of the Roll Light Company, remembered,

> At four o'clock in the morning we arrived near the island; everything was put in order in the boats that rowed swiftly to shore. The French batteries opened a fierce fire, but our warships and gunboats answered so surely that the enemy had to abandon them and take refuge in the fort of Ischia. We landed at once, pursued the French on all sides, and took many prisoners, but without much bloodshed.[30]

As many of the fugitives scattered into the island, troops had to be sent after them, bringing in prisoners throughout the day, the Roll company getting to Casamicciola on the north coast of the island. However, in general, the main task for the officers was to prevent the soldiers from drinking too much of the local wine which was cheap and plentiful; unfortunately by the evening the whole of the 81st Foot were drunk.[31] Meanwhile the Grenadier Battalion secured Procida. That night heavy guns were landed on Ischia to commence the siege of the fort, that stood on a naturally strong position, and the riflemen that formed part of the King's German Legion Light Companies occupied a hill to harass the enemy's gunners. The rest of the 2nd Light Battalion marched to the south of the island to Testaccio (Barano d'Ischia) where it stayed for a few days before being sent to the force's headquarters, a mile outside Ischia town, to replace the 1st Light Battalion, due to the latter's indiscipline.[32] Once viable batteries had been completed on 30 June the commander of the fort surrendered. But news of an Austrian reverse at Wagram on 2 and 3 July and renewed activity of the French navy at Toulon persuaded Stuart to return to Sicily. The evacuation began on 23 July, the coastal batteries were blown up and the enemy's guns spiked and thrown into the sea. On 25 July the 2nd Light Battalion was one of the last units to embark and the fleet sailed the next day.

While Stuart had been making his way towards the Gulf of Naples, an attempt led by Lieutenant Colonel Haviland Smith had been made to destroy the enemy's posts on the Calabrian coast and capture Scilla. This failed and Smith withdrew to Messina on 20 June but, when the enemy had to send troops

---

30   Gugelberg (ed.), *Bündners*, p.32.
31   Gugelberg (ed.), *Bündners*, p.32, the regiment is given as the 87th but it was the 81st that was present.
32   Gugelberg (ed.), *Bündners*, p.32; Watteville described the headquarters as being at Bagni d'Ischia (BiG: Watteville Diary 29 June).

north in response to the threat posed to Naples by Stuart, they abandoned Scilla on 2 July, blowing up the works. It appears that a detachment of two or three companies were about to be sent to Calabria to exploit the enemy's retreat as Major Vogelsang, Captains Joseph Glutz and Lewis Steiger and five subalterns, are shown as having been embarked between 6 to 8 July, but the deployment did not take place.[33]

Stuart's expedition arrived off Milazzo late on 29 July and the troops disembarked except for both the light battalions, the Royal Corsican Rangers, 81st Foot and Watteville that remained on their transports, under Smith's command.[34] On 19 August the 15 transports, convoyed by the brig-sloop HMS *Delight* and six gunboats, set sail in light winds from Milazzo to make their way northward. As Gougelberg recalled, the flotilla cruised, 'from Calabria to Naples, making small landings here and there, destroying various enemy batteries and entrenchments, burning magazines and taking prisoners. It was very entertaining for us to keep the enemy on the move as they never knew where we were going to attack.'[35] The flotilla returned to Milazzo on 30 September with the advent of stormy weather and, after a fortnight's delay, the troops disembarked. The 2nd Light Company returned to the east coast of Sicily and were stationed over the winter between Messina and Taormina; the Roll Light Company at the latter town.

As the year, 1809, progressed the Regiment de Roll went through a transformation. On 31 May it was joined by 182 recruits, including seven sergeants, who arrived from Portugal under the command of Captain Augustus Curren, 3rd Line Battalion, King's German Legion. Then, on 25 November, 745 more, including 26 sergeants, arrived from England under the command of Major Charles Philip de Bosset, along with seven of the regiment's recently appointed subalterns.[36] The recruits of both detachments originated from Portugal the year before.

Among Junot's troops were a number of foreign units of the French army, including the 2e Bataillon of the 2e Régiment Suisse, almost 1,200 men, and the 1er Bataillon of the 4e Suisse, that had been reinforced by 308 men of the 2e Bataillon to bring it to a strength of 1,270 men.[37] At the time of the British landing, the 4e Suisse was sent from Almeida, where it left a depot of 200 men, to Peniche while the 2e Suisse remained at Elvas, where it had been since April 1808, but some of the battalions' flank companies served with Junot's field army.[38] The Convention of Cintra applied to Junot's garrisons, as well as the field army, and all were to embark at Lisbon except for those from Almeida who would be evacuated from Oporto. The troops were to be shipped in three divisions and the first started embarking on the

---

33 TNA: WO 12/11993: Stoppages for sea rations.

34 BiG: Watteville Diary, 6 August.

35 Gugelberg (ed.), *Bündners*, p.34.

36 TNA: WO 17/1933: Army return; WO 12/11993: Pay list.

37 Henri de Schaller, *Histoire des troupes suisses au service de France sous le règne de Napoléon 1er* (Lausanne; Payot, 1883), modern edition (Gollion: Infolio éditions, 2012), p.86.

38 Guy Dempsey, *Napoleon's Mercenaries: Foreign Units in the French Army under the Consulate and Empire, 1799–1814* (London: Greenhill Books, 2002), pp.281, 289.

15 September, those from the garrisons were to be included in the last.[39] In all 24,735 men, 215 women, 116 children and 759 horses were embarked on British transports and returned to France.[40]

Louis Bégos, an officer of the 2e Suisse, states that it was only after an order had arrived from Junot himself that the Elvas garrison, 1,400 strong of which almost 1,000 were Swiss, agreed to quit the fortress on 1 October.[41] The column arrived at Lisbon on 6 October and the following morning the men began to embark on the transports allocated for them. Bégos, a Napoleon loyalist, while describing how well the troops were treated by the British soldiers, complained of the poor conditions on the vessels. While some of this may be because he had not experienced conditions on a transport before it would indeed have been cramped as only five transports were allocated for the Elvas garrison on the, erroneous, basis that it was 1,000 strong.[42]

At this point the British commander, Lieutenant General Harry Burrard, was approached by a Swiss officer in British service,

> He stated, 'that they were his countrymen – that he had found means of discovering their political sentiments – and that, if authorized to form a corps of them, or to incorporate them in other Swiss regiments in the British service, he was certain he could overcome the many difficulties that were in the way of getting them on shore, where they could enlist into our service with propriety.'[43]

Burrard regarded the obstacles as significant but he 'authorized him to enlist as many of these foreigners (his countrymen) as he could, without breaking the articles of the Convention, or creating any disorder or confusion.'[44] The officer was Bosset, from Neuchâtel, who had been commissioned in the Regiment de Meuron in 1796 but had served in diplomatic and related roles, notably with Wickham in Switzerland in 1799. Promoted captain in the King's German Legion in 1803, he was posted to the 2nd Line Battalion and served with it through its various campaigns culminating in its arrival in Portugal in August 1808, just before the signing of the Convention of Cintra.

Bosset was not perhaps the first to recognise the chance to recruit from the Swiss soldiers in French service. According to one source, when the companies in the field army, the first to arrive at Lisbon, waited to embark sergeants from the Regiment de Roll went among them to try to persuade

---

39   Anon., *A History of the Campaigns of the British Forces in Spain and Portugal, undertaken to relieve those Countries from the French Usurpation; comprehending Memoirs of the Operations of this Interesting War, Characteristic Reports of the Spanish and Portuguese Troops, and Illustrative Anecdotes of Distinguished Military Conduct in Individuals, Whatever their Rank in the Army* (London: T. Goddard, 1812), vol.II, p.217.

40   Anon., *A History*, p.222 reproducing the return.

41   Louis Bégos, *Souvenirs des Campagnes du lieutenant-colonel Louis Bégos* (Lausanne: Libraire A. Delafontaine, 1859), pp.52–54.

42   Anon., *A History*, p.220.

43   Charles Philip de Bosset, *Parga and the Ionian Islands; comprehending a refutation of the various mis-statements on the subject: with a report of the trial between Lieut.-Gen. Sir Thos. Maitland, Lord High Commissioner, and the Author* (London; Rodwell and Martin, 1822,) p.133, reproducing Burrard's letter dated Horse Guards, 13 April 1809.

44   Bosset, *Parga*, p.133, Burrard's letter.

the soldiers to enlist in the British service. However according to *Lieutenant* David Braemy, 4e Suisse, 'they only persuaded a few bad subjects to enlist, whose departure was more desirable than regrettable'[45] – soldiers who had previously served in the British Army having warned their comrades of the strict discipline they would face. The delays in gathering the last of the French troops at Lisbon and then more, due to the weather, provided Bosset with better opportunities to induce men to desert. Bégos, naturally, objected to this activity and considered the delays and conditions on the transports as ploys to encourage recruitment. The flotilla of transports sailed with about 4,000 men in early December, but storms forced it to return to the Tagus after 12 days at sea. The ships needed repairs and it was only on 14 January 1809 that the transports sailed once more. Bégos wrote, 'At the moment of definitively leaving for France, we went on land; there all the means imaginable were employed to excite desertion ... Moreover, violence was employed towards our men, rather than persuasion.'[46] His bitterness is understandable as his battalion, excluding the grenadiers who had returned earlier, only had 315 men when it arrived in France.[47] The matriculation registers for the Swiss regiments, with brief personal records of the soldiers, follow a similar line to Bégos, recording many men as 'removed' or 'taken by force.'[48]

In all, over 910 men, mainly Swiss and German, enlisted in the British service at Lisbon through Bosset's efforts and they were assembled at Almada, on the south bank of the Tagus.[49] Meanwhile it appears Curren recruited at Oporto and two sergeants and 57 privates of his detachment have been identified in the register of the 4e Suisse, where they are shown as 'taken by force' at Oporto. However, others appear with other fates, including another of the sergeants, Xavier Einhardt, who was entered as having died on 16 October.[50] Several of Curren's recruits apparently came from other units, such as Private Judeus Vandamme, with a Dutch or Flemish name.[51]

Most of the men Bosset assembled at Almada were sent to England to be distributed to various foreign units in British service. In general the Germans, Dutch and Belgians went to the 60th Foot and King's German Legion and the French and Italians to the Chasseurs Britanniques, while all the Swiss were allocated to the Regiment de Roll on 25 December 1808.[52] They were sent to Portchester Castle, at the head of Portsmouth Harbour, under the command

45   Albert Maag, *Geschichte der Schweizertruppen im Kriege Napoleon I in Spanien und Portugal (1807–1814)* (Biel: Ernst Kuhn, 1892), vol.I, p.486. Although three sergeants were recruiting in the period, location not shown, Braemy's account may be apocryphal given Bosset's subsequent mission.

46   Bégos, *Souvenirs*, p.57.

47   Bégos, *Souvenirs*, p.62.

48   Service historique de la Défense, Vincennes (SHD): GR 23 Yc 170: 2e Suisse and GR 23 Yc 177: 4e Suisse.

49   Bosset, *Parga*, p.133, Burrard's letter gives the number of men as 913 and a return from the Adjutant General's Office of 24 April 1809 gives number of recruits as 916 (*Reports also accounts and papers* (London: House of Commons, 1809), vol.IX, p.164).

50   SHD: GR 23 Yc 177: 4e Suisse.

51   TNA: WO 12/11993: Paylists 1809.

52   TNA: WO 25/669: Foreign Description and Succession Book 1806–1809.

Portchester Castle, near
Portsmouth. (Author's photo)

of Bosset who was appointed supernumerary major in the Regiment de Roll on 15 October 1808.[53] Of the 26 sergeants in Bosset's detachment, 20 are identified as having been in the Swiss regiments in Portugal, 18 'removed by force' from the 2e Suisse at embarkation, another by the same means from the 4e Suisse and one, Christian Stuntz, had deserted from the 4e Suisse on 4 September 1808. The provenance of five of the sergeants is unknown while another transferred from the King's German Legion in England. Of the 40 corporals and 470 privates in the detachment, 227 have been identified as 'taken' from the 2e Suisse and 23 from the 4e Suisse. It should be noted that a further 166 from the 2e and 51 from the 4e Suisse were recorded as 'taken' but have not been matched with names listed in either Bosset's or Curren's detachment.[54]

At Portchester Castle Bosset oversaw the training of the men and they were inspected by Major General Arthur Whetham, Lieutenant Governor at Portsmouth, who described them to the Baron de Roll in a letter of 9 July 1809,

> The men are young, stout, and healthy; they were perfectly steady, and went through all the most useful manoeuvres, according to his Majesty's regulations, with promptitude and precision. … Major de Bosset … has made the detachment perfectly fit for actual service; and I am convinced, that, either with the body of the regiment or separately as a detached corps, they would distinguish themselves …[55]

On 2 September 1809 the detachment boarded three transports for the voyage to Sicily, the embarkation return shows that on the *William* were six sergeants and 209 rank and file with Bosset, Lieutenant Michael Krumm and Ensign Charles Pannach, along with Captain Frederick Matthey (Meuron)

53   TNA: WO 12/11993: Paylist 1809.
54   SHD: GR 23 Yc 170 and GR 23 Yc 177; TNA: WO 12/11993: Paylists 1809.
55   Bosset, *Parga*, p.134, Whetham to Roll, 9 July 1809.

and Assistant Surgeon Augustus Stromeyer (Watteville). On the *Mathilda* were 12 sergeants and 368 rank and file with Lieutenant Sorgenfrey and Ensigns George Peter Maule and Maximilian d'Escher; on transport *No.99* there were three sergeants and 112 rank and file with Lieutenant Hector de Salis and Ensign Conrad Christian Holl.[56]

Bosset brought a further 47 men with him from Portsmouth, apparently recruited at the very last moment as they were only approved, the last stage of enlistment, once they had arrived in Sicily.[57] These men would appear to have been among the prisoners of war held at Portsmouth or Portchester Castle and it seems, from their names, that not all of them were Swiss.

The augmentation had a profound effect on the regiment. On 1 May 1809 it had had a total of 655 rank and file and on 25 December it had 1,507. It was now significantly larger than any other British Army unit in Sicily, the next infantry battalion in size being the 1/44th Foot with 1,042 rank and file.[58] Perhaps even more significantly it returned the regiment to something like its original composition with a large proportion of the soldiers being Swiss. Indiscriminate recruiting, notably among deserters from the French and prisoners found in the Mediterranean, had caused the regiment to become little different in personnel from other foreign regiments serving there, such as the Chasseurs Britanniques, Watteville and Dillon. The regiment's size and its more homogenous composition appear to have changed the way the regiment was to be regarded and deployed, with companies, singly or in small detachments detached to provide a reliable element in garrisons or to strengthen units.

1810

Another expedition had left from Sicily in 1809, commanded by Brigadier General John Oswald it sailed from Messina on 23 September to capture the Ionian Islands, with the exception of the largest, Corfu, which was too strongly defended. Vice Admiral Cuthbert Collingwood, the naval commander in the Mediterranean, had pressed for this to happen for a number of reasons including to provide safe anchorages for his ships that were operating in the Adriatic. Oswald had about 1,800 men from the 1/35th Foot, Royal Corsican Rangers, and a detachment from the 1/44th Foot, along with supporting arms.[59] With the active co-operation of the Royal Navy, Zakynthos (Zante) was taken on 2 October. Two days later, as the British ships approached Kefalonia, the garrison evacuated Argostoli, the capital, and withdrew to the Castle of Agios Georgios (Saint George) eight kilometres to the south-east, where they surrendered promptly after the first summons.

---

56 TNA: WO 27/93: Embarkation returns. It is recognised that the numbers in this return are lower than those shown in the pay list and army return, furthermore Lieutenant Frederick Baring is shown as being on the *Mathilda* but he did not sail (TNA: WO 2/55 and 56: Correspondence).
57 TNA: WO 12/11993: Paylist (recruitment account).
58 TNA: WO 17/1933: Sicily returns.
59 TNA: WO 1/307: Embarkation return 22 September 1809.

Detail of officer's gorget – gilt, engraved with crowned GR royal cypher surrounded by a laurel wreath and suspended on celestial blue ribbons. (Item 4827 B, Musée de l'Empéri, dépôt du Musée de l'Armée, Centre de documentation du Musée de l'Empéri, courtesy of Jérôme Croyet)

Ithaca was taken on 8 October followed by the most southerly, Kythira (then known as Cerigo), on 12 October after some resistance.[60] Significant proportions of the enemy's garrisons were men of the Régiment Albanais, principally formed from Souliots and other refugees from the mainland who had fled the attacks of Ali Pasha, the local Ottoman viceroy, many of whom immediately volunteered to join the British which Stuart authorised in a letter of 23 October 1809.[61] Captain Richard Church, with other officers of the Royal Corsican Rangers, formed these men in what was to be called the Greek Light Infantry.

On 17 January 1810 Major de Bosset embarked with two companies of the Regiment de Roll for Zakynthos to join the British forces on the islands. The companies were those of Henry Ryhiner (No. 4) and Barbier (No. 6), along with both captains, there were four lieutenants, two ensigns, Assistant Surgeon John Herring, 11 sergeants, three drummers, 13 corporals and 250

---

60   *The London Gazette*, 2 and 5 December 1810.

61   TNA: WO 1/307: Stuart to Oswald, 23 October 1809. Such a transition was not unprecedented as the Régiment Albanais had been formed from a unit in Russian service before 1807.

privates.[62] They sailed in company with 300 men of the Calabrian Free Corps and replaced the detachment of the 44th Foot.[63]

Meanwhile the Regiment de Roll's Light Company remained at Taormina and the rest of the unit was at Messina, but supplying detachments to various duties. On 25 January Lieutenant Auguste de Courten, a drummer, a corporal and 13 privates were at Forte Gonzaga; a sergeant, a corporal and 17 privates were stationed at the tower, or lighthouse, on the Faro point; a sergeant and nine privates were in 'public employ'; a corporal and eight privates served on the Army Flotilla, gunboats principally operating in the Straits of Messina with Sicilian sailors and British soldiers and gunners; and five privates 'with the Garrison Company.'[64] This last unit had been formed for foreign soldiers who were unfit for active duty but could perform sedentary duties and so were retained in service as they could not be returned home, due to Napoleon's hegemony in Europe. It would appear that soldiers of the regiment were exposed to tuberculosis at the time, as of the eight men who died between 25 December 1809 and 24 April 1810 six were shown as having been 'consumptive.'[65]

The next island Oswald planned to seize was Lefkada (know by the British by its former Venetian name of Santa Maura). He gathered a force at Zakynthos with elements from the 35th Foot, Royal Corsican Rangers, Greek Light Infantry and 'a Battalion of Detachments, consisting of Two Companies of the Royal Marines … Two Companies of the Roll's under Major de Bosset, and Two Companies Calabrian Free Corps under Major [Robert] Oswald.'[66] The battalion was commanded by Major Charles William Clarke of the 35th Foot. The force sailed from Zakynthos early in the morning of 21 March and arrived off Lefkada that evening.[67] The troops began to disembark at daybreak to the south of the town of Lefkada and the defenders soon abandoned their coastal batteries on the appearance of the warships and gunboats that had accompanied the expedition. The Corsicans Rangers led the advance with the Greek Light Infantry on the flank, the latter driving some of the Régiment Albanais from the nearby heights. The French garrison abandoned Lefkada town and withdrew to the Fortress of Agias Mavras (Santa Maura), which stands astride the spit connecting the island with the mainland, Oswald described it thus,

> The Fortress of St. Maura is situated upon a narrow sandy Isthmus, of Three Miles in length, which joins it to the island, and it has, besides, a direct Communication with the Town by a singularly narrow Causeway, nearly a Mile in Length. The Neck of Land is defended by Two strong Redoubts and an Intrenchment regularly

---

62   TNA: WO 17/803: Return for 25 January 1810 where they were noted as 'Embarked for the island of Zante.' The paylist, WO 12/11994, indicates they were present on the muster of the same date.

63   TNA: WO 1/308: Stuart to Liverpool, 11 February 1810; WO 17/1934: Monthly returns; WO 31/1563: Memo of Joseph Barbier on 5 December 1815.

64   TNA: WO 17/803: 25 January 1810.

65   TNA: WO 25/2291: Regimental casualty record, afterwards the recording of the cause of death fell into disuse.

66   *The London Gazette*, 19 June 1810, Oswald to Stuart, 24 March 1810.

67   *The London Gazette*, 31 July 1810, George Eyre to Charles Cotton, 18 April 1810.

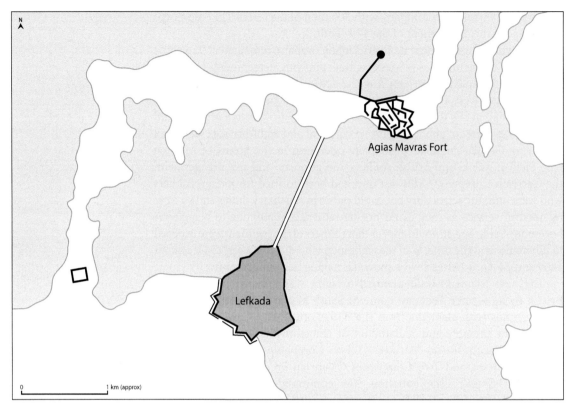

Agias Mavras Fort

Lefkada

0   1 km (approx)

Lefkada.

constructed, and capable of such a Resistance as led the Enemy to declare they would arrest our Progress for a Month at least.[68]

Leaving troops in the town, Oswald went onto the spit where he found Church had already taken the outermost redoubt, armed with two guns, with four of his Greek Light Infantry companies and saw the enemy falling back to the next entrenchments which were being strengthened. Due to their earlier good conduct, Oswald entrusted the attack on the next position to the Greeks and brought the Battalion of Detachments from the town as their support. The position extended across the spit and was 'mounted with Four Pieces of Cannon well flanked; had a wet Ditch and Abattis in Front; manned by about Five Hundred Infantry; and was so defiled from the Sea as to render it almost secure from the Fire of the Shipping.'[69] The troops advancing in columns were initially screened by the lie of the terrain, however as soon as they approached the position they came under 'a heavy and well directed Fire of Grape and Musquetry.'[70] The Greeks threw themselves to the ground and Church and his officers could not get them to push on with the speed and dash that was required.[71] So Major Clarke with his

68   *The London Gazette*, 19 June 1810, Oswald to Stuart, 24 March 1810.
69   *The London Gazette*, 19 June 1810, Oswald to Stuart, 24 March 1810.
70   *The London Gazette*, 19 June 1810, Oswald to Stuart, 24 March 1810.
71   This behaviour drew criticism, even derision, from British officers, Captain John Slessor, although not a witness, noting, 'The Albanians in our service behaved badly, the rascals.' (Hayter (ed.), *The Backbone*, p.233). Nevertheless, Oswald was more generous describing it

battalion was directed to drive through with the attack, with the marines at their head.

> The Royal Marines … broke through the Abattis and charged into the Intrenchments; they were nobly supported by the Roll's, under Major Bosset; … [the Calabrian Free Corps followed]. The Contest was not of long Duration; the Enemy fled at all Points, pursued with the Bayonet from Work to Work; and such was his Precipitation that he not only abandoned the Camp and Cannon of the attacked Line, but left his remaining strong Position, followed by Major Clarke's Command even to the Gates of the Fortress.[72]

The attack had been supported by the riflemen and two companies of the Royal Corsican Rangers with one from the 35th Foot that advanced along the narrow and exposed causeway, on the other side of the lagoon. According to Oswald's despatch the casualties incurred in the attacks on the outworks were one officer and 12 rank and file killed, 16 officers and 78 other ranks wounded and 17 rank and file missing. The Regiment de Roll had a sergeant and eight rank and file wounded.[73] The fortress was strong, due to its site and design, and was defended by about 1,000 men, Oswald needed reinforcements and additional supplies. Stuart received Oswald's request for assistance on 30 March and responded rapidly, 'in the course of the following day six flank companies of the Foreign Regiments belonging to the Army together with a Detachment of Artillery and a supply of Ordnance Stores … embarked and sailed'.[74] The reinforcements were commanded by Lieutenant Colonel Fischer and were 645 men from four companies of the 2nd Light Battalion (those of Roll, Watteville, Chasseurs Britanniques and Dillon), the Grenadier Companies of Roll and the Chasseurs Britanniques and 40 men of the Royal Artillery. Gougelberg sailed with the Roll Light Company, now commanded by Captain Nicholas Müller, while the regiment's Grenadiers Company was commanded by Lieutenant Charles de Sury, its captain, Albert Steiger, being on staff duties.

The vessels from Sicily reached Zakynthos on 4 April and continued their voyage two days later, after briefly anchoring at Ithaca due to strong winds, arriving off Lefkada on 7 April.[75] In the meantime naval guns had been landed and placed in batteries which began firing on the fortress in the morning of 8 April.[76] The same day the Roll flank companies disembarked and camped above their landing place, it was on 11 April that they marched to Lefkada town. Gougelberg described their duties when they got there,

as 'their accustomed and in many Situations appropriate Mode of Fighting' by which he meant skirmishing (24 March 1810).

72 *The London Gazette*, 19 June 1810, Oswald to Stuart, 24 March 1810.
73 *The London Gazette*, 19 June 1810, Oswald to Stuart, 24 March 1810. The missing were riflemen of the Royal Corsican Rangers who had been driven by the enemy's fire from the causeway into the water.
74 TNA: WO 1/308: Stuart to Liverpool, 24 April 1810.
75 Gugelberg (ed.), *Bündners*, p.35.
76 *The London Gazette*, 31 July 1810, George Eyre to Charles Cotton, 18 April 1810.

Our service was very difficult. We had to open trenches, build new batteries with sandbags, haul in ammunition, mortars and cannons and at the same time man the picquets in the trenches and outposts, all of which was very dangerous since the fort is built on a promontory, in several places barely a pistol shot wide, so we had to get very close to the enemy guns. But most of the work was done at night and we did not lose many men.[77]

At noon on 15 April the Roll Light Company received the order to assemble, after sunset, by the British approach battery in light order, without their knapsacks but with their water canteens. They were to join an attack to clear the enemy from an entrenchment less than 300 metres from the fort's rampart so that a site for a breaching battery could be surveyed. The troops were commanded by Lieutenant Colonel Lorenzo Moore, 35th Foot, who 'encouraged the men to be brave and gave the necessary orders.'[78] The men were not to load their muskets but to attack with the bayonet. The Roll Light Company was on the left flank of the spit, detachments of Corsican riflemen and marines in the centre and the 35th's Grenadier Company was on the right flank. In his report Oswald described the action, 'The Corps pushing undauntedly through a heavy Fire of Grape and Musquetry, carried the Enemy's Line at the Point of the Bayonet.'[79] Gougelberg adds some further detail of the advance,

After a short while the French started firing at close range and canister shots killed some men and smashed the guns of others. Immediately we formed line, ran forward with shouts of hurrah, bayonets toward the enemy, and drove them into the fortress, which then fired at us heavily with artillery and small-arms fire, but without harming us much, since we were too close to the fort for the cannons and the trenches that had been thrown up covered us from small-arms fire.[80]

As the position could be held, Moore was ordered to stay put, and entrenchment tools were brought forward, along with grog and bread for the men. As Oswald wrote, 'by incessant and judicious Labour during the Night, the Intrenchment was converted into a second Parallel, from whence the Fire of the Enemy, however severe, could not dislodge it.'[81] Meanwhile the British artillery maintained a heavy bombardment. Gougelberg who, with 40 men, had been ordered even closer to the rampart described some of the bombs falling short and bursting near his position, but with no harm due to the parapet they had constructed.[82]

---

77   Gugelberg (ed.), *Bündners*, pp.35–36. Gougelberg states the village they had stayed at, and by implication, had disembarked was named 'Irine.' It has not been identified but Eyre states that he had had to send the transports with the initial expedition to 'a Port Six or Seven Miles' away from Lefkada town (18 April 1810).
78   Gugelberg (ed.), *Bündners*, p.36.
79   *The London Gazette*, 19 June 1810, Oswald to Stuart, 17 April 1810.
80   Gugelberg (ed.), *Bündners*, p.36.
81   *The London Gazette*, 19 June 1810, Oswald to Stuart, 17 April 1810.
82   Gugelberg (ed.), *Bündners*, p.37.

The following day the French garrison surrendered. The casualties among Moore's troops in the evening's attack were comparatively light, one sergeant and two rank and file had been killed and a further seven wounded, two of whom were from the Regiment de Roll. One of these, Corporal John Eykhold, who was Flemish, was to die of his wounds on 25 July.[83] Under the capitulation, the men of the garrison were to be taken to Malta as prisoners of war while their officers were to be landed at Ancona in Italy and released on parole. That evening the grenadiers of the 35th Foot were sent into the fort to guard the gates. On 17 April the French garrison began boarding transports with their wounded to follow the next day. Roll's Light Company and the grenadiers of the Chasseurs Britanniques had relieved those of the 35th and had to camp within the fort as all the dwellings had been rendered uninhabitable by the British bombardment and the casemates were full of the French wounded.[84] After the batteries had been dismantled and the artillery taken on board, the troops embarked on 25 April and sailed the following day, leaving Lowe and the Royal Corsican Rangers in garrison at Lefkada. The convoy reached Zakynthos on 27 April and the troops landed before those who had been sent as reinforcements sailed for Sicily on 1 May, arriving at Messina on 8 May.

The officers and soldiers from the Regiment de Roll who took part in the expedition were entitled to the prize money raised from the public property that had been captured. The distribution was according to the class apportioned by their rank and made in two parts, the first in 1815. For the regiment the captains, being in the third class, received £5-8-6, the subalterns (including Sury) £2-16-10, the sergeants £1-8-10 and the other ranks, in the final sixth class, four shillings and two pence in each instalment.[85]

The regiment's Grenadier Company joined its headquarters at Milazzo, it having left Messina in March. The 2nd Light Battalion, on the other hand, had a different destination, Enna, then called Castro Giovanni, which, due to its naturally strong position, had been identified by the British, as early as 1806, as a secondary defensive position should an enemy gain a foothold on the coast. The battalion marched along the coast to Taormina, had two days' rest and continued south to Catania where it turned inland to its destination; its heavy equipment, meanwhile, was brought to Augusta by gunboats and placed in storage.[86]

Austria's defeat had allowed Murat to renew his plans to seize Sicily and during the spring and early summer he began to assemble troops and material in Lower Calabria. Napoleon, on the other hand, seems to have had an equivocal attitude to the plans but he recognised that the mere threat to Sicily prevented British troops being deployed elsewhere, indeed Stuart refused to release troops to Spain and Portugal for this very reason.[87] He had 16,000

83   TNA: WO 25/2291: Regimental casualty register.
84   Gugelberg (ed.), *Bündners*, pp.37–38.
85   TNA: WO 164/217 and 164/547: Prize money registers.
86   Gugelberg (ed.), *Bündners*, p.38.
87   Desmond Gregory, *Sicily, the Insecure Base: A History of the British Occupation of Sicily, 1806–1815* (London and Toronto: Associated University Presses, 1988), pp.85–86.

Johann Conrad Müller (1770–1833) adjutant of the Regiment de Roll from 1804 (ensign 1804 and lieutenant 1807); he is shown wearing the Sultan's Medal, issued only to officers, despite having served in the 1801 campaign as sergeant major of the regiment. (Historisches Museum, Basel inv. 1966.2, courtesy of Jean-Philippe Ganascia)

men in the north east of Sicily stationed between Milazzo, through Messina, to Taormina and by mid-July Murat had gathered about 25,000 men on the opposite coast, with 500 or so boats to carry them across the straits. The British troops were brought to the highest state of readiness and, despite obstruction from the court at Palermo, local people willingly assisted in the construction of coastal defences. Raids were sent from Sicily to destroy the enemy's boats while Murat's forces made several feints simulating the start of an attack that led inevitably to false alarms. Adjustments were made to the British dispositions so they could react to a landing. In July the Regiment de Roll left Milazzo and was stationed on the heights above the village of Curcuraci, at a place to be known as Campo Inglese near which fortifications were built later in the nineteenth century. This position gave commanding views over the Faro point and its surrounding area as well as across to the Calabrian coast opposite. A German soldier who was stationed in the same 'large barracks' in 1812 recalled,

In front of us we had a most delightful view of the channel of Messina, of Reggio and Scylla; the whole of Calabria lay before us; farther to the left we beheld Italy and the Island of Lipari; to the right was the valley of Messina, and the harbour, and the stupendous Mount Etna, with its top covered with eternal snow. … in short, the prospect was so rich and varied that we were never weary of gazing on it. The surrounding vineyards were frequently visited by us, and figs and other delicious fruits were here in abundance.[88]

The 2nd Light Battalion moved from Enna and, by mid-July, was stationed on the coast south of Messina at the Benedictine monastery of San Placido Calonèro at Briga Marina.[89] Gougelberg remembered, 'Here we were almost daily spectators of the skirmishes of our warships with the French.' The troops stood to every morning before daybreak.[90]

A real attack finally took place in the early hours of 18 September. About 3,000 Neapolitan troops had embarked at Reggio in 60 or so sloops the evening before, commanded by Jacques-Marie Cavaignac, a general in Murat's service. The first notice the British had of their approach was

---

88   Johann Christian Maempel, *Adventures of a Young Rifleman: the Experiences of a Saxon in the French & British Armies During the Napoleonic Wars* (Driffield: Leonaur Ltd., 2008), pp.170–171.

89   TNA: WO 12/12027: Watteville pay list 1810 and BiG: Watteville Diary.

90   Gugelberg (ed.), *Bündners*, p.41.

when one of the sloops fired upon a cavalry picquet at Santo Stefano. The Neapolitan troops came ashore between Santo Stefano and Galati Marina and immediately climbed onto a ridge, which was covered by a vineyard, above the beach. In response to the alarm, to the north, the 21st Foot and the 3rd Battalion, King's German Legion, along with two guns, took up a position around Mili. To the south, the 2nd Light Battalion had been turned out, and could see the progress of the attack by the fire of the British picquets, including that of the Regiment de Roll commanded by Lieutenant Stephen Planta, as they retired before the enemy. Fischer immediately sent the Dillon and Chasseurs Britanniques companies into the mountains to prevent the enemy advancing further inland and Lieutenant Frederick de Rousillion, with a patrol, to reconnoitre the enemy. Captain Müller advanced with part of the Roll company to fall on the enemy's flank, while, as Gougelberg recalled, 'Colonel Fischer with the Watteville Company and part of ours, which I commanded, stood ready at the foot of the mountains to receive the enemy.'[91]

Major General Campbell had been informed of the attack at 4.15 a.m. and immediately went to Mili. As he approached the village he heard the exchange of fire between the advanced positions. As dawn broke Campbell could see that the enemy were still landing and making their way onto the ridge above. Then he saw a change,

> I observed not only a Hesitation and Period to his further Advance upon the Heights, but that he was actually hastily re-embarking his Troops nearest the Beach, occasioned, I have no Doubt by the spirited and unexpected Manner in which he was brought to Action by the 2nd Light Infantry, under Lieutenant-Colonel Fischer, which, moving from its Cantonments of St. Placido, hung upon his Rear and Left.[92]

Campbell then ordered the troops at Mili to advance along the coastal road and the enemy's retreat descended into flight. As the boats hastened to put to sea and pull from the shore, troops were abandoned on the beach including the rear guard, a battalion of the Regimento Real Corso. As the defenders, including Planta's and Rousillion's detachments, pressed forward the Corsicans had no option but surrender. About 800 men, including a number of staff officers, were taken prisoner and others, who tried to slip away, were brought in by 'the Peasantry of the Country, who, with Arms, and every other Weapon of Offence they could collect, flocked to our immediate Assistance.'[93] Indeed some sought sanctuary with the British troops in fear of being massacred by the Sicilians. The British casualties were light, and none are shown for the 2nd Light Battalion. Lieutenant Planta, the first onto the ridge, discovered a Neapolitan flag that had been hastily buried in the vineyard where the Corsicans had surrendered.[94]

---

91   Gugelberg (ed.), *Bündners*, p.42.
92   *The London Gazette*, 20 November 1810, Campbell to Stuart, 18 September 1810.
93   *The London Gazette*, 20 November 1810, Campbell to Stuart, 18 September 1810.
94   Gugelberg (ed.), *Bündners*, p.42.

Meanwhile the main body of the enemy's troops, opposite the Faro, had embarked and were seen to leave the Calabrian shore, the landing south of Messina appeared to have been simply an attack on the flank. However, what would have been the main thrust did not materialise. The French commanders, receiving their instructions directly from Napoleon, decided they would not commit to the attack and their troops returned to shore. Murat considered himself betrayed and wanted nothing more to do with the venture despite Napoleon wanting the threat to Sicily to be maintained, but paid for by the Neapolitan treasury. Boats began to quit the Calabrian coast on 28 September and by 1 October almost all had left, and the shore batteries had been dismantled. The proportion of the British forces in Sicily involved in the action of 18 September had been very small, however Stuart in his despatch to London wanted the efforts of the whole to be recognised,

> … every Department and Rank of this Army, during a long Period of Four Months, in which the Contiguity and constant Menaces of an enterprising Enemy have demanded from us a System of unabating Vigilance, to which every Mind has submitted with Cheerfulness, but which your Lordship will believe has not been without its Fatigue.[95]

With the reduced threat, the Regiment de Roll returned to Milazzo from the Curcuraci Heights by 25 October.[96] However the 2nd Light Battalion remained where it was, on the coast south of Messina, until April 1811.[97] Stuart's refusal to release units to the Spanish theatre had been vindicated in the short term, however the British Government were determined that they would go. Dissatisfied with the decision, and the reduced command that would be the result, Stuart offered his resignation on 16 October, soon leaving for Malta to await its acceptance.

In November 1810 there were a series of courts martial involving officers of the Regiment de Roll which were the culmination of events that had begun over 12 months before. On the face of it they do not cast the regiment's cadre in the best light, however it is likely that a continued desire to retain justice and related matters within the regiment, rather than have them dealt with by external authorities, lay at their heart. Some of the events are unclear but what can be inferred is that they began when Captain Fuchs acted as spokesman for the officers over the funding of the regimental band. The band was paid for by subscriptions raised from the officers and as there was already £400 in the fund, held by Lieutenant Colonel Sonnenberg, the officers considered that their payments should be reduced. Considering he had an amicable relationship with Sonnenberg, Fuchs raised the issue with him and the officers' contributions were reduced by a half. However, this seems to have soured the relationship between the two men and led to Fuchs feeling he was being treated unfairly especially when, in October 1809, Sonnenberg ordered him to quit his lodging in Messina. Fuchs appealed to Brigadier

---

95   *The London Gazette*, 20 November 1810, Stuart to Liverpool, 22 September 1810.
96   TNA: WO 17/803: Monthly returns.
97   Gugelberg (ed.), *Bündners*, p.42.

General White, the commandant, who rescinded it. This not only widened the gulf between the two but also between Fuchs and his fellow officers who refused to associate with him. This reaction indicates they considered Fuchs had broken an expected code of behaviour.

The quarrel, if this is what it was, was taken up by the lieutenant colonel's nephew, James, who, after threatening to do so, severely wounded Fuchs's dog. When the latter confronted him about it, Sonnenberg took exception to the language used and so demanded satisfaction from Fuchs in a duel. Feeling that he had no honourable option but to take up the challenge, Fuchs sought a second but all his fellow officers refused, even after he had made a request in a general letter, finally he managed to get the recent arrival, Ensign Richard Wall, to take the role. The officers fought their duel when shots were exchanged and the seconds declared that Sonnenberg had received ample satisfaction, nevertheless the latter immediately wanted a further duel but this did not happen, apparently after Wall informed Fuchs that he could not risk associating with him any further. Lieutenant Colonel Sonnenberg called a meeting of the regiment's officers, Fuchs was not informed and he and Lieutenant Sonnenberg were not present. At the meeting the commanding officer stated that Fuchs had refused to give his nephew satisfaction, Fuchs's position was not represented. The lieutenant colonel asked if the matter should be settled within the regiment or referred to White, the officers agreed to the latter course. One of White's first actions was to put both officers under arrest for duelling but, after Stuart felt that no further action should be taken, he simply reprimanded them both. Fuchs was then ostracised by his comrades as witnessed by British officers in the garrison and White continued, unsuccessfully, to bring the situation to a close.

In February 1810 Fuchs took leave to go to England and sailed on the transport, *Flora*. At the same time Lieutenant Sonnenberg, also on leave, sailed on another transport, *Perseverance*, along with Lieutenant Holl who had been 'sent out of the Regiment de Roll for dishonourable conduct.'[98] On the voyage, young Sonnenberg not only associated with Holl but brought him into the society of other officers who were passengers and was 'privy to and an Accomplice in several acts of Atrocity' by Holl.[99] What these were is not specified but Sonnenberg was to write a letter admitting, at the least, knowledge of Holl's threats to commit them.[100] Both Fuchs and young Sonnenberg returned to Sicily on the troopship, HMS *Leyden*, and this voyage, between 8 September and 12 October, brought things to a head.

On 9 November a court martial sat at which Fuchs faced a variety of accusations laid by Lieutenant Sonnenberg. After four days of evidence, Fuchs was acquitted, the court having found the allegations made against him, 'groundless, frivolous, vexatious, and malicious.'[101] Three days later Fuchs was again in court, now facing charges brought by the senior Sonnenberg.

98 TNA: WO 91/3: Record of Commander-in-Chief's decisions on courts martial.
99 TNA: WO 91/3: Record.
100 TNA: WO 71/222: Trial of Captain Fuchs, 9 to 12 November 1810, copy of letter from Lieutenant Sonnenberg dated 15 April 1810.
101 TNA: WO 71/222: Trial of Captain Fuchs, 9 to 12 November 1810.

These related to written complaints he had made to senior officers, in which he had reported that Sonnenberg had supported the officers in refusing to do duty with him and had made 'cruel and unjust assertions towards his [Fuchs's] person.'[102] The court found him not guilty of the first charge but guilty of the second but, given his treatment by the officers of the regiment and his previous service his only sentence was to receive a reprimand. Then, on 21 November, it was Lieutenant Sonnenberg's turn to stand before a court martial. He faced five charges, three relating to his behaviour towards Fuchs and two to his behaviour with Holl on the transport. Apparently, no evidence was provided to the court relating to the charges regarding Fuchs however he was found guilty of the two others and was sentenced to be cashiered. In London the Judge Advocate General recommended he be pardoned, with an admonishment, however the Commander-in-Chief having taken into consideration Lieutenant Sonnenberg's behaviour towards Fuchs in the round declined to allow this. On 6 April 1811 the sentence of the court was confirmed and Sonnenberg was cashiered.[103]

Fuchs's position in the regiment must have been untenable and, despite having previously asking to be transferred, preferably to a British regiment, he exchanged with Captain Anthony Courant of the Meuron Regiment in March 1811. Unfortunately, the ill will from his fellow officers in Roll followed him to his new regiment, nevertheless he continued to serve with it until it was disbanded in 1816.[104]

In the last three months of 1810 an eleventh company was added to the Regiment de Roll, an addition that had been authorised a year before on 25 November 1809. Captain Nicholas Müller's (No. 5) Company became a rifle company while the new company (No. 11) was formed as the regiment's new Light Company, commanded by Captain Amantz de Sury. However, it was to be some time before the conversion of Müller's Company was completed as the additional allowance for rifles only commenced on 25 February 1811.[105]

1811

The behaviour of the royal court at Palermo, in receipt of a generous subsidy, had become an issue not only for the British command on the island but also for political discourse in Britain.[106] To address the issues, on 25 February 1811 Lord William Cavendish Bentinck was appointed both minister plenipotentiary in Sicily and commander-in-chief in the Mediterranean with Frederick Maitland as his second-in-command; they were both given the local rank of lieutenant general on 1 March 1811.[107] Bentinck arrived in July and within five weeks had gathered enough information to convince him

102 TNA: WO 71/222: Trial of Captain Fuchs, 15 to 19 November 1810.
103 TNA: WO 91/3: Record.
104 *Army Lists*, Courant is shown as joining the Regiment de Roll on 10 March and Fuchs Meuron on 21 March 1811.
105 TNA: WO 380/5: Establishment book; WO 12/11994: Paylist 1810.
106 Gregory, *Sicily*, pp.94–95.
107 *Army List*, 1811.

De Bosset Bridge, Argostoli, Kefalonia. (Author's photo)

that he needed to fully brief the government and receive additional powers in order to deal with the court at Palermo. Thus he returned to London, leaving Maitland in charge, and only returned, armed with new powers, on 7 December 1811.

Two companies (No.4 and 6) of the Regiment de Roll remained in the Ionian Islands. After the capture of Lefkada they had been placed in garrison on Kefalonia with Major de Bosset as governor with military and civil command. Captain H. Ryhiner commanded the largest body at Argostoli, the island's capital, while Captain Barbier commanded the contingent at its second town, Lixouri. Other detachments, from both companies, were posted at the Castle of Agios Georgios, Sami and Assos; by June detachments were no longer at the last two posts but at Kerameies instead.[108] Bosset used his tenure as governor, which ceased when he returned to England in early 1814, to improve the infrastructure on the island. The most ambitious improvement was the construction of what is now known as the De Bosset Bridge across the Koutavos Lagoon. Almost 690 metres long, it provided a direct link between Agostoli and the main body of the island across the lagoon removing the need to travel the almost five kilometres along its shore.

Meanwhile the rest of the regiment was on Sicily. What was now the Rifle (No.5) Company commanded by Captain N. Müller remained with the 2nd Light Battalion that, on 11 April, moved along the coast to Taormina.[109] The battalion lost the companies from the Chasseurs Britanniques and the Watteville Regiment as well as its commander, Lieutenant Colonel Fischer, to service in Spain, command passing to Fischer's second-in-command, Major Daniel Mahony, 58th Foot. By October the battalion was posted at Rometta, between Milazzo and the Faro point, when the Regiment de Roll's Albert Steiger, who had been brevetted major on 4 June 1811 and ended his staff appointment, took command of the battalion. A few months before Gougelberg, as a senior lieutenant, had been recalled to the regiment to take

---

108   TNA: WO 12/11995: Paylist 1811.
109   Gugelberg (ed.), *Bündners*, p.42; TNA: WO 12/11995: Paylist 1811.

command of Steiger's Company (No.7) where he 'was warmly welcomed by the officers of the regiment, from whom I had been detached since September 1808.'[110]

The regimental headquarters, and other companies had begun the year at Milazzo but transferred to Taormina in March, with two companies, including the new Light Company (No.11) at Scaletta, and later another was placed at San Placido. Although it was a comparatively quiet period, the Army Flotilla continued to be in action which resulted, on 28 April, in one of the regiment's privates, Ulrich Pferdshofer, dying of wounds that he had received 'on the Calabrian Shore.'[111] During the year some men were sent to England to join the 2nd Invalid Company at the Foreign Depot at Lymington and others were invalided from the regiment, so that in all 160 or so men left the regiment. These were replaced by recruits either raised in Eastern Spain, apparently from prisoners or deserters from the Italian contingent serving with the Imperial army, or within the Mediterranean command. In the month ending on 25 May, 10 sergeants and 70 rank and file arrived from Spain, via Gibraltar, seven more direct from Tarragona and nine from the Ionian Islands and on 14 June 21 joined the regiment from Malta.[112] This allowed, by June, the formation of a twelfth company, which had been authorised on 25 October 1810. The official establishment of the Regiment de Roll was now 1,602 all ranks with 77 sergeants, including a sergeant major, drum major and three staff sergeants, 23 drummers, two fifers and 1,368 privates.[113] On 25 December 1811 it was marginally over the establishment of soldiers with 75 sergeants, 26 drummers and 1,440 rank and file.[114] As for senior officers, as has been seen, Bosset was the third, supernumerary, major, and on 7 March 1811 a supernumerary lieutenant colonel was appointed.[115] He was Frederick, Baron Eben, or Friedrich Christian Freiherr von Eben und Brunnen, who had had a varied career in the armies of his native Prussia, Britain and Portugal and was on the staff in the Peninsular, he never served with the Regiment de Roll.

Over the years Napoleon sought to force the authorities in Switzerland to ensure that the only military service their countrymen would enter would be his own. Bowing to this pressure, on 2 July 1807 the Swiss Diet had forbidden any other recruitment than French. However, enforcement rested with individual cantons and so was tempered by individual and family influence as well as local attitudes to Napoleon's hegemony.[116] This continued to be a source of frustration for the emperor, his Swiss regiments struggled to attract recruits and, when serving in Spain, lost men to desertion. He blamed the Swiss regiments in British service for this, considering them to be 'veritable

110 Gugelberg (ed.), *Bündners*, p.43. He is shown as commanding the company in the casualty return ending 24 April 1812 (TNA: WO 25/2291).
111 TNA: WO 25/2291: Casualty returns.
112 TNA: WO 17/803: Regimental monthly returns.
113 TNA: WO 24/887: Authorised estimates.
114 TNA: WO 17/1934: Monthly returns.
115 *Army List*, 1811.
116 Édouard Guillon, *Napoléon et Les Suisses 1803–1815* (Paris and Lausanne: Plon and Payot et Cie., 1910), pp.332–333.

agencies of desertion that work upon our Swiss.'[117] Finally, after a meeting in which Swiss deputies had faced Napoleon's wrath, the Diet decided on 8 July 1811 that the Swiss in British service would have to return to their homeland before the end of the year and that those who refused would be stripped of their citizenship, both cantonal and national, as well as their property. It was formally forbidden to enter British service.[118] It is not clear when the regiment received news of this declaration but their compatriots in the Watteville Regiment at Cádiz heard of it on 27 October.[119] Apparently the only officer of the Regiment de Roll who responded to the decree was Captain Charles de Sury who, on 1 December 1811, was granted six months' leave but gave notice that, should he not return by the following 31 May, he resigned his commission.[120] He did not return and his replacement was appointed on 29 October 1812.

In August the Regiment de Roll returned to the garrison at Messina for the rest of the year, so it was present when a conspiracy to hand over the citadel as well as other key parts of the defences to the French was discovered. On 2 December several officers in the Bourbons' service were arrested followed by *Capitano* Rossaroll, chief of the secret police at Messina, on 6 December.[121] Rossaroll's brother, Guiseppe, was a senior officer in Murat's army and although, on enquiry, little of weight was unearthed, he was to be something of a scapegoat and was executed, perhaps to protect more senior figures from culpability.[122] The captain's family originated from Switzerland and he seems to have had good relations with the Regiment de Roll, Gougelberg 'knew him and his family quite well' and Rossaroll's daughter had married Francis Ziegler, the regiment's sergeant major who was later commissioned ensign.[123] According to Gougelberg two Frenchmen in the Regiment de Roll had been drawn into the conspiracy and, having tried to desert, they were subsequently transported to New South Wales.[124] Although there is no evidence among the regimental records to directly support this, two men were shown as 'Prisoner in the Present' for every muster of 1812 until discharged, with no further details shown, on 24 August; they were Sergeant Lewis Lointier and Private Henry Dubois.[125]

117 Guillon, *Suisses*, p.333.
118 Guillon, *Suisses*, pp.333–334.
119 BiG: Watteville Diary, 27 October 1811.
120 TNA: WO 31/1561: Officers' memoranda.
121 Virgilio Ilari, Piero Crociani and Giancarlo Boeri, *Le Due Sicilie nelle Guerre Napoleoniche (1800–1815)* (Rome: Stato Maggiore dell'Esercito, 2008), vol.II, p.823.
122 Gregory, *Sicily*, pp.92–95.
123 Gugelberg (ed.), *Bündners*, p.43. Guiseppe Maria Rossaroll (1775–1825) had thrown in his lot with the French early in the Revolutionary Wars and was much later, when in command at Messina, to distinguish himself in support of the constitutional cause in the Kingdom of Two Sicilies.
124 Gugelberg (ed.), *Bündners*, p.44.
125 TNA: WO 12/11996: Paylists 1812.

8

'Well behaved and not drunken'

1812 – Adriatic

The year 1812 was to see elements of the Regiment de Roll deployed much further afield. The island of Vis, then called Lissa, in the Adriatic had for some time been used as a base by British warships operating in the region despite French attempts to prevent it. The Royal Navy was keen to share responsibility for its defence with a British Army garrison. Its occupation offered several other benefits. One, that had already been agreed by Bentinck as early as August 1811, was as a base for raising Italian troops in British service. Called the Italian Levy the units were to be led by officers who had been in Austrian service but been dismissed, on demand by the French, as they were from territories annexed by Napoleon.[1] The levy finally consisted of three regiments, the basis of a fourth, as well as a number of independent companies. Its formation fitted with a policy of supporting Italian nationalist insurrectionists against Napoleon, something that the Austrians had sought to do in 1809, and that chimed with Bentinck's own liberal views.

In February 1812 troops were assembled at Kefalonia, under the command of Lieutenant Colonel George Duncan Robertson of the Sicilian Regiment, to be sent to Vis. They were a detachment from the Royal Artillery, two companies of the 35th Foot, two from the Royal Corsican Rangers, one from the Calabrian Free Corps and Captain Barbier's (No.6) Company of the Regiment de Roll.[2] This last consisted of Barbier, Lieutenants John Peter Sorgenfrey and Otto Henry Salinger, four sergeants, five corporals, two drummers and 97 privates.[3] Due to a false report that a French squadron had slipped out from Toulon and might be heading for the Adriatic and then adverse winds, the convoy only arrived off Vis on 25 April and the troops landed two days later.[4] Robertson ensured he could defend the island, as he reported to Bentinck, 'immediately on our landing we lost no time in

---

1   Virgilio Ilari and Piero Crociani, *L'Armata italiana di Lord Bentinck 1812–1816* (self-published, 2010), pp.231–232.

2   TNA: WO 1/311: Memorandum, 25 February 1812.

3   TNA: WO 12/11996: Paylist, 24 June 1812.

4   Malcolm Scott Hardy, *The British and Vis: War in the Adriatic 1805–15* (Oxford: Archaeopress, 2009), p.65; TNA: WO 1/311: Robertson to Bentinck, 26 April 1812.

commencing Field works, & throwing up Field lines, to cover ourselves against any sudden attempt of the enemy, every man was employed and in three days they were finished; I am now not in the least uneasy.'[5] At first the troops camped 'under canvas,' and Ensign John Hildebrand of the 35th Foot, a teenager at the time, was to later recall waking cold and drenched after a sudden storm had carried away his tent. 'Barracks ... and other necessary buildings were run up hastily, and indeed in a manner which showed that they were not intended for permanent occupation ... we were soon under the temporary roofs provided by our engineer.'[6] Hildebrand's memory, at least in terms of the timing was at fault as the barracks were only completed at the end of September.[7]

On 29 May Robertson put Barbier in charge of 'civil affairs,' effectively policing, at Vis.[8] Undoubtedly it would have been no sinecure as the population is estimated to have grown from 4,000 to 11,000 within two years, as the British occupation brought prosperity through trade and employment in building permanent fortifications, the shipyard and serving the needs of the visiting sailors and garrison.[9] A clear example of this last activity was the 14 taverns and six billiard rooms that sprung up along the small waterfront of Vis town.[10] Robertson also raised a local militia, of 500 men, among the islanders which was apparently placed under the command of Barbier.[11] Towards the end of the year, 1 and 24 November 1812, there were two episodes of men from his company deserting, three at a time, from Vis; of the six, four were German, one from Alsace and one was Swiss.[12] These were the only examples of desertion from No.4 or 6 Company during this period.

1812 – Sicily

When Bentinck returned with additional powers, he resolved to act decisively in pushing through reforms to Sicily's constitution that the British considered necessary for the alliance to continue effectively. He moved his headquarters from Messina to Palermo and ordered five battalions to the city, including the 2nd Light Infantry that disembarked there on 3 January.[13] Meanwhile the staff and main body of the Regiment de Roll remained in

---

5   TNA: WO 1/311: Robertson to Bentinck, 14 May 1812.

6   Gareth Glover (ed.), *Fighting Napoleon: The Recollections of Lieutenant John Hildebrand 35th Foot in the Mediterranean and Waterloo Campaigns* (Barnsley: Frontline Books, 2016), p.51.

7   Hardy, *British and Vis*, p.79.

8   TNA: WO 31/1563: Barbier's memorandum of 5 December 1815.

9   Hardy, *British and Vis*, p.100.

10   Tom Pocock, *Remember Nelson: The Life of Captain Sir William Hoste* (London: Collins, 1977), p.184.

11   D. W. King, 'A Note on the Operations of George Duncan Robertson's Force from Lissa at Trieste and in Northern Italy, 1813–1814' *Journal of the Society for Army Historical Research*, vol.56, no.227 (Autumn 1978), p.175. Remarkably Barbier does not mention this appointment in his memorandum of 5 December 1815 (TNA: WO 31/1563).

12   TNA: WO 25/2291: Casualty returns.

13   TNA: WO 1/311: Bentinck to Earl Liverpool, 11 February 1812; WO 12/11996: Paylist 1812.

the garrison of Messina until moving just outside the city, to Contesse, in June.[14] One of Bentinck's reforms was to have the size of the Sicilian army reduced. This was to ensure the available finance could be used to properly equip and pay the remaining troops so that they could operate in the field with British forces, it being agreed later that a brigade would be available to serve within the Mediterranean theatre.[15] The army was now to contain only Sicilians or Neapolitans, the regiments formed of the latter being named *estero* (foreign). All the other soldiers were dismissed and 900 who were identified as Germans, many originating from German and Swiss regiments that had formerly served in the Bourbon army at Naples, offered to join the British Army, mostly in the King's German Legion. A similar number of Italians were used to begin the formation of the 2nd Regiment of the Italian Levy.[16] The Regiment de Roll received 39 Swiss from this source, recruited at Palermo on 21 and 23 May, a significant number given that the total number recruited in the year of 1812 was 47 men.[17]

In his recollections Ensign Hildebrand of the 35th Foot, made some observations about the officers of the foreign regiments of the British Army at this time,

> Their officers … were not generally very young men; but many above middle age. These were mostly unfortunate noblemen and their kindred who had been driven from their homes and country by the sad and disastrous war with Napoleon; and most of them, having served in the army in some way, were but too glad to take service in the British Army, in positions and ranks often much below what they might have attained to in their own, but affording the means of living. An ensign of 40, or even older, years of age was no very unusual thing to meet with: the captains were generally so, gentlemen, good soldiers, always ready for any undertaking and although bearing a contrast with our much more youthful officers, and therefore perhaps not quite so ardent and active: steady, brave, experienced and *always to be relied on* in any duties committed to them.[18]

In the Regiment de Roll, alongside the young men that arrived from Switzerland, there were indeed such subalterns. One example was Francis von Hundheim who had been appointed ensign on 23 January 1810 when he was 41 years old and joined the regiment in Sicily in July that year. He had begun his career as a *sous-lieutenant* in the Régiment Royal Deux-Ponts of the French Royal Army aged 16, was a subaltern in a light infantry corps of the United Provinces in 1794 before serving as lieutenant in the Riflemen Regiment of the Dutch Brigade in British pay until 1802.[19] Promoted lieutenant in the Regiment de Roll on 27 February 1811, he died the following 15 June

---

14   TNA: WO 17/1935: Monthly returns.
15   Gregory, *Sicily*, pp.109–110.
16   TNA: WO 1/311: Bentinck to Liverpool, 25 May 1812.
17   TNA: WO 12/11996: Paylists 1812.
18   Glover, *Fighting Napoleon*, pp.38–39.
19   SHD: GR 1 Ye 28905: Dossier des sous-lieutenants; *Etat militaire* 1791; *Naamregister der Heeren militaire Officieren, den Capitein generaal, de Generaals, Lieutenant-Generaals, Generaals-Major, Colonels, Lieutenant-Colonels, Majors, Capiteins, Lieutenants en*

1812 while serving with the Rifle Company at Palermo.[20] His belongings were sold by auction and the list provides not only some indication of what a junior officer possessed but also what was most valued among his peers, Hundheim's canine hunting companion gaining the highest price.

Table 13: Possessions of Lieutenant von Hundheim, auctioned on 20 June 1812 and money received.[21]

		Pounds	Shillings	Pence
2	Uniforms	7	1	–
1	Great Coat	1	7	7
1	Cap		3	9
8	Pantaloons	1	7	–
6	Waist Coats		14	–
2	Sashes	1	–	7
1	Sword, Belt and Knot	2	8	1
1	Gorget		3	7
12	Shirts	2	13	5
12	Pairs of stockings		5	6
11	Neck Cloths		15	6
8	Handkerchiefs		7	1
3	Pairs of gloves		1	6
4	Towels		2	6
2	Pairs of shoes		5	11
2	Pairs of boots	1	10	–
1	Bedstead		13	3
1	Mattress	1	17	7
2	Pairs of sheets	1	3	1½
2	Blankets		6	10
2	Portmanteaus	1	10	8
	Several books	1	–	–
2	Razors		7	9
1	Fowling piece	2	5	–
1	Pointer [dog]	3	8	3
1	Knapsack		4	6
	Sundry small articles	3	5	8½
	Cash	10	16	–

1812 – Spain

Bentinck was placed under pressure to contribute troops to the British intervention in Portugal and Spain while still balancing the needs of his own mission. In anticipation of this General Arthur Wellesley, Earl (later Duke) of Wellington, commander-in-chief in Spain and Portugal, while besieging Badajoz, wrote to him on 24 March 1812.

Vaandrigs… Vermeerded mit eene Lyste der Chefs van alle de Regimenten, zo Cavallery, als Infantery, zedert den Jaare 1713. Mart 1794; TNA: WO 2/55 and 56: Correspondence.

20 TNA: WO 17/1935: Monthly returns 1812.
21 TNA: WO 25/2291: Casualty return.

> The most essential object on which the troops under your command could be employed on the Eastern coast of Spain, would be the siege of Barcelona, or, if that could not be undertaken, the siege of Tarragona ... Upon the whole, however, I should doubt the sufficiency of your Lordship's force ... to undertake such an operation as the siege of Barcelona ... You are certainly much more equal to the attack of Tarragona, ...[22]

This is despite Wellington, four days earlier, having informed Lord Liverpool, the Secretary of State for War, 'the attack of Tarragona or of Barcelona appears ... most desirable. I think it probable, however, that neither ... will succeed.'[23] As far as Wellington was concerned Bentinck, in co-operation with Spanish forces, was simply to prevent the French forces in Eastern Spain, commanded by *Maréchal* Louis-Gabriel Suchet, interfering with his forthcoming campaign, anything else would be a bonus. In mid-June Wellington started to advance from Portugal into Spain, a campaign marked by his remarkable victory at the Battle of Salamanca on 22 July.

On 7 June the first division destined for Spain, about 3,000 men, sailed from Palermo and arrived at Mahón 10 days later.[24] Menorca was the rendezvous for the expedition and British and Portuguese artillery, from Wellington's command, arrived on 24 June.[25] The second division of the troops from Sicily, consisting of units from Messina and Milazzo, had been expected to arrive a fortnight or so behind the first. However, having collected troops from Messina adverse winds delayed passage through the straits and so, having embarked more at Milazzo, it only reached Palermo on the night of 24 June.[26] There it was joined by the expedition's commander, Lieutenant General Frederick Maitland, Bentinck having chosen to remain in Sicily. Problems with horse transports that were to join the convoy meant that it only left Palermo on the night of 28 June. It then headed for Palma Bay on the south-western coast of Sardinia and arrived there on 9 July. The first division was already waiting in the bay, having arrived the day before from Menorca after two days at sea.[27] Bentinck had made this convoluted arrangement in case, at the last minute, an opportunity had emerged to use his troops in Italy.[28] He finally gave up such an idea when *Generalmajor* Laval Nugent von Westmeath, an Irish born officer in Austrian service, arrived to inform him that following the alliance of the Treaty of Paris, of 14 March 1812, any attack on French territory adjoining that of Austria would bring the latter into the conflict. Bentinck was advised that this was something

---

22 John Gurwood (ed.), *The Disptaches of Field Marshal the Duke of Wellington, during his various campaigns in India, Denmark, Portugal, Spain the Low Countries, and France, from 1799 to 1816* (London: John Murray, 1838), vol.IX, pp.5–6.

23 Gurwood (ed.), *Dispatches*, vol.IX, p.3.

24 TNA: WO 1/311: Bentinck to Liverpool, 9 June 1812; Anon., *Historical Record of the Eighty-First Regiment, or Loyal Lincoln Volunteers* (Gibraltar: The Twenty-Eighth Regimental Press, 1872), p.102.

25 S.G.P. Ward (ed.), 'The Diary of Lieutenant Robert Woollcombe, R.A., 1812–1813' *Journal of the Society for Army Historical Research*, vol.52, no.211 (Autumn 1974), pp.161–162.

26 TNA: WO 1/311: Bentinck to Liverpool, 25 and 29 June 1812.

27 Anon., *Historical Record*, p.103.

28 TNA: WO 1/311: Bentinck to Liverpool, 9 June 1812.

Austria wanted to avoid so he should commit his troops to Spain.[29] As a result Maitland arrived at Mahón on 14 July followed by all the transports with the troops from Sicily two days later.[30]

The units from Sicily were the 1/10th, 1/58th and 1/81st Foot, the 4th and 6th Line Battalions of the King's German Legion and detachments from the Regiment de Roll, Dillon, Calabrian Free Corps and the 20th Light Dragoons as well as supporting arms, including the Foreign Hussars – 6,688 all ranks.[31] The detachments from Roll and Dillon were to form a provisional battalion, generally referred to as the Roll-Dillon Battalion, under the command of Lieutenant Colonel John Potter Hamilton, 2/10th Foot. It had three companies from Roll and five from Dillon, the embarkation return of 25 June 1812 showing the respective strengths from Roll as three captains, seven lieutenants, an ensign, 14 sergeants, six drummers, 300 rank and file, a servant and six women – 338 in total – and from Dillon, a major, five captains, 10 lieutenants, an ensign, a surgeon, 26 sergeants, 10 drummers, 500 rank and file and eight women – 562 in total.[32]

The Regiment de Roll's companies were those of Captains Anthony Mohr (No.1), Henry Ryhiner (No.2 grenadiers) and Amantz de Sury (No.11 light).[33] Mohr immediately took up field officer duties with the battalion, he had been brevetted lieutenant colonel from 1 January 1812, as Major John Boutaud, of Dillon, was found to be no 'longer fit for the active duties of the Field' due to his long service, previous wounds, the climate 'and indeed from his time of life'.[34]

Finally on 28 July the expedition sailed from Menorca, as Lieutenant Robert Woollcombe, Royal Artillery, recalled,

> Blue Peters hoisted and signal-guns fired for sailing … The whole fleet sailed from Mahon consisting of about 75 sail (not including men-of-war) of transports. The destination of the expedition remains unknown further than we are going to the coast of Spain … The expectation of every individual in the fleet is now raised to the highest pitch …[35]

On the morning of 1 August the fleet anchored in the bay, between Palamós and Sant Feliu de Guixols, on the Catalan coast, east of Girona, and so distant from Barcelona, let alone Tarragona.[36] That afternoon, and the following day, an intention to land was signalled as enemy troops assembled on the shore in

---

29   TNA: WO 1/311: Bentinck to Liverpool 29 June 1812.

30   Ward (ed), 'Woollcombe', pp.163–164.

31   TNA: WO 1/311: embarkation return dated 25 June 1812, showing both divisions.

32   TNA: WO 1/311: embarkation return 25 June 1812.

33   TNA: WO 12/11996: Paylist 1812.

34   TNA: WO 27/118: Inspection report 20 May 1813; Boutaud was described in the report as 'a meritorious old French officer.' Antione-Jean de Boutuad had had around 20 years' service in the French army in the Régiment d'Armagnac before the revolution upon which he emigrated and joined the Loyal Emigrants on its formation.

35   Ward (ed), 'Woollcombe', p.165.

36   TNA: ADM 51/2569: Captain's journal HMS *Malta*, 2 August; ADM 51/2478: Captain's journal HMS *Implacable*, 1 August 1812, in which the latter is shown as 'San Philion.'

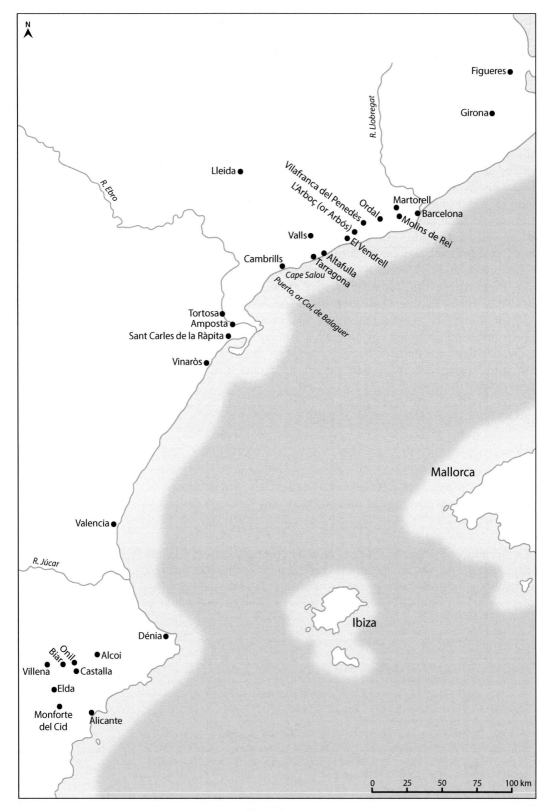

Eastern Spain.

growing numbers.[37] No landing took place and on 3 August the fleet sailed for Alicante. The timing was fortuitous as the local Spanish commander, Joseph O'Donnell, had been routed at Castalla on 21 July. This had left Alicante, the only harbour, other than the smaller naval port of Cartagena, held by the allies on the East Coast of Spain vulnerable to attack. When, on 8 August, the fleet arrived at Alicante there were reports that the enemy were approaching in strength to the northwest.[38]

The troops began to disembark on 10 July. The Roll-Dillon Battalion was placed in the Reserve Division, forming its second brigade with the 81st Foot under the command of Lieutenant Colonel Patrick McKenzie, of the latter regiment.[39] The next day Maitland's troops, about 15,000 in all, were distributed among villages north of Alicante and across the road to Castalla. The British were at Sant Vicent del Raspeig and El Palamó and the two Spanish divisions equipped and paid for by Britain, commanded by Philip Keating Roche and Samuel Ford Whittingham, to their right at Sant Joan d'Alacant and Mutxamel.[40] On 15 August the army advanced from Alicante to Monforte del Cid and then Elda where a defensive position in front of the town was taken on 18 August. The Roll-Dillon Battalion is not specifically mentioned in any of the sources but Woollcombe noted that the 81st Foot was placed on a hill in advance of the position and then when the army began to retreat, overnight 21/22 August, it did so 'with the rear-guard of Dillon and some Spanish cavalry'.[41] The troops returned to their earlier positions around Alicante. The operation had been marked by poor staff work but finally abandoned due to a lack of horses and waggons to bring up supplies. The previous positions were again adopted.

Meanwhile Wellington's victory at Salamanca and his subsequent advance on Madrid had forced the French armies in Spain to concentrate. He was anxious that Suchet, at least, should not join them for which he needed Maitland to be a continuing threat from Alicante. Throughout August Wellington, who had been authorised to command Maitland while he was in Spain, wrote to him and in a letter of 30 August he was unequivocal, 'understand that I expect you to maintain yourself at Alicante as long as possible.'[42] Frederick Maitland, his health broken by stress, asked Bentinck to relieve him of his command, so Major General William Henry Clinton sailed from Sicily on 3 October to take command in Spain.[43] However Maitland did not wait and on 22 September he handed command to the senior officer present, Major General John Mackenzie, and left for Sicily.

It was during this period, on 30 September, that Captain Antoine Courant of the Regiment de Roll, serving on the army's staff as Assistant Adjutant General since May, was taken prisoner of war. Despite attempts to have him

37 Charles Oman, *A History of the Peninsular War* (London: Greenhill Books, 1996), vol. V, p.566; Ward (ed.), 'Woollcombe', pp.165–166, see also Gleig (ed.), *The Hussar*, vol.II, pp.26–28.
38 Ward (ed), 'Woollcombe', p.166.
39 Anon., *Historical Record*, p.103.
40 Ward (ed), 'Woollcombe', p.167.
41 Ward (ed), 'Woollcombe', p.170.
42 Gurwood (ed.), *Dispatches*, vol.IX, p.387.
43 TNA: WO 1/312: Bentinck to Bathurst 5 October 1812.

released immediately by a local exchange of prisoners, he was taken to France where he was held at Verdun on parole.[44]

On the evening of 4 October five companies of the 81st Foot and the Grenadier Company of the Regiment de Roll under the command of Major General Rufane Shaw Donkin, the Quartermaster General, embarked in secrecy on HMS *Fame* (74) and *Cephalus* (brig) to attack the Castle at Dénia, north of Alicante. The following morning the troops landed near the castle and, the Light Company of the 81st at their head, 'drove in the outposts of the enemy, pressing them so closely, that they were nearly entering the castle with the fugitives'.[45] Having rushed forward too far and ignoring the bugle call to withdraw, a sergeant had to bring them the order to retreat onto the main body. Donkin realised that the castle could not be taken by assault and withdrew his men to the beach where, under the cover of the guns of the *Cephalus*, they re-embarked. The cost was one man killed and two officers and 15 men wounded; the only loss from the Roll grenadiers was Private Joseph Gallot, from Piedmont, who was later recorded as having been taken prisoner.[46] In his order of the 6 October Donkin expressed 'his approbation of the conduct of the troops during the operations on shore yesterday. … Captain Ryhner's [*sic*] support of that advance with the grenadiers of De Roll's, was very handsome'.[47]

Renewing their activity on 8 October, the French drove in the Anglo-Spanish advanced posts at Tibi and Jijona and then attacked those in front of Sant Vicent del Raspeig with all arms.[48] The attack was not pressed as it was simply to screen a realignment of the French armies.[49] On 24 October Clinton arrived and he continued the occupation of the pocket of territory around Alicante that expanded and contracted as opportunity and the enemy permitted, resulting in some minor clashes among the outposts.

Other than the raid on Dénia the service of the three Roll companies was, at this stage, uneventful. However, there were a series of desertions, particularly from Mohr's company from which 19 men deserted between August and December. Except for one Italian, all of them were Spanish, several of whom were from the region in which they were now serving and appear to have been enlisted after Trafalgar. This pattern of behaviour was also seen in the Chasseurs Britanniques when several of the Spaniards in its ranks deserted soon after arrival in their homeland, not to quit soldiering or join the enemy, but to join Spanish units.[50] This appears to be also the case in the Regiment de Roll and, apparently to address this issue, eight privates were transferred from Mohr's company to the Spanish Army on 24 December 1812.[51] The only others who deserted from the regiment in this

44   TNA: ADM 103/468: Register of British prisoners of war held in France.
45   Anon., *Historical Record*, p.104.
46   TNA: WO 25/2291: Casualty return.
47   Anon., *Historical Record*, pp.105–106.
48   Anon., 'Operations', given as 10 October Mackenzie to Wellington 11 October 1812 and 8 October in Mackenzie to Torrens, War Office, 22 October 1812.
49   Oman, *Peninsular War*, vol.VI, p.92.
50   Nichols, *Mongrel Regiment*, p.71.
51   TNA: WO 12/11997: Pay lists 1813.

period were two Poles and one German who quit the Grenadier Company in November.[52]

Since the beginning of October Bentinck had been planning to send a reinforcement from Sicily to Spain. Just over 4,500 men finally sailed on 15 November, under the command of Major General James Campbell, and arrived at Alicante on 2 December. Bentinck was expected to follow shortly and in the meantime Campbell commanded the expeditionary army. The infantry reinforcements were the Grenadier Battalion, the 2nd Light Infantry Battalion commanded by Major Albert Steiger that included the Regiment de Roll's Rifle Company, the 1/27th Foot, 2nd Italian Regiment and a battalion of Sicilian grenadiers.[53] A muster held on 24 December at 'St Vincente near Alicante' shows that the Roll Rifle Company had three officers, Captain Nicholas Müller and Lieutenants Stephen de Planta and Anton Segesser, six sergeants, six corporals, two buglers and 103 privates (five being at the General Hospital at Alicante).[54] Lieutenant Frederick Rusillion had, the previous month, left the company to serve as aide de camp to Brigadier General Vittorio Sallier de la Tour, or della Torre, of the Italian Levy.[55]

January to June 1813 – Eastern Spain

More reinforcements, among them Sicilian cavalry and infantry with detachments of the Calabrian Free Corps followed by the 1st Italian Regiment and 2/27th Foot, arrived to boost the size of the army.[56] However confidence in the multi-national composition of the army was severely shaken between 8 and 10 February when, on the back of mass desertion, a plot was discovered within the 2nd Italian Regiment to hand over Jijona during a French attack. The regiment was disarmed and placed on transports before being reformed after the malcontents had been weeded out.[57] A few days earlier incidents of desertion occurred from Müller's Rifle Company when seven privates, all Swiss but for one German, deserted on 30 January followed by two more, a Swiss and a German, on 6 February. There is no indication of why or where this happened which is frustrating given that they were the only desertions from that company throughout the period.

On 25 February Lieutenant General Sir John Murray arrived at Alicante from England. He had been appointed as second in command to Bentinck but instructed to immediately go to Alicante to take command there and take his orders from Wellington.[58] The new commander set about reorganising the

---

52 TNA: WO 25/2291: Casualty return. One of the Spaniards, Private Joseph Flores, a native of Cartagena, who had deserted on 20 September returned four days later.

53 TNA: WO 1/312: Embarkation return 14 November 1812.

54 TNA: WO 12/11996: Paylists 1812.

55 TNA: WO 17/1935: Monthly returns 1812.

56 TNA: WO 1/312: Embarkation return 5 December 1812 and Bentinck to Bathurst, 9 December 1812.

57 Ilari and Crociani, L'Armata italiana, pp.247–248.

58 TNA: WO 6/57: Earl Bathurst to Murray, 4 December 1813. Should Bentinck be at Alicante, or arrive later, Murray was to go to Sicily where he was to follow the former's instructions.

army, Woollcombe writing, 'Since the arrival of Sir John Murray, the orderly books have been filled with General Orders altering all the arrangements made by his predecessors.'[59] One of his first acts, the order being dated 25 February, was to break up the Light Battalion. Dillon's Light Company joined the Roll-Dillon Battalion but the Roll Rifle Company, despite being officially assigned to the battalion as well, was to always serve separately.[60] Albert Steiger was appointed Murray's only aide de camp.[61]

In the forthcoming campaign it is difficult to provide a comprehensive account of the movements and role of the Regiment de Roll's companies. It is conceivable that the Rifle Company formed part of the advance or light brigade, commanded by Colonel Frederick Adam, as did the rifles of the 3rd and 8th battalions of the King's German Legion, despite the absence of evidence to support or contradict it. As for those in the Roll-Dillon Battalion, it is clear that it still formed a brigade with the 1/81st Foot that was initially posted at Monforte del Cid.[62] In the order of battle provided by Oman, and used by subsequent writers, both battalions of this brigade are shown as being in Clinton's division, however evidence from the general himself shows this to be incorrect as, on 20 May, he wrote of Roll-Dillon, 'The Battalion has not been attached to the Division under my command above three weeks.'[63]

Murray opened the campaign, in cooperation with Spanish forces, by trying to encircle a French brigade at Alcoi, however the movements did not go to plan and the enemy brigade slipped away on 6 March. The Roll-Dillon Battalion was probably involved as Murray blamed the failure on the drunkenness of a detachment of the 81st.[64] Murray then placed Whittingham at Alcoi and posted the rest of his army around Castalla. This provided Suchet an opportunity to counter-attack and so, ignoring Whittingham, he transferred all his available troops to his right and, defeating the Spanish forces before him, he reached Villena on 11 April.

A road ran from Villena eastwards to Biar and from there climbed, through a gap in the surrounding steep hills, to emerge in the northeast corner of a valley which is bound, to the south, by a parallel line of hills. This latter line, however, soon peters out to the east, ending with a distinct hill on which the castle of Castalla stands. As soon as Villena was threatened Murray placed Adam's brigade at Biar while the rest of his forces lined the opposite side of the valley. Suchet, pursuing his success, advanced on Biar. Oman wrote,

> The combat of Biar, which filled the midday hours of April 12th, was one of the most creditable rearguard actions fought during the whole Peninsular War. Colonel Adam … had prepared a series of positions on which he intended to fall back in succession, as each was forced … the enemy turned Biar on both flanks;

59   Ward (ed), 'Woollcombe', p.172.
60   TNA: WO 12/11997: Paylists 1813; WO 27/118: Battalion inspection 20 May 1813.
61   TNA: WO 43/413: Steiger memorandum 24 August 1825; WO 17/2478: Army return 25 April 1813.
62   Anon., *Historical Record*, p.112.
63   Oman, *Peninsular War*, vol.VI, p.748; TNA: WO 27/118: Battalion inspection 20 May 1813.
64   Fortescue, *British Army*, vol.IX, p.38, footnote, Murray to Wellington 4 March 1813.

its garrison retired unharmed, but the turning columns came under the accurate fire of the troops [placed by Adam] above, and the attack was again checked. Suchet, angered at the waste of time, then threw in no less than nine battalions … The Light Brigade had, of course, to retire; but Adam conducted his retreat with great deliberation and in perfect order, fending off the turning attack … and making the column on the high road pay very dearly for each furlong gained … after five hours' fighting the Light Brigade marched back in perfect order to the position beside Castalla which had been assigned to it. Its final retirement was covered by three battalions which Murray had sent out to meet it, at the exit from the pass.[65]

These last were the Roll-Dillon, 1/81st and one of Whittingham's Spanish battalions.[66] Murray's line was formed with Clinton's division at Castalla, Roche to his right and immediately to his left Mackenzie, then Adam and finally Whittingham on the western flank. It is likely, given their role the day before, that the Roll-Dillon Battalion and the 1/81st were in reserve behind Adam's Brigade and the Roll Rifle Company was in the skirmish line in front of that brigade, at the centre of the line. Suchet delayed his attack until 13 April when his infantry, preceded by skirmishers, assaulted the left and centre of Murray's position, held by Whittingham and Adam. Although the enemy columns managed, at times, to reach the crest of the hills they were driven back and eventually retreated to the plain. By the end of the day Suchet withdrew towards Biar but Murray declined to pursue him.

The casualty return, attached to Murray's published victory despatch, combined the losses of 12 and 13 April, the total being 145 killed, 481 wounded and 42 missing.[67] While the 1/81st Foot had no casualties, the Roll-Dillon Battalion had four rank and file killed, a sergeant and 14 rank and filed wounded and nine rank and file missing. The Roll Rifle Company, listed separately, is shown as having had the following wounded: Lieutenant Segesser (slightly), a sergeant and four rank and file. The regimental returns, compiled later and listing killed, dead or missing, shows that all the Regiment de Roll's losses were in Sury's Light Company from the action of 12 April. These were Private Andrew Sexer who was killed that day and Private Baptiste Jaeger who died of his wounds on 14 April, both were Swiss; furthermore five privates were missing, having been taken prisoner.[68] Dillon's return shows two privates killed in action and two more taken as prisoners of war on 12 April, one killed on 13 April and another on 14 April.[69] The support the Roll-Dillon Battalion provided to Adam's brigade was clearly a more significant action than the historiography conveys.

Suchet slipped away northwards to concentrate his forces on the River Júcar, Murray did not respond although there is a hint that the Roll Rifle Company clashed with the enemy as two men were listed as missing on 16

---

65   Oman, *Peninsular War*, vol. VI, pp.288–289.
66   Oman, *Peninsular War*, vol. VI, p.289, footnote; Anon., *Historical Record*, p.113.
67   *The London Gazette*, 18 May 1813, Murray to Bathurst, 14 April 1813.
68   TNA: WO 25/2291: Casualty returns.
69   TNA: WO 25/2271: Casualty returns.

April.[70] Murray appears to have been waiting for clear instructions from Wellington as to how he should proceed in the next campaign. On 14 April, before he had received news of Castalla, Wellington wrote a detailed memorandum which spelled out what he wanted in the forthcoming campaign from Murray and the Spanish armies facing Suchet. Their task was, once again, to prevent Suchet from intervening in Wellington's advance and, if possible, to clear the enemy from the province of Valencia and the lower Ebro and capture of Tarragona. Wellington was adamant that the primary object would only be achieved if all elements of the allied forces in Eastern Spain were not defeated.[71] For his part of the plan Murray, as soon as further Spanish forces arrived to take his place facing the French on the Júcar, was to embark with at least 10,000 men for the attack on Tarragona.

Prior to this deployment some reorganisation took place in his army and about 1 May the Roll-Dillon Battalion was placed in Clinton's division and the Roll Rifle Company in the advance corps which, on 8 May, was at Biar.[72] On 20 May Clinton inspected the Roll-Dillon Battalion at Onil. His observations were limited by the short time it had been under his command and that the inspection was taking place in the field, the men being in 'light marching order' and 'crowded in small houses' they were little better off than bivouacking.[73] The field officers present were Lieutenant Colonels Hamilton, commanding, and Mohr, of whom Clinton wrote, 'as far as I am enabled to judge … attentive to his Duty and is an Officer of a good deal of experience'.[74] He continued,

> The Captains of this Battalion appear for the most part very good officers, those of Roll Grenadiers & Light infantry particularly so. Captain Ryhiner, of the Grenadiers, is an Officer of very long standing in our Service & from the Report made to me of him, & the excellent appearance of his Company, I have reason to think very favourably of him.[75]

Of the private soldiers, he wrote,

> Generally speaking they are a fine body of men, the two flank companies of De Roll are as fine as any I ever recollect to have seen and are as I am told very well conducted … The Battalion generally seems to be well drilled and, as far as I can judge, the men are well behaved and not drunken.[76]

70   TNA: WO 25/2291: Casualty returns.
71   See Nick Lipscombe, *Wellington's Eastern Front: The Campaigns on the East Coast of Spain 1810–1814* (Barnsley: Pen and Sword Military, 2016), pp.112–123, for a discussion of the memorandum.
72   TNA: WO 12/11997: Muster roll 8 May 1813.
73   TNA: WO 27/118: Battalion inspection 20 May 1813.
74   TNA: WO 27/118: Battalion inspection 20 May 1813; Major Boutaud was sick at Alicante and would later retire.
75   TNA: WO 27/118: Battalion inspection 20 May 1813.
76   TNA: WO 27/118: Battalion inspection 20 May 1813.

Clinton, despite his reservations about the variety of nationalities in the Dillon companies, was content, sure that the battalion, 'may be looked to for the achievement of distinguished services.'[77] Perhaps another sign of confidence in the Regiment de Roll was the commissioning of Sergeant Frederick Blatter, of the Rifle Company, as ensign in the 1st Italian Regiment on 14 April 1813, he was subsequently promoted lieutenant on 5 May 1814.[78]

The Roll-Dillon Battalion embarked on 28 May at Alicante and the convoy set sail three days later so that Murray's expedition of about 16,000 men coincided with Wellington's advance from Portugal.[79] With favourable winds the convoy arrived off Cape Salou on the evening of 2 June but before it anchored a small force parted company, this was commanded by Lieutenant Colonel William Prevost, 2/67th Foot, and consisted of his battalion, Roll-Dillon, the Roll Rifle Company and an artillery detachment.[80] While the rest of Murray's troops landed on 3 June to commence the siege of Tarragona, Prevost's mission was to capture the fort, Fuerte de San Felipe, which dominated the coast road to the south as it squeezed between the mountains and the sea at the Puerto, or Col, de Balaguer. Possession of this fort would prevent the enemy using the road, the only viable route for artillery to Tarragona, from Tortosa and the south.

The detachment landed at about 11.00 a.m. on 3 June and it was joined by two battalions from the Spanish forces in Catalonia. Prevost immediately sent Captain Müller with the 67th's Light Company and the Light and Rifle Companies of the Regiment de Roll, 'to invest the Fort as closely as possible, which he did so completely by two o'clock, that the enemy could not shew himself before his parapet.'[81] The riflemen climbed an adjacent slope which dominated the fort to bring more effective shots upon the defenders. A number of Royal Navy vessels had been allocated to assist Prevost and the sailors brought up guns to provide cover while preparations were made to commence constructing the breaching battery. On the night of 4/5 June, 'the whole of the seamen and troops were employed, the former in bringing up five 24-pounders, shot, powder, &c. for the battery, whilst the troops constructed the work.'[82] The work was almost completed but the nature of the ground prevented it being finished. The following evening the Roll Light Company began work filling sandbags to provide protection for the guns in the breaching battery which was expected to be in action by 2:00 a.m. and to have immediate results, so that an assault by the three companies under Müller's command was planned. However further work was halted by a tremendous thunderstorm and heavy rain, Lieutenant Hector de Salis, of the Roll Light Company, noted in his journal, 'This was a frightful night.'[83] On the evening of 6 June, two mortars from the bomb-vessel HMS

---

77   TNA: WO 27/118: Battalion inspection 20 May 1813.
78   TNA: WO 12/11997: Paylists 1813; WO 1/285: Levy correspondence.
79   TNA: WO 12/11997: Paylists 1813, officers' stoppages; *The London Gazette*, 20 July 1813, Murray to Wellington, 9 June 1813.
80   Prevost was in fact promoted colonel on 4 June 1813.
81   *The London Gazette*, 20 July 1813, Prevost to Murray, 7 June 1813.
82   *The London Gazette*, 20 July 1813, Prevost to Murray, 7 June 1813.
83   Bürkli, 'Das Schweizerregiment', p.30

Stromboli were placed alongside the breaching battery and that night the Roll Light and Rifle Companies occupied the heights on which the naval guns were placed. Before the break of day, the mortars commenced firing during which an expense magazine was destroyed. That evening, 7 June, as the breaching battery was about to open fire, a white flag was raised over the fort. The garrison surrendered and Müller's three companies immediately took possession of the fort.

The riflemen and naval guns covering the siege works had kept the number of casualties down. In total, the Spanish lost an officer who died of his wounds and seven rank and file were wounded. The British Army had five killed and 32 wounded. Private Ulrich Rohrer of the Roll Rifle Company was killed in action on 4 June and the company is shown as having had a sergeant and three rank and file wounded between 3 and 7 June. During the same period the Roll-Dillon Battalion is shown as having an officer and one rank and file killed with a drummer and 17 rank and file wounded.[84] Both the men who were killed were from Dillon, Private Pietro Raffi on 6 June and Lieutenant Frederick Delatre by one of the last shots from Fuerte de San Felipe.[85] Salis states that the Roll Light Company only had one man wounded throughout the operations.[86] In Prevost's despatch he brought notice to 'the admirable conduct of the whole of the Officers, Non-commissioned Officers, and soldiers … Their labour and exertion has been severe' and also the contributions of the navy personnel; among the officers he gave particular notice to 'Captain Muller, of the advance.'[87] Lieutenant Colonel Mohr was placed in command Fuerte de San Felipe, which had been taken in a good state of defence, with a garrison of a captain, a lieutenant and 200 men from various units present.[88]

Prevost's brigade remained at the fort and in the Puerto de Balaguer and so was not involved in the debacle of the siege of Tarragona and Murray's ignominious flight on 12 June. The convoy with Murray's troops arrived off Balaguer late on 13 June. However, rather than immediately embark Prevost and his troops, Murray spent the next few days unsure of what to do. Finally on 17 June, after a council of war, the army was preparing to embark when Bentinck arrived from Sicily and, as an eye-witness recalled, 'the joy of the Army and of the Sailors was notified by three cheers.'[89] Bentinck immediately relieved Murray of command, ordered the troops to embark and Fuerte de San Felipe to be destroyed. The Regiment de Roll companies embarked on to the transports; the rifles on *The British Hero* and the others on *The Recovery*. The convoy departed the coast on 19 June but struck by storms it only arrived at Alicante around 26 June.[90] Murray soon left for Sicily and then

84   TNA: WO 25/2291: Casualty returns; *The London Gazette*, 20 July 1813, Prevost to Murray, 7 June 1813.
85   TNA: WO 25/2271: Casualty returns (Dillon).
86   Bürkli, 'Das Schweizerregiment', p.31.
87   *The London Gazette*, 20 July 1813, Prevost to Murray, 7 June 1813.
88   Bürkli, 'Das Schweizerregiment', p.31.
89   Lipscombe, *Eastern Front*, p.139, quoting the diary of Major Thomas Scott, RA, entry of 17 June 1813.
90   TNA:12/11997: Paylists 1813.

England, and, without employment, Steiger soon joined the Honourable William Stewart, now lieutenant general and commanding the 2nd Division of Wellington's army, near Pamplona.[91]

The news of Wellington's victory at Vitoria on 21 June and King Joseph's retreat towards the French frontier began to filter through to both Bentinck and Suchet; the latter's position in Valencia was untenable. However, Napoleon's victories at Lützen and Bautzen had led the coalition allies in Central Europe to seek an armistice which was agreed at Pläswitz on 4 June. As it was far from certain that Austria would join the coalition, there was a chance that French troops could be released from Germany for the emperor's forces to regain the initiative in Spain.

January to June 1813 – Ionian Islands and the Adriatic

Vis depended on supplies from the Dalmatian coast so when privateers, operating from the adjacent island of Lastovo (known as Lagosta), preyed on them something had to be done. On 18 January 1813 Robertson left Vis with an expedition of 300 men from the garrison for Lastovo which was quickly secured however the privateers had escaped to the adjacent, and larger, island of Korčula (known as Curzola) which was also captured. In his despatch Robertson made special mention of Captain Francis May, of the 35th, a Swiss officer who had begun his British career in the Minorca Regiment. He was an older brother of Victor, who had served as an officer in the Regiment de Roll from 1810 until 1812 before he joined his step-brothers in the Watteville Regiment.[92] The only units mentioned in the operations are the 35th Foot and the Calabrian Free Corps, however soldiers from Captain Barbier's No.6 Company of the Regiment de Roll appear to have been also present. The muster of 24 January shows Lieutenant Sorgenfrey, Sergeants Lorenz Muzio and Carl Schmidt, a corporal, a drummer and 32 privates on Korčula and two corporals and 10 privates on Lastovo. These numbers were soon reduced, so the following month there was only Corporal Adam Kaiff with a drummer and 13 privates on Korčula and Corporal Johann Robe, alone, on Lastovo.[93] These commitments continued throughout the spring and into the summer of 1813.

The dispatch of substantial numbers of British troops from Sicily to Eastern Spain had meant that the remaining, reduced, manpower in the wider Mediterranean theatre had to be redistributed. This process took time as each movement needed to be balanced with the need to maintain sufficient numbers at any given station as well as the availability of transports. As early as October 1812 Bentinck had planned to have No.4 Company, now commanded by Captain Joseph Glutz, return to Sicily for which purpose it was moved from Kefalonia to Zakynthos, leaving Sergeant John Bollinger

---

91 TNA: WO 43/413: Steiger memorandum 24 August 1825; Steiger states he was 'recalled' by Stewart but it is not clear in what capacity he was with him.
92 *The London Gazette*, 5 June 1813 and *Army Lists*.
93 TNA: WO 12/11997: Paylists 1813.

and Private John Cheminant behind 'on command.' However, it was only on 4 May 1813 that the company finally sailed from Zakynthos for Sicily, the men split between two transports.[94] Individual officers of the Regiment de Roll remained on the Ionian Islands, Major de Bosset in command on Kefalonia and Lieutenant Michael Krumm as Lieutenant General Campbell's military secretary at Zakynthos.[95] On 9 April Bentinck created a unified military command under Campbell in the Adriatic and Ionian Islands to provide co-ordination and quicker decision making.[96]

1813 – Sicily

On 25 January 1813 the headquarters and main part of the Regiment de Roll were at Contesse, where they had been since June 1812 and remained throughout 1813, except between March and May when they returned to Messina.[97] As part of the redistribution of troops, on 28 April Major Vogelsang, brevetted lieutenant colonel since 25 July 1810, and three companies, those of Captains Albert Steiger (No.7 commanded by Lieutenant Gougelberg), Louis Steiger (No.9 commanded by Lieutenant Joseph Tugginer) and Benoit Ryhiner (No.10) were ordered to be ready to embark for Malta complete with their heavy baggage and wives.[98] Anticipating the arrival of Glutz's company, Vogelsang's detachment embarked on 1 May. However, when the transports from Zakynthos arrived at Messina on 15 and 16 May the troops were placed in quarantine at the port's Lazaretto due to the presence of plague in the Balkans.[99]

On 18 May 1813 Major General Peter Du Plat, of the King's German Legion, carried out a review at Messina but could only inspect the regimental staff and the three companies of Captains Lewis Müller (No.3), Antoine Courant (No.8 commanded by Lieutenant Jost Müller) and Francis Glutz (No.12). In his confidential report he was positive about Sonnenberg's command, describing him as 'a very able Officer who keeps the Regiment in excellent order, he having had the same for a considerable time under his direction; the good state of discipline, their being sufficiently versed in the Field Exercise and Manoeuvres are the best proofs of his capacity.'[100] He was also complimentary about the two captains who were present. As for the drummers, musicians and privates, Du Plat wrote,

> Drummers and Musicians appear intelligent and attentive to their duty, and expert in the Qualities they are to possess of, the Number of the latter is according to Regulations, and they are trained also to the Ranks.

---

94   TNA: WO 1/311: Bentinck to Bathurst, 26 October; WO 17/1935: Bentinck to Torrens, 28 October 1812; WO 12/11997: Paylists 1813, officers' stoppages.
95   TNA: WO 12/11997: Paylists 1813; WO 17/1937: Returns 1814.
96   TNA: WO 1/313: Bentinck to Bathurst, 9 April 1813.
97   TNA: WO 17/1935: Monthly returns.
98   Gugelberg (ed.), *Bündners*, p.40; TNA: WO 12/11997: Paylists 1813.
99   TNA: WO 12/11997: Paylists 1813.
100 TNA: WO 27/118: Inspection 18 May 1813.

The Men of the Companies present have in general a good appearance of health and Cleanliness, they are of proper Standard … they are a sober and well behaved set of Men of orderly and soldierlike conduct.[101]

As far as he could judge, given the small numbers present, Du Plat reported that movements and drills conformed strictly to the regulations. He continued, 'In firing Ball the Men have been practised and much improved in hitting their aim, also have they been trained to the Great Guns; but both has not been repeated shortly on account of the few Troops present and the heavy duty laying upon them.'[102]

He noted that a new chaplain had been appointed; John Becker, who had not been present since the end of the Gibraltar epidemic, having been placed on half pay. However his replacement William Peter McDonald had not arrived, 'meanwhile such of the men as profess to the Roman Catholic Religion frequent the Churches of the Country, and the German Protestants attend Divine Service with those of the King's German Legion; and the Sick are attended by these different Clergymen in the same manner.'[103] Lastly Du Plat confirmed the regiment had a school, each regiment in the British Army being required to have one since November 1811, 'and all the Children attend regularly.'[104] The Schoolmaster was Sergeant Christian Stuntz, recruited in Portugal in 1809.[105]

Francis Glutz (1782–1821), officer in the Regiment de Roll from 1805 to 1816. (Photograph by José R. Martinez, Solothurn, courtesy of Historisches Museum Blumenstein, Solothurn, inv. no. 1955.63)

The troop movements meant that the Regiment de Roll, on 25 January had had 754 rank and file on Sicily, out of a total of 1,426 rank and file, on 25 June only 424 were on the island out of 1,365.[106]

The Baron de Roll had not only remained active as the agent and companion to the Comte d'Artois, heir to the French throne, but also in regimental business. Indeed in 1812, prompted by Prince Edward, Duke of Kent, he had proposed that the three Swiss regiments of the British Army be formed into a Royal Swiss Brigade with the Duke as colonel-in-chief, however it was rejected on the grounds that such a brigade would provide no additional benefits to the service.[107] In the summer of 1813 the baron accompanied the Comte d'Artois and his son, the Duc d'Angoulême, to the allied headquarters at Kołobrzeg in Pomerania, however they were not permitted to remain for fear of antagonising Austria which may or may

---

101 TNA: WO 27/118: Inspection 18 May 1813.
102 TNA: WO 27/118: Inspection 18 May 1813.
103 TNA: WO 27/118: Inspection 18 May 1813; McDonald finally arrived at Messina on 24 August 1813.
104 TNA: WO 27/118: Inspection 18 May 1813.
105 TNA: WO 12/11997: Paylists 1813.
106 TNA: WO 17/1936: Monthly returns.
107 See Nichols, *Switzers*, pp.141–142.

not join the coalition against Napoleon.[108] Very shortly after returning to England, on 27 August, the baron died at his country residence, Bounds, near Bidborough, Kent and was interred at the local parish church of Saint Lawrence.

On 16 October Sonnenberg, brevetted colonel since 4 June 1811, submitted a memorandum to the Duke of York applying for the regimental colonelcy. He outlined his service, that he had not been absent from the regiment since its creation and the positive reports of the regiment under his command. In addition he undertook, 'to endeavour in the present Circumstances, to maintain the Regiment as much as is possible, with Officers & Soldiers of his Nation. He is confident that this Appointment will please every Swiss, on witnessing that the Promotion in His Majesty's Service, devolve upon the true Swiss of the Nation.'[109] Notably, despite the length of time he had served in the British Army, while he described himself as being 'acquainted with the German, French & Italian Languages' he could only claim to 'understand a little the English.'[110] Unfortunately, his was always going to be a losing cause, regimental colonelcies were by custom the preserve of general officers. Indeed Louis de Watteville's appointment to his regiment's colonelcy the year before had drawn public criticism and had relied on the intercession of his friend from service in Sicily, Bunbury, who was now Military Undersecretary for War.[111] The new colonel of the Regiment de Roll was Major General Francis Baron Rottenburg (or Rottenburgh), his appointment being dated from 2 September 1813.[112] Rottenburg, born in Gdańsk, Poland, had begun his career in the French Royal Army and after the revolution he had had extensive experience in the British Army as well as being a proponent of the use of light infantry tactics and rifles in the army. By 1813 he was serving in Canada and, as was customary, would not take actual command of the regiment. Despite his appointment the Regiment de Roll retained its name.

1813 – Malta

Vogelsang's detachment disembarked at Valletta on 4 May.[113] Among other reductions to the garrison, the Regiment de Meuron left for Canada the next day and Gougelberg only had a moment to see his cousin, John Theodore de Misani, a lieutenant in Meuron, who 'was in such a hurry to embark that welcome and farewell coincided.'[114] Despite being sent the 3rd Garrison Battalion from Britain, Lieutenant General Hildebrand Oakes, in command on Malta, had requested Bentinck for two or three companies of the Regiment

108 Kirsty Carpenter and Philip Mansel (ed.), *The French Émigrés in Europe and the Struggle against Revolution, 1789–1814* (Basingstoke: Macmillan Press, 1999), pp.10–11.
109 TNA: WO 31/1562: Memorandum Sonnenberg to Duke of York, 16 October 1813.
110 TNA: WO 31/1562: Memorandum Sonnenberg to Duke of York, 16 October 1813.
111 See Nichols, *Switzers*, pp.157–158.
112 *The Army List*, 1814.
113 Gugelberg (ed.), *Bündners*, p.45; TNA: WO 380/5. The regimental record states that part of the detachment had landed a few days before, on 30 April.
114 Gugelberg (ed.), *Bündners*, p.45.

Regimental Seal, the legend reads – LOUIS . BARON . DE ROLL . COLONEL . DU REGIMENT . DE SON NOM. (Historisches Museum, Basel inv.1948.395, courtesy of Jean-Philippe Ganascia)

de Roll, having been authorised to do so, 'should [he] find the Duties of the Garrison press too hard upon his numbers.'[115] The Roll companies were initially quartered in barracks within Fort Saint Elmo however they were soon transferred to buildings formerly used by the Knights of Saint John: the officers in the Auberge de Castile and the men in the Auberge d'Italie.[116]

Events were to prove Oakes to have been wise in requesting an augmentation to his garrison. On their first evening on shore, the Roll officers learned that there were signs of an epidemic in Valletta and communication between the soldiers and the citizens was immediately prohibited.[117] On 5 May it was publicly announced that plague was in the city and restrictive measures began however, in the interim, many people had already left for the countryside so the sickness spread across the island.[118] Strict regulations were applied in the city, including the isolation of all those who had been exposed to infection at Fort Manoel, across Marsamxett Harbour from the city, and soon wooden barracks were constructed in the fort's ditches for additional accommodation. The fort was chosen as it was adjacent to the Lazaretto, where the sick were treated, and when, by the end of June, the Lazaretto was full the fort was also used to house the sick, so tents were pitched for those who were isolating.[119] At one stage, according to Gougelberg, there were 10,000 people in or around Fort Manoel.[120]

---

115   TNA: WO 6/57: Bathurst to Bentinck, 3 February 1813. Bentinck was instructed to comply with such a request.

116   Gugelberg (ed.), *Bündners*, p.45.

117   Gugelberg (ed.), *Bündners*, p.45.

118   James D. Tully, *The History of Plague, as it has lately appeared in the Islands of Malta, Gozo, Corfu, Cephalonia &c.* (London: Longman, Hurst, Rees, Orme and Brown, 1821), p.41.

119   Tully, *History of Plague*, p.54.

120   Gugelberg (ed.), *Bündners*, p.46.

Civilians were temporarily employed to enforce the regulations but soldiers were posted at key places. A detachment of the Regiment de Roll, under Lieutenant Joseph Tugginer, was sent as a guard for Fort Manoel where, as Gougelberg related, 'As an eyewitness, he saw unbelievable, shocking scenes.'[121] Tugginer remained at the fort throughout the epidemic and his fellow officer noted the assistance he provided to the sick and isolating who were about him, many of whom suffered through the lack of food. Gougelberg commanded a detachment doing duty at the Porta Reale, or City Gate, the only landward access to Valletta. On 28 June three of his men complained of severe headaches and fever soon followed, shortly afterwards one died, the cause confirmed as bubonic plague.[122] The two men who were ill were placed in a secluded tent and any soldier who had had contact with the sick was sent to an observation house. As Gougelberg was among the latter he had to quarantine himself in his quarters for 54 days, his only contact being his servant, during which time,

> They sent me mercurial pills, censers, oil, vinegar and God knows what, and asked how I was feeling every day. I did not take the pills, but stuck to the numerous bottles of the best port wine that the artillery mess sent me and rubbed myself often with oil. Otherwise quite healthy, I only had a raging headache for 2 days and a small swelling appeared on the left side; but I said nothing, had a brick heated up in the evening, which I put on the swelling, drank a bottle of port wine, fell asleep, and when I woke up the swelling had disappeared and the headache had also subsided considerably.[123]

Detachments of the Regiment de Roll, apparently made up of men from different companies, were isolated from each other at Fort Manoel, Porta Reale and in quarters at the Auberges. Care was taken to prevent plague spreading among the troops, 'The men were examined twice a day, had to rub themselves with oil, wash with vinegar, and be extremely clean'.[124] The steps were effective and not many succumbed to the disease, Gougelberg recalled that 18 fell ill, of whom 11 died.[125] The casualty returns support this, showing that, between 28 June and the end of October, 11 men died in the three companies, the first being Private Jacob Weber on 28 June who, although with Gougelberg, was from No.9 Company.[126]

Meanwhile, on 23 July, the British Government changed the status of the British presence on the island, declaring Malta to be a Crown Colony and on 5 October Lieutenant General Thomas Maitland arrived as governor. The outbreak of plague was on the wane, but Maitland took even stricter measures to finally extinguish it. These included building barriers around Qormi, where earlier regulations had been ignored and the plague continued

---

121 Gugelberg (ed.), *Bündners*, p.48.
122 Gugelberg (ed.), *Bündners*, p.49.
123 Gugelberg (ed.), *Bündners*, p.50.
124 Gugelberg (ed.), *Bündners*, p.50.
125 Gugelberg (ed.), *Bündners*, p.50, he indicates that this was during his quarantine.
126 TNA: WO 25/2291: Casualty returns.

to flourish, with troops stationed to ensure no one broke through the cordon. Similar steps were immediately taken in February 1814 when an outbreak occurred on Gozo, which had previously escaped plague, with the result that only 96 people died in a population of 15,000.[127] On Malta itself the island was considered free of plague by the end of January 1814 with the final restrictions lifted in March. Although Gougelberg estimated that 8,000 people had died modern estimates put the figure at around 4,500.[128]

July to December 1813 – Adriatic

For the British uncertainty about Austria's position, as well as a lack of manpower, had restricted offensive operations in the Adriatic but this changed when it joined the coalition against Napoleon and finally declared war on 12 August 1813. An Austrian army was sent into Italy and *Generalmajor* Nugent was sent with a brigade to secure the Istria peninsula and so isolate Napoleon's forces that remained in Croatia. The Royal Navy was soon co-operating with him and on 26 August Fremantle arrived at Rijeka (then known as Fiume) with his squadron, the same day Nugent's troops entered the town.[129] Croatian troops deserted en masse to the allies, sometimes delivering the French or Italian troops they had been serving alongside as prisoners. On 7 September Major John Henry Slessor, 35th Foot, arrived at Rijeka to liaise with Nugent, bringing with him an offer from Robertson to join him with part of the Vis garrison that was accepted.[130]

Nugent, with other Austrian forces, pressed their advantage and on 5 October the enemy were driven across the Soča, or Isonzo, river. Istria was clear of them, except for the garrison at Trieste which was blockaded. On 10 October Fremantle landed marines from his squadron in preparation for a siege and he was soon joined by Nugent. On 12 October the town itself was taken and the garrison withdrew to defend the Castello di San Giusto and outlying works. The next day Robertson arrived at Trieste, having sailed from Vis on 10 October, with a detachment of 500 men.[131] They included Lieutenant Sorgenfrey, three sergeants, two corporals and 56 privates from the Regiment de Roll.[132] Other elements came from the 35th Foot, under Captain May, Royal Corsican Rangers, Calabrian Free Corps, Royal Artillery and the Italian Levy. This last consisted of an independent Illyrian Company of Croatians who had deserted the enemy; Sergeant Lorenz Muzio of the Regiment de Roll served as its adjutant.[133] The weather was wet and the work of constructing and arming the batteries took time so it was only completed

---

127 Tully, *History of Plague*, p.74.

128 Gugelberg (ed.), *Bündners*, p.49.

129 *The London Gazette*, 19 October 1813, Fremantle to Admiralty, 4 September 1813.

130 Hayter (ed.), *The Backbone*, p.254; *The London Gazette*, 23 November 1813, Fremantle to Pellew, undated extract.

131 King, 'Robertson', pp.175–176.

132 TNA: WO 12/11997: Muster list 24 October 1813.

133 TNA: AO 3/67: Paylist German Chasseur Battalion. There was also an Italian Company which appears to have been formed after Robertson had landed.

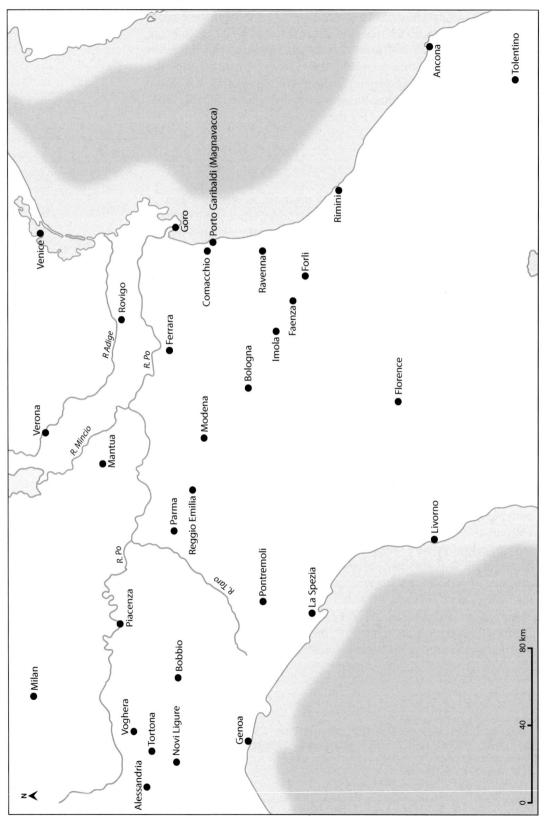

Northern Italy.

on 23 October, however the resulting fire soon caused the enemy garrison to surrender on 29 October, so that the planned assault, in which Robertson and his men were to have taken part in, was not required.[134]

In November the main Austrian army advanced and forced Napoleon's viceroy in Italy, Eugène de Beauharnais, to retreat westwards from Udine; as the Austrians advanced Venice was bypassed but blockaded. Nugent's command was to land on the Italian coast, south of the Po, as part of the blockade as well as to provide a threat to Beauharnais's right flank. On the night of 9/10 November his 2,700 men, including those with Robertson, embarked in a convoy of locally hired transports with an escort of Royal Navy warships.[135] After making a detour to hide their destination and being delayed by contrary winds, the convoy anchored off Goro, just south of the Po delta, in the evening of 14 November. The following morning the troops landed and Nugent's units, Croatian border troops of the Grenz-Infanterie-Regiment No.5 Warasdiner Kreuzer and Hungarian infantry regiment No.52 Herzog Franz Carl, established a sizeable beachhead, entering Ferrara on 18 November and Robertson's battalion-sized force apparently reached the city a day or so later. Nugent's advance reached Rovigo, north of the Po, on 19 November where they soon linked up with elements of the main Austrian army.

Beauharnais soon ordered forces to counter Nugent's incursion. While they advanced on Ferrara, about 750 Italian troops marched from Ravenna on Comacchio to cut Nugent's communication with the sea. On 24 November they attacked the fort at Magnavacca (now called Porto Garibaldi), which was defended by British marines and Croatians, the attack was driven off by the defenders, the gun brig HMS *Wizard* and the people of Comacchio. Nugent was at Ferrara with about 1,000 men when on 26 November the enemy drove in the Austrian outposts and attacked the city's southern gate, the Porta Paola.[136] This was the point defended by Robertson who, unmasking his batteries at the last moment, stopped the assault 50 paces from the city walls as well as a further attempt that night.[137] However, threatened with encirclement, Nugent withdrew from the city, taking a defensive position closer to the sea. Despite again threatening to attack Comacchio from Ravenna and capturing Rovigo on 3 December, the enemy's counter-offensive went no further, and Rovigo was immediately evacuated. Some or all of the detachment of the Regiment de Roll was with Robertson at Ferrara as two privates deserted there on 27 November, apparently when it was evacuated, but Sorgenfrey was serving at Comacchio where he signed the muster roll on 25 November.[138]

Nugent received reinforcements including a detachment of 70 men, of which 15 were privates of the Regiment de Roll, that had left Vis on 27 November with Major Slessor. The latter had had command of the island

---

134   *The London Gazette*, 11 December 1813, Nugent to Bathurst, 1 November 1813.

135   Ilari and Crociani, *L'Armata italiana*, pp.259–260.

136   The gate had been named after Pope Pius V, so during the French rule in Italy had been renamed the Porta Reno, the name used by, for example, in King 'Robertson', p.177.

137   Ilari and Crociani, *L'Armata italiana*, p.261.

138   TNA: WO 12/11997: Detachment muster rolls, 1813.

since Robertson's departure, and this now devolved to Barbier. Having initially sailed to Trieste Slessor's detachment landed at Magnavacca on 4 December. He noted the effects of that winter's weather, 'Dec 5th. Marched to Commacchio [*sic*] four miles, most part of the way above our ankles in mud. ... Called on General Nugent, who gave me an account of his retreat from Ferrara. He spoke in high terms of Col. Robertson and his detachment.'[139] On 6 December Nugent took the offensive again and by the next day his advance entered Ravenna. Robertson was not part of this initial push southwards but at the outposts covering the flank. However, his detachment marched to Ravenna on 26 December, entering the city the following day, where the British troops were greeted with, 'the acclamations of the inhabitants.'[140]

Nugent's operations had taken place in the shadow of Neapolitan forces approaching from the south. Since January, when the remains of Napoleon's army had emerged from Russia, Murat had made approaches to the coalition allies as he tried to ensure he retained his throne at Naples. These had been briefly interrupted when he returned to the Emperor's side during the Armistice of Pläswitz but he had soon returned to pursue his regal ambitions. However, his intentions were not settled when his army had reached Ancona at the end of December, with the Austrians occupying Forli with advance posts at Rimini, as he was reaching out to Beauharnais at the same time.

While these events had been taking place on the Italian mainland, the Royal Navy vessels and especially the frigate HMS *Bacchante*, commanded by Captain William Hoste, were involved in clearing the enemy garrisons from the eastern seaboard and islands of the Adriatic. In mid-October when Hoste made his first attempt to seize Kotor, on the coast of Montenegro, he was accompanied by Captain Pearce Lowen of the Royal Corsican Rangers who had command of Korčula, with a detachment of his garrison, although the soldiers' contribution to the operation was, at most, minimal.[141] Soon attention turned to Dubrovnik where local insurgents were attempting a blockade to starve the garrison into surrender and wished support, in any form, from the British. According to the now, Lieutenant Hildebrand, who commanded on Lastovo, Lowen who could only provide 50 rank and file, persuaded the former to join him with 15 more from his garrison.[142] They were landed by Hoste at Cavtat (then Ragusa Vecchia) to the south east of Dubrovnik to join the insurgents, however it became clear very quickly that their blockade was somewhat haphazard and their politics complicated. Hildebrand recounts that Lowen remained at Cavtat with all the troops they had brought with them as a reserve while he, alone, joined the insurgents.[143] Finally after the arrival of Austrian troops and then the return of Hoste, who landed cannon to fire on the city, the garrison surrendered on 28 January 1814.

---

139 Hayter (ed.), *The Backbone*, pp.258–259.
140 Hayter (ed.), *The Backbone*, p.259.
141 *The London Gazette*, 8 January 1814 Hoste to Fremantle, 16 October 1813.
142 Glover, *Fighting Napoleon*, pp.85–87.
143 Glover, *Fighting Napoleon*, p.97.

Detail of the tails of an officer's coat, some decoration differs from that included in the colour plates. (Item 4827 B, Musée de l'Empéri, dépôt du Musée de l'Armée, Centre de documentation du Musée de l'Empéri, courtesy of Jérôme Croyet)

The presumption has been, given Lowen and Hildebrand's units, that the troops they brought with them were only from the Royal Corsican Rangers and the 35th Foot. However, Sergeant Schmidt, Corporal Kaiff and 16 privates – 17 of the 65 rank and file who were present – were from the Regiment de Roll. At the musters of 24 November and 24 December 1813 they were recorded as 'on command at Ragusa [Dubrovnik],' having been shown at Korčula the month before.[144]

July to December 1813 – Eastern Spain

One of Bentinck's first actions after his troops arrived at Alicante was to adjust the army's formation. For the forthcoming campaign his field army was to have three infantry divisions, the First, commanded by Clinton, had four brigades: the Advance Brigade, commanded by Adam, of the 2/27th Foot, Calabrian Free Corps, Roll Rifle Company and, as future events showed, the Rifle Company of the 4th Battalion, King's German Legion; the Right Brigade of two Sicilian (Estero) battalions; the Centre of two British battalions and the Left of the 1st and 2nd Italian Regiments. The Second Division was commanded by Whittingham and was made up of his own troops while the Reserve Division had two brigades, the first commanded by Colonel Lemuel Warren was of the 1/10th and 1/27th Foot and the second, Colonel Patrick McKenzie, the 1/81st Foot and Roll-Dillon Battalion.[145]

Following news of Wellington's victory at Vitoria, Suchet retreated northwards and by 12 July he was established along the line of the Ebro. Then, learning that French forces were retreating over the Pyrenees, he continued to withdraw and reached Tarragona on 17 July with a field army of about 15,000 men. However, he left sizable garrisons behind in a number of strongholds should the tide of war turn once more in his favour. Bentinck's ability to follow was hampered as he only had around a quarter of the transport he needed and a lack of supplies meant that his Spanish allies were prevented from concentrating with him.[146] Although his foremost units reached Valencia on 9 July, a week had passed before his Anglo-Sicilian army of about 16,000 men moved from there, along the coast road. Bentinck had reached Vinaròs on 20 July when he was informed that Suchet was about to leave Tarragona and abandon Catalonia. He felt compelled to act to prevent Suchet being able to join forces against Wellington, which was, after all, the purpose of the intervention in Eastern Spain. Bentinck's immediate plan was to seize Tarragona for which Clinton was to go by sea with the First and Reserve Divisions and land at the city while the rest of the Anglo-Sicilian army, the Second Division and cavalry, was to cross the Ebro around Amposta and march along the coast road. The Roll-Dillon Battalion had reached Sant

144   TNA: WO 12/11997: Detachment muster rolls 1813.
145   Based on Salis, Bürkli, 'Das Schweizerregiment', pp.31–32, there are some minor variations between this and the order (without brigades) given by Oman, *Peninsular War*, vol.VII, pp.532–533.
146   Oman, *Peninsular War*, vol.VII, pp.63, 79.

Carles de la Ràpita, on the southern extremity of the Ebro delta, by 24 July where it embarked three days later.[147]

However, when Clinton came in sight of Tarragona it was evident that the city remained firmly in French hands. The information Bentinck had received was incorrect, the main body of Suchet's troops were in fact cantoned between Tarragona and Barcelona, waiting to be joined by reinforcements of around 8,000 to 10,000 from the rest of Catalonia. Clinton withdrew to the Puerto de Balaguer where he was joined by Bentinck who, although unsure of where Suchet was, decided to press on to surround Tarragona.

Bentinck's march on Tarragona was disputed as Landsheit, with the Foreign Hussars and operating with Adam's Advance Brigade, remembered, 'The enemy seemed reluctant to abandon the ground between Tortosa and Tarragona, and were not removed from it without frequent encounters between our advanced parties and their rear-guard.'[148] On 30 July the Roll Rifle Company was involved in such an encounter when one private was killed, another was missing after being wounded, and several more men were wounded, including Ensign Edward Tugginer who was to be hospitalised, on board ship, for at least two months.[149] The next day, 31 July, Tarragona was invested and preparations began to besiege the city. However Bentinck, now aware of how close the French forces were, did not land his heavy artillery. McKenzie's brigade of the Reserve was posted on the western side of the city, along the Francoli river, close into the walls in the cover of some banks.[150] The men certainly came under fire as a soldier from one of the Dillon companies was killed in action on 2 August.[151] Meanwhile Adam's brigade was posted on the eastern side, on the coast road to Barcelona, around Altafulla.[152] On 13 August Suchet was finally joined by the reinforcements and the next day he moved on Tarragona, hoping to trap Bentinck in a pincer movement. However the column that he sent along the coast road was stopped at Altafulla by Adam, who had been reinforced by the Second Brigade of the Reserve although the latter appears to have suffered no casualties.[153] Bentinck, although he had been joined by more Spanish troops, decided to avoid a full engagement and, on the night of 16 August, he retreated to Cambrils, with the strong position at the Puerto de Balaguer in his rear and his flank protected by British warships offshore. Suchet, in turn, decided Bentinck was too strongly posted to attack so he withdrew to Vilafranca del Penedès, abandoning Tarragona on the night of 18 August.[154] In doing so the city's magazines were destroyed along with much of the defences, in what Landsheit described as, 'an explosion … that shook the very earth beneath our feet. The sound was louder than the loudest thunder; and the effect … resembled that of an earthquake.'[155]

---

147   TNA: WO 12/11997: Paylists 1813 officers' stoppages.
148   Fortescue, *British Army*, vol.IX, p.373; Gleig (ed.), *The Hussar*, vol.II, p.118.
149   TNA: WO 12/11997: Paylists 1813; WO 25/2291: Casualty returns.
150   Anon., *Historical Record*, pp.120–121.
151   TNA: WO 25/2271: Casualty returns (Dillon).
152   Gleig (ed.), *The Hussar*, vol.II, p.119.
153   Anon., *Historical Record*, pp.121–122.
154   Oman, *Peninsular War*, vol.IV, pp.83–87.
155   Gleig (ed.), *The Hussar*, vol.II, p.134.

Bentinck remained in his positions with much of the Anglo-Sicilian troops, the Spanish troops having been sent to the rear due to a lack of provisions. On 25 August the Reserve, including the Roll-Dillon Battalion, was encamped at the Puerto de Balaguer while the Advance had pushed on to La Canonja, close to Tarragona.[156] Then, after Suchet had retreated to the Llobregat valley, west of Barcelona, Bentinck occupied Tarragona, making it the logistical centre for his army and the fleet. The Reserve's Second Brigade was posted around Altafulla until the 5 September when Bentinck, informed that Suchet's strength had been reduced, advanced to Vilafranca.[157] On the morning of 12 September Bentinck ordered Adam to occupy the Pass of Ordal, through which the Barcelona road crossed the mountainous ridge of the Serra d'Ordal. His brigade was accompanied by four guns and some cavalry and so amounted to about 1,500 to 1,600 men.[158] It appears that Bentinck intended to bring the rest of the Anglo-Sicilians up from Vilafranca during the day but instead Adam was reinforced by Spanish troops, three infantry battalions – Tiradores de Cádiz, Voluntarios de Aragon and the grenadier companies of the Regimiento Ultonia – with about 2,300 in the ranks and more cavalry.[159] Facing towards the east, and the direction of Molins de Rei, the position was strong, above a deep defile that extended across its front which the road crossed on a bridge, the Pont del Lledoner. Its importance had been recognised earlier when the Spanish had constructed earthworks that flanked the road, but they had been ruined three years ago.

By nightfall Adam had placed the Calabrian Free Corps, commanded by Lieutenant Colonel Octavius Carey, on the hill on his left flank, his guns in an elevated position on the road, the Spanish battalions in line to the right of the road and the 2/27th Foot on the far right covering a track that climbed the slope from the defile. Captain Müller commanded four companies – the rifles of the Regiment de Roll and 4th Battalion, King's German Legion, and two from the 2/27th – in the foremost earthwork. Due to the losses of 30 July and sickness, the Roll Rifle Company had three officers and 87 other ranks present under arms.[160] Critically Adam did not place any troops, not even a cavalry vidette, on the Pont del Lledoner. Meanwhile Suchet had gathered his forces at Molins de Rei in order to attack Bentinck at Vilafranca. One column, of about 7,000 infantry with some cavalry, was to take the road to the north and so appear on Bentinck's flank while Suchet advanced along the road via the Pass of Ordal with 10,000 infantry and 1,500 cavalry. The columns set off in the evening of 12 September and Suchet's made good progress. Finding the Pont del Lledoner undefended he pressed on, sending a battalion to his left flank to cross the defile by the previously mentioned track. At about 11:00 p.m. his advance ran into a Spanish cavalry patrol that raised the alarm.

156   TNA: WO 17/2478: Army return 25 August 1813.

157   Anon., *Historical Record*, pp.122–123; Oman, *Peninsular War*, vol.IV, p.98.

158   Oman, *Peninsular War*, vol.IV, p.99.

159   Miquel Miró, 'The Combat of the Ordal Cross: 13th September 1813', *The Napoleon Series* <https://www.napoleon-series.org/military-info/virtual/c_ordal.html>, accessed 9 February 2023.

160   Bürkli, 'Das Schweizerregiment', p.33.

Soon the French guns were in action providing covering fire as Suchet's column made a frontal attack and skirmishers swept round to the flanks. Müller's detachment was immediately in action, as he reported,

> We resisted a considerable time the repeated attacks of the Enemy, but our Ranks being at last much thinned, whilst the attacks of the Enemy became more and more impetuous, we were at last driven from the old Redoubt. I rallied the Troops about 60 paces in rear of it behind some old ruins, from which place we succeeded twice to retake the higher part of our old position, attacking in conjunction with the Spanish Brigade which was close on our left and which fought and charged with the greatest intrepidity.[161]

In the fighting Lieutenant Anton Segesser was shot and killed and Lieutenant Stephen de Planta, noted for his short stature, considered he owed his life to his lack of height when a shot grazed the top of his head and killed the man immediately behind him. Having lost his shako, Planta picked up Segesser's and placed it on his head.[162]

The position was finally lost. In the darkness it was impossible for the defenders to assess the enemy's strength or intentions. The confusion was made worse by Adam being severely wounded and carried to the rear at a very early stage of the combat. The next most senior officer was Lieutenant Colonel George James Reeves of the 27th and on taking command he was concerned how the contest was going and ordered the guns to retire before himself being wounded and taken to the rear. Without further direction, the officer in charge of the artillery, Captain Frederick Arabin, decided to remain in support of the Spanish troops.[163] Meanwhile the main body of the 27th, on the right of the position, was suffering heavy casualties, principally from artillery fire and that of the skirmishers that were working round its flank.[164]

After about an hour and a half of combat, Müller was informed by a staff officer, Nicolas de Goumoëns, that he should direct the troops until Carey could be contacted, as Adam and Reeves were both wounded.[165] Müller wrote,

> I immediately proceeded to the right where the 27th Regiment was posted, and desired some of my party to follow me. I had scarcely joined them that I was informed that the Enemy were turning our right flank. I occasioned it to be

161 University of Southampton, Hartley Library, Special Collections (HLS): MS61/WP/1/376 folder 8: Müller to Carey, 15 September 1813. This and the accompanying letters were published in *The London Gazette*, 5 October 1813.

162 Bürkli, 'Das Schweizerregiment', p.33, using Salis's journal as the source.

163 HLS: MS61/WP/1/376 folder 8: Arabin to Major Williamson, RA, 17 September 1813.

164 HLS: MS61/WP/1/376 folder 8: Captain John Waldron, 27th Foot, to Carey, 15 September 1813.

165 Goumoëns, named by both Müller and Carey, was a Swiss officer who had previously served in the Austrian army and, with a Spanish commission, was on Bentinck's headquarters staff (Adolf Bürkli, 'Biographie von Niklaus Emmanuel Friedrich von Goumoëns, Oberst im Niederländischen Generalstab 1790–1832', *Neujahrsblatt der Feuerwerter-Gefellschaft*, vol. LXXXIII 1890, pp.3–14).

reinforced, but it was in vain they attempted to withstand any longer, the Enemy continuing to gain ground. At the same moment I saw the Spanish Brigade on our left retiring. There was not a moment to be lost and I ordered the 27th Regiment to retire. We gained the main road for the purpose of arriving at a hill in rear of the first position before the Enemy could get possession of it; in this we succeeded. I am however concerned to state that many men continued to follow by the main road and could not be brought to turn left when it was ordered.[166]

The French cavalry broke through along the road where the retreat of the allied troops became a rout. One of the troopers delivered a blow at Planta's head, but he was saved by Segesser's shako and only fell into the ditch where he stayed until the cavalry had passed. Segesser had placed a metal circle in the top of his shako for just such an occasion and was mocked for it by his comrades for doing so, for which one of them owed his life.[167]

At about 2:00 a.m. Goumoëns found Carey whose Calabrians, on the left flank, had not been engaged and informed him of the situation. Carey brought his troops across to attack the enemy's column on the flank however seeing, 'The Enemy had already succeeded in turning the Right of the Position and the Troops that had defended that flank had been obliged to retire, I therefore determined to fall back'.[168] In the confusion the French cavalry took the British guns as they retired on the road, but most of the gunners were able to slip away. The darkness was to provide safety for many of the allied soldiers who took to the wooded hills. Carey led his Calabrians northwards where they ran into the flank of Suchet's other column, so he turned towards the coast. Müller's party kept close to the road in the hope that the enemy's pursuit would stop at some time but with continued contact, he led it over the wooded ridge to Olesa de Bonesvalls and to join the rest of the army,

> Our march was of the most fatiguing nature that can be imagined, many men worn out by fatigue remained behind, so that the party with which I joined the first division (by about 2 o'clock in the afternoon) consisted only of about 70 men, but I can assert that a great number are still in the woods and will be able to join.[169]

The sounds of combat had stirred Bentinck and at daybreak he had drawn his troops up in battle array in front of Vilafranca. However, Suchet soon threatened to turn the left flank at the village of Sant Cugat Sessgarrigues. Although the Roll-Dillon Battalion is not directly mentioned, the history of the 81st Foot describes the part played by the brigade in the day's events,

> The ground in front affording too great a scope for the play of the enemy's cavalry, the army retired, and the first battalion Eighty-first regiment, with the division of reserve, covered the movement, retiring in such fine order by the passing of

166 HLS: MS61/WP/1/376 folder 8: Müller to Carey, 15 September 1813.
167 Bürkli, 'Das Schweizerregiment', p.34.
168 HLS: MS61/WP/1/376 folder 8: Carey to Bentinck, 15 September 1813.
169 HLS: MS61/WP/1/376 folder 8: Müller to Carey, 15 September 1813.

alternate lines, under a heavy fire of artillery, as to excite the praise of Marshal Suchet himself.[170]

Suchet's cavalry and horse artillery had a clear numerical advantage over those of Bentinck. The retreat continued towards a strong position just behind L'Arboç (or Arbós),

> Preparations were made for destroying the bridge of Arbos as soon as the army had passed over, and the Eighty-first regiment, with its brigade, formed on the left of the road to cover the retreat, but the enemy's cavalry pressing close on the rear, it became necessary to repel them to afford time for the Twenty-seventh and Tenth regiments to pass the ravine. This was gallantly effected by the Brunswick Hussars ... The troops having passed the bridge, it was destroyed, and the reserve division retired in echelon to its position in line, the Eighty-first regiment being the last to withdraw ... In the affair of the thirteenth the troops displayed the greatest steadiness and discipline. They were under a cannonade from daylight till nearly three o'clock in the afternoon ...[171]

Suchet declined to assault such a strong position and withdrew his main force, ultimately, to his original positions on the Llobregat. Bentinck stayed in position until the evening when he fell back to El Vendrell and, on 14 September, continued via Altafulla to Tarragona. Despite secondary sources indicating that contact between the opposing forces ended on 13 September, it appears that it continued until Bentinck had reached Tarragona.[172]

Table 14: Allied losses, Combat of Ordal, 12–13 September 1813.[173]

	Killed		Wounded		Missing		Total
	Officers	Men	Officers	Men	Officers	Men	
Staff	–	–	2	–	–	–	2
2/27th	1	31	8	76	1	247	364
4th KGL Rifles	–	24	2	11	–	–	37
Roll Rifles	1	18	–	9	–	22	50
Calabrians	–	–	1	–	1	50	52
Royal Artillery	–	–	–	–	–	12	12
Spanish (all ranks)	–	87	–	239	–	132	458
Oman explains the variations thus, 'In the two Rifle companies, the 4th K.G.L. evidently put down their 'missing' as all dead, while De Roll did not. The Calabrese entered their dead and wounded as 'missing,' all having fallen into the hands of the French, so did the R.A.'							

The regimental records show the Regiment de Roll's Rifle Company lost 19 men killed – a lieutenant, a sergeant, two corporals and 15 privates – and 22 missing, among whom a corporal and eight privates were recorded as

---

170 Anon., *Historical Record*, p.124.

171 Anon., *Historical Record*, pp.125–126.

172 Landsheit paints a picture of the retreat being something of a rout, Gleig (ed.), *The Hussar*, vol. II, pp.194–197.

173 Oman, *Peninsular War*, vol.IV, p.533.

having been left behind after being wounded including Privates Martin Dariel and Joseph Donde, both Frenchmen, who returned to the regiment in July 1814. The other missing, in the combat or retreat, were two sergeants and 11 privates.[174] The losses of the three other Roll companies were men who were shown as missing, indicating that they were in contact with the enemy at the time. These were: No.1 (Mohr): three privates on 13 and one private on 16 September; No.2 (H. Ryhiner, Grenadier): a corporal, a drummer and four privates on 13 and seven privates on 14 September and No.11 (A. de Sury, Light): a bugler and three privates on 13 and one private on 14 September.[175]

Having satisfied himself that Suchet had retreated, on 22 September Bentinck left the army for Sicily and he arrived at Palermo on 3 October. William Clinton, who resumed command of the Anglo-Sicilian army, was not inclined to resume the offensive and was satisfied to consolidate his position in and around Tarragona, indeed Wellington was later to remark that he, 'Did nothing in particular – and did it pretty well.'[176] By 24 September the Reserve Division, including the Roll-Dillon Battalion, were in cantonments at Valls, north of Tarragona, where the battalion supplied three sergeants and 36 rank and file, including men from the three Roll companies, to a detachment sent to the 'Castle of St. Barbaro' which was presumably Castell de Barberà, north of Valls.[177] Then on 22 October, after the headquarters had transferred to Vilafranca, the division moved to El Vendrell, where the Roll Rifle Company was also posted.[178]

Suchet had remained inactive until he received orders from Napoleon, dated 25 November, to evacuate his garrisons that still remained in the Ebro fortresses. In an attempt to dispose of the Anglo-Sicilian army first, on 2 December he marched on Vilafranca by the same roads as in September, however Clinton, warned of this movement, withdrew to the L'Arboç position. Suchet, once again, declined to attack and soon both armies returned to their original positions.[179]

174 TNA: WO 25/2291: Casualty returns.
175 TNA: WO 25/2291: Casualty returns.
176 Quoted in Oman, *Peninsular War*, vol. VII, p.109.
177 TNA: WO 17/2478: Army return, 25 September 1813; WO 12/11998: Paylists.
178 TNA: WO 12/11997: Muster roll, 24 September to 24 December 1813; Anon., *Historical Record*, p.126.
179 Oman, *Peninsular War*, vol. VII, pp.407–408.

9

'Scattered to all corners'

1814 - Spain

On 24 January 1814 the strength of the four companies of the Regiment de Roll in Spain was:

> No.1 (Mohr) – captain (brevet lieutenant colonel), two lieutenants, one ensign, six sergeants, three corporals, one drummer and 44 privates.
> No.2 (H. Ryhiner, Grenadier) – captain (brevet major since 4 June 1813), two lieutenants, four sergeants, five corporals, one drummer and 82 privates.
> No.5 (Müller, Rifle) – captain, two lieutenants, three sergeants, three corporals, two buglers and 50 privates.
> No.11 (A. de Sury, Light) – captain, two lieutenants, five sergeants, six corporals, one bugler and 96 privates.[1]

The losses in Müller's company had principally been caused by combat while in Mohr's it was by the desertion of the Spanish soldiers. The Roll-Dillon Battalion was still at El Vendrell and the Advance Brigade, with Roll's Rifle Company, at La Gornal, just south of L'Arboç.[2]

Suchet had to send troops to help Napoleon to defend the frontiers of France in the north and east and so on 1 February he quit his position on the Llobregat for Girona, leaving a well-supplied garrison of 7,500 men in Barcelona. On 3 February Clinton, alongside Spanish troops, but without a siege train, invested the city. On 7 February the Reserve Division was quartered at Esplugues de Llobregat, just west of Barcelona, with picquets pushed up closer to the walls.[3] In the meantime the French garrison of Lleida, and two other posts, had been tricked into quitting their posts in the belief that Suchet had signed a convention by which they had free passage to Barcelona. Although apparently not party to the ploy, Clinton had determined that the French could approach no further than Martorell, where the road from Lleida passes through a narrow mountain pass. On 17 February the Roll-Dillon's brigade marched via Molins de Rei to Martorell

---

1   TNA: WO 12/11998: Paylists 1814.
2   TNA: WO 17/2478: Army return 25 January 1814.
3   Anon., *Historical Record*, p.130.

where the French garrisons arrived on 18 February. Halted by the British troops, the column was surrounded by the Spanish and forced to surrender, only the accompanying women and children were allowed to continue to Barcelona.[4] After this somewhat inglorious mission, the Second Brigade returned to Esplugues.[5]

On 23 February the Barcelona garrison made a strong sortie to test the strength of the investment on a section held by Spanish troops but it was repelled with losses on each side.[6] Then, on 6 March, Suchet evacuated Catalonia, withdrawing to Figueres, and on 30 March, the Anglo-Sicilian army participated in a large military display Molins de Rei.[7] It was described by Landsheit,

> … an order was issued for the whole army, Spaniards as well as English, to form in a long double line along the main road. The troops stood by brigades – here a brigade of Spanish infantry – there a brigade of British infantry – here a body of horse – there a detachment of artillery – all the troops of all the allied nations being interlaced, and all extending to a great distance … The lines had been formed perhaps an hour and a half, and each man asked his neighbour what was going to happen, when some staff-officers came at full speed from the front, and passed the word to mount and draw swords. We did so, of course, and presently the thunder of artillery, as brigade after brigade fired its salute, warned us that some great personage was approaching. All eyes were accordingly turned in the proper direction, and in due time two horsemen made their appearance, followed at an interval of perhaps ten or twelve paces by a very numerous staff. One of these persons we instantly recognised as Sir Wm. Clinton – the other was pointed out to us as Ferdinand VII, the King of Spain.[8]

Ferdinand had been released from captivity in France by Napoleon in the forlorn hope he would turn his country against Britain, his return became a ceremonial progress after entering Catalonia on 24 March.

On 6 April, Clinton prepared to break his army up, the war was over. On 31 March Paris had surrendered to the coalition allies and on 6 April Napoleon resigned himself to abdicate unconditionally. Suchet learned of these events on 13 April, the day that Napoleon ratified the Treaty of Fontainebleau that formally stripped him of his powers.[9] Five British battalions, including the 1/81st, left on 14 April to join Wellington in France and the rest of the British and Sicilian units marched to Tarragona to embark for their destinations.[10]

---

4   Anon., *Historical Record*, pp.130–131; for details of the trick see Oman, *Peninsular War*, vol. VII, pp.415–421.

5   TNA: WO 17/2478: Army return 25 February 1814.

6   Oman, *Peninsular War*, vol.VII, p.430. Bürkli, 'Das Schweizerregiment', p.34 states that the regiment had 15 men killed in this sortie. However, in the returns no men are shown as killed in or around 23 February 1814 from either the Regiment de Roll or Dillon, supporting Oman's statement that Spanish troops were involved in this action.

7   Bürkli, 'Das Schweizerregiment', p.35, apparently using Salis's journal as the source.

8   Gleig (ed.), *The Hussar*, vol.II, pp.232–234.

9   Oman, *Peninsular War*, vol.VII, p.429.

10   Anon., *Historical Record*, p.132.

The four companies of the Regiment de Roll sailed on 25 April in HMS *Malta* and the transport, *General Graham*.[11]

On 11 May 1815 the Regiment de Roll was granted permission, 'to bear on its Colors and Appointments … the Word "Peninsula," in consideration of the good Conduct of the Officers and Men of a portion of that Regiment while employed in Spain.'[12]

1814 – Italy

January 1814 began with Robertson's force at Ravenna, with some elements still on the Adriatic coast. On 12 January Slessor wrote, 'A great many deserters come daily over to us, principally Poles and Germans. Col. Robertson has permission to form them into a separate Corps. Active, fine fellows they are, and shew much animosity towards their late rulers.'[13] Six companies of this corps, the German Chasseurs Battalion, were formed in the month following 25 December 1813. Lieutenant Sorgenfrey, commanding the Regiment de Roll's detachment, appears to have been given the additional responsibility of organising the battalion and was acting captain of its First Company; he was assisted by two of the regiment's sergeants, Lorenz Muzio who was appointed ensign and commanded the Second Company, and Johann Boshardt who was the battalion's adjutant.[14] The Regiment de Roll detachment was left with one sergeant, along with two corporals and 53 privates; to be joined in the next month or so by another sergeant, a drummer and one more private.[15]

On 11 January Murat finally signed a treaty with Austria which saw him retain his crown and his army occupied Rome on 16 January and was at Florence at the end of the month. Bentinck, cognisant of Bourbon rights, was reluctant to meet Murat's demands fully so, on 3 February, they only concluded an armistice but this allowed the campaign to commence. The weather, however, was atrocious, the British liaison officer at the main Austrian headquarters remarked, 'Nature herself is hostile. Italy does not remember

Officer's shako plate 1815–1816, gilded with the Sphinx and Peninsula honours in sliver. (Historisches Museum, Basel inv. 1948.392, courtesy of Jean-Philippe Ganascia)

---

11   TNA: WO 12/11998: Paylists 1814; Bürkli, 'Das Schweizerregiment', p.35.
12   TNA: WO 123/137: Memorandum 11 May 1815. The regiment had been missed off the memorandum of 29 March 1815 granting this honour to other units which was published in *The London Gazette* on 18 April 1815.
13   Hayter (ed.), *The Backbone*, p.262. One of the enemy units facing Nugent's division was a battalion of the 1er Régiment Etranger.
14   TNA: AO 3/67: Paylists, German Chasseurs Battalion.
15   TNA: WO 12/11998: Paylists 1814.

such a wintry season. Alternate snows and rains render communication almost impracticable. The lightest carriage ... requires twenty draught oxen.'[16] On 18 February he noted, 'The weather is cold enough for bears to go to sleep in.'[17]

North of the Po, Beauharnais abandoned Verona and the line of the Adige and withdrew to Mantua and the Mincio while Nugent had marched on Bologna. The British contingent followed, leaving Ravenna early on the morning of 4 February and marching via Forli, Faenza and Imola to reach Bologna five days later. Slessor noted that during the march,

> We were cheered by the people, tho' in truth but a motley sample of British troops: 150 only of the 35th, the rest composed of detachments from De Rolls, Corsicans, Italians, Calabrians and deserters from the enemy, altogether amounting to under 1000 men.[18]

The following day, 10 February, Robertson marched on to Modena before continuing to Reggio Emilia and then Parma, which he reached on 14 February.[19] The aim was that the Neapolitans and Nugent would march through Emilia and so threaten Beauharnais's line of retreat. To this aim Nugent had his advance cross the Taro, just west of Parma, to push onto Piacenza on 17 February, an exposed position until the Neapolitans came up in support. On the night of 18 February, there was a false alarm of an attack from the direction of Mantua, and the British at Parma, 'remained under arms all night, bitter cold work in the snow.'[20] Despite the agreements, the Neapolitans appeared ambivalent and on 22 February Slessor wrote, 'Our situation rather critical, between the enemy and the doubtful Neapolitans, with so small a force.'[21] On 27 February Nugent's advance was driven from Piacenza back to the Taro but he did not quit Parma, the British bivouacking outside the city. On the morning of 2 March the French attacked over the Taro. Slessor wrote,

> We retreated on Reggio, keeping up a brisk and regular fire, in good order. Rain and wind all day. The ground was well contested, but numbers prevailed. The rascally Neapolitans never came into action. The enemy were reported to be 20,000: our force little more than half that number.[22]

It is not clear how involved the British contingent was, in the fighting, but there are no signs of any loss from the Regiment de Roll detachment. The

---

16   Robert Wilson, *Private Diary of travels, personal services, and public events, during mission and employment with the European armies in the Campaigns of 1812, 1813, 1814* (London: John Murray, 1861), vol.II, p.301. Entry 23 January 1814, Vicenza.
17   Wilson, *Private Diary*, vol.II, p.322.
18   Hayter (ed.), *The Backbone*, p.264, entry 8 February 1814.
19   Hayter (ed.), *The Backbone*, p.264. The dates are those provided by Slessor's journal, they vary slightly from those in King, 'Robertson', pp.177.
20   Hayter (ed.), *The Backbone*, p.265.
21   Hayter (ed.), *The Backbone*, p.265.
22   Hayter (ed.), *The Backbone*, p.266.

firing ceased at daybreak the next day and Nugent continued to retreat to Modena, with the heavy baggage sick and wounded sent back as far as Ferrara. By 4 March the French were close to Modena but halted as Murat's troops now became active, their king having renegotiated his alliance to his advantage. On 6 March Nugent and Murat advanced and in the early hours of the next day they drove the French into Reggio Emilia; just as the city was surrounded and the allied artillery began to fire on it, Murat agreed to a truce and permitted the French to leave unmolested. On 8 March Nugent's advance entered Parma and the following day Robertson's contingent resumed their quarters in the city, the enemy having crossed the Taro. However, alarms caused them to remain under arms overnight on 10 and 12 March.

Meanwhile, Bentinck mounted an expedition from Sicily and on 11 March the first division, commanded by Henry Tucker Montresor, now major general, disembarked at Livorno which was already occupied by Neapolitan troops. Two days later Bentinck arrived at Reggio Emilia to negotiate with the Austrian commander and Murat.[23] On 18 March Bentinck ordered Robertson and his men to join the troops from Sicily and the next day he reviewed the detachment at Parma when, as Slessor wrote, 'he appeared much satisfied, and much pleased with the report made by General Nugent of our conduct while under his command.'[24] Montresor moved north and by 30 March had secured the Gulf of Spezia as a secure base for operations against Genoa and with communication with Parma, over the Apennines, via Pontremoli where Robertson was by this time.[25] On 7 April, the second division having arrived at Livorno from Sicily, Bentinck decided to advance on Genoa so his troops were at Sturla, on the eastern outskirts of the city, on 13 April. As a result of these movements, Robertson who was still at Pontremoli on 8 April, was ordered to march in a north westerly direction to Bobbio.

On 16 April, following Napoleon's abdication, Beauharnais signed a treaty with the Austrians which would see the French evacuate Italy by the end of the month. Meanwhile Bentinck prepared to attack Genoa, but with the impending peace, it capitulated on 18 April. Robertson by forced marches, via Voghera, had reached Tortona, east of Alessandria, that same day.[26] From there he marched by Novi Ligure to join Bentinck at Genoa on 25 April.[27]

Despite not having arrived before the capitulation four sergeants, including Muzio and Boshardt, and 61 other ranks of the Regiment de Roll shared in the allocation of prize money.[28] The only losses from the detachment since landing at Trieste had been 12 desertions, seven of which had been once it was known that there would be general peace: two on 13 April, four on 14 April and one more on 20 April.[29] Another private, Georg Adamscheck, did

---

23   Hayter (ed.), *The Backbone*, p.268; Fortescue, *British Army*, vol.X, pp.61–62.
24   Hayter (ed.), *The Backbone*, p.268. Slessor obtained leave on 21 March so did not serve with the detachment after this date.
25   TNA: WO 12/11998: Muster list 24 March 1814, indicates the detachment of the Regiment de Roll, at least, was still at Parma on that date.
26   King, 'Robertson', pp.177.
27   TNA: WO 17/1937: Army returns.
28   TNA: WO 164/236: Genoa prize roll 1818/19.
29   TNA: WO 25/2291: Casualty returns.

not return, having been left sick at Parma.[30] The men of the Regiment de Roll and 35th Foot were soon sent to Sicily but unfortunately no source gives the date of this. However it is possible that they sailed with the four companies of the Regiment de Roll from Spain, that arrived at Genoa on 4 May and were transhipped to continue their voyage to Sicily, disembarking at Messina on 18 May.[31] The German Chasseurs were ordered to be disbanded and, having undoubtedly administered this process, Sorgenfrey's departure was delayed, sailing from Genoa on 22 May to arrive at Messina on 10 June.[32]

1814 – Sicily and Malta

By 25 January 1814 the Regiment de Roll's staff and its four companies (Numbers 3, 4, 8 and 12) on Sicily had moved from Contesse to Catania. There they remained until July when, having been joined by the detachments from Spain and Italy, they moved to Messina. Sonnenberg, who was brevetted major general on 4 June 1814, joined the staff at that rank as commander of the citadel from July until December, when he retired.[33]

On 18 July, Bentinck, on leaving Sicily for the last time, relinquished his civil powers in Sicily but remained military commander in the Mediterranean. Thus, on 10 August, he was sent instructions from London to immediately evacuate the British troops from Sicily. They were to be sent to Malta, the Ionian Islands, as well as Genoa, where a garrison was to be maintained. It was specified that the Regiment de Roll should provide five companies to the Malta Garrison, so adding to the three already there, while the remainder of the regiment was to be sent to the Ionian Islands. The instructions concluded,

> Upon the final breaking up of the Army which has served so long and so meritoriously in His Sicilian Majesty's Dominions, I am commanded by The Prince Regent to desire that Your Lordship will convey to the General Officers, Officers and Men, the thanks of His Royal Highness for the exemplary conduct which they have manifested upon all occasions, and which has enabled a comparatively small force to secure Sicily by preserving the respect and good will of the Inhabitants.[34]

However, King Ferdinand succeeded in persuading the British Government to keep troops on Sicily on the grounds that the powers, sitting at the Congress of Vienna, were yet to decide the fate of his kingdom and that of Murat.[35]

Thus, only three Roll companies were on Malta throughout 1814, still at Valletta carrying out garrison duties. From March the regiment provided the city's Key Corporal, for the first three months this duty fell to Corporal Francis Satanofsky before Sebastian Etter fulfilled the role until the end

---

30   TNA: WO 12/11999: Paylists.
31   TNA: WO 17/1937: Army returns; WO 12/11998: Paylist.
32   TNA: WO 17/1937: Army returns; WO 12/11998: Paylist.
33   TNA: WO 17/1937: Army returns.
34   TNA: WO 6/57: Bathurst to Bentinck, 10 August 1814.
35   Gregory, Sicily, p.127.

of 1815.[36] Gougelberg, for one, despite generally enjoying his stay, found inactivity only added to his frustration about the progress of his career.[37] He had been lieutenant since 1804 and was the most senior of the rank after Rusillion's promotion on 24 April 1814 but with the peace and the potential disbanding of the regiment he had little prospect of promotion to captain which would have increased his annual income from £136-17-6 to £191-12-6. When field officer vacancies occurred in the Regiment de Roll, wealthy British officers purchased them for promotion, thus preventing men like Captain Mohr, brevet lieutenant colonel since 1812, and Gougelberg gaining a step up in rank. So, when Sonnenberg retired he was replaced as lieutenant colonel by Fleming Thomas Roberts on 31 December 1814, followed by The Honourable John Maitland who became major on 2 February 1815 on Capol's retirement.[38] Maitland, formerly captain in the 10th Foot, had been aide de camp to Thomas, his uncle, the governor of Malta.[39]

In anticipation that the British Government would be considering discontinuing the service of the foreign units in its service, a suggestion was drafted at Horse Guards that, before any steps were taken to disband the three Swiss regiments, consideration should be given to transferring them to the service of France or the Netherlands. The Regiment de Roll was described as 'almost entirely [changed to 'chiefly'] composed of Swiss, and is reported in a prefect state of discipline.'[40] Nothing came of it as the two other regiments, Meuron and Watteville, were in Canada as the war with the United States of America continued.

The year ended with the return of Captain Antoine Courant who, no longer a prisoner of war at Verdun, travelled to Genoa where on 21 December he took a passage to Sicily.[41]

1814 – Adriatic

At the start of the year Barbier remained in command at Vis, the much-reduced garrison included only a sergeant, two corporals and 20 or so privates from the Regiment de Roll.[42] As has been seen, most of his company was with Robertson and, in January and February Lieutenant Salinger was also on command in Italy, probably on the coast as he was not with Robertson's detachment, furthermore there were the few men at Dubrovnik. The Royal Navy was using Trieste as their base so, in January, its stores and provisions were removed from Vis and Barbier was given charge of the

---

36 TNA: WO 17/2128–17/2129: Army returns.
37 Gugelberg (ed.), *Bündners*, p.53.
38 *The Army List* 1814. Although it did not take place, in December 1815 Barbier arranged to sell his captaincy to Lieutenant Francis Stenton, 35th Foot (TNA: WO 31/1563: Memos of 5 December 1815).
39 TNA: WO 17/2128: Army returns.
40 TNA: WO 1/658: York to Bathurst, 2 May 1814.
41 TNA: WO 12/11999: Paylists.
42 TNA: WO 12/11998: Paylists.

dockyard and arsenal.[43] The Austrians were strengthening their hold on the Dalmatian coast and wanted the British to hand over all the islands they occupied, including Vis. In January Barbier had refused to accept an Austrian garrison, in his opinion any decision to hand over territory was a matter for governments to decide, not local commanders. Rear Admiral Sir John Gore, who had arrived to command the squadron in the Adriatic, took the same approach and pressed for instructions from the British Government. The answer he received in April was a little opaque, but the essence was that the other islands may be handed over but not Vis, for the present, as it was taken before Britain and Austria were allies. Its future was to be yet another topic for the Congress of Vienna.[44]

The British Government's primary concern in the region was the Ionian Islands, of which only Corfu was not yet in its control, so the Foreign Secretary, Robert Stewart, Viscount Castlereagh, directed Campbell to take possession of it.[45] However when Gore and Campbell arrived at Corfu on 11 May, the news the war had ended had only just been received and the island's commander, *Général de division* François-Xavier Donzelot, refused to relinquish the island without instructions from France's new rulers as it had not been taken before the cessation of hostilities. Although Donzelot's stance was not hostile and entirely reasonable, Gore, who had returned to Trieste, received orders from Castlereagh on 2 June, 'to give instructions and assistance to General Campbell to force the surrender of Corfu.'[46] Gore immediately wrote to Robertson, who had now returned to Vis with some of the original garrison, to request that he send as many troops as he could from Vis, Korčula and Lastovo to assist in the effort. On 9 June the frigate, HMS *Tremendous*, anchored at Vis and the next day '150 troops' embarked; she immediately sailed and arrived off Corfu on 12 June.[47] Among the troops on board was Sergeant Henri Kunert with two corporals and 27 privates of the Regiment de Roll.[48]

Some British troops had landed on Corfu, without hinderance, and appear to have camped at Analipsi, just south of Corfu town, but Donzelot maintained his stance.[49] Then on 16 June the impasse was broken when Louis XVIII's commissioner arrived with instructions for Donzelot to relinquish the fortifications of Corfu to the British. The handover was incremental allowing a brief period when the troops from each side socialised in apparent harmony before the island was officially ceded by the French on 24 June and Campbell took possession of it 'in the name of the Allied Powers'.[50] The troops on board the *Tremendous* had landed on 21 June, two days later French troops began to embark on French warships and British transports and soon sailed for home.[51] The British garrison on Corfu was formed of the

43 Hardy, *British and Vis*, pp.109–110.
44 Hardy, *British and Vis*, pp.112–113.
45 TNA: WO 1/315: Bentinck to Bathurst, 22 and 25 May 1814.
46 Hardy, *British and Vis*, p.114.
47 TNA: ADM 51/2896: HMS *Tremendous* Captain's journal.
48 TNA: WO 12/11998: Paylists.
49 Glover, *Fighting Napoleon*, p.157.
50 TNA: WO 1/315: Campbell to Bentinck, 24 June 1814.
51 TNA: ADM 51/2896: HMS *Tremendous* Captain's journal.

SCATTERED TO ALL CORNERS'

35th and 75th Foot, to be joined by the Royal Corsican Rangers in December. The men of the Regiment de Roll on Corfu did not return to Vis but went on to Sicily. The regiment's presence on Vis dwindled, so by the end of the year there was only Barbier, brevetted major on 4 June, Lieutenant Salinger, a sergeant, a drummer, a corporal and 11 privates from the Regiment de Roll.[52]

On 25 December 1814, as part of the peacetime reductions, the authorised strength of each company in the regiment was reduced to five sergeants, two drummers, five corporals and 95 privates, from six, two, six and 114 respectively.[53] However as 12 companies were retained and the staff was not reduced, the number of officers remained the same. In contrast many of the foreign regiments in the British Army had already been disbanded and others that remained in service had had the number of their companies reduced. The reductions in the Regiment de Roll had little real effect as, that same day, it had 57 sergeants, 21 drummers and 1,093 rank and file due to the numbers who had been discharged, as the term of their service had expired or due to ill-health, as well as other reductions.[54]

1815

The first few months of 1815 passed quietly for the Regiment de Roll companies on Sicily, the reduced size of the British presence meant, however, wider responsibilities for them. Although posted at Messina, detachments served at Milazzo, Scaletta and Sant'Alessio Siculo, north of Taormina, and men undertook a broad range of duties, such as Sergeants Charles Schmid 'in the Post Office' and John Roux who was Town Sergeant at Messina.

Then came the news that Napoleon had slipped from exile on Elba and returned to France on 1 March 1815. The British Government hesitated to form a strategy for the Mediterranean until the course of events became clearer so it was only 29 March that instructions were issued to Bentinck. They were stark, as it was recognised that, 'The British Troops in the Mediterranean are at present unequal to do more than garrison certain Fortresses, which are so distant from each other, and unconnected' that they should not be under a single command.[55] In the Mediterranean itself the security of Malta was paramount and, while troops were to remain at Genoa, only the fortress of Messina was to be defended on Sicily. In the Adriatic, Campbell, 'must be instructed to collect as large a Proportion of His Force as possible in Corfu … He will provide everything necessary for defending that Fortress to the last Extremity.'[56] The element of the Regiment de Roll on Sicily was to join Campbell in the Ionian Islands and once Bentinck had issued the required orders his command ceased. The commander on Sicily, Lieutenant General

---

52 TNA: WO 17/1937: Army returns; WO 12/11998: Paylists.
53 TNA: WO 380/5: Regimental record.
54 TNA: WO 17/1937: Army returns for Sicily, and including Malta. Of the rank and file, 586 were present under arms, 30 were sick and 477 on command.
55 TNA: WO 6/57: Bathurst to Bentinck, 29 March 1815.
56 TNA: WO 6/57: Bathurst to Bentinck, 29 March 1815.

Robert Macfarlane, was given additional instructions, 'you should lose no time in carrying into effect as far as may be in your power, the provisions of this Instruction, particularly in what relates to the reinforcing Malta and Corfu and the concentrating the British Troops which remain, for the special Defence of Messina.'[57]

Events overtook the implementation of these instructions as Murat had decided to act in concert with Napoleon. On 15 March he declared war on Austria and his forces marched into the Papal States and Tuscany. However his attempt, on 7 April, to cross the Po was defeated, shattering his army's morale; as he retreated, he learned Bentinck had ended the armistice.[58] Once again Sicily was a base for offensive operations against Naples as Macfarlane gathered troops for an expeditionary force, of which half were Sicilian. The British contingent consisted of the 10th and 31st Foot; the Regiment de Roll's Grenadier, Rifle and Light Companies; the Rifle Companies of the 6th and 7th Battalions, King's German Legion and detachments from the 20th Light Dragoons, Royal Artillery, Royal Engineers and Staff Corps – 2,283 officers and men in all. The strengths of the Regiment de Roll companies were:

> Grenadier: 1 captain, 2 lieutenants, three sergeants, two drummers and 100 rank and file.
> Rifle: 1 captain, 2 lieutenants, three sergeants, one bugler and 59 rank and file;
> Light: 1 captain, 1 lieutenant, four sergeants, one bugler and 73 rank and file.[59]

On 15 May the Roll companies, commanded by Brevet Lieutenant Colonel Mohr, embarked at Milazzo on two transports: Mohr, with the Light (Captain Amantz de Sury) and Rifle (Lieutenant Jost Müller) Companies on the *Minerva* and the grenadiers (Captain Joseph Glutz) on the *Providence*.[60] Jost Müller commanded the rifles as his brother, Nicholas, was attending an Army Medical Board for the wound he sustained in Egypt in 1807, for which he received a year's pay.[61] Macfarlane's expedition sailed on 18 May and landed at Naples six days later, however the campaign was already over. On 2/3 May Murat had been decisively defeated at Tolentino and his army fell apart. He reached his capital in disguise on 19 May and fled to Corsica; the following day his generals sued for peace and a British squadron entered the Bay of Naples.[62] On 23 May the Austrians entered Naples and King Ferdinand was soon restored to his throne. Macfarlane's force was broken up, the 10th Foot leaving for Malta on 28 May, however the Roll companies remained at Naples a little longer, returning to Sicily between 25 June and 1 July.[63] Meanwhile,

57   TNA: WO 6/57: Bunbury to Macfarlane, 31 March 1815.
58   Digby Smith, *Murat's Army: The Army of the Kingdom of Naples 1806–1815* (Solihull: Helion & Company, 2018), pp.9–10.
59   TNA: WO 17/1938: Return dated 18 May 1815.
60   TNA: WO 12/11999: Paylists, officers' rations. These show that two officers were with each company, differing from the embarkation return (WO 17/1938).
61   TNA: WO 2/58: Out letters, 31 March and 18 April 1815.
62   *The London Gazette*, 13 June 1815, Burghesh to Castlereagh, 23 May 1815.
63   TNA: WO 17/1938: Return, note; WO 12/11999: Paylists. Although no date is given for their return, the companies are shown on 25 June at Naples but Captain Joseph Glutz signed the

apparently part of the same operation, the companies of Captains Courant (No.8) and Francis Glutz (No.12) landed in Calabria and were stationed at Reggio on 25 June but returned to Messina by 3 July.[64]

On 27 August Brevet Major Albert Steiger returned to the regiment at Messina. After serving in Wellington's army until September 1813 and then travelling to England, he had been given permission to go to France to offer to raise troops in Switzerland for the new royal army. The offer was accepted but Napoleon's return had, for the time being, halted the project so he made his way to Genoa and sailed from there.[65]

On Malta the three Regiment de Roll companies remained in garrison at Valletta but there were changes in command of the detachment. On 1 May Major Vogelsang returned to Sicily and so command briefly fell to Henry Ryhiner, who had arrived to take command of No.9 Company, before Major Maitland joined in June. On 25 December the detachment consisted of Maitland, Captains Henry and Benoit Ryhiner, five lieutenants, two ensigns, 12 sergeants, three drummers, and 249 rank and file.[66]

For the officers and men of the Regiment de Roll on Vis, the resumption of hostilities brought a surprising bonus, 'four Vessels laden with Grain, the property of … General Murat, captured by … the Garrison of Lissa' on 9 May.[67] The circumstances are not stated but it is notable that they were captured by the army and not the Royal Navy suggesting the vessels arrived, or had already been, at Vis when taken. The lion's share of the prize money from the capture went to Robertson as the commanding officer but Brevet Major Barbier's share, £192-11-8 equated to just over 10 months' pay; the rest of the personnel of the Regiment de Roll, Lieutenant Salinger, Sergeant Francis Suihs, Corporal John Rohner, a drummer and nine privates received shares according to their rank.

Finally, around 7 June, instructions arrived for the islands in the Adriatic that were still held by British troops to be handed over to the Austrians, Korčula was evacuated on 20 July and Vis a week later.[68] The officers and men, 23 of the Royal Artillery, 18 from the Royal Corsican Rangers along with the above mentioned contingent from the Regiment de Roll arrived at Corfu on 5 August.[69] On 23 August Barbier's (No.6) company was reunited at Corfu when the rest, under Lieutenant Sorgenfrey, joined from Messina after nine days at sea, it was then sent to Lefkada where it garrisoned the citadel.[70] On 25 December the company had three officers, four sergeants, six corporals, two drummers and 75 privates at Lefkada.[71]

voucher for his company's pay at Messina on 1 July.

64   TNA: WO 12/11999: Paylists.
65   TNA: WO 43/413: Memos of 24 August 1825 and 14 November 1827; WO 12/11999: Paylists.
66   TNA: WO 17/2129: Army returns; WO 12/11999: Paylists.
67   TNA: WO 164/397: Prize money Lissa 1815.
68   Hardy, *British and Vis*, pp.117–118.
69   TNA: WO 17/1939: Army returns.
70   TNA: WO 17/1939: Army returns; WO 12/11999: Paylists; WO 31/1563: Barbier's memo 5 December 1815.
71   TNA: WO 12/11999: Paylists.

The eight companies and staff of the Regiment de Roll left on Sicily embarked at Messina on three transports, the *Wyton*, *Zephyr* and *Zodiac*, on 9 October and sailed the following day. They, and two companies of the 7th Line Battalion, King's German Legion, were the last British Army troops to leave the island. The transports arrived at Corfu on 17, 21 and 25 October, respectively.[72] On shore, the companies were dispersed to various cantonments.

The question of what was to happen to the Ionian Islands was not settled at Vienna but in the Second Peace of Paris, 20 November 1815 – as the United States of the Ionian Islands they were to be a British protectorate that lasted until 1863.[73]

1816

The peace that followed Napoleon's defeat at Waterloo and exile to Saint Helena meant that the Regiment de Roll's fate was inevitable. The British Army was being radically reduced and on 27 January 1816 the Prince Regent signed the warrant for the regiment to be disbanded.[74] As a result, the three companies that had been on Malta since 1813 left on 19 February 1816 for the Ionian Islands but they did not join the rest of the regiment, which was now commanded by Lieutenant Colonel Roberts, on Corfu. Instead, No.7 and 9 Companies landed at Zakynthos under Major Maitland's command on 29 February while No.10 Company arrived at Kefalonia on 4 March. Benoit Ryhiner, the company commander, was accompanied by his brother as the field officer for the detachment.[75] Barbier's company (No.6) remained on Lefkada.

This arrangement is explained by the appearance of plague on Corfu. The British troops posted on the island had suffered from malaria during the summer of 1815 but it had declined in the winter, an annual occurrence on Corfu in that period, the cause of which was yet to be recognised. William Goodison, Assistant Surgeon of the 75th Foot, wrote on 26 December 1815, 'I have had a good deal to do since my arrival here, a severe fever having prevailed in the regiment during the whole of the hot weather' but as he closed his letter, he added, 'I am sorry to inform you that there are grounds to suspect that the plague has made its appearance in this island'.[76]

On 18 December the British authorities were informed that a number of people had died of disease in the tiny village of Marathias in the south of the island and the following day Deputy Inspector James Tully arrived to find that 13 people were dead, the first on 15 November. There was some hesitation

---

72   TNA: WO 12/11999: Paylists; WO 17/1938: Army returns.
73   Hardy, *British and Vis*, p.116.
74   TNA: WO 380/5: Regimental record.
75   TNA: WO 12/11999: Paylists.
76   William Goodison, 'Observations on the Remittent Fever, and on the Plague which prevailed in the Island of Corfu during 1815 and 1816', in *The Dublin Hospital Reports and Communications in Medicine and Surgery* (Dublin: Hodges and McArthur, 1817), vol.I, pp.192–194.

to identify the disease as plague, despite it being present in nearby Albania, because the village was some distance from the sea and the population had no apparent connection with seafaring. Nevertheless it was clear that it was virulent and contagious so a cordon of militia was placed around the village with an outer cordon placed across the island, from shore to shore, the easterly end being at Mesongi.[77] It was soon found that the disease, now generally accepted to be plague, had spread to the villages surrounding Marathias, so on 25 December troops were sent to reinforce the inner and outer cordons. Three companies, No.5, 11 and 12, of the Regiment de Roll were deployed to the cordons, reflecting the preference for light troops to carry out these duties.[78] It appears the Rifle Company was posted at Mesongi with the other two companies within the infected area.

The policy was 'seclusion and separation,' the sick being placed in hospital and those who may have had contact with them in camps, under the supervision of medical officers.[79] The risks the troops ran were clear but Tully, who was in charge of the district, observed,

Sketch of cockade strap, cockade and plume of the bicorne belonging to Henry Ryhiner derived from a drawing of an original formerly in the Historisches Museum, Basel; the Sphinx was gilt and the Peninsula bar silver. (Author's collection)

It is worthy of remark that, of the numerous troops dispersed all over the district with disease hourly before them (and that too before experience had taught them to estimate and guard against danger), not more than thirteen fell victim to plague; and in every case the source of contagion was most satisfactorily traced. In one instance it was proved, before a military commission, that an entire guard had entered an infected house for the purpose of plunder. The penalty of law was inflicted on the most guilty, whilst many of the others suffered under the hand of Providence. This salutary example sufficed to check an alarming evil, from which the most destructive consequence might have resulted.[80]

Although he does not identify the troops, and other evidence is sparse, it appears the incident he described involved men of No.12 Company of the Regiment de Roll, posted at Chlomos. On 11 January Private Jacob Till, a Swiss, was 'shot by sentence of a General Court Martial' and six other privates from the company died of plague between that date and 24 January.[81]

---

77   Tully, *History of Plague*, pp.86–91.
78   TNA: WO 12/12000: Paylists.
79   Tully, *History of Plague*, p.98.
80   Tully, *History of Plague*, p.102.
81   TNA: WO 25/2291: Casualty returns, three of the six were Swiss and the others were a German, a Slovenian and a Frenchman.

Otherwise the troops were remarkably healthy, despite being under canvas in the winter weather and having testing duties, including escorting people to the hospitals and camps, so they, 'were issued a liberal daily allowance of provisions and spirits, and such other articles as were calculated to ensure safety, and afford comfort for the soldiers.'[82]

Despite some success, the disease continued to progress with about 300 people dying in the first two months. In February Sir Thomas Maitland arrived on Corfu as Lord High Commissioner and, from his experience on Malta, instructed Tully to take more draconian measures, 'nothing short of the jealous eye of authority, and the overawing presence of a military force, thrown up to every door in an infected town, could ever ensure safety, or guarantee the due fulfilment of those measures, which were necessarily resorted to for the extinction of the contagion of plague'.[83] A single hospital was established for the sick as well as only one camp for the segregated and soldiers were posted within villages to prevent people mixing. More troops were deployed to the area and in March the Regiment de Roll's No.4 Company was brought inside the outer cordon, apparently to join the Light (No.11) Company at Lefkimmi, while No.1 Company was posted outside the cordon at Benitses.[84] The severity of the measures now taken is illustrated by an entry in the regimental causualty return for Private Anton Joseph of No.12 Company that reads, 'deserted from the plague hospital on the 23 February & was killed on the 29th ditto.'[85] In time, the measures worked and the last, isolated, case of plague was recorded on 6 May; the disease had been restricted to within the outer cordon and the total death toll to 414.[86]

The number of men of the Regiment de Roll who died from plague between 17 January and 26 March was 19: a corporal, a drummer and 13 privates from No.12 Company and four privates from No.4 Company. Then, as the district remained in quarantine, the companies were struck by malaria. Between 25 June and 16 August a corporal and seven privates of No.4 Company died of the disease as did four privates of the Rifles (No.5), a corporal and a private of the Light (No.11) Company and three privates of No.12 Company; 17 men in all.[87] Despite these cases, the regiment's men on Corfu appear to have been otherwise healthy, with only three rank and file sick on 25 June and two the following month.[88]

In the meantime, the process of disbanding the Regiment de Roll had begun to run its course. On 2 May the detachment on Zakynthos, No.7 and 9 Companies, embarked on the transport *Minerva* that had arrived from Malta. They were under the command of Lieutenant Gougelberg as Major

82 Tully, *History of Plague*, p.103.

83 Tully, *History of Plague*, pp.108–109. Maitland is shown as in command on 25 February, Campbell taking leave on 1 March (TNA: WO 17/1940: Army return).

84 TNA: WO 12/12000: Paylists.

85 TNA: WO 25/2291: Casualty return.

86 Tully, *History of Plague*, p.138; Goodison, 'Observations', p.197.

87 TNA: WO 25/2291: Casualty returns.

88 TNA: WO 17/1940: Army returns. Bürkli, 'Das Schweizerregiment', p.36, states that 150 men of Vogelsang's command were hospitalised in June however it is not clear his source as the officers whose journals he had relied on were not with the detachment.

Maitland remained on the island. Two days later the *Minerva* arrived at Kefalonia where a company of the 14th Foot was landed to relieve No.10 Company that embarked. On 10 May Barbier's No.6 Company was taken on board at Lefkada before the *Minerva* sailed on to Corfu arriving on 13 May.[89]

Major Henry Ryhiner, who commanded the combined detachments, was instructed to, 'be careful on his arrival at Corfu, not to have any communication, which might subject the Transport, to the Quarantine laid on Vessels from that Island.'[90] Gougelberg related that he and his comrades had wanted to land but were unable to, 'To our deepest sorrow, this made it impossible for us to say goodbye to our friends and comrades there, whom it was certain we would never see again. Since they were only allowed to approach us up to a certain distance because of the plague, we could only greet them from afar and wave to them.'[91] On 23 May the Grenadier (No.2), No.3 and No.8 Companies embarked. The next day three transports left Corfu, the *Minerva* and *Nearchus* for Venice and the *Prince of Orange* for Malta. The latter presumably with men from all seven companies who were to take their discharge on that island or continue to England to return home to countries in the near continent, such as Belgium and the Netherlands.

Table 15: Embarkation return of detachments of the Regiment de Roll, 23 May 1816.[92]

	Minerva	*Nearchus*	*Prince of Orange*	**Total**
Captains	3	1	–	4
Lieutenants	4	2	4	10
Ensigns	–	1	–	1
Surgeons	–	1	–	1
Sergeants	8	6	4	18
Drummers	3	6	2	11
Corporals	12	9	1	22
Privates	197	172	26	395
Servants	5	–	1	6
Women	10	9	6	25
Children	6	7	7	20
Total	248	214	51	513

Despite the precautions all those who arrived at Venice were taken by barge to the Lazzaretto and required to spend 23 days in quarantine. In anticipation of this, Lieutenant General Maitland had authorised the NCOs and other ranks discharged on 24 May and returning home by Venice to receive 20 days' pay in addition to the regulation two months' pay on discharge.[93] Released from quarantine, 'the Germans, Swiss and Italians were brought to Fusina [on the shore of the lagoon] by boat, the officers, on the

---

89   Gugelberg (ed.), *Bündners*, p.54.
90   TNA: WO 12/12000: Paylists, quoting General Orders 20 April 1816.
91   Gugelberg (ed.), *Bündners*, p.54.
92   TNA: WO 17/1940: Army returns.
93   TNA: WO 12/12000: Paylists.

Régiment de Steiger in 1818 by Tanconville, 1910 illustrating L to R – musician, *sergent major de voltigeurs*, *fusilier*. Red coats with black facings and brass buttons, yellow voltigeur distinctions, musician with dark blue coat and red and white lace. (courtesy of Yves Martin)

other hand, with the few Venetians, went to Venice, while the Hungarians, Russians, Poles and Austrians were taken to Trieste by ship, those who formed the regiment were scattered to all corners.'[94]

The men of the remaining companies on Corfu, under Vogelsang's command, were discharged as their duties permitted, No.1 Company on 24 July and the other four, No.4, 5, 11 and 12, the following month. It would appear that No.1 Company, at least, returned to the continent at Genoa, with some men again being sent to Malta.[95]

While something can be traced of officers' later lives and careers, those of almost all the other ranks fade from the records. A few officers continued a military career in the French kingdom's new Swiss regiments. The most prominent being Albert Steiger who raised and commanded the 3e Suisse, otherwise known by his name, and ended his career as a *maréchal de camp*, and Eugène de Courten who resumed military service after the death of his wife, Eugénie, in 1814. Having served in cantonal and federal forces in Switzerland, he re-entered French Royal service as *lieutenant-colonel* and then *colonel* in the Swiss regiments of the *Garde Royale* and commanded two battalions in the French intervention in Spain in 1823 as a *maréchal de camp*.[96] Some former Roll soldiers would certainly have served in France, however, some preferred the British service, an example being Peter Biery or Büry. He had served as private in the Regiment de Roll from 1808 until discharged in May 1816 with the Grenadier Company. The following year he enlisted in the 35th Foot, after five days being promoted to corporal, and served until 1820 when he transferred to the 81st Foot and was discharged, having served as sergeant for the last seven years, with a pension on 22 July 1828.[97]

Some of the officers and men of the Regiment de Roll remained in the Ionian Islands. In 1814 Bosset had left Kefalonia for England and was soon assisting the raising and equipping of new troops in Belgium with the brevet rank of lieutenant colonel until the peace when he returned to England in September 1814. On 8 December 1815 he was made Companion in the Order of the Bath before he returned to the Adriatic, arriving at Corfu in March 1816, where Sir Thomas Maitland placed him as commander at Zakynthos.[98] On 19 October 1816 his appointment, dated from the previous 24 March, as one of four 'Inspecting Field Officers of the Militia in the Ionian Islands' was published in *The London Gazette*; one of the others was another half pay Roll officer, The Honourable John Maitland.[99] However Bosset soon discovered that, for some reason, he had become the target of Sir Thomas Maitland's animosity, which led to a legal case and printed accusations. One of the disputes arose over Bosset being forced from his post as inspector of militia on the grounds that the Charter

94   Gugelberg (ed.), *Bündners*, p.55.
95   TNA: WO 12/12000: Paylists.
96   The later careers of officers can be found in the biographical notes to be published on the website fortisetfidelis.com.
97   TNA: WO 97/905/69: Discharge record.
98   Bosset, *Parga*, pp.3–5; *The London Gazette*, 9 December 1815.
99   *The London Gazette*, 19 October 1816.

Charles Philip de Bosset (1773–1845), major in the Regiment de Roll. The medal he is wearing appears to be that presented by the councillors of Kefalonia now held in the British Museum, inv. M.5398, along with a collection of ancient Greek coins he bequeathed. (Author's collection)

of the Ionian Constitution of 1817 prevented the selection of anyone who was not a native born Briton or Ionian for such a post.[100] Later Maitland's biographer concluded that Bosset 'had been shamefully bullied' and that in this affair, 'Maitland cut a sorry figure.'[101]

Gougelberg, promised a good position by Maitland himself, had returned to Corfu where, on 7 November 1816, he had been appointed a sub-inspector of militia with the rank of captain. He was unfortunately caught in the wake of the affair.[102] On 8 November 1817 the local General Orders noted that his appointment had been 'discontinued' on the grounds that it was deemed his 'services in that capacity [were] inexpedient.'[103] This was despite Gougelberg's, and indeed Bosset's, appointment pre-dating the charter and, furthermore, the very same orders published the appointment of Lieutenant Michael Krumm among six new sub-inspectors. Krumm, another half pay

100 Bosset, *Parga*, pp.469–470.
101 Walter Frewen Lloyd, *Sir Thomas Maitland: The Mastery of the Mediterranean* (New York: Longmans, Green & Co., 1897), pp.207, 209.
102 Gugelberg (ed.), *Bündners*, pp.54–58; TNA: WO 25/756: Half pay return.
103 Bosset, *Parga*, p.462, quoting General Orders of 8 November 1817.

officer from the Regiment de Roll and a German, who also acted as chief of police in Corfu town, remained in post until he resigned in 1824.[104]

Sergeant John Bollinger and Private John Cheminant had been left on Kefalonia when the regiment was disbanded.[105] In 1824 Sergeant William Wheeler, 51st Foot, was posted to the island and on 7 August he wrote home,

> My next door neighbour is an old Switzer, he has been a Serjeant in one of the Sicilian [garrison's] Regiments, but is now out of the army, he holds the civilian situation of Clerk of the works, aged about sixty. His wife, a young Greek about twenty eight. His family consists of himself, wife, seven children, a dog, two cats, and a monkey, a fine hawk, several pigeons, canaries, turkeys and fowls, a little army of guinea pigs and rabbits. Last Sunday his youngest child was christened. I and my family were invited. ... [after the ceremony] we regaled ourselves in a back apartment over plenty of excellent old wine that had been kept for the purpose.
>
> Bullinger [*sic*] was no starter, I believe he would drink an hogshead without being drunk, so we kept it up until the cock crew more than thrice, there was an abundance left, so we had another turn at it the night after. Bullinger is one of the most singular characters I ever met with, ... In bottom he is a good hearted old fellow. ...
>
> This is the sort of character I generally spend an hour with every evening.[106]

Two veterans of the Napoleonic Wars enjoying each other's company over a glass seems a fitting end to the long and distinguished service of the Regiment de Roll.

---

104 *The London Gazette*, 14 February 1824; *Saint James's Chronicle*, 20 November 1821.

105 TNA: WO 12/12000: Paylists.

106 B.H. Liddell Hart (ed.), *The Letters of Private Wheeler 1809–1828* (London: Michael Joseph, 1931), pp.240–242.

10

Colours and Uniforms

Colours

Bürkli considered that the regiment's first flags were red with a white cross edged in yellow, a description that has been generally agreed since.[1] As with earlier units that had been raised without cantonal capitulations, there is a possibility that it bore the Baron de Roll's personal arms on the cross, above the centre, or on the upper left-hand quarter.[2] An alternative, given the symbols used later, is a version of the flag described as being carried by Bachmann's regiment of the Swiss Corps namely a red flag with a white cross bearing an 'all-seeing' eye of Providence with the motto *Schwebe über uns und segne unsere Treue* 'Hover over us and bless our loyalty' below.[3] Presumably each of the two battalions had such a flag.

If it had not been received earlier, a British style King's Colour, consisting of a Union flag, is likely to have been issued at the time the regiment was reformed in 1798. What is clear is that the regiment had had such a colour before 1801, when the saltire of St Patrick was incorporated into the Union flag, as the Historisches Museum at Basel possesses a remnant colour of this earlier pattern.[4] That segment does not show whether the flag bore any regimental symbol. In 1802 the regiment received a King's Colour with the new version of the Union flag.[5]

The Regimental Colour remained the original flag until at least the end of 1805 by which time it was, 'very much worn.'[6]

Soon the regiment received the pair of colours as illustrated in Alexandr Chernushkin's colour plate. These were replaced on at least two subsequent occasions as those in use in 1813 were described as, 'in conformity to the King's Regulations and in good Condition.'[7] Presumably the last set are those now held at the National Army Museum, Chelsea, although, if this is the case it is worthy of note that they do not bear the honour 'PENINSULA' which

---

1   For instance, Grouvel, *l'émigration française*, vol.I, p.311, his source however is not cited.
2   McCormack, *One Million Mercenaries*, p.68.
3   Grouvel, *l'émigration française*, vol.I, p.324.
4   Historisches Museum Basel, inventory number 1948.390.a–b.
5   TNA: WO 27/88: Inspection 10 April 1804.
6   TNA: WO 27/89: Inspection 1 December 1805.
7   TNA: WO 27/118: Inspection 18 May 1813.

was granted to the regiment on 11 May 1815. The remarkable feature is the use of Masonic symbols, as regimental badges, on both colours, apparently recognising the baron's membership of the Freemasons.

Samuel Milne in *Standards and Colours of the Army*, illustrated a yellow flag that has been ascribed to the Roll-Dillon Battalion.[8] The flag is in the form of a Regimental Colour in the centre of which is a silver 'all-seeing' eye in a golden garter bearing the motto *Schwebe über uns und segne unsere Treue*, below which is a sphinx and EGYPT, all three are surrounded by a green wreath. Above these is an R, surrounded by another smaller wreath and surmounted by a crown. It has been ascribed to the battalion as Dillon's facings were yellow and the eye and motto probably pertain to Roll, the honours being common to both regiments. It is quite possible that this flag was just a proposal and was never made as the Roll-Dillon Battalion had no colours in May 1813.[9]

Uniforms

There is no contemporary illustration of the earliest uniforms of the Royal Etranger or Regiment de Roll, however table four of the 9 December 1794 capitulation goes into some detail about the equipment and uniform of the soldiers. The uniform follows the pattern of the French émigré White Cockade regiments. The Marquis de Toustain, an officer in one such regiment, raised like Roll in Germany, described the jackets and greatcoats as being like that of the Austrian army in style and cut.[10]

The capitulation described the uniforms thus,

> Habit veste (short jacket) buttoned as far as the waist, without lapels, madder red colour, buttonholes with white thread lace an inch wide and three and half inches long, celestial blue piping or edging, turnbacks white laced in celestial blue, celestial blue cuffs and collar. Waistcoat of white cloth and with sleeves. Celestial blue breeches 'en pantalon.' Black half gaiters with yellow buttons. Felt hat in the form of a crumpled helmet a bit like Henry IV style. Greatcoat of dark-grey cloth, cuffs and collar of celestial blue. The blue of the trousers flecked in white [so like modern denim]. The officers with long habits and three-corned hats etc.[11]

Toustain described the soldiers' headgear, which was in shape like a modern top hat, as having a turban of cloth around the crown and a strip of 'bear skin

---

8   Cecil C.P. Lawson, *A History of the Uniforms of the British Army* (London: Kaye & Ward Limited, 1967), vol.V, p.130, citing Samuel Milne in *Standards and Colours of the Army: From the Restoration of 1661 to the Introduction of the Territorial System 1881* (Leeds: Goodall & Suddick, 1893).

9   TNA: WO 27/118: Battalion inspection 20 May 1813.

10   Marquise de Perry de Nieüil, *Mémoires du Marquis de Toustain 1790–1823* (Paris: Plon, 1933), p.53.

11   TNA: HO 50/386: Table four.

which, passing over the top [front to back], formed a helmet.'[12] To resemble the 'Henry IV style' the front of the peak would have been turned up above the face. What was unique to the Royal Etranger was the blue trousers, laced buttonholes and the facings of 'bleu celeste' (celestial blue), matching those of the former Gardes Suisses, which is of a richer, darker, hue than the lighter, even, watery sky-blue (bleu ciel) some recent artists have used.

The three-cornered hats of the Royal Etranger officers, like those of the White Cockade regiments, were of the 1786 ordnance of the French royal army and so were closer to a bicorne with a more prominent central fold than a tricorne of an earlier age. It seems they wore white waistcoats and breeches, silver buttons and lace as well as 'French-style epaulettes.'[13] It seems that, unlike their French counterparts whose long-tailed coats were single-breasted like the other ranks, those of the Royal Etranger officers had lapels from the start (see below for what they may have looked like). On 30 January 1795 Dürler asked Major Dieffenthaller to send his complete uniform, adding 'It is very essential that the [coat] sleeves are exactly à l'anglais.' It is clear that he meant that they should have buttons and inverted chevron, or herring-bone, lace as worn by senior British officers. It seems that it is this coat that Dürler is shown wearing in the engraving used at the front of Wolfgang Friedrich von Mülinen's book *Das Französische Schweizer-Garderegiment am 10. August 1792* reproduced in Chapter 1. In the same letter he also requested blue cloth for a greatcoat.

The officers were armed with sabres carried on waistbelts, and *sergent majors* with halberds and sabres borne on shoulder belts. *Sergents* were armed with muskets and sabres, the *caporaux, grenadiers* and *fusiliers* were armed with muskets and wore crossed shoulder belts (although not mentioned, a belt plate may have been worn) with a cartridge-pouch and bayonet, the *caporaux* additionally carried a sabre. The *chasseurs* were to be armed with a 'carbine', with a loose sling as opposed to the tense slings of the muskets, and a 'hunting knife' and equipped with 'a cazaquiere [presumably a wide flat pouch like a Corsican *carchera*] worn at the front of the lower stomach.'[14]

The Landesmuseum at Zürich possesses a watercolour (reproduced in Chapter 3) reconstructing the uniform of a grenadier of the Regiment de Roll in 1797. However, given the regiment's service up to that date and that the uniforms, worn both before and afterwards, were much simpler, the ornate features, especially a jacket that matches, but in white lace, the one previously worn by Dürler makes it doubtful as a true representation. It should be noted that the herring-bone ornamentation on the sleeves may have only been worn by Dürler, and not by the other officers, to denote his rank.

It seems that the regiment, like Dillon, adopted the standard British infantry uniform of cylindrical shako and single-breasted jacket, with lace buttonholes across both sides of the body, at the time they were reformed in Portugal in 1798 and certainly before the Egyptian campaign of 1801. In the

---

12   Marquise de Perry de Nieüil, *Mémoires du Marquis de Toustain 1790–1823* (Paris: Plon, 1933), p.53. Toustain was in the Régiment de Vioménil.

13   Perry de Nieüil, *Toustain*, p.53.

14   TNA: HO 50/386: Table four.

case of the Regiment de Roll the facings remained celestial blue and a line of the same blue ran along the white lace, the buttons were spaced singly and, according to Bosset's chart of 1803, the buttonhole laces ended in a spearhead.

Around 1900 the artist Henri Garnier, known as Tanconville, found in Baden-Baden two, apparently contemporary, watercolours depicting the Regiment de Roll in Egypt in 1801 the details shared with Lawson and Grouvel. One showed, quite indistinctly, a group of soldiers with two officers in the foreground, the distinguishing feature of all are their hats which Lawson described as being of straw. These are black and shaped like a top hat but the only decoration are white plumes with red bases, on the front or left side. The other, seemingly by the same hand, is of an officer with powdered hair in a walking out dress. His grey hat, which has no plume, has a lower crown than the others and the rim that is slightly turned down making it appear to have been made of felt, its only decoration is a black or dark grey ribbon or band around the base of the crown. He wears a white waistcoat, breeches and stockings with gold buckled shoes; he has no weapons, having only a cane or walking stick. His red coat appears of a much older style, such as would have been worn in 1795, which may have been reserved for off-duty occasions having had the collar re-tailored. The coat is only fastened at the chest and so reveals the waistcoat. The collar, which is open and flat, is blue as are the round cuffs and lapels, which are quite narrow and end just below the waistcoat in square ends. The white lining appears on the turnbacks. Both collar and cuffs are decorated by two short, perhaps silver, laces which are reminiscent of the short lace buttonholes described in the capitulation. On his shoulders he has black velvet shoulder straps that end with a simple fringe; Lawson states that the fringes are silver but in Grouvel's notes, which are accompanied by detailed sketches, they are described as gold.[15] Around the officer's neck is a black cravat and a prominent lace shirt frill appears below, through the coat fastening. When Tanconville produced a fine plate depicting the Regiment de Roll in Egypt in 1801, used on the front cover of this book, he rather fudged the soldiers' jackets illustrating them as something between a contemporary British style coat and the original style but, for some reason, adding the facing colour to the turnbacks.

It seems that while at Gibraltar the regiment adopted further refinements to its uniform, indeed it may be in this period that lace triangles were added to the ends of the buttonhole laces, in imitation of those worn by the former Gardes Suisses. When Courten returned to the regiment at Gibraltar he remarked on the expense, and complexity, of the uniform he had to have, including a blue frock coat and blue trousers; officers only wearing white trousers when on duty, made of cashmere in winter and bazin (a thick cotton fabric) in summer. The shirts for all ranks had to be cropped and have a frill that was visible though the coat.[16]

The 1804 inspection shows that the Regiment de Roll's sergeants were armed with muskets and the grenadiers did not have additional caps,

15   Lawson, *A History of the Uniforms of the British Army*, p.127.
16   Courten, *Souvenirs*, 10 November 1803 to Eugénie.

indicating that all companies wore the shako.[17] The regiment received new clothing in March and November 1805 and by the end of the year the sergeants were equipped with halberds and fusils, as was normal among British line regiments, and the grenadiers with caps, and it appears these continued to be used throughout the regiment's service. That year one man per company was designated as a pioneer and, from 1 February 1806, received their additional equipment: a cap, apron, axe, pouch and saw.[18]

By and large, from this stage on, the uniforms of the Regiment de Roll followed the same pattern and changes of the British line regiments, as confirmed by a set of two contemporary watercolours held by the Landesmuseum at Zürich illustrating the uniforms of a variety of men from the regiment in Sicily, apparently around 1815, which are reproduced in the colour plates.

---

17   TNA: WO 27/88: Inspection 10 April 1804.
18   TNA: WO 27/89: Inspection 1 December 1805.

Notes on Colour Plates

Plate 1 – Officer *petite uniforme*, Régiment des Gardes Suisses. The celestial blue facings of the Royal Etranger and the Regiment de Roll and, later, the use of small triangles at the end of the buttonhole lace on the coats provided a link with the Régiment des Gardes Suisses of the French *ancien régime*.

Plate 2 – Louis de Flüe (1752–1817), *lieutenant de grenadiers* of the Régiment de Salis-Samade, later *capitaine* in the Royal Etranger. Flüe commanded a detachment of 32 *grenadiers* of the Régiment de Salis-Samade that was sent to join the garrison of the Bastille in Paris immediately before it was captured in 1789. Later he was *capitaine* in the Royal Etranger until 1798.

Plate 3 – *Chasseur*, Royal Etranger 1795. A reconstruction of the earliest uniforms worn by the regiment, from the 1794 capitulation which is described in Chapter 10.

Plate 4 – King's and Regimental Colours, Regiment de Roll, c.1806–1816, over time the colours borne by the regiment followed the pattern of other units of the British Army, although the explicit use of Masonic symbols distinguished them.

Plate 5 – Assistant Surgeon William Heyn (c.1777–1840) assistant surgeon in the Regiment de Roll 1804–1815. Heyn was born at Salzwedel, Prussia (now Saxony-Anhalt), he appears to have already lost his right arm at the taking of Saint Lucia in 1804, before his appointment to the regiment. He wears the simpler uniform of his role, but with the regiment's distinctive facings and lace on his collar and cuffs.

Plate 6 – Charles de Sury (1782–1834), lieutenant commanding the Grenadier Company, Regiment de Roll, from 1808 to 1811. Examples of similar belt plates as that worn by Sury are held by the Historisches Museum, Basel (reproduced in Chapter 6), and the National Army Museum, London (item 1974-02-24-1). It is silver with a gilt eye and crowned garter, with the motto *Schwebe über uns und segne unsere Treue*. The silver grenade with a gilt flame on his wing and another above his belt plate are distinctions of the Grenadier Company, the officers of the battalion companies would have worn a small gilt Sphinx above their belt plates. The bearskin cap in the background would have had silver cords and a gilt plate which, according to Grouvel, would have had the same decoration as the belt plate.[1]

Plate 7 – Regiment de Roll, 1805–1816, contemporary watercolour by the Sicilian artist Letterio Subba (1787–1868). Left to right: The furthest left is a drummer in a celestial blue coat embellished with white and red lace. It is likely that the regiment's musicians would have been dressed in a similar manner. The drum case has, at the front, a blue panel with a white Sphinx surrounded by a green wreath. Then, a little in the background, is a group of officers in a variety of dress with a Rifle Company officer in the centre.

The central group consists of (left to right) the drum major, a grenadier, sergeant of a flank company (seated), two grenadiers, rifleman. The grenadiers, and drum major, are shown with brass square belt plates with the crowned GR cypher. They all wear the full dress bearskin cap with white cords and plume, the plate as described above. The half-turned grenadier shows the pouch without decoration and a water canteen which appears to be marked with RS in white. The seated sergeant is from a flank company as he wears wings but no plume or other distinction provides more information. The distinctions of his rank, stripes on the sleeves and a crimson sash with a celestial blue central stripe are clearly visible. The rifleman is clothed as a soldier of the light battalions of the King's German Legion, including the black facings, and armed and equipped as other riflemen in the British Army. He wears the 'Belgic' shako of the latter stages of the war, with a brass hunting horn at the front and has grey trousers. It is of note that all these figures have moustaches and the drum major, first grenadier and rifleman all appear to be wearing white gloves.

Finally on the far right, in the background, there are soldiers marching away with a battalion company sergeant. Although lacking detail the latter can be seen to be armed with a halberd and sword and wears the 'Belgic' shako apparently with a white on red plume. The rear of his pack seems to be marked with a cartouche in white within which are three indistinct letters.

Plate 8 – Regiment de Roll, 1805–1816, contemporary watercolour by Letterio Subba.

Shows a similar group of figures as Plate 7. The seated figure appears to be a grenadier in full dress, as he is wearing white gloves, wearing a shako with white plume which is curious given that all the other grenadiers in this pair of paintings are portrayed in bearskin caps.

The group of officers confirm the use of the different styles of coat and headgear as in the British line regiments. Most of the red-coated officers appear to be carrying their swords on waistbelts, the plate of which would have been gilt, square and with the crowned GR cypher, surrounded by a wreath, all in silver. The rifle officer wears the green hussar-style dolman with black cords as his contemporaries in the 95th Rifles and other rifle units.

---

1   Grouvel, *l'émigration française*, vol.I, p.309.

His shako is of the earlier 'stovepipe' pattern, the green plume placed at the front. It is decorated with a Sphinx and above it a scroll – which may well be the PENINSULA honour. He is wearing white trousers, perhaps in full dress in Sicily. Whereas in the other painting only the rifle officer clearly has a moustache, all three officers are depicted with them. An unusual feature for a British regiment, although common in some foreign units such as the King's German Legion and the 5/60th Foot, it is worthy of note that none of the officers sitting for portraits have a moustache.

Plate 9 – Edmund Tugginer (1787–1849), lieutenant in the Grenadier Company, Regiment de Roll, from 1812 to 1816. Tugginer wears similar wings to Sury. His portrait which is oil on canvas and dated 1821 so the Spanish medals he is shown wearing may have been painted at the same time rather than added later. They are, L to R – the First Army, the Castalla (otherwise identified as the Seville) and the Tarragona Medals. Edmund's brothers, *Frédéric* Joseph (1786–1857) and Edward (1791–1865) also served in the Regiment de Roll. Sury and Tugginer were both from Solothurn and it is plausible that their portraits were painted by the same artist, explaining why, in both cases, the blue facings have, over time, become black.

Plate 10 – Officer's coat, Light Company, Regiment de Roll c.1816. Although the blue facings are now a little faded, the coat held by the Château de Morges has several fine details.

Plates 11–13 – Wing, cuff and trunbacks detail from the officer's coat. The wings indicate that it would have been worn by an officer of the Light Company as they bear a gilt hunting horn as well as the 'PENINSULA' honour that was granted in 1815.

Bibliography

Archives

Service historique de la Défense, Vincennes (SHD)
GR 1 Ye Dossiers individuels des sous-lieutenants recrutés dans l'infanterie et
    cavalerie 1781–1790
GR 15 Yc 95 contrôle, Régiment de Reinach
GR 23 Yc 170 and 177 registres matricules, 2e and 4e Suisse

Archives du Musée Condé, Château de Chantilly Fonds Grouvel (AMC)
1 GR 142 Troupes suisses

Bibliothek am Guisanplatz, Bern (BiG)
Diary of Major General Louis de Watteville.

Archives de l'Etat du Valais (CH AEV)
Xavier de Riedmatten, P 298–310
Courten Papers Cn B 16/1–2 and CN B 30/2–3

Courten family papers (Courten)
Souvenirs à Gibraltar 1803–1805, transcriptions of letters written by Eugène de
    Courten

Staatsarchiv Graubünden, Chur (StAAG)
XV 2c/12, 'Hochgebiethende gnädige Herren und Oberen!'

Staatsarchiv Luzern (SL)
PA 639/22 Schumacher papers

National Archief, The Hague (NA)
2.21.008.01/IN – 19: Journal de Constant Rebecque, Volume 1

British Library, London (BL)
Add MS 32168, Relation de Monsieur de Durler Capitaine au Régiment des Gardes-
    Suisses et commandant environ 500 hommes qui se sont défendus sur l'Escalier
    de la Chapelle et dans l'Intérieur du Château, le 10 Août 1792
Add MS 20190 Original letters addressed to Colonel Lowe
Add MS 34902–34992 Correspondence and papers of Admiral Horatio Nelson
Add MS 37050 Correspondence of General the Hon. Henry Edward Fox
Add MS 37842–37935 Windham Papers

Add MS 58929–58931 Dropmore Papers
Add MS 50851 Correspondence of William Windham

Hampshire Record Office, Winchester (HRO)
38M49 Wickham Papers

University of Southampton, Hartley Library, Special Collections (HLS)
MS61/WP/1/376 folder 8 Wellington Papers

The National Archives, Kew (TNA)
ADM 51 Admiralty: Captains' journals
ADM 103 Prisoner of War Department and predecessors: Registers of Prisoners of War
AO 3 Auditors of the Imprest and Successors: Various accounts
FO 20 Home Office: General Correspondence, Corsica
FO 29 Foreign Office: Political and Other Departments: General Correspondence, Missions to the Armies in Austria, German States and Prussia
FO 74 Foreign Office: Political and Other Departments: General Correspondence, Switzerland
HO 42 Home Office: Domestic Correspondence, George III
HO 50 Home Office: Military Correspondence
PMG 6 Paymaster General's Office and predecessors: Army Establishment: Foreign Half Pay, Pensions, etc.
WO 1 War Office and predecessors: Secretary-at-War, Secretary of State for War, and Commander-in-Chief, In-letters and Miscellaneous Papers
WO 2 War Office and predecessors: Indexes to Out-letters
WO 4 War Office: Secretary-at-War, Out-letters
WO 6 War Department and successors: Secretary of State for War and Secretary of State for War and the Colonies, Out-letters
WO 7 War Office and predecessors: Various Departmental Out-letters
WO 12 Commissary General of Musters Office and successors: General Muster Books and Pay Lists
WO 17 Office of the Commander in Chief: Monthly Returns to the Adjutant General
WO 24 War Office: Papers concerning Establishments
WO 25 War Office and predecessors: Secretary-at-War, Secretary of State for War, and Related Bodies, Registers
WO 27 Office of the Commander-in-Chief and War Office: Adjutant General and Army Council: Inspection Returns
WO 28 War Office: Records of Military Headquarters
WO 31 Office of the Commander-in-Chief: Memoranda and Papers
WO 42 War Office: Officers' Birth Certificates, Wills and Personal Papers
WO 43 War Office: Secretary-at-War, Correspondence, Very Old Series (VOS) and Old Series (OS)
WO 65 War Office: Printed Annual Army Lists
WO 71 Judge Advocate General's Office: Courts Martial Proceedings and Board of General Officers' Minutes
WO 91 Judge Advocate General's Office: General Courts Martial Reports, Confirmed at Home
WO 97 Royal Hospital Chelsea: Soldiers Service Documents
WO 123 Ministry of Defence and predecessors: Army Circulars, Memoranda, Orders and Regulations
WO 164 Royal Hospital Chelsea: Prize Records
WO 380 Office of the Commander-in-Chief and War Office: Adjutant General's Office: Designation, Establishments and Stations of Regiments, Returns and Papers

Contemporary Newspapers and Journals

Cobbett's Weekly Political Register
Giornale di Sardegna
Ipswich Journal
The London Gazette
Oxford University and City Herald
Public Ledger and Daily Advertiser
Staffordshire Advertiser
Saunders's News-Letter

Contemporary Registers

A List of the Officers of the Army and Marines, with an Index, a Succession of Colonels; A List of the Officers of the Army and Marines on Half-Pay, also with an Index (The Army List) (annual editions)
Etat Militaire de France (annual editions 1753–1793)
Naamregister der Heeren militaire Officieren, den Capitein generaal, de Generaals, Lieutenant-Generaals, Generaals-Major, Colonels, Lieutenant-Colonels, Majors, Capiteins, Lieutenants en Vaandrigs…Vermeerded mit eene Lyste der Chefs van alle de Regimenten, zo Cavallery, als Infantery, zedert den Jaare 1713. (annual editions)

Published Works

Allen, Rodney, *Threshold of Terror, the Last Hours of the Monarchy in the French Revolution* (Stroud: Sutton Publishing, 1999)

Anderson, Aeneas, *Journal of the Forces which sailed from the Downs , in April 1800, on a Secret Expedition under the Command of Lieut.-Gen. Pigot, till their arrival in Minorca, and continued through the subsequent transactions of the Army under the Command of the Right Hon. Sir Ralph Abercromby, K.B. in the Mediterranean and Egypt* (London: J. Debrett, 1804)

Anon., *A Faithful Journal of the late Expedition to Egypt … by a Private on Board the Dictator* (London: J. Lee, 1802)

Anon., *A History of the Campaigns of the British Forces in Spain and Portugal, undertaken to relieve those Countries from the French Usurpation; comprehending Memoirs of the Operations of this Interesting War, Characteristic Reports of the Spanish and Portuguese Troops, and Illustrative Anecdotes of Distinguished Military Conduct in Individuals, Whatever their Rank in the Army* (London: T. Goddard, 1812)

Anon., *Historical Record of the Eighty-First Regiment, or Loyal Lincoln Volunteers* (Gibraltar: The Twenty-Eighth Regimental Press, 1872)

Anon., *Reports also accounts and papers* (London: House of Commons, 1809) vol. IX

Anon., *The Royal Military Calendar or Army Service and Commission Book* (London: A. J. Valpy, 1820)

Aspinall, Arthur (ed.), *The later correspondence of George III, 1793–1810* (Cambridge: Cambridge University Press, 1962–1970)

Baldwin, George, *Political Recollections relative to Egypt* (London: Privately published, 1802)

Bancroft, Edward Nathaniel, *An Essay on the disease called Yellow Fever, … partly delivered as the Gulsonian Lectures, before the College of Physicians, in the Years 1806 and 1807* (Baltimore: Cushing and Jewett, 1821)

Bégos, Louis, *Souvenirs des Campagnes du lieutenant-colonel Louis Bégos* (Lausanne: Libraire A. Delafontaine, 1859)

Bosset, Charles Philip de, *Parga and the Ionian Islands; comprehending a refutation of the various mis-statements on the subject: with a report of the trial between Lieut.-Gen. Sir Thos. Maitland, Lord High Commissioner, and the Author* Second Edition (London; Rodwell and Martin, 1822)

Bouillé, Louis-Joseph-Amour Marquis de, *Souvenirs et fragments pour servir aux mémoires de ma vie et de mon temps* (Paris: Société d'histoire contemporaine, 1908)

Brenton, Edward Pelham, *Life and Correspondence of John, Earl of St. Vincent, G.C.B., Admiral of the Fleet, &c. &c. &c.* (London: Henry Colburn, 1838)

Bunbury, Henry, *Narratives of some Passages in the Great War with France, from 1799 to 1810* (London: Richard Bentley, 1854)

Bürkli, Adolf, 'Biographie von Niklaus Emmanuel Freidrich von Goumoëns, Oberst im Niederländischen Generalstab 1790–1832', *Neujahrsblatt der Feuerwerter-Gefellschaft*, vol.LXXXIII 1890, pp.3–14

Bürkli, Adolf, 'Das Schweizregiment von Roll in englischen Dienste 1795 bis 1816', *Neujahrsblatt der Feuerwerter-Gefellschaft*, vol.LXXXVIII 1893, pp.3–39

Burnham, Robert and McGuigan, Ron, *The British Army Against Napoleon: Facts, Lists and Trivia 1805–1815* (Barnsley: Frontline Books, 2010)

Cannon, Richard, *Historical Record of the Tenth, or the North Lincolnshire, Regiment of Foot* (London: Parker, Furnivall & Parker, 1847)

Carpenter, Kirsty and Mansel, Philip (eds), *The French Émigrés in Europe and the Struggle against Revolution, 1789–1814* (Basingstoke: Macmillan Press, 1999)

Castella de Delley, Rodolphe de, *Le Régiment des Gardes-Suisses au service de France du 3 mars 1616 au 10 août 1792* (Fribourg : Éditions Universitaire, 1964)

Cazotte, Jacques Scévola, *Témoignage d'un Royaliste* (Paris: Adrien Le Clerc et Cie., 1839)

Church, E.M., *Chapters in an Adventurous Life: Sir Richard Church in Italy and Greece* (Edinburgh: William Blackwood and Sons, 1895)

Corbett, Julian S. (ed.), *Private Papers of George, Second Earl Spencer, First Lord of the Admiralty 1794–1801* (London: Naval Records Society, 1913)

Dacombe, M.R., Rowe, B.J.H. and Harding, J. (eds), 'The Adventures of Serjeant Benjamin Miller, during his service in the 4th Battalion, Royal Artillery, from 1796 to 1815', *Journal of the Society for Army Historical Research*, vol.7, no.27 (January 1928), pp.9–51

Delavoye, Alexander M., *Life of Thomas Graham, Lord Lynedoch* (London: Richardson & Co., 1880)

Dempsey, Guy C., 'Mutiny at Malta, The Revolt of Froberg's Regiment April 1807', *Journal of the Society for Army Historical Research*, vol.67, no.269 (Spring 1989), pp.16–27

Dempsey, Guy, *Napoleon's Mercenaries: Foreign Units in the French Army under the Consulate and Empire, 1799–1814* (London: Greenhill Books, 2002)

Dunfermline, James Abercromby Lord, *Lieutenant-General Sir Ralph Abercromby K.B. 1793–1801* (Edinburgh: Edmonston and Douglas, 1861)

Ede-Borrett, Stephen, *Swiss Regiments in the service of France 1798–1815* (Warwick: Helion and Company, 2019)

Farmer, Henry George, 'Scots Duty: The Olde Drum and Fife Calls of Scottish Regiments', *Journal of the Society for Army Historical Research*, vol.24, no. 98 (Summer, 1946), pp.65–70

Finley, Milton, *The Most Monstrous of Wars: The Napoleonic Guerrilla War in Southern Italy, 1806–1811* (Columbia: University of South Carolina Press, 1994)

Fischer, Frederick Augustus, *Travels in Spain in 1797 and 1798* (London: T. N. Longman and O. Rees, 1802)

Fortescue, The Honourable J.W., *A History of the British Army* (London: Macmillan and Co., 1906–1920)

Giddey, Ernest, 'James Francis Erskine et son Régiment Suisse (1779–1786)', *Revue suisse d'histoire*, vol.4 (1954), pp.238–259

Gleig, G.R. (ed.), *The Hussar*, (London: Henry Colburn, 1837)

Glover, Gareth (ed.), *Fighting Napoleon: The Recollections of Lieutenant John Hildebrand 35th Foot in the Mediterranean and Waterloo Campaigns* (Barnsley: Frontline Books, 2016)

Glover, Gareth, *The Forgotten War against Napoleon: Conflict in the Mediterranean 1793–1815* (Barnsley: Pen & Sword Military, 2017)

Glover, Gareth (ed.), *The Military Adventures of Private Samuel Wray 61st Foot 1796–1815* (Godmanchester: Ken Trotman Publishing, 2009)

Goodison, William, 'Observations on the Remittent Fever, and on the Plague which prevailed in the Island of Corfu during 1815 and 1816', in *The Dublin Hospital Reports and Communications in Medicine and Surgery* (Dublin: Hodges and McArthur, 1817), vol.I, pp.191–203

Gould, Robert, *Mercenaries of the Napoleonic Wars* (Brighton: Tom Donovan, 1995)

Gregory, Desmond, *Sicily, the Insecure Base: A History of the British Occupation of Sicily, 1806–1815* (London and Toronto: Associated University Presses, 1988)

Gregory, Desmond, *The Ungovernable Rock: A History of the Anglo-Corsican Kingdom and its role in Britain's Mediterranean strategy during the French Revolutionary War (1793–1797)* (London; Associated University Press, 1985)

Gretton, G. le M., *The Campaigns and History of the Royal Irish Regiment From 1684 to 1902* (Edinburgh: William Blackwood and Sons, 1911)

Grouvel, Vicomte Robert, *Les corps de troupes de l'émigration française* (Paris: Les Éditions de La Sabretache, 1957–1964)

Gugelberg von Moos, Marie (ed.), *Erlebnisse eines Bündners im Regiment Roll (1804–1819)* (Maienfeld: Privately published, c.1910)

Guillon, Édouard, *Napoléon et Les Suisses 1803–1815* (Paris and Lausanne: Plon and Payot et Cie., 1910)

Gurwood, John (ed.), *The Dispatches of Field Marshal the Duke of Wellington, during his various campaigns in India, Denmark, Portugal, Spain the Low Countries, and France, from 1799 to 1816* (London: John Murray, 1838)

Hardy, Malcolm Scott. *The British and Vis: War in the Adriatic 1805–15* (Oxford: Archaeopress, 2009)

Harley, John and Glover, Gareth (ed.), *The Veteran or 40 Years' Service in the British Army: The Scurrilous Recollections of Paymaster John Harley 47th Foot - 1798–1838* (Solihull: Helion & Company, 2018)

Hayter, Alethea (ed.), *The Backbone: Diaries of a Military Family in the Napoleonic Wars* (Bishop Auckland: The Pentland Press Ltd., 1993)

Ilari, Virgilio and Crociani, Piero, *L'Armata italiana di Lord Bentinck 1812–1816* (self-published, 2010)

Ilari, Virgilio, Crociani, Piero and Boeri, Giancarlo, *Le Due Sicilie nelle Guerre Napoleoniche (1800–1815)* (Rome: Stato Maggiore dell'Esercito, 2008)

Jackson, Sir William G.F., *The Rock of the Gibraltarians: A History of Gibraltar* (Grendon: Gibraltar Books Ltd., 1987)

James, William, *The Naval History of Great Britain, from the Declaration of War by France in 1793, to the Accession of George IV* (London: Richard Bentley, 1847)

Jollivet, Maurice, *Les Anglais dans la Méditerranée (1794–1797) Un Royaume Anglo-Corse* (Paris: Léon Chailley, 1896)

Kaulek, Jean, *Papiers de Barthélemy, ambassadeur de France en Suisse, 1792–1797, publiés sous les auspices de la Commission des Archives des Affaires étrangères* (Paris: Félix Alcan, 1889)

King, D.W., 'A Note on the Operations of George Duncan Robertson's Force from Lissa at Trieste and in Northern Italy, 1813–1814', *Journal of the Society for Army Historical Research*, vol.56 no.227 (Autumn 1978), pp.174–177

Lane-Poole, Stanley, *Sir Richard Church C.B., G.C.H.: Commander-in-Chief of the Greeks in the War of Independence* (London: Longmans, Green and Co., 1890)

Lawson, Cecil C.P., *A History of the Uniforms of the British Army* (London: Kaye & Ward Limited, 1967)

Liddell Hart, B.H. (ed.), *The Letters of Private Wheeler 1809–1828* (London: Michael Joseph, 1931)

Lipscombe, Nick, *Wellington's Eastern Front: The Campaigns on the East Coast of Spain 1810–1814* (Barnsley: Pen and Sword Military, 2016)

Lloyd, Walter Frewen, *Sir Thomas Maitland: The Mastery of the Mediterranean* (New York: Longmans, Green & Co., 1897)

McCormack, John, *One Million Mercenaries: Swiss Soldiers in the Armies of the World* (London: Leo Cooper, 1993)

McGuigan, Ron and Burnham, Robert, *Wellington's Brigade Commanders* (Barnsley: Pen & Sword Military, 2017)

Mackesy, Piers *British Victory in Egypt: The end of Napoleon's Conquest* (New York: Taurus Parke, 2010)

Mackesy, Piers, *The War in the Mediterranean 1803–1810* (Cambridge: Harvard University Press, 1957)

Maempel, Johann Christian, *Adventures of a Young Rifleman: the Experiences of a Saxon in the French & British Armies During the Napoleonic Wars* (Driffield: Leonaur, 2008)

Mansell, Philip, *Louis XVIII* (Stroud: Sutton Publishing, 1999)

Martin, Yves, *The French Army of the Orient 1798–1801* (Solihull: Helion & Company, 2017)

Maule, Francis, *Memoirs of the Principal Events in the Campaigns of North Holland and Egypt* (London: F. C. and J. Rivington, 1816)

Maurice, J.F., *The Diary of Sir John Moore* (London: Edward Arnold, 1904)

Miles, Alfred H. (ed.), *With Fife and Drum* (London: Hutchinson & Co., 1899)

Minto, Countess of (ed.), *Life and Letters of Sir Gilbert Elliot First Earl of Minto from 1751 to 1806* (London: Longmans, Green and Co., 1874)

Mugnai, Bruno, *The Ottoman Army of the Napoleonic Wars, 1784–1815: A Struggle for survival from Egypt to the Balkans* (Warwick: Helion & Company, 2022)

Maag, Albert, *Geschichte der Schweizertruppen im Kriege Napoleon I in Spanien und Portugal (1807–1814)* (Biel: Ernst Kuhn, 1892) Vol. I

Nichols, Alistair, 'The Raising of the White Cockade Regiments, 1794–1802', in Robert Griffith (ed.), *Armies and Enemies of Napoleon 1789–1815* (Warwick: Helion & Company, 2022), pp.111–134

Nichols, Alistair, 'The Soldiers Are Dressed In Red': The Quiberon Expedition of 1795 and the Counter-Revolution in Brittany* (Warwick: Helion & Company, 2022)

Nichols, Alistair, *Wellington's Mongrel Regiment: A History of the Chasseurs Britanniques Regiment 1801–1814* (Staplehurst: Spellmount Limited, 2005)

Nichols, Alistair, *Wellington's Switzers: The Watteville Regiment in Egypt, the Mediterranean, Spain and Canada* (Godmanchester: Ken Trotman Publishing, 2015)

Nichols, Alistair with Antoine de Courten, Antoine de (eds), 'The Letters of Major de Courten of the Roll Regiment, Gibraltar, 1803–1805', *Journal of the Society for Army Historical Research*, vol.94 no.379, pp.177–192 and no.380, pp.276–293

Nicolas, Sir Nicholas Harris, *Dispatches and Letters of Vice Admiral Lord Viscount Nelson* (London: Henry Colburn, 1845)

Nicoll, Daniel, *Sergeant Nicoll: The Experiences of a Gordon Highlander during the Napoleonic Wars in Egypt, the Peninsula & France* (Milton Keynes: Leonaur, 2007)

Oman, Charles, *A History of the Peninsular War* (London: Greenhill Books, 1996)

Ompteda, Christian Baron and Hill, John (trans.), *A Hanoverian-English Officer a hundred years ago* (London: H. Grevel & Co., 1892)

Petrides, Anne and Downs, Jonathan (eds), *Sea Soldier: An Officer of Marines with Duncan, Nelson, Collingwood and Cockburn* (Tunbridge Wells: Parapress, 2000)

Pfyffer d'Alitshoffen, Charles (ed.), *Récit de la conduit du régiment des Gardes Suisses, à la journée du 10 Août 1792* (Geneva: Chez Abraham Cherbuliez, 1824)

Pinasseau, Jean, *L'Émigration Militaire campagne de 1792 Armée Royale Notices D à Z* (Paris: Éditions A. et J. Picard et Cie, 1964)

Pocock, Tom, *Remember Nelson: The Life of Captain Sir William Hoste* (London: Collins, 1977)

Poole, James, *A Narrative exposing a variety of Irregular Transactions in one of the Departments of Foreign Corps during the Late War* (London: J Parson and Son, 1804)

Ræmy, *Abbé* Charles, *Le Chevalier d'Appenthel* (Fribourg: Libraire J. Labastrou, 1879)

Reiset, Vicomte de, *Les Reines de l'Emigration, Louise d'Esparbès, Comtesse de Polastron* (Paris: Emile-Paul, 1907)

Rovéréa, Ferdinand de, *Mémoires de F. de Rovéréa* (Bern, Zurich and Paris: Fréd. Klinchsieck, 1848)

Schalbetter, Jacques, 'Le Régiment Valaisan au service de l'Espagne 1796–1808', *Annales valaisannes: bulletin trimestriel de la Société d'histoire du Valais romand*, vol. 15 no. 3 (1969), pp.283–369

Schaller, Henri de, *Histoire des troupes suisses au service de France sous le règne de Napoléon 1er* (Lausanne; Payot, 1883) modern edition (Gollion: Infolio éditions, 2012)

Schaller, Henri de, 'Le Régiment de Watteville au service de l'Angleterre', *Revue historique vaudoise*, November 1894, pp.321–334 and December 1894, pp.353–370

Smith, Digby, *Murat's Army: The Army of the Kingdom of Naples 1806–1815* (Solihull: Helion & Company, 2018)

Sparrow, Elizabeth, *Secret Service British Agents in France 1792–1815* (Woodbridge: The Boydell Press, 1999)

Stewart, David, *Sketches of the Character, Manners, and the present State of the Highlanders of Scotland* (Edinburgh: Archibald Constable and Co., 1822)

Tully, James D., *The History of Plague, as it has lately appeared in the Islands of Malta, Gozo, Corfu, Cephalonia &c.* (London: Longman, Hurst, Rees, Orme and Brown, 1821)

Vallière, Paul de, 'Histoire du régiment des Gardes Suisses de France (1567–1830)', *Revue Militaire Suisse*, no.5 Mai 1911, pp.381–406

Vallière, Paul de, *Honneur et Fidélité Histoire des Suisses au Service Étranger* (Lausanne: Les Editions d'art Suisse ancient, 1940)

Vincenz, P.A. (ed.), 'Il regiment svizzer de Roll en survetsch ingles: 1795 entochen 1801: tenor il diari de sergent Giachen Gius. Tomaschett de Trun', *Annalas da la Societad Retorumantscha*, Year 11 (1897), pp.285–318

Vogel, Franz Adam, *Code Criminel de l'Empereur Charles V, vulgairement appellé La Caroline: contenant les Loix qui sont suivies dans les Jurisdictions Criminelle de l'Empire; et à l'usage des Conseils de Guerre des Troupes Suisses* (Maastricht: Jean-Edme Dufour & Phil. Roux, 1779)

Walsh, Thomas, *Journal of the Late Campaign in Egypt: including descriptions of that Country, and of Gibraltar, Minorca, Malta, Marmorice and Macri* (London: T. Cadell and W. Davies, 1803)

Ward, S.G.P. (ed.), 'The Diary of Lieutenant Robert Woollcombe, R.A., 1812–1813', *Journal of the Society for Army Historical Research*, vol.52 no.211 (Autumn 1974), pp.161–180

Whittingham, Ferdinand (ed.), *A Memoir of the Services of Lieutenant-General Sir Samuel Ford Whittingham* (London: Longmans, Green and Co., 1868)

Wickham, William, *The Correspondence of the Right Honourable William Wickham from the year 1794* (London: Richard Bentley, 1870)

Wilson, Robert Thomas, *History of the British Expedition to Egypt; to which is subjoined, a Sketch of the present state of that Country and its means of defence* (London: T. Egerton, 1802)

Wilson, Robert, *Private Diary of travels, personal services, and public events, during mission and employment with the European armies in the Campaigns of 1812, 1813, 1814* (London: John Murray, 1861)

Unpublished material

Foerster, Hubert, *Die Gründung des Regiments von Roll im Dienste Englands 1795–1796* (unpublished article)

Musteen, Jason R., *Becoming Nelson's Refuge and Wellington's Rock: The Ascendancy of Gibraltar during the Age of Napoleon (1793-1815)* PhD dissertation, Florida State University, 2005

Internet sources

Anon., 'Operations on the East Coast of Spain 1812–13', *The Waterloo Association*, <https://www.waterlooassociation.org.uk/2021/09/17/operations-on-the-east-coast-of-spain-1812-13/>, accessed 28 December 2022

Miró, Miquel, 'The Combat of the Ordal Cross: 13th September 1813', *The Napoleon Series*, <https://www.napoleon-series.org/military-info/virtual/c_ordal.html>, accessed 9 February 2023

From Reason to Revolution – Warfare 1721-1815

http://www.helion.co.uk/series/from-reason-to-revolution-1721-1815.php

The 'From Reason to Revolution' series covers the period of military history 1721–1815, an era in which fortress-based strategy and linear battles gave way to the nation-in-arms and the beginnings of total war.

This era saw the evolution and growth of light troops of all arms, and of increasingly flexible command systems to cope with the growing armies fielded by nations able to mobilise far greater proportions of their manpower than ever before. Many of these developments were fired by the great political upheavals of the era, with revolutions in America and France bringing about social change which in turn fed back into the military sphere as whole nations readied themselves for war. Only in the closing years of the period, as the reactionary powers began to regain the upper hand, did a military synthesis of the best of the old and the new become possible.

The series will examine the military and naval history of the period in a greater degree of detail than has hitherto been attempted, and has a very wide brief, with the intention of covering all aspects from the battles, campaigns, logistics, and tactics, to the personalities, armies, uniforms, and equipment.

Submissions

The publishers would be pleased to receive submissions for this series. Please contact series editor Andrew Bamford via email (andrewbamford@helion.co.uk), or in writing to Helion & Company Limited, Unit 8 Amherst Business Centre, Budbrooke Road, Warwick, CV34 5WE

Titles

About the author

Alistair Nichols is a former police officer with a social science degree from Portsmouth University. Over the last 20 or so years he has researched and written about the foreign units in the British Army during the French Revolutionary and Napoleonic Wars. His work includes books on the history of the Chasseurs Britanniques (2005), the Watteville Regiment (2015) and the Independent Companies of Foreigners (2018). For Helion he has contributed a chapter to *The Sword and the Spirit: Proceedings of the first 'War & Peace in the Age of Napoleon' Conference* (2021), co-authored *For God and King: A History of the Damas Legion 1793–1798: A Case Study of the Military Emigration during the French Revolution* (2021), and written *The Soldiers are Dressed in Red: The Quiberon Expedition of 1795 and the Counter-Revolution in Brittany* (2022).

About the artist

Alexandr Chernushkin lives in Poznan, Poland and for more than 20 years has been engaged in military history, specialising in the uniforms of various European armies during the 17th-19th centuries. His particular interest is the history of military and civil uniforms of the Russian Empire and Poland.